THE HIDDEN STRUCTURE OF INTERACTION

Emerging Communication

Studies in New Technologies and Practices in Communication

Emerging Communication is publishing state-of-the-art papers that examine a broad range of issues in communication technology, theories, research, practices and applications.
It presents the latest development in the field of traditional and computer-mediated communication with emphasis on novel technologies and theoretical work in this multidisciplinary area of pure and applied research.
Since Emerging Communication seeks to be a general forum for advanced communication scholarship, it is especially interested in research whose significance crosses disciplinary and sub-field boundaries.

Editors-in-Chief
Giuseppe Riva, Applied Technology for Neuro-Psychology Lab., Istituto Auxologico Italiano, Verbania, Italy
Fabrizio Davide, TELECOM ITALIA Learning Services S.p.A., Rome, Italy

Editorial Board
Luigi Anolli, State University of Milan-Bicocca, Milan, Italy
Cristina Botella, Universitat Jaume I, Castellon, Spain
Martin Holmberg, Linköping University, Linköping, Sweden
Ingemar Lundström, Linköping University, Linköping, Sweden
Salvatore Nicosia, University of Tor Vergata, Rome, Italy
Brenda K. Wiederhold, Interactive Media Institute, San Diego, CA, USA
Luciano Gamberini, State University of Padua, Padua, Italy

Volume 7

Previously published in this series:

ISSN 1566-7677

The Hidden Structure of Interaction

From Neurons to Culture Patterns

Edited by

Luigi Anolli
State University of Milan-Bicocca, Milan, Italy

Starkey Duncan JR.
University of Chicago, Chicago, IL, USA

Magnus S. Magnusson
University of Iceland, Reykjavik, Iceland

and

Giuseppe Riva
Catholic University of Milan, Milan, Italy

IOS
Press

Amsterdam • Berlin • Oxford • Tokyo • Washington, DC

ISBN 1-58603-509-6
Library of Congress Control Number: 2005923351

Publisher
IOS Press
Nieuwe Hemweg 6B
1013 BG Amsterdam
The Netherlands
fax: +31 20 687 0019
e-mail: order@iospress.nl

Distributor in the UK and Ireland
IOS Press/Lavis Marketing
73 Lime Walk
Headington
Oxford OX3 7AD
England
fax: +44 1865 750079

Distributor in the USA and Canada
IOS Press, Inc.
4502 Rachael Manor Drive
Fairfax, VA 22032
USA
fax: +1 703 323 3668
e-mail: iosbooks@iospress.com

The Hidden Structure of Interaction
L. Anolli et al. (Eds.)
IOS Press, 2005
v

PREFACE

Even though unaided observers often perceive human behaviour in interactions as somewhat structured and repetitive, they find it difficult or impossible to specify what kinds of patterns are being repeated or when. The approach adopted here, therefore, assumes that the temporal structure of a complex system of behaviour is largely unknown, at least consciously.

Thus, ideas or hypotheses are needed concerning kinds of patterning for which detection methods must then be found, adapted, or created...

Behind the pattern definition lies the hypothesis that both hidden and manifest behaviour patterns may involve similar relations among their parts. The T-pattern definition, therefore, attempts to abstract some of these relations in order to create an algorithm for the detection of hidden patterns. Examples of well-known patterns that may serve as models are, for example, standard phrases, which are sequences of words that, in turn, are sequences of phonemes.

Magnusson, 2000

The idea of complexity states that most things – e.g., packs of wolves, immune systems, and human cultures – tend to organize themselves into recurring patterns, even when these patterns are not immediately visible to an external observer. The more general name for the scientific field concerned with the behaviour over time of a dynamic system is "complexity theory". The dynamic systems – systems capable of changing over time – are the focus of this approach, and its concern is with the predictability of their behaviour.

The systems of interest to complexity theory, under certain conditions, perform in regular, predictable ways; under other conditions they exhibit behaviour in which regularity and predictability is lost. As underlined by the physicist and Nobel Laureate Ilya Prigogine, almost undetectable differences in initial conditions lead to gradually diverging system reactions until eventually the evolution of behaviour is quite dissimilar. The most known example of this phenomenon is the oft-quoted assertion that the flapping of a butterfly's wing can in due course decisively affect weather on a global scale.

The concepts of stable and unstable behaviour are part of the traditional repertoire of physical science. What is novel is the concept of something in between – chaotic behaviour. For *chaos* here we refer to systems which display behaviour that, though it has certain regularities, defies prediction. A classical example is weather forecasts: despite the many efforts, success in predicting the weather has been quite limited, and forecasts get worse the further ahead they are pitched. How does the order emerge from the chaos? How can we predict the behaviour of a chaotic system? Over the last 30 years and more, trying to identify the hidden patterns behind chaotic behaviour became the focus of attention in a number of scientific disciplines. These range as widely as astronomy, chemistry, evolutionary biology, geology and psychology.

However, at the heart of "the science of complexity" we always find the descriptive power of mathematics: mathematics reveals hidden patterns that help us understand the world around us. Striking applications of mathematics have emerged across the entire landscape of natural, behavioural and social sciences. From medical technology (CAT scanners) to economic planning (input/output models of economic behaviour), from genetics (decoding of DNA) to geology (locating oil reserves), mathematics has made an indelible imprint on every part of modern science, even as science itself has stimulated the growth of many branches of mathematics.

This book shows that the understanding of behaviour may benefit from the power of mathematics, too: one basic type of hierarchical time pattern – called a "T-pattern" – and the corresponding detection and analysis software – THEME – are here proposed as new tools for the detection of hidden behaviour patterns. T-patterns are probabilistic, repeated, recursive (self-similar and hierarchical) synchronic and/or sequential structures that may involve any number of individuals and behavioural, physiological and/or environmental event types. However, the book does more than present and review different researches made using the same methodology: it offers a series of recommendations, based on extensive evidence from research, about how to investigate the human and the animal behaviour.

The wide array of perspectives described in the six Sections strengthens the importance of T-patterns for understanding behaviour. As this approach continues to develop, it is largely expected a wider comparison with existing methods. In order to achieve this goal, an interdisciplinary approach is essential. Moreover the integration of knowledge coming from different disciplines, such as mathematics, clinical, social and cognitive psychology, neuroscience and chemistry will be crucial to incorporate ongoing insights from these fields into powerful future-generation forecasting methods.

In the end, we hope that the contents of this book will stimulate more research on the hidden patterns behind human and animal behaviours and on how best use mathematics in understanding their structure. Future potential applications of T-patterns are really only limited by the imagination of talented individuals. In this sense, understanding how to shape and exploit the full potential of this new approach is an exciting challenge for both developers and researchers. This book wants to help them in identifying some key paths for reaching this goal.

Prof. Marcello Fontanesi

Rector Magnificus
University of Milan-Bicocca
Milan, Italy

FOREWORD

This book begins with God and the Bible, which, in nowadays world, should boost its US career. But, fortunately and as usual in science, God is vanishing soon and lets the flow to language and interaction. These are more scientifically correct topics!

Simple general questions, however ambitious, complex and puzzling to answer, are the only very best questions in science. So when, in the early 80's, a tonic Viking dropped in my Paris office just saying: "I play drums, work with psys, write a program to detect any sequence of events characterized by Ids, sequence *and* events spacing in sequences, and I would like to work about it around here", I did not hesitate to offer him the first opportunity to go on.

Sequence analysis and drums witnessed a coherent global, professional and private approach. Sequence analysis and pattern detection, mixing qualitative data-order and quantitative-spacing was a challenge. Working with French psys was even worse and only an aboriginal descendant of my Normandy ancestry such as Magnusson could dig with that! So, I just settled him in the Musée de l'Homme, in the room where, three-four years before, two anonymous post docs – Jean-Marc Lalouel and Mark Lathrop! – fixed the multipoint linkage analysis method, which permitted to produce the genetic map of the human genome, a pre-requisite to the sequencing HUGO project. This sequencing was another good basic question, even if THEME's use in today's molecular genetic research just proves that it was less general because potentially included within the THEME program while the genetic method exclusively fit the genetic problematic. Of course, the bureaucracy of French research refused to really invest both in the genetic project and in Magnus's one, so that more pragmatic institutions from US to Iceland got the whole payback of these brain investments!

The table of contents of this book shows that Magnus was fully right when thinking that THEME was an interdisciplinary tool able to solve a number of fundamental assessment problems in nearly all possible scientific areas. Beyond the content of this book about ethology, medicine, psychology, communication sciences etc, THEME made its proves in subjects ranging from Human Genome to the demography of Inuit migrations. There is no doubt that this is just a beginning: interaction and pattern description, both qualitative and quantitative, are the most basic problem and method overall sciences. So that applications can be expected through a variety of first importance fields, from climate evolution to economic cycles, neurobiology, media's impact or evolutionary medicine.

It is not the less interesting fact that psychology and very "soft sciences" were those which permitted these technical developments while the "hard" field of molecular genetics, which needed it so much, failed to address it correctly. By the way, this story repeats that of factorial analysis in the first half of the twentieth century. This must remind us that techno-sciences very often wear blinkers that prevent them from dealing with good simple ideas and sink them in non-communicant sophistication.

Thanks to Magnus, it is demonstrated here that humanities can still have an efficient leadership over many fields... provided that they are combined with knowledge and capacity in the last technical developments, a *sine qua non* condition that they unfortunately don't satisfy systematically...

André Langaney

Professor of Genetics,
University of Geneva,
Geneva, Switzerland

Paris National Museum of Natural History,
Paris, France

INTRODUCTION

Interaction is everywhere and always. In the Bible it is written: "In the beginning was the Word, and Word was with God, and the Word was God" (John, 1:1). "Word" is the English translation of the Greek term "Logos", and Logos, besides word, means also: "connection, correspondence, analogy, relationship". Then, it is meaningful to think: "In the beginning was the interaction", as interaction is the basis of the life genesis and the bond for every kind of evolution and change.

Whatever the beginning of the world might be, first was the chaos. Should have been a primary Big Bang or not, certainly it was a primordial complexity. Very likely there was a huge catastrophe but, as Thom argued, each catastrophe is at the same time a creation of new structures. In its nature, catastrophe is morphogenetic. By disintegrating, the cosmos organizes itself, as a seismogenetic process is contemporarily a morphogenetic one. Order comes from disorder, since partial deviations transform the dispersion process into a concentration one, as Prigogine effectively showed within the dissipative structures.

Transition from disorder to order passes through interactions which are mutual actions able to modify the behaviour or the nature of objects, organisms and systems. Interactions presuppose elements which may meet each other, imply a set of meeting constraints, obey the opportunities and bonds at the stake, and, given specific conditions, originate organization of some kind. Once elements are organized, they, as an ordered system, are able to face and to put up with a large number of troubles and disorders. In such a way, organization, born from disorder, is stronger than disorder itself. Needless to say, every organization is far from being perfect, and, then, it necessarily generates disorder. Chaos is coming back again. Morin called this bidirectional process the "great game" between disorder and order, between chaos and unity.

In this eternal game, disorder, interaction, order and organization are four basic elements, which are at the same time complementary, concurrent and antagonistic. They act together and each of them is unthinkable without the others. Consequently, unlikelihood turns into local likelihood however remaining unlikelihood. Human beings are compelled to life in an uncertain universe, where the dialogue between order and disorder is the general rule and makes up the "reality". Disorder is everywhere, since there are disorders into order as well as into disorder. Nevertheless, disorder is not absolute. From it some elements start to interact due to the plain action of the probabilistic law.

In such a way interactions may originate a system, described as "a set of unities with relationships among them" (according to the perspective of von Bertalanffy), or as "a organized totality formed by unanimous elements which are defined by mutual relationships" (according to the perspective of de Saussure). Therefore, interactions give rise to the relationships which, in turn, generate a given organization. Organization is characterized by a basic *unitas multiplex*, that is, a paradox: from the standpoint of the whole, it is homogeneous; from the standpoint of the constituents it is heterogeneous. Unity is such only within difference.

Moreover, totality is more than the addition of the single parts because of the superadditive composition rule, proposed by von Foerster. As he highlighted, composition of interacting components is superadditive. This phenomenon is strictly connected with the emergence process, as emergence is a new quality referring to the system constituents. Such quality can neither be reduced into previous elements nor be deduced from them. It is a new condition of the system, unforeseeable in its becoming. Consequently, the whole and the elements are strictly tied and mutually interconnected. Already Pascal pointed out that it is impossible to know the parts without knowing the whole, as well as it is impossible to know the whole without knowing the parts. However, each totality is grounded on the competition among its elements and involves the struggle among them.

Within such a perspective, it is worth deepening on how organization is organized. Certainly, it shows a surface order, observable from everybody, in special circumstances only by the experts. In any case, such order implies invariance or stability, stratified in different layers, which enable further organizations. Organization cannot be portioned into clear-cut and discrete parts, or compartments insulated in character. Moreover, it should be noticed that organization is an active process, changing unceasingly referring to the contingent conditions of the environment. Then, organization organizes itself by means of set of assembly rules, of connections, and of transformations. It is an open and contemporarily closed system, since it interacts with the context by assuming a given identity which is circumscribed by specific borders.

In any case, organization shows patterns to obtain its goals, to face and overcome difficulties, to produce outcomes, and the like. Obviously, patterns and their detection are essential for understanding the nature and evolution of organization, as well as for communication. The competence in recognizing organizational patterns is crucial for an organism's survival, as it is a premise for foraging, danger avoidance, mate selection, and, in the whole, associating specific responses with particular events and objects.

Generally, such patterning is manifest and gives a certain shape to organization. As a rule, a manifest patterning has a macroscopic nature, easily readable from outside time by time. However, as Eibl-Eibesfeldt argued, "behaviour consists of patterns in time. Investigations of behaviour deal with sequences that, in contrast to bodily characteristics, are not always visible". Often, ever always, these hidden patterns are basic for an adequate and effective understanding of behaviour organization, since they build up its design. It is obvious that, before examining the function and evolution of any pattern, it must be first detected. Often it is impossible to detect hidden recurrent action patterns on the basis of order alone in an organization because it is characterized by a large complexity and by a great variability in the number of behaviours occurring between their components.

The purpose of this book is to highlight a new device able to discover and recognize hidden real-time patterns in intra- and inter-individual streams of behavioural events, which may include physiological and environmental events. This device, called THEME and its pattern detection algorithms were created by Magnusson on the basis of his model, called the T-system, concerning the real-time structure of behaviour and interactions. THEME has turned out to be an effective and flexible way to analyze and understand a very large range of interactive processes. The current book intends to show some of the possible applications of THEME, starting from hidden patterns in a population of neurons to cultural patterns passing through the detection of hidden patterns in non-verbal communication.

We have put a great deal of thought and effort into the definition of the structure of the book and the sequence of the contributions, so that those in search of a specific reading path will be rewarded. To this end we have divided the book into six main Sections comprising 18 chapters overall:

I.   *Theoretical framework*
II.   *Hidden patterns in neuronal and physiological activity*
III.   *Hidden patterns in courtship interaction*
IV.   *Hidden patterns in non-verbal communication within therapeutic conversation*
V.   *Hidden patterns in non-verbal communication with atypical children*
VI.   *Hidden patterns in social and cultural contexts.*

Each section will be introduced by a brief presentation, in which the main points included in it will be highlighted.

We think it is worthwhile to spend some words on THEME. The development of THEME itself started around 1980 after a number of preparatory steps. Having graduated in 1975 with a thesis on social organisation and communication in social insects and primates, Magnusson focused his doctoral research tutored by Melvin Lyon at the Psychological laboratory of Copenhagen University on verbal and non-verbal communication in humans. He thus came face-to-face with the daunting complexity of human and animal interactions. With as background the heated debates of those years among linguists, behaviourists and ethologists, he was particularly inspired by the French ethologist Hubert Montagner's discoveries of social interaction mechanisms in both social insects and humans and, in the USA, psychologist Starkey Duncan's discovery of para-verbal and non-verbal mechanisms in human turn taking. Long lasting collaboration with both resulted.

In this situation, the computer revolution, which would soon lead to the personal computer (PC), clearly offered unprecedented possibilities, and Magnusson consequently experimented with the use of a various standard multivariate statistical methods and software helped by his countryman and statistician Agnar Hoskuldsson at the Danish Technical University. Magnusson also carried out a wide ranging search for specialized behavioural analysis software in Europe and the USA, but the testing of the very few programs found indicated that new models, algorithms, and software were needed to harness this new source of power for behavioural research. Consequently, in 1979 Magnusson received a medal from the University of Copenhagen for a thesis concerning computational and ethological analysis of children's interactions seen as multivariate streams of sequential and parallel events. In this thesis he put forward some of the elements that since have grown into a combination of algorithms and a mathematical model concerning the temporal organization of behaviour and interactions.

In 1983 Magnusson accepted an invitation from André Langaney at the National Museum of Natural History in Paris to continue his work at the Anthropological Laboratory at the Musée de l'Homme in Paris where he thus came to work as associate professor and finally as deputy director until 1989. During this period, close collaboration, lasting to this day, was started with research teams at the Universities of Paris V, VIII and XIII, where he in all cases later held temporary positions as invited professor. This includes the Speech Research Group directed by Rodolphe Ghiglione at the Psychology Department of the University of Paris VIII, the Laboratory for Experimental Ethology and Sociobiology at the University of Paris XIII with Claude Baudoin et al., and finally, cognition and communication research with Janine Beaudichon et al. at the (Alfred Binet) Psychological laboratory, University of Paris V, in the Sorbonne.

On returning to his native country Iceland, Magnusson founded in 1991 the Human Behaviour Laboratory (http://www.hbl.hi.is), which he currently directs as a Research professor at the University of Iceland in Reykjavik. In 2000 he created the company PatternVision Ltd (http://www.patternvision.com), which has taken over the technical development of THEME under his direction, but THEME is currently marketed and supported worldwide by Noldus Information Technology in Holland (http://www.noldus.com).

This book may be seen as the most recent result of collaboration between research groups at a number of European universities connected by a formal inter-university convention named "Methodology for the Analysis of Social Interaction" (MASI). The group collaborates closely with researchers in the US and Japan. The formal convention, aimed at the testing of Magnusson's analytical model and the development of new methods for the analysis of social interaction, was initially created and based at the Psychological laboratory of the University of Paris V at the Sorbonne in Paris under the direction of Pr. J. Beaudichon. The MASI convention has since then been extended to include more universities and is currently based at the University of Paris VIII and is headed by Pr. A. Blanchet, President of the French Psychological Association.

The Editors gratefully acknowledge the assistance of a number of people and institutions without whose help this project could not have been carried out. We are thankful to the University of Milan-Bicocca for its support. We also acknowledge the *Fondazione Piera, Pietro e Giovanni Ferrero*, Alba, Italy, for the grant given to the Centro per gli Studi Avanzati nelle Scienze dell Comunicazione *(CESCOM – Centre for Advanced Research in Communication Sciences)* of the University of Milan-Bicocca, Italy (e-mail: cescom@unimib.it).

We are also grateful to Valentino Zurloni, Marcello Mortillaro and Linda Confalonieri, who helped the Editors in the difficult editorial process in the preparation of the current book. A final thank goes to Prof. Susanna Mantovani, Dean of the Faculty of Education Science at the University of Milan-Bicocca, and to Prof. Ugo Fabietti, Head of the Department of Epistemology and Education Hermeneutics at the same university.

Finally, we hope that the contents of this book will stimulate further integrated research by using the THEME approach to the detection of hidden real-time patterns in different scientific domains. In particular, we hope that in the near future a new deal of research on interaction and order organization may be enhanced to better understand the different phenomena and processes which define our human world.

Luigi Anolli, Ph. D.   Starkey Duncan, Ph D.   Magnus Magnusson, Ph. D.   Giuseppe Riva, Ph. D.
University of   *University of*   *University of*   *Catholic University*
Milan-Bicocca,   *Chicago,*   *Iceland, Reykjavik*   *of Milan,*
Italy   *USA*   *Iceland*   *Italy*

CONTRIBUTORS

Alessia AGLIATI, Ph. D.
Researcher in Communication Psychology
Faculty of Education Science, University of Milan-Bicocca
Milan, Italy

Maria Teresa ANGUERA, Ph. D.
Professor, Department of Methodology and Behaviour Science
Faculty of Psychology, University of Barcelona
Barcelona, Spain

Luigi ANOLLI, Ph. D.
Professor of Communication Psychology
Faculty of Education Science, University of Milan-Bicocca
Milan, Italy

Benjamin Isaac ARTHUR, Jr., Ph. D.
Research Scientist for Behavior Neurogenetics
Zoologisches Museum, University of Zurich
Zurich, Switzerland

Martine BATT, Ph. D.
Researcher in Psychology
Faculty of Psychology, University of Nancy 2,
Nancy, France

Alain BLANCHET, Ph. D.
Professor of Clinic Psychology
Faculty of Psychology, University of Paris 8
Saint Denis, France

Jonathan BLOOMFIELD, BSc
Department of Sport, Health & Exercise Science, University of Hull
Hull, United Kingdom

Starkey DUNCAN, Jr., Ph.D.
Professor of Psychology
University of Chicago
Chicago, IL, USA

Didone FRIGERIO, Ph. D.
Konrad Lorenz Research Station for Ethology,
Gruenau, Austria
University of Vienna
Vienna, Austria

Christina HARDWAY, Ph. D.
Adjunct Professor of Psychology
Suffolk University
Boston, MA, USA

Toshikazu HASEGAWA, Ph. D.
Professor of Cognitive and Behavioral Psychology
Graduate School of Arts and Sciences, The University of Tokyo
Tokyo, Japan

Véronique HAYNAL-REYMOND, Ph. D.
University Psychiatric Hospitals,
Geneva, Switzerland

Katharina HIRSCHENHAUSER, Ph. D.
Konrad Lorenz Research Station for Ethology,
Gruenau, Austria
University of Vienna
Vienna, Austria

Kenneth HOULAHAN, MSc
Sport and exercise development consultant

Gudberg K. JONSSON, Ph. D.
Human Behavior Laboratory, University of Iceland
Reykjavik, Iceland
Department of Psychology, University of Aberdeen
Aberdeen, United Kingdom

Keith M. KENDRICK, Ph. D.
Laboratory of Cognitive & Behavioural Neuroscience
The Babraham Institute, Babraham Research Campus,
Cambridge, United Kingdom
Gresham Professor of Physic (and the other biological sciences), Gresham College,
London, United Kingdom

Sabine C. KOCH, M.A., D.T.R.
Social Psychologist and Communication Researcher
University of Heidelberg
Heidelberg, Germany

Lenelis KRUSE, Ph. D.
Professor of Environmental and Social Psychology
Fernuniversität Hagen
Hagen, Germany
Honorary Professor, University of Heidelberg
Heidelberg, Germany

Magnus S. MAGNUSSON, Ph. D.
Research Professor,
Director of the Human Behavior Laboratory, University of Iceland
Reykjavik, Iceland

Laurence MASSE, Ph. D.
Associate Professor of Social Psychology
Faculty in Psychology, University of Paris 8
Saint Denis, France

Jörg MERTEN, Ph. D.
Lecturer in Clinical Psychology
Faculty of Empirical Human Sciences, Saarland University
Saarbrücken, Germany

Stephanie M. MÜLLER, Ph. D.
Research Assistant,
Department of Language and Social Psychology, University of Heidelberg
Heidelberg, Germany

Alister NICOL, Ph. D.
Laboratory of Cognitive & Behavioural Neuroscience
The Babraham Institute, Babraham Research Campus
Cambridge, United Kingdom

Peter O'DONOGHUE, Ph. D.
Lecturer in Sport and Exercise Science
Department of School of Sport, PE & Recreation, University of Wales Institute Cardiff
Cardiff, United Kingdom

Marie-Hélène PLUMET, Ph. D.
Lecturer in Developmental Psychology,
Institute of Psychology, University Paris 5-René Descartes,
Paris, France

Remco POLMAN, Ph. D.
Lecturer in Sport and Exercise Psychology
Department of Sport, Health & Exercise Science, University of Hull
Hull, United Kingdom

Giuseppe RIVA, Ph. D.
Associate Professor in Communication Psychology
Faculty of Psychology, Catholic University
Milan, Italy

Kikue SAKAGUCHI, Ph. D.
Graduate School of Arts and Sciences, The University of Tokyo
Tokyo, Japan

Sylvia SASTRE-RIBA, Ph.D.
Professor of Developmental Psychology
Faculty of Humanities and Education, University of La Rioja
Logroño, Spain

Antje SCHROEER, M.A.
Linguist and Communication Researcher
University of Heidelberg
Heidelberg, Germany

Frank SCHWAB, Ph. D.
Scientific Assistant in Media- and Organizational Psychology
Faculty of Empirical Human Sciences, Saarland University
Saarbrücken, Germany

Carole TARDIF, Ph. D.
Lecturer in Developmental Psychopathology,
Department of Psychology, University of Provence Aix-Marseille I,
Aix-en-Provence, France

Caja THIMM, Ph. D.
Professor of Communication and Media Studies,
University of Bonn
Bonn, Germany

Alain TROGNON, Ph. D.
Professor of Social Psychology
Faculty of Psychology, University of Nancy 2
Nancy, France

Dagmar C. UNZ, Dr. rer. Soc.
Scientific Assistant in Media- and Organizational Psychology
Faculty of Empirical Human Sciences, Saarland University
Saarbrücken, Germany

Antonietta VESCOVO
Researcher in Communication Psychology
Faculty of Education Science, University of Milan-Bicocca
Milan, Italy

Joerg ZUMBACH
Educational and Instructional Psychologist
University of Heidelberg
Heidelberg, Germany

Valentino ZURLONI, Ph. D.
Researcher in Communication Psychology
Faculty of Education Science, University of Milan-Bicocca
Milan, Italy

Contents

SECTION I

THEORETICAL FRAMEWORK

Behind the pattern definition lies the hypothesis that both hidden and manifest behaviour patterns may involve similar relations among their parts. The T-pattern definition, therefore, attempts to abstract some of these relations in order to create an algorithm for the definition of hidden patterns

Magnusson, 2000

From proteins to human individuals, to large companies or whole cities, most of the interaction processes that take place around us and within us are hidden to our naked eyes and ears. The reasons for this differ considerably as interactions take place concurrently within the invisible world of molecules, cells and tissues and deep within hives or cities of insects. Such phenomena clearly raise methodological problems, since only adequate models, methods and tools may allow the detection of such patterns.

The current section aims to provide an initial insight and reference point for the concept of "hidden patterns" and the methods used to detect them. In particular, in this session is assumed that hidden patterns do share some structural characteristics with well-known everyday patterns; some of their structural aspects have been abstracted and combined to create a general and scale independent pattern-type. The final goal of the session is double, that is, to allow readers an effective search for hidden patterns and provide elements for a new kind of "grammar" concerning the real-time structure of behavior and interactions.

To achieve this goal, chapter 1, written by MAGNUSSON, underlines the importance of discovering hidden patterns to better understand social interactions. How interactions organize into a working system seems to be a common subject of molecular biology and human interaction research. The discovery of the essence of biological heredity involved a methodological progression from the quantitative to the structural. Quantitative measures allowed the detection of particularly high concentrations of a molecular substance in certain places and helped bringing the focus upon it.

Then gradually deeper structural analysis, first brought out the cyclical structure of that substance and then the combinatorial system hidden within it as well as some of its "auto-interactive" aspects. The analysis of human interactions appears to be following this general methodological path, that is, after focusing on the purely quantitative, the focus is turning further towards structure and a search for sequences, hierarchical/syntactic patterns, new kinds of "grammars", and even "programs". Following such paradigm, the more formal definitions of the T-pattern, the derived "T-system", and the discovery of a mathematical algorithm are outlined in this chapter.

Chapter 2, by ANOLLI, focused on analyzing the hidden design of meaning. According to the author, meaning turns out to be the local outcome of a large and consistent multiplicity of distinctive semantic facets, some of which are apparent and immediately understandable, while others are latent and concealed. As a result, meaning is not given once and for all and for any circumstance; instead, it should be recognized and defined each time within a specific situation.

The present chapter aimed at facing this complex subject by developing a course through three subsequent steps. First, the meaning complexity was deepened considering different theoretical standpoints: the truth-conditional semantics, the structural semantics, and the cognitive semantics. Second, the dilemma between variability and stability of meaning was examined. Obviously, meaning is a flexible and contingent matter, insofar as it is subjected to a wide range of semantic phenomena like the defeasibility of semantic traits, fuzzy boundaries, the radial categorization, the semantic gradualness and polysemy, context dependence, and so on. Third, on this platform it was worth analysing the compositionality of meaning in its different versions. Particularly, the feature semantics, the extended prototype theory, and the type-pattern framework will be focused.

Within such theoretical framework, the author highlighted how the type-pattern concept, proposed by Magnusson for a wide range of interactions and events, is also very useful for semantic analysis and understanding. Within the communicative sequence of exchanges between interlocutors, there seems to be some chances to initiate a new path to detect, recognize, and interpret meaning in an empirical way, adhering to the contingent situation in a given cultural system. In particular, the present chapter advanced and illustrated a new model based on the T-patterns detection, as, based on empirical observations extracted from the flow of communicative events, it seems to arrange quite well both with the variability and the stability of meaning. The detection of T-patterns enables to appreciate the hidden design of meaning encompassed in an utterance or in a nonverbal item not generally and in an abstract way but locally and in a contingent manner. The attention is focused on the local management of meaning, as each moment communicators have the opportunity of organizing, regulating, managing and monitoring their communicative interaction through the most effective choice between different semantic routes.

In chapter 3, ANGUERA analysed the relationships between the structure of data gathered from a recording of an interactive situation and the temporal patterns (T-patterns) obtained through use of THEME software. The specific question that constitutes the *leitmotif* of the present chapter is the study of the hidden structures underlying an interactive situation: the way in which temporal patterns are able to reveal those aspects of social interaction which are not immediately observable. Every interactive flow is governed by behavioural structures of varying stability that can be visualized by obtaining temporal patterns (T-patterns). More in detail, the chapter deepens the following three issues. First, the enormous wealth of information contained within every interactive situation and the great power of the THEME software in detecting hidden patterns, which are then visualized and analyzed through knowledge of their structure. Second, the great versatility of T-patterns, which are subject to multiple recording contingencies such as the duration of behaviours in each episode and/or the type of recording, etc Finally, the chapter suggests the existence of an 'isomorphism' between symmetry/asymmetry which arises in each interactive situation and inside the T-patterns obtained.

1. Understanding Social Interaction: Discovering Hidden Structure with Model and Algorithms

Magnus S. MAGNUSSON

Abstract. The dynamics of interaction between actors making up an organized system is a complex matter where myriads of events are constantly happening within ever changing spatial and temporal contexts that determine the ultimate meaning, effect and function of each event. For the understanding of such systems quantification alone is not enough, matters of pattern and structure must be considered. It is pointed out that most of the behavioural sciences have traditionally accepted repeated patterns among their central concerns. However, tools based on relevant and adequate models and methods have been hard to find in this area and easily available standard statistical methods generally developed for different tasks therefore direct research away from structural approaches. The importance of considering not only order but also real-time when searching for hidden interaction structure is underlined and a real-time model, called the T-system, is advanced together with specifically created detection algorithms and commercially available software (THEME). A particular pattern type, called T-pattern, is the core of the model and its detection is based on the definition of a so called critical interval relation among series of points on a single dimension such as time. It is argued that repeated patterns of the T-pattern type are frequent at highly different levels of organization from information molecules to proteins, neurons, and human verbal and non-verbal interaction. Examples are presented of T-patterns detected in children's interaction as well as interactions among neurons in brain tissue. References are provided to applications of T-pattern analysis within psychology, psychiatry, psychopharmacology, sports science, ethology, and neuroscience. A "bird's eye view" is thus advocated in the search for essential features exemplified by those conserved in genetic materials across all living species where even some genes may be found among practically all life forms. It is suggested that behavioural research is following a logical progression from quantitative to structural analysis somewhat similar to that leading to the discovery of the patterns on DNA molecules, the genetic code and then genetic control programs. It is pointed out that pattern detection is already producing new data for quantitative analysis, classification and diagnostics. It is finally suggested that intelligence may always presuppose interaction and interaction patterns.

Keywords: Context; quantitative; structural; real-time; T-system; detection; neurons; DNA; THEME.

Contents

1.1   Introduction

When two or more individuals interact, whether they are humans, monkeys, mice or fruit flies, many things are happening at the same time. Trunks, heads, limbs and various extremities are moving, sounds and odours are emitted and perceived while whole bodies change postures and locations relative to each other and the environment. All this is occurring at the same time as numerous events of various types occur concurrently and sequentially within and across individuals in countless ways. They are clearly not just ordered as letters or words in lines of text. And the same is actually true for the multitude of events in the sound stream of speech, where linguistic and paralinguistic events are mixed in time and paralinguistic elements sometimes modify or even annul the meaning or effect of verbal ones and vice-versa. Little or none of this is, however, visible in the highly abstract coding in written text. It is after at least tens of thousands of years of talking together that humans have recently become able to transform their speech sounds streams into longer lasting objects, i.e., to produce text. Similarly, the rich and rigorous structure of spoken language, some of which is now expressed in grammars, remained largely unnoticed through thousands and thousands of years. It seems therefore quite possible that much structure in human interactions remains undiscovered, but it also appears that trying to order all that's happening into a simple string may result in misleading oversimplification. But even if this was attempted there would surely be a myriad of ways to do it and only deep understanding of what is essential could guide such an undertaking. That understanding will have to deal with complex real-time streams of behaviour concurrently produced by two or more individuals. The model and methods outlined below were aimed at this task. They are based on an attempted "bird's eye view" as a way to learn from structural analogies across highly different levels of biological organization. Such analogies are assumed to be of special importance and point to something essential just as various stretches of DNA molecules, i.e., some genes, are practically identical across all species and thus point to something essential for life. It seems, moreover, that some structural types, analogous to those in DNA, occur also in the time domain, that is, as patterns in both individual behaviour and interactions and at various time scales.

1.1.1   Actors and Interaction

In this text it is assumed that *interaction* implies more than one party where, minimally, one is influencing one other, while *social* implies some kind of *system* within which each interaction takes place, involving different types of entities, individuals or *actors* (sometimes also called agents, parties, players, etc.). Within a cell the actors may be proteins (see below); in body tissue they are cells; in insect hives or human cities they are individual insects or humans. All have particular shapes and special parts they can move at various characteristic speeds and change postures or shapes thereby changing their attractiveness and relationships with others. And all are sensitive to such aspects in others (for example [1]). The function and place of an individual within the interaction system is affected by its interactions and in turn shapes them and when an individual enters into existence the time and place as well as the system's state at that moment is necessarily beyond the individual's control, but often essential for the individual's fate.

1.1.2   Individual, Whole and the Invisible

"In the existing sciences much of the emphasis over the past century or so has been on breaking systems down to find their underlying parts, then trying to analyze these parts in as much detail as possible. And particularly in physics this approach has been sufficiently successful that the basic components of everyday systems are by now completely known. But just how these components act together to produce even some of the most obvious features of the overall behaviour we see has in the past remained an almost complete mystery" [2, p.3]

Interactions of individuals often become coordinated into a functional whole that at a higher level of organization may be an actor again. This necessitates a flow of control up and down the organizational levels. It may be all the way from proteins to human individuals to large companies or whole cities. However, most of the interaction processes that take place around us and within us are hidden to our naked eyes and ears. The reasons for this differ considerably as interactions take place concurrently within the invisible world of molecules, cells and tissues and deep within hives or cities of insects and humans difficult or forbidden to observe. Others are too complex and/or extended in time and/or space. There seems little doubt that only a tiny fraction of the interaction mechanisms involved in any and all of the biological interaction systems humans are aware of is currently known and that the vast majority is hidden to the eyes, ears, instruments, and methods of modern humans. Figure 1.1 illustrates how difficult it can be to detect patterns directly even under very simple and fairly ideal circumstances, and, surprisingly, for various more complex cases, adequate statistical methods are not readily available to aide in their discovery.

What then if interaction patterns essential for the understanding of our own behaviour and communication go undetected? This also poses problems regarding the most elementary and easily detected behavioural elements since a complex hidden pattern could be the context determining their meaning. Such phenomena clearly raise methodological problems that call for adequate models, methods and tools to allow the detection of such patterns.

1.1.3 From Quantitative to Structural

The discovery of the essence of biological heredity involved a methodological progression from the quantitative to the structural (see, for example [3]). Quantitative measures allowed the detection of particularly high concentrations of a molecular substance in certain places and helped bringing the focus upon it.

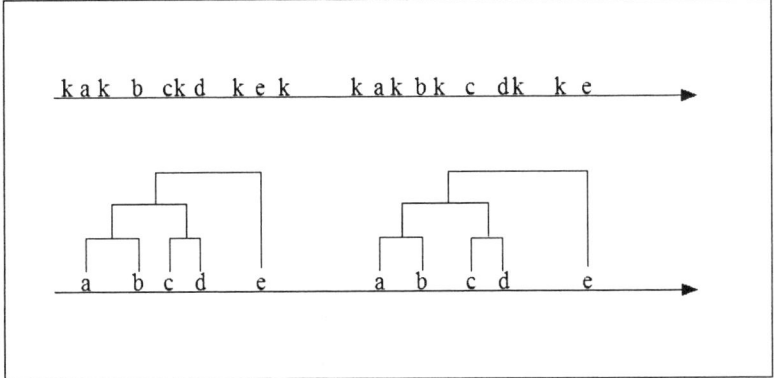

Figure 1.1 This figure illustrates how little it takes for a repeated pattern of the T-pattern type to become invisible to the unaided observer. The upper axis and its letter pattern is a copy of the lower one, but with only a few instances of "k" added.

Then gradually deeper structural analysis, first brought out the cyclical structure of that substance and then the combinatorial system hidden within it as well as some of its "auto-interactive" aspects. Thus was discovered the essential DNA structure [4] (see also [5, 6]) and the genetic code and then feed-back interactions between its parts mediated through their own products, proteins, thus creating control programs [7].

As witnessed amongst other by the chapters of this volume, the analysis of human interactions appears to be following this general methodological path, that is, after focusing on the purely quantitative, i.e., frequencies and durations and then frequency waves, the focus is turning further towards structure and a search for sequences, hierarchical/syntactic patterns, new kinds of "grammars" (see below), and even "programs" (see, chapter 14 in this volume).

This development has been slow to be adopted within Psychology as witnessed by the following rather dramatic quote, but this seems partly true for some related areas such as, for example, ethology:

"Only about 8% of all psychological research is based on any kind of observation. A fraction of that is programmatic research. And, a fraction of that is sequential in its thinking" [8, p. 184].

Early research on "face-to-face" interaction [9, 10] showed how regularities in such behaviour may come to light through the use of adequate methods. Such discoveries depend increasingly on recent technologies to "fix the object (behaviour)", i.e., film and video, and then to code and to deal with the complex information obtained from their in-depth analysis, i.e., interactive multimedia programs and algorithms implemented in easily accessible software. But for such work to succeed the models (structural ideas or hypotheses), methods and technology applied in the search for hidden structure or regularities must be adequate and powerful. In the opposite case the situation can become a bit like using a hammer to search for square planetary orbits; a hopeless undertaking no matter how hard one works. Theoretical and methodological issues are no doubt particularly important in studies of interaction systems because their complexity is unforgiving. In spite of this, easy access to standard statistical software often seems to decide the choice of approach in behavioural and interaction studies.

The present work, which has evolved over a considerable period [11-18] was initially inspired in very different ways by theoretical and empirical research concerning the structure of behaviour and interactions with special focus on real-time, probabilistic, functional and sequential aspects as well as hierarchical/syntactic structure, creativity, routines and planning (for example, [19-26]).

1.1.4   Interaction and Algorithms

Convergence between views and methodologies at such very different levels of biological organization do not end here but continues into studies of "social" interaction systems:

"A modern view of molecular biology is concerned with *organization* in time and space. How do the molecules of life arrange themselves amongst the cell's compartments, how are they shifted around, how do they communicate so as to synchronize their action? We can ask these questions only because we can now inspect the working cell at the molecular level, taking measurements and snapshots of molecules going about their business. And so the cell becomes a community" [27, p. 44].

How interactions organize into a working system thus seems to be a common subject of molecular biology and human interaction research and this is further underlined by the following quote from the same source:

"Molecular biology is not difficult in the way theoretical physics is difficult – *the concepts are not unfamiliar, abstract, or mathematically abstruse. The difficulty arises because there is so much going on at once.* We react with surprise and shock when things go wrong with our own molecular machinery, but it is far more astonishing that the machinery works at all. Frequently it does so because it is designed to be robust in the face of the world's vicissitudes. There are checkpoints, safety mechanisms, back-up plans, careful record-keeping" [27, p. 44] (Emphasis added).

The fact that the concepts are not difficult but familiar surely reflects their common use regarding human activity within human communities and cities. The problem of "too much going on at the same time" may also be a fundamental problem associated with the study of the true complexity of interaction systems rather than focusing on their elements and splitting them ever finer and thereby eliminating interaction possibilities.

1.1.5   Algorithms vs. Equations

How to deal with the overwhelming complexity of interaction systems? It seems obvious that without the still ongoing computer revolution any attack on the real complexity of social interaction systems would be futile.

Much hope seems to lie in new and better algorithms and ever more powerful and cheaper computers. Algorithms, considered among mathematics' greatest inventions, what are they:

"An algorithm is a finite procedure, written in a fixed symbolic vocabulary, governed by precise instructions, moving in discrete steps, 1, 2, 3, ..., whose execution requires no insight, cleverness, intuition, intelligence, or perspicuity, and that sooner or later comes to an end" [28, p. xviii].

And the analogy with social interaction processes is immediately noticed:

"After all, what is a bureaucracy but a social organization that has since at least the time of the ancient Chinese patiently undertaken the execution of complicated algorithms?" [28, p. xii].

It is often said that the difference between, for example, social insects and humans in this respect is that humans are conscious about what they are doing. But consider, for example, a simple clerk in a vast (ancient Chinese) bureaucracy. How conscious would he/she be about the ultimate effect of his/her activity? The individual would surely be conscious of each act of "pushing paper", but not even the director of a whole branch of a bureaucracy might know that its current activity is a part of a strategic move, for example, to deal with a political problem or overtake some neighbouring country. By analogy with proximal and distal causes, one might possibly talk of proximal and distal consciousness, which clearly do not always go together: "Human society contemplated with a tranquil and disinterested eye appears at first to display only the violence of powerful men and the oppression of the weak; the mind is revolted by the harshness of the strong; one is impelled to deplore the blindness of the weak..." [29, p. 17].

From a theoretical and methodological standpoint, it seems that in science the consequences of the computer revolution with its focus on algorithms may go very deep indeed:

"Tree centuries ago science was transformed by the dramatic new idea that rules based on mathematical equations could be used to describe the natural world. My purpose in this book is to initiate another such transformation, and to introduce a new kind of science that is based on the much more general types of rules that can be embodied in simple computer programs" [2, p. 1].

1.1.6   Model Pattern and a Detection Algorithm

The problem of "too much happening at the same time", even within a few minutes of face-to-face interaction between two toddlers provided more than sufficient inspiration and material for the theoretical, methodological and technical development that has led to the definition of a particular but very general time pattern type called T-pattern, which can be seen as a hypothesis concerning the real-time structure of behaviour and interactions. Corresponding detection algorithms and software (THEME) have been developed. The main definitions and some of the motivations behind them are outlined here, but a more thorough description with a list of references amongst other to applications in a number of areas has appeared elsewhere [16] (www.hbl.hi.is also contains a regularly updated list of references).

The behavioural sciences have long considered repeated patterns as an essential aspect of behaviour. Clearly, in Linguistics and Ethology repeated temporal patterns are amongst central concerns and radical behaviourism deals with real-time contingencies, i.e., patterns also with a focus on repetition. In Anthropology, Social Psychology and Sociology repeated temporal patterns such as, for example, scripts, plans, routines, strategies, rituals and ceremonies are important concerns. Within the arts and music, in particular, repeated real-time patterns are omnipresent and often fascinate humans to the highest degree. Generally, the patterns in question are not only patterns of elements as their various components are also patterns as, for example, any common phrase that is a repeated pattern of words, which again are composed of letters, etc. Note that, as we go from the phrase to the letter the patterns in question become increasingly frequent, that is, in a standard phrase, each of its words are more frequent than the phrase, and any letter more frequent than a word. On the other hand, there are far more different words than letters.

But behaviour is not always as plain to see as words and letters on a page:

"*Behaviour* consists of *patterns in time*. Investigations of behaviour deal with sequences that, in contrast to bodily characteristics, are *not always visible*" [30, p.1] (Emphasis added).

Perceptual aids like the microscope and the telescope were developed to deal with detection of phenomena beyond direct human perception. Similarly, behavioural patterns that escape direct human detection call for new perceptual aids ("behaviourscopes"?) based on adequate ideas concerning their structure.

A basic assumption here is that hidden patterns in behaviour do share some structural characteristics with well-known everyday behaviour patterns. Some structural aspects of such patterns were therefore abstracted and combined to create a general, scale independent pattern-type. The aim is double, that is, to allow effective search for hidden patterns and possibly to provide elements for a new kind of real-time probabilistic "grammar" concerning the structure of behaviour and interactions. Here, some characteristics of a few everyday patterns can serve to illustrate the main aspects.

"How are you?" An intra-individual verbal pattern.

"How are you? Fine, thank you." An inter-individual verbal pattern.

Bill says: "Pass me the salt Jack" followed by Jack passing him the salt. An an inter-individual mixed verbal/non-verbal pattern.

"If..then..else" is a verbal pattern with slots (here indicated with dots) that may be filled in various ways.

A typical dinner (in the western world) is also such a pattern of components which themselves are patterns, for example, a person "(1) sits down at table...(2) has a starter...(3) a main course...(4) a dessert...(5) coffee...(6) stands up from table". See figure 1.2.

As in "if..then..else", each of the components of the dinner is itself a pattern and there are also the "free" (dotted) time slots where various other behavioural elements may occur in various numbers. It is exactly this last aspect that makes the detection of such patterns so difficult using sequential analysis methods based exclusively on the sequential order of events, but the algorithm described below deals with that problem by considering, simultaneously, the order of events, the time distances between them, their positions on a real-time scale and the average probability of occurrence per time unit of each and every component at all hierarchical levels.

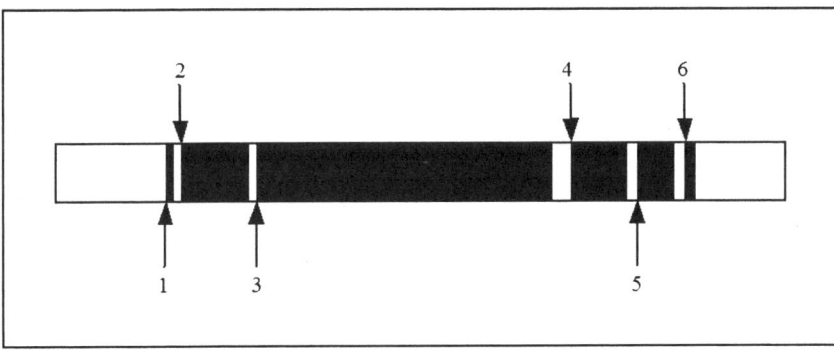

Figure 1.2 This figure, which could be called a "dinner-gene" can be interpreted in different ways, explained in the text. The numbers 1 to 6 show where its six component patterns begin. The figure should be thought of as being flexible or elastic, such that the object and/or any number of its dark and light parts could be stretched and squeezed changing their relative lengths but to a limited extent, i.e., as a rubber band. See text.

In each of these patterns, the components occur in a particular order and the temporal distance from one to the next is of an approximate length that is characteristic for the particular pattern. If these time distances between components become too short or too long the pattern becomes strange or disappears altogether. Squeezed and stretched too much, a spoken sentence or a melody will cease to be. The same is actually true for the great molecules of life, they are quite flexible, but can only be stretched to a limit. The limits of flexibility are typically quite strict making the occurrence of patterns of this kind highly improbable a priori, that is, they would hardly ever recur with such similarity if their components were simply occurring independently and randomly with their observed frequencies.

These constrains are here essential for the detection of patterns often impossible to detect on the basis of component order alone because of the highly varied number of other behaviours that occur between their components. This is especially true if the pattern is complex and rare as often is the case for important phenomena.

When considered in this way, as patterns on a single dimension, which may be either temporal or spatial, the above everyday patterns seem to correspond to a large class of patterns in individual and inter-individual behaviour as well as patterns within information molecules such as DNA.

1.2   The T-pattern

In the following sections the more formal definitions of the T-pattern and the derived "T-system" are outlined (for further details see [16]). The T-pattern definition refers to a particular, but essentially well known data type.

1.2.1   The data type

An *event-type* here refers to some behaviour that occurs or not at a particular point on a discrete time scale, but has no duration otherwise: For example, "Bill begins walking" (or short: bill,b,walk) and Sue ends talking (sue,e,talk) are event types. They may also be further qualified, for example, bill,b,walk,fast; sue,e,talk,loud,bill (Sue ends talking loudly to Bill). The behaviour is coded in terms of the occurrence times of such beginnings and endings (points) on a discrete time scale. Each beginning and/or ending thus occurs or not at a discrete time point. Any number of event-types may occur at the same point (i.e., basic time unit). The time unit can be of any size, for example, milliseconds or days (see, for example, chapters 4 and 5 in this volume), but can also be years, decades, etc., depending on the system being studied. The occurrences of all event-types within a given continuous observation period thus constitute the type of multivariate time point process (see, for example, [31]), here called T-data or T-dataset, that is referred to by the T-pattern definition. Event types can also be other than behavioural in the strict sense such as, for example, it begins to rain, heart-rate increases, car breaks down, earthquake begins, alarm clock rings, shares fall, storm ends, temperature decreases, the sun comes out, etc.

Figure 1.3 shows an example of a T-dataset with 82 event type occurrence series. This particular data is the result of coding approximately 13.5 min of interaction between two children using interactive multimedia software and 1/15 s as the time unit (i.e., one video frame in this case) and a pre-existing list of behavioural categories [32].

1.2.2   The T-pattern structure

A T-pattern with m components $X_{i..m}$ (each an event type or a T-pattern) can be noted as:

$$X_1 \, [d_1, d_2]_1 \, X_2 \, [d_1, d_2]_2 \, .. \, X_i \, [d_1, d_2]_i \, X_{i+1} \, .. \, X_{m-1} \, [d_1, d_2]_{m-1} \, X_m$$

$[d_1, d_2]_i$ stands for the interval within which the characteristic distances vary. $X_i \, [d_1, d_2]_i \, X_{i+1}$ thus means: if X_i ends at t, it is followed within $[t+d_1, t+d_2]_i$ by the beginning of component X_{i+1}. Furthermore, any T-pattern can be described as a binary tree by splitting it recursively (top-down) into left and right halves until the event-type level is reached. Thus, for detection purposes, the T-pattern definition is narrowed to a binary tree of *critical intervals* between left and right branches:

$$X_{left} \, [d_1, d_2] \, X_{right}$$

Where X_{left} stands for the first part, ending at t, followed within $[t+d_1, t+d_2]$ by the beginning of X_{right}; where $0 \leq d_1 \leq d_2$. In $[d_1, d_2]$, t is omitted to simplify notation. Note that, when the two branches are concurrent, $0 = d1 = d2$.

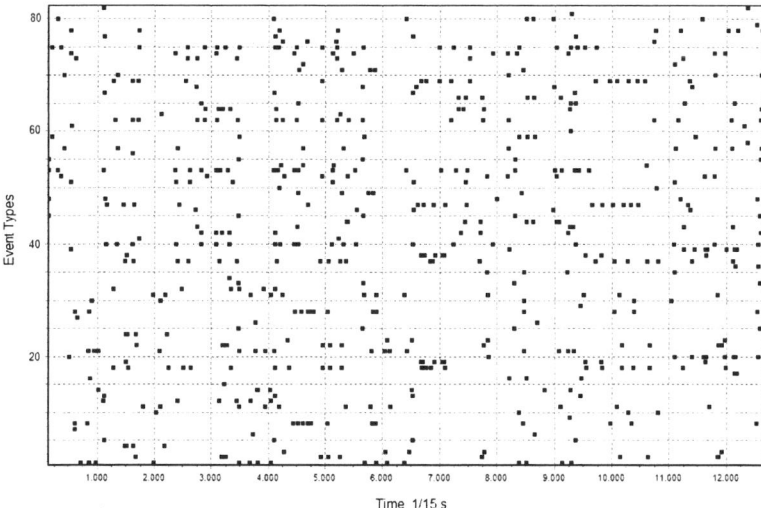

Time 1/15 s

Figure 1.3 This figure shows a typical data set of the kind that is referred to by the T-pattern definition and is the input to the T-pattern detection algorithm. It shows the occurrence times (point) series of the 82 event types coded from a video recording of two five-year-olds 13.5 min dyadic object play.

1.2.3   The detection algorithm

In behaviour records with a hundred event-types each occurring at least twice, the number of possible patterns involving, for example, ten event-types is colossal, that is, far greater than 100^{10}. Trying out all possible sequences of all lengths is thus not an option. Instead, the algorithm reveres the above top-down recursive splitting and performs bottom-up construction. Beginning with T-data it uses a critical interval detection algorithm to build binary T-pattern trees.

The *critical interval algorithm* measures the time from each occurrence (end) of X_{left} to the first following or concurrent occurrence (beginning) of X_{right}. Using this distribution and some preset significance level, it searches for the longest possible interval $[d_1, d_2]$ such that (X_{left}) (ending at t) is, significantly more often than expected by h0, followed within $[t+d_1, t+d_2]$ by the beginning of another component (X_{right}); where h0 is that (X_{right}) is independently randomly distributed over the observation period $[t_1, t_2]$ with a constant probability per time unit $= N(X_{right}) / (t_2-t_1+1)$; where $N(X_{right})$ is the number of occurrences of X_{right}. If found, the critically related instances of each of the two components are connected and added to the data as the occurrences of a new T-pattern, which later in the process may become the (left or right) part of a more complex pattern. Increasingly complex patterns may thus be detected as patterns of patterns of patterns, etc.

However, a T-pattern of length > 2 may be represented as a binary tree in various ways, for example, ABCD as ((A (B C)) D), ((A B)(C D)), (((A B) C) D), etc. Complex T-patterns existing in the data may thus be detected (constructed) in many different ways. This can easily lead to numerous partial and/or redundant detections. To deal with this, patterns are automatically compared and those occurring only as parts of other more *complete* patterns are dropped. The search ends when no more critical intervals can be found.

At very low preset significance levels no patterns are found. At some higher level (often near 0.005) all the most complex patterns have been detected, while at still higher levels the same patterns are redundantly discovered as more and more binary trees become significant for each underlying pattern. Pattern *growth* (construction) and completeness *competition* thus often lead to the *evolution* of both simple and complex patterns that are the result of the search process.

1.2.4   Regular vs. similar

Repetition is essential in the current definition of the T-pattern type. A single instance of a T-pattern is typically not regular in any way and such regularity is not a defining characteristic. For a given T-pattern, even if none of its instances are regular, they are all similar in the particular way specified by the above definition that relates to the overall frequency of the components and their hierarchical/syntactic relations. From other points of view, the instances of a T-pattern may be seen as not similar at all.

1.2.5   Statistical methods and T-patterns

The essential T-pattern algorithms were initially developed [11, 12] after careful consideration of standard statistical methods and especially those commonly used in behaviour analysis (see, for example, [33-35]) and implemented in various statistical packages and in behaviour analysis software (for example, [36, 37]). Such methods were not, however, developed for and do not allow the detection of complex T-patterns. They neither provide a T-pattern definition, automatic critical interval detection, multi-ordinal bottom-up pattern construction nor pattern evolution through completeness competition.

1.2.6   The T-system

Other terms have consequently been derived from the T-pattern to gradually form the so called, *T-system*, which is proposed as the possible beginning of a kind of probabilistic "grammar" for the description and analysis of the real-time structure of behaviour and interaction. Definitions of the main terms derived from the T-pattern follow.

T-set: all the patterns detected within the same T-dataset.

T-marker: a T-pattern component that rarely occurs independently of that pattern and thus strongly indicates its occurrence (presence) [38].

T-associate, positive or negative (+/-): some behaviour (event-type or pattern) that is *not* a component of a T-pattern Q, but with significant positive vs. negative tendency to occur within or near Q. It may thus serve as an indicator of the occurrences of Q; a *T-satellite* of Q is a positive T-associate occurring exclusively with Q, while a *T-taboo* of Q is a negative T-associate that never accompanies Q.

T-attraction zones of a pattern Q (positive and negative). A positive zone stretches from zp1 time units before to zp2 time units after each occurrences of Q and is the smallest zone where positive associates of Q are found. Thus if $[a_i, b_i]$; $i=1..NQ$ is the series of durations intervals of Q, then $[a_i - zp1, b_i + zp2]$; $i=1..NQ$ is its series of positive attraction intervals. Similarly, $[a_i - zn1, b_i + zn2]$ is its series of negative attraction intervals.

T-packet: a T-pattern with its positive and negative associates and +/- attraction zones.

T-drifters are behaviours belonging to none of the other categories of the system.

T-coverage of a pattern is the total amount of time when the pattern is in progress (its total duration) that can be expressed as a percentage of the observation period.

T-composition: for a given initial set X of patterns (such as the T-set) it refers to the sub-set of alternating non-overlapping patterns that has the highest combined coverage of all possible sub-sets of X.

T-path: when the event types of a T-pattern correspond to points in space, a T-pattern defines a path in that space called a T-path (see figure 1.7).

T-path network: two or more paths belonging to the same T-set (see figure 1.8).

1.3   Research application and the THEME software

Special software, called THEME, has been developed for the detection and analysis of T-patterns and an increasing number of other T-system elements. Its development continues at PatternVision Ltd (see www.patternvision.com) in collaboration with the Human Behavior Laboratory, University of Iceland (see www.hbl.hi.is).

T-pattern analysis with THEME has been applied in a number in different research areas such as psychology, psychiatry, ethology, psychophysiology and sports science (for example [39-56]).

International marketing and support for THEME is in the hands of Noldus Information Technology (see www.noldus.com, which also maintains a data-base of THEME application references).

1.3.1   T-pattern Examples and Diagrams

In this section T-patterns detected in human interaction (figures 1.4 and 1.5) and in interactions between neurons in brain tissue (figures 1.6 and 1.7) are presented using diagrams specially developed to make even complex T-patterns as accessible as possible. A diagram of this kind shows the binary tree structure, i.e., how a T-pattern has been gradually detected as pairs of already detected patterns or event types. It also shows the occurrences time series of the original event types (as in figure 1.3) involved in the pattern and which occurrences of each were connected to form the pattern.

The first example concerns a pattern detected in an interaction between two five-year-old girls playing with a toy, a handheld viewer for viewing picture cards. The T-dataset is that shown in figure 1.3, but figures 1.4 and 1.5 present in different ways the longest (highest value of m) T-pattern detected in this data.

In figure 1.4, the left box shows the full sequence (string) of event-types (i.e., $X_1..X_{m;}$ here $m = 27$) and the binary tree relations between them. Level-by-level, from level 0 (initial event types) to level 9, the event types of the pattern are connected into patterns of growing complexity (length). Note that some of the event types are repeated within the terminal string (sequence) of 27 event types, but different instances are involved. Moreover, in all but the last occurrence of this particular pattern, its last event is the first event of its next occurrence. The right box shows the occurrence times of each of the 27 event types in the pattern immediately to its right (some of these series are thus repeated). Connection lines, corresponding to the tree on the left, show how the critically related instances of event-types and/or sub-patterns are connected on the basis of detected critical interval relationships. Sub-patterns occurring sometimes outside the full pattern are also visible.

The upper box in figure 1.5 is the same as the right box of figure 1.4 except that its height has been reduced and it has been aligned with a different presentation shown in the lower-box, which only shows occurrences of the complete T-pattern tree and in a manner similar to the trees in the lower part of figure 1.1, but without the labels. (Note that when event-types occur concurrently within a pattern, lines overlap and branching disappears.)

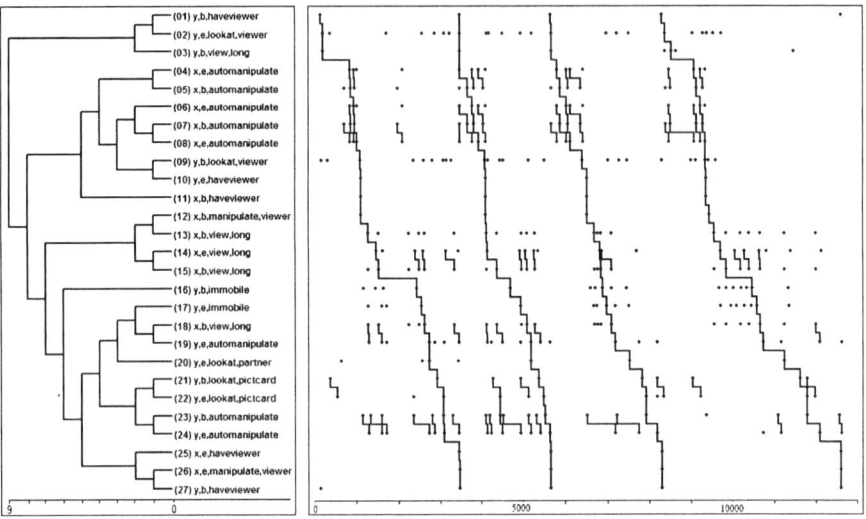

Figure 1.4 This figure shows a pattern detected by the T-pattern detection algorithm in the data shown in figure 1.3. See text on how to read this kind of pattern and explanations of label meanings.

The event type labels of figure 1.4 are composed in the following way:

x and y represent the two five-year-olds actors.

b and e mean, respectively, begins and ends.

The list from 1 to 27 means: 1) y begins having the viewer; 2) y ends looking at the viewer; 3) y begins looking for a long time, i.e., per definition, > 3s; 4) x ends touching herself (i.e., her hand touches any part of her body); 5) x begins touching herself; 6) x ends touching herself; 7) x begins touching herself; 8) x begins touching herself; 9) y begins looking at viewer; 10) y ends having viewer; 11) x begins having the viewer; 12) x begins manipulating the viewer; 13) x begins viewing for a long time, >3s; 14) x ends viewing for a long time; 15) x begins viewing for a long time; 16) y begins being immobile, no visible movement, i.e., she "freezes"; 17) y ends being immobile; 18) x begins viewing for a long time; 19) y ends touching herself; 20) y ends looking at the other (her partner); 21) y begins looking at a picture card (not in the viewer); 22) y ends looking at a picture card; 23) y begins touching herself; 24) y ends touching herself; 25) x ends having the viewer; 26) x ends manipulating the viewer; 27) y begins having the viewer.

At the first level the following pairs are connected: (1-2), (4-5), (7-8), (9-10), (12-13), (14-15), (18-19), (21-22), (23-24), (26-27); at the second level, for example, ((1-2)-3), ((12-13)-(14-15)), (17-(18-19)), (25-(26-27)); at third level, for example, ((17-(18-19))-20), etc.

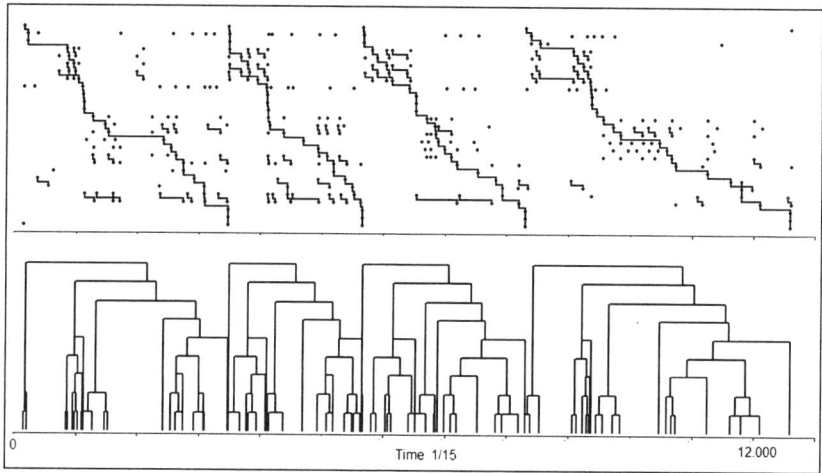

Figure 1.5 This figure's upper part is the same as figure 1.4 except that the box on the left has been removed and the height of right box has been reduced. The lower part gives a corresponding binary tree view of the occurrences of the pattern. The tree is the same as that in figure 1.4 but is here turned, the labels removed, and the shape of the tree follows the real-time shape of the pattern instances much as the binary trees in the lower part of figure 1.1.

1.3.2 T-patterns and T-paths in Neuronal Interactions

Results described notably in other chapters in this book suggest that T-patterns are examples of such structural types that can be found across different levels of organization involving different actors, i.e., not only humans but also, for example, neurons or drosophila. The most recent test of the relevance of the T-pattern structure across areas and levels of biological interaction systems is a search for T-patterns in interactions between individual neurons, i.e., brain cells, within a living brain (see chapter 4 in this volume). Figures 1.6, 1.7 and 1.8 give an idea of the kind of patterns found and illustrate relations between T-patterns, T-paths and T-path networks. Figures 1.6 and 1.7 both represent the same T-pattern, respectively, as a time pattern and as a spatial (here 2D) path on a 2D grid of electrodes. Each electrode registers the spikes from a few individual neurons. The numerical event type names therefore represent the locations of individual neurons. The neurons are the actors and they have only one behaviour: firing; and this event has a particular location in both time and space. (That is, the behaviour is always of the same kind, but the actors and positions change.)

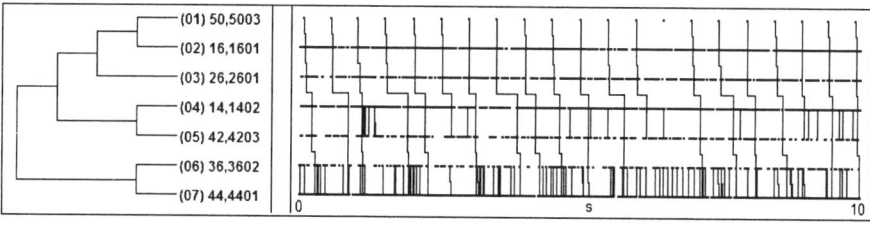

Figure 1.6 This figure shows a T-pattern detected in the interactions between individual neurons within the brain of a rat while presented with odour for 10 seconds and breaths in and out during this time. The event types 50,5003 stands for "breaths in" while other event types refer to various individual neurons. See chapter 4 in this volume.

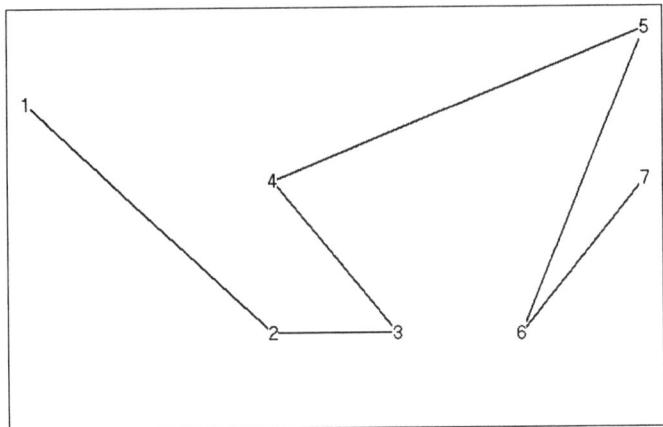

Figure 1.7 This figure shows the T-path of the pattern in figure 1.6 on the electrode grid used to register the activity of individual neurons. See chapter 4 in this volume.

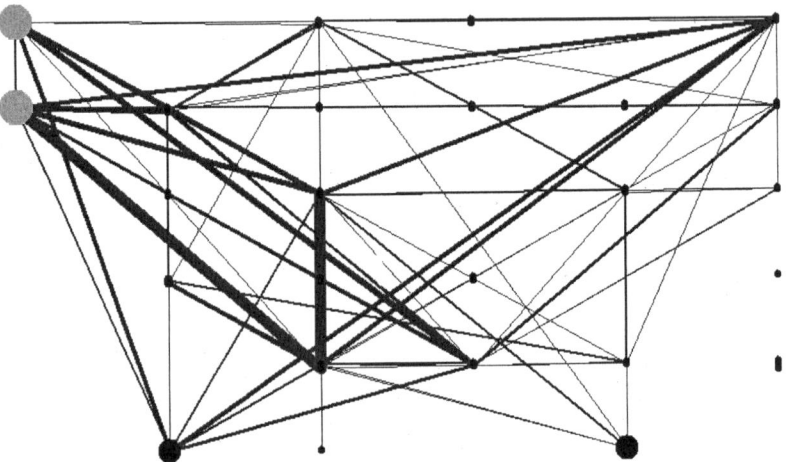

Figure 1.8 This figure combines all the 49 different T-paths (T-patterns) involving inhalation detected within 10 seconds of interactions between neurons. The paths are drawn one over the other and the more often a line is drawn (in the more frequent direction) the thicker the line. See chapter 4 in this volume.

1.3.3   T-patterns in DNA & proteins

The elements used to code information along the DNA molecules contained in chromosomes are themselves molecules called *bases*. These are of only four kinds commonly referred to as G, T, C, and A. The so-called backbone of the DNA molecule is a cyclical structure of alternating molecules, somewhat like the ticks on a scale (or a ticking clock), with a base occurring at each tick. Much as a byte in a computer has 8 bits that can be arranged in 256 different ways to represent letters and various other symbols, the series of bases are translated three at the time, i.e., in triplets called *codons*. Each codon is translated into one of 20 different *amino acid* molecules (thus conveniently referred to by letters of the alphabet, a coincidence?) and a protein is a particular chain of such molecules.

A (structural) *gene* is a stretch of DNA containing a particular series of codons, which at various moments is translated into varying numbers of copies of a particular protein. Different chains thus make up the great number of proteins in a cell that is called its *proteome*, i.e., its population of proteins at each moment.

Actually, in complex organisms such as Drosophila and humans, the series of codons in a stretch of DNA corresponding to a gene is often interrupted by nonsense segments as if a paragraph of text were repeatedly interrupted by various nonsense series of letters, or a serious discussion or a speech by periods of small talk or chat. The alternating meaningful and nonsense segments of a gene are, respectively, called exons and introns. When a gene is transcribed into a protein only the exons are used, but the non-coding introns define distances and possibly some effective content between the exons characteristic for the gene. But this is also one of the essential aspects of a T-pattern, where time distances of characteristic lengths but with more or less free content separate the components, which frequently are T-patterns themselves. Moreover, within the exons in terms of codons or equivalently amino acids there are so called *motives*. These can again show this same kind of structure where some particularly important stretch is fixed (occurs across species) while stretches separating them can vary freely. Moreover, since the genes are also separated by introns, the whole genome can be seen as a massively repeated T-pattern within the cells of the organism, influencing from within the internal functioning and thereby the behaviour of each cell as a whole.

DNA and proteins are typically depicted as strings of equally spaced letters like in a line of text, but in reality the molecules are *flexible*. The real distances between and within exons and introns, i.e., within a gene, can thus vary even if the number of elements separating them remains the same (see, for example [57]) and this is in particular true for proteins [1, p. 46]. This further strengthens the analogy with temporal behaviour patterns as described by the T-pattern model. Moreover, only 2% of human DNA contains genes and:
"Genes appear to be concentrated in random areas along the genome, with vast expanses of noncoding DNA between. Stretches of up to 30,000 C and G bases repeating over and over often occur adjacent to gene-rich areas, forming a barrier between the genes and the *junk DNA*. These CpG islands are believed to help regulate gene activity." Copied 14/10/04 from www.ornl.gov/sci/techresources/Human_Genome/project/info.shtml

This appears to mean that from chromosomes, to gene rich areas to genes to exons and motives, the whole structure is analogous to the T-pattern time structure of common every-day behaviour patterns as described by the T-pattern model. It remains to be established whether T-pattern detection can therefore be of important use in the search for unknown structure in information molecules. Initial analysis has identified T-patterns in proteins and in DNA often showing good correlation with well-known patterns while other highly statistically significant cases are being evaluated (Magnusson & Oskarsson, in preparation, Icelandic Research Center, grants: 013220001 and 013220002).

Figure 1.2 illustrates the kind of structural analogy discussed here between genes and behavioural T-patterns as it can be read in two entirely different ways: as a description of a dinner composed of six shorter patterns numbered 1 to 6 and separated by flexible time-slots with unspecified or "free" content, or as a common graphical representation of a gene (see, for example, [58, p. 33]) here composed of six exons numbered 1 to 6 and separated by introns, which can be seen as flexible space-slots with mostly non-essential freely varying content.

Moreover, regulatory mechanisms exist such that special proteins get attached to DNA and modify a gene's effect (how it is expressed) within the internal community of the cell. It is therefore tempting to note that particular events may also occur during or around a dinner (disputes, flirting, etc) that may influence the unfolding of that dinner and its effect on future interactions and relations within a community.

1.3.4   Strings, Traces and Control in Cells and Cities

The molecular information chains (strings) such as DNA and RNA are produced by cell organs and are more or less durable traces of their behaviour. In that context, it is interesting to note that earlier in evolution cell organs leaving those traces may have been independent organisms and to recall that a common analogy used to describe the patterning of information molecules is text, also a more or less durable trace of behaviour. Here, information molecules and text will therefore be referred to as *information objects*.

The complete set of information objects (DNA) in a cell is referred to as its *genome* and it is typically stored within a central place (core), but only a tiny fraction or approximately 2% contains the essential genes while the rest is considered mostly "junk". The genome is to a large part composed of highly repeated meaningless segments, but these may serve an important function in separating other parts. Moreover, in the community of cells making up a body, practically all the cells carry identical copies of the same genome and various stretches of its string (genes) are turned into different proteins. But, in "cell city", these proteins are a) the specialized "actors" that perform most life functions or b) construction materials. Some of these molecules are enzymes:

"If the cell is a city, enzymes are the workers. To keep the city running, raw materials are imported and converted into useful items. Enzymes populate the cellular factories in which this is done. One curious aspect of this manufacturing industry is that it includes factories for making the workers themselves: enzymes too are put together on a production line" [27, p. 46].

Replacing the word "worker" here by "specialized individual" then, in human cities, such factories could be, for example, schools, where various kinds of "specialized individuals" (including teachers) are created by other specialized individuals (notably teachers) mostly by exposing them to particular verbal materials, spoken and written, typically within a process of patterned face-to-face verbal and nonverbal interaction.

While the genome of a cell is stable, the composition of its protein population (its proteome) at each moment results from fluctuating rates of translation of different genome fractions under complex environmental influence, which includes interactions with the current proteome (population). A typical modern human city also has its information objects, most notably texts, and essential parts are also carefully stored in central places (libraries). The totality of text within a community could be called a "textome" and again a large part has little or no information value. Its various fractions (knowledge) also make it possible to create (educate) at varying rates the various specialized actors needed by the city as well as to produce a multitude of materials and tools requiring complex prescriptions no single person could remember. Particular parts of the textome, such as a holy script, a constitution, and particular elements of history, law, regulations, etc. are also shared by the majority of the individuals of the city providing them amongst other with the essential religious and political standpoints of the particular society. And human societies seem deeply dependent on such standard information objects:

"Yet religions have persisted in almost every society in the world – and where they have not they have been replaced by systems of political dogma..." [59, p. 2].

Within a society, information objects may be dispersed at first but later become concentrated in particular locations somewhat like the evolution from primitive cells (prokaryotes) where the genome is spread throughout the cell to the more advanced ones (eukaryotes) where nearly all of it is kept within a central core.

1.4   Discussion and conclusion

The information value of a single newly discovered T-pattern can vary greatly. It may be impossible to make sense of or it may tell about well known phenomena, but it may also provide new insight into some particular type of interaction and together with other T-patterns discovered in the same or different interactions it may be useful or even the missing brick in shaping a global picture. (Regarding the complex matters of meaning see chapter 2 in this volume.)

This search for patterns was begun with the hope of finding rather fixed and universal repeated patterns in human interaction, but even if some such can of course be found, a much more striking aspect is the apparently endless creativity. That is, two interactions never seem to be the same. This is true, even if the participants interactively co-construct new patterns which they then repeat in a similar way within that interaction, while in each new interaction more or less different patterns are formed and repeated.

But why do the T-patterns differ so much between interactions relating the same kind of individuals even in very similar conditions? Does this mean that very different underlying rules or processes are operating? According to findings within other areas this does not have to be the case as many dynamic systems have been found to be highly sensitive to the most minute differences in conditions (see, for example, [60]). Social interaction may simply be highly sensitive to internal (physiological) and external conditions, which well corresponds with common sense.

"The patterns detected in social interactions are often quite complex, but does this mean that the underlying rules must also be complex? Apparently, this does not have to be the case at all, as it has been shown that even the simplest rules can produce great complexity" [2, p. 28].

As pointed out notably by Duncan and colleagues [61], there has been a tendency to look at the analysis of interactions as a means to other ends such as the detection of effects of external variables rather than as a subject of study in its own right. To this can be added that, for results to be considered acceptable at all, it is sometimes required that the external variables relate to differences between groups and, moreover, have a clinical or diagnostic quality. What consequences could such viewpoints have had for the demanding research leading to the discovery of the structure of DNA and the genetic code, undoubtedly amongst the most important discoveries in the history of humanity? But that discovery, purely about structure and pattern, has opened fascinating new perspectives in a multitude of areas and in particular those related to health.

Structural and quantitative analysis does of course combine naturally, but it is worth underlining that this can work in both directions, that is, through structural analysis new entities may be discovered and provide a new basis for quantification. As witnessed, for example, by a number of chapters in this volume, detected patterns rather than just elements can be counted and measured, thus allowing the detection of otherwise hidden effects of independent variables.

It appears that structures of the T-pattern type exist in behaviour and interactions not only across species, but also across time and space, thus suggesting considerable global conservation of a structural principle. If so, this seems to call for careful attention: Does the real-time organization of overt human behaviour reflect to this extent the spatial structure of the DNA molecules present within each of the trillion cells in a human body?

A long list of questions is waiting to be answered: Is there some kind of "code" analogous to that of biological heredity involved in social interactions and then of what kind, in what sense, how? Are the seemingly omnipresent repeated patterns of social interaction integrated parts of a global system of organic codes (see [62]) ranging from DNA to cultural patterns? Are there possibly fairly few, simple and discoverable rules behind the generation of much of the regularities we know or sense directly and those we begin to detect with the help of special models and algorithms? What about the T-system as a candidate for a new kind of grammar? Do the T-pattern model and algorithms in any way reflect the nature of underlying regular processes or is the relationship arbitrary and entirely superficial? How can hidden interaction programs be discovered and described? How to answer such questions?

In any case, colossal tasks lie ahead:

"Deriving meaningful knowledge from the DNA sequence will define research through the coming decades to inform our understanding of biological systems. This enormous task will require the expertise and creativity of tens of thousands of scientists from varied disciplines in both the public and private sectors worldwide." Copied 10.10.2004 from www.ornl.gov/sci/techresources/Human_Genome/project/info.shtml

Discovering and deciphering the integrated systems of information objects and real-time interaction patterns within human social systems seems an analogous and no lesser task that has also just begun and holds limitless promises such as a better understanding of the mechanisms behind the age old and painful social problems of inequality, injustice, and violence. It will probably also be at least as dependent on structural hypotheses and automation, i.e., on the development and application of specially designed models (patterns) and algorithms, but given the analogies between the tasks at different levels of biological organization there seems to be to much hope for useful cross-fertilization.

Finally, about intelligence and with one eye on the above neuronal interaction patterns: Is there really any use for the term "collective intelligence", i.e., is all intelligence really collective? Is there ever any intelligence without interaction? And is there ever without interaction patterns?

1.5   References

[1]   G. A. Petsko and D. Ringe, *Protein Structure and Function*. London: New Science Press, 2004.
[2]   S. Wolfram, *A New Kind of Science*. Champaign: Wolfram Media Inc, 2002.
[3]   J. D. Watson, *DNA: The Secret of Life*. New York: A. A. Knopf, 2003.
[4]   J. D. Watson and F. H. C. Crick, A Structure for Deoxyribose Nucleic Acid, *Nature* **171** (1953) 737-738.
[5]   R. Franklin, *Rosalind Franklin and DNA*. New York: Norton, 1975.
[6]   F. H. C. Crick, *What Mad Pursuit: A personal view of scientific discovery*. New York: Basic Books, 1988.

[7]   F. Jacob and J. Monod, Genetic Regulatory Mechanisms in the Synthesis of Proteins, *Journal of Molecular Biology* **3** (1961) 318-356.

[8]   R. Bakeman and J. M. Gottman, *Observing interaction: An introduction to sequential analysis.* Cambridge: Cambridge University Press, 1997.

[9]   S. D. Duncan and D. W. Fiske, *Face-to-face interaction: Research, methods and theory.* Hillsdale N.J.: Lawrence Erlbaum Associates, 1977.

[10]   H. Montagner, *L'enfant et la communication.* Paris: Stock/Pernoud, 1978.

[11]   M. S. Magnusson, Temporal Configuration Analysis: detection of an underlying meaningful structure through artificial categorization of a real-time behavioral stream. Paper presented at Workshop on Artificial Intelligence, University of Uppsala, 1982. Part of a "Magisterkonferens" at the Psychological Laboratory, Copenhagen University, 1983.

[12]   M. S. Magnusson, THEME and Syndrome: two programs for behavior research, in *Symposium in Applied Statistics,* D. Edwards and A. Hoskuldsson, eds. Copenhagen: NEUCC, RECKU & RECAU, 1983, pp.17-42.

[13]   M. S. Magnusson, Le temps et les patterns syntaxiques du comportement humain: modèle, méthode et programme THEME, *Revue des Conditions de Travail* (hors série), (1988) 284-314.

[14]   M. S. Magnusson, Structure syntaxique et rythmes comportementaux: sur la détection de rythmes cachés, *Sciences et Techniques de l'animal du Laboratoire* **14** (1989) 143-147.

[15]   M. S. Magnusson, Hidden Real-time Patterns in Intra- and Inter-Individual Behavior: Description and Detection, *European Journal of Psychological Assessment* **12**(2), (1996) 112-123.

[16]   M. S. Magnusson, MS Discovering Hidden Time Patterns in Behavior: T-Patterns and their Detection, *Behavior Research Methods, Instruments and Computers* **32**(1), (2000) 93-110.

[17]   M. S. Magnusson, Analyzing Complex Real-time Streams of Behavior: Repeated Patterns in Behavior and DNA, in *L'éthologie appliquée aujourd'hui, Volume 3 - Ethologie humaine,* C. Baudoin, ed. Levallois-Perret, France: Editions ED, 2003, pp. 25-36.

[18]   M. S. Magnusson, Repeated Patterns in Behavior and Other Biological Phenomena, in *Evolution of Communication Systems: A Comparative Approach,* D. K. Oller and U. Griebel, eds. Cambridge: The MIT Press, 2004, pp. 111-128.

[19]   N. Chomsky, Review of Skinner, Verbal Behavior, *Language* **35** (1959) 26-58.

[20]   N. Chomsky, *Syntactic structures.* The Hague: Mouton, 1965.

[21]   J. Cosnier, *Clefs pour la psychologie.* Paris: Seghers, 1971.

[22]   Dawkins R Hierarchical organisation: a candidate principle for ethology, in *Growing Points in Ethology,* P. P. Bateson and R. A. Hinde, eds. Cambridge: Cambridge University Press, 1976, 7-54.

[23]   R. A. Hinde, *Non-verbal Communication.* Ney York: Cambridge University Press, 1972.

[24]   G. A. Miller, E. Galanter and K. H. Pribram, *Plans and the Structure of Behavior.* Stanford: International Thomson Publishing, 1960.

[25]   B. F. Skinner, *Verbal Behavior.* New York: Appleton-Century-Crofts, 1957.

[26]   N. Tinbergen, On the aims and methods of ethology, *Zeitschrift fur Tierpsychologie* **20** (1963) 410-433.

[27]   P. Ball, *Stories of the Invisible: A guided tour of molecules.* New York: Oxford University Press, 2001.

[28]   D. Berlinski, *The Advent of the Algorithm.* New York: Harcourt, 2000.

[29]   J. J. Rousseau and M. Cranston, *A discourse on inequality.* London: Penguin Books, 1985 (reprint edition).

[30]   I. Eibl-Eibesfeldt, *Ethology: The Biology of Behavior.* New York: Holt, Rinehart and Winston, 1970.

[31]   D. J. Daley and D. Vere-Jones, *An Introduction to the Theory of Point Processes.* Berlin: Springer, 1988.

[32]   W. C. McGrew, *An Ethological Study of Children's Behavior.* London: Academic Press, 1972.

[33]   P. W. Colgan, *Quantitative Ethology.* New York: John Wiley & Sons, 1978.

[34]   P. R. Monge and J. N. Cappella, Multivariate Techniques in Human Communication Research. New York: Academic Press, 1980.

[35]   K. R. Scherer and P. Ekman, *Handbook of Methods in Nonverbal Behavior Research.* Cambridge & Paris: Maison des Sciences de l'Homme & Cambridge University Press, 1982.

[36]   R. Bakeman and V. Quera, *Analyzing Interaction: Sequential Analysis with SIDS and GSEQ.* New York: Cambridge University Press, 1995.

[37]   L. P. J. J. Noldus, The Observer: a software system for collection and analysis of observational data. *Behavior Research, Methods, Instruments & Computers* **23** (1991) pp. 415-429.

[38]   M. S. Magnusson and J. Beaudichon, Détection de "marqueurs" dans la communication référentielle entre enfants, in *Conversation, Interaction et Fonctionnement Cognitif,* J. Bernicot, J. Caron-Pargue and A. Trognon, eds. Nancy: PUN, 1997, pp. 315-331.

[39]   M. T. Argilaga and G. K. Jonsson, Detection of Real-Time Patterns in Sports: Interactions in Soccer, *International Journal of Computer Science in Sport* **2** (2003) 118-121.

[40]   J. Beaudichon, S. Legros and M. S. Magnusson, Organisation des régulations inter et intrapersonnelles dans la transmission d'informations complexes organisées, *Bulletin de Psychologie, édition speciale: Les processus de contrôle dans la résolution de tâches complexes: développement et acquisition* **399**(44), (1991) 110-120.

[41]   A. Blanchet and M. S. Magnusson, Processus cognitifs et programmation discursive dans l'entretien de recherche, *Psychologie Française* **33**(1/2), (1988) 91-98.

[42]   A. Borrie, G. K. Jonsson and M. S. Magnusson, Temporal pattern analysis and it's applicability in sport: an explanation and preliminary data, *Journal of Sport Science* **20**(10), (2002) 845 - 852.

[43]   K. Grammer, K. B. Kruck and M. S. Magnusson, The courtship Dance: Patterns of Nonverbal Synchronization in Opposite-Sex Encounters, *Journal of Nonverbal Behavior* **22**(1), (1998) 3-29.

[44]   K. Hirschenhauser, D. Frigerio, K. Grammer and M. S. Magnusson, Monthly Patterns of Testosterone and Behavior in Prospective Fathers, *Hormones and Behavior* **42** (2002) 172-181.

[45]   M. Lyon and A. S. Kemp, Increased temporal patterns in choice responding and altered cognitive processes in schizophrenia and mania, *Psychopharmacology* **172** (2004) 211-219.

[46]   M. Lyon, N. Lyon and M. S. Magnusson, The importance of temporal structure in analyzing schizophrenic behavior: some theoretical and diagnostic implications, *Schizophrenia Research* 13 (1994) 45-56.

[47]   M. Martaresche, C. Le Fur, M. S. Magnusson, J. M. Faure and M. Picard, Time structure of behavioral patterns related to feed pecking in chicks, *Physiology and Behavior* **70**(5), (2000) 443-451.

[48]   J. Merten, *Beziehungsregulation in Psychotherapien. Maladaptive Beziehungsmuster und der therapeutische Prozeß*. Stuttgart: Kohlhammer, 2001.

[49]   H. Montagner, M. S. Magnusson, C. Casagrande, A. Restoin, J. P. Bel, P. N. M. Hoang, V. Ruiz, S. Delcout, G. Gauffier and B. Epoulet, Une nouvelle méthode pour l'étude des organisateurs de comportement et systèmes d'interaction du jeune enfant, *Psychiatrie de l'Enfant* **33**(2), (1990) 391-456.

[50]   S. Pastor and E. Sastre, Patrones de interacción adulto-niño en la construcción del significado: Aplicación del programa THEME, in *Observación de la conducta interactiva en contextos naturales: Aplicaciones*, M. T. Anguera, ed. Barcelona: E.U.B, 1999, pp. 125-150.

[51]   S. Sastre and E. Pastor, Modalidades de tutela de "gestión cognitive" en bebés trisómicos, *Infancia y Aprendizaje* **93** (2001) 35-52.

[52]   F. Schwab, *Affektchoreographien. Eine evolutionspsychologische Analyse von Grundformen mimisch-affektiver Interaktionsmuster*, Dissertation am FB 5.3 Empirische Humanwissenschaften der Universität des Saarlandes, 2000.

[53]   T. Sigurdsson, *Relation de Tutelle entre Parents et Enfants Handicapés Mentaux de Quatre a Six Ans*. Lille: Presses Universitaires de Septentrion, 2000.

[54]   C. Tardif, M. H. Plumet, J. Beaudichon, D. Waller, M. Bouvard and M. Leboyer, A micro-analysis of social interactions between autistic children and normal adults in semi-structured play situations, *International Journal of Behavioral Development* 18 (1995) 727-747.

[55]   C. Tardif and M. H. Plumet, La détection des répertoires d'interaction sociale propres à chaque enfant autiste: enjeux pour la recherche et la clinique, in *Autisme: Perspectives actuelles*, V. Gérardin-Collet and C. Riboni, eds. Nancy: L'Harmattan-IRTS, 2000.

[56]   S. H. N. Willemsen-Swinkels, M. J. Bakermans-Kranenburg, M. H. van Ijzendoorn, J. K. Buitelaar, H. van Engeland, Insecure and disorganised attachment in children with a pervasive developmental disorder: Relationship with social interaction and heart rate, *Journal of Child Psychology and Psychiatry* 41 (2000) 759-767.

[57]   A. I. Grosberg and A. R. Khokhlov, *Giant Molecules*. New York: Academic Press, 1997.

[58]   A. J. F. Griffiths, W. M. Gelbart, J. H. Miller, and R. C. Lewontin, *Modern Genetic Analysis*. New York: W. H. Freeman, 1999.

[59]   R. A. Hinde, *Why Gods Persist*. London: Routledge, 1999.

[60]   J. Gleick, *Chaos: Making a New Science*. New York: Penguin Books, 1988.

[61]   S. Duncan, D. W. Fiske, K. Oatley and A. Manstead, *Interaction Structure and Strategy*. Cambridge: Cambridge University Press, 1985.

[62]   M. Barbieri, *The organic codes: An introduction to semantic biology*. Cambridge: Cambridge University Press, 2003

2. The Detection of the Hidden Design of Meaning

Luigi ANOLLI

Abstract. Meaning is a marvellous and dreadful matter, as it is neither totally intelligible nor totally unintelligible. It cannot be considered as an univocal, closed and fixed entity, atomic in nature, universally shared and invariable in time. Rather, meaning has a complex design, composed by different facets: a referential, an inferential, and a differential one. This standpoint, which overcomes the truth-conditional semantics as well as the structural one, entails that meaning is patterned in nature, based on the encyclopaedic knowledge and connected with mental concepts. The meaning dilemma between variability and stability is crucial for every semantic theory, as meaning flexibility, grounded on the daily experience, displays a large range of linguistic phenomena like the defeasibility of semantic traits, fuzzy boundaries, radial categorization, semantic gradualness and polysemy, the interconnection between the literal and non-literal semantic domain as well as the context dependence. The semantic variability calls for an inferential process, as modal meaning is not an immediate and fully evident datum; rather, it is generated by communicators during their interaction in a dynamic way in the light of the principle of semantic and pragmatic synchrony. At the same time, meaning shows stability over time owing to its conventional nature. Without semantic stability it would be ungraspable. As patterned, meaning is coded in some way and follows at least some standard features to be taken by default. Presumptive meanings basically depend on context regularity and communicative formats. On this platform the meaning compositionality appears to be a critical issue. Traditionally, such compositionality has been faced by the feature semantics in which meaning is composed by a finite set of necessary and sufficient conditions. More recently, the prototype theory in its extended version afforded another explication of meaning compositionality by proposing the distinction between essential and typical features. In the present chapter a new model based on the T-patterns detection has been briefly advanced and illustrated, as, based on empirical observations extracted from the flow of communicative events, it seems to arrange quite well both with the variability and the stability of meaning. The detection of T-patterns enables to appreciate the hidden design of meaning encompassed in an utterance or in a nonverbal item not generally and in an abstract way but locally and in a contingent manner. The attention is focused on the local management of meaning, as each moment communicators have the opportunity of organizing, regulating, managing and monitoring their communicative interaction through the most effective choice between different semantic routes.

Keywords: Meaning; verbal and non-verbal communication; semantic features.

Contents

2.1   Introduction

Among specie-specific properties of human kind, meaning is certainly one of the principal, if not the principal one. From the evolutionary standpoint, meaning is the access to the symbolic domain and is the way through which individuals become able to communicate each other their internal states of mind. By means of symbols the human interaction has been unbelievably enhanced and has reached layers of multiplicative complexity through an endless process which enables more and more sophisticated communication patterns.

Dating from 17,000 to 18,000 years ago, in caves near Lascaux, in France, hundreds of aurochs bulls (ancient oxen), horses, and deer, along with mysterious dots and geometric figures were painted on the walls by humans of that time. Previously, approximately 25,000 years ago an anonymous artist sculpted the so-called "Willendorf Venus", found in Austria, one of the earliest non-tool artefacts yet discovered. This ancient expression, made of fine limestone and 11 cm tall, plainly details a bountiful mother figure. On the inclined head is designed a complicated hairstyle made of parallel curls extending to the neck. Both wrists are decorated with ragged arm-rings.

Quite likely, since the origin of the *Homo sapiens* in Africa, human beings were endowed with some kind of symbolic representation and were provided with the basic ability of mind-reading in order to grasp the other's intentions and goals. Similarly, the emergence of language about 150,000 years ago gave an enormous and exclusive advantage to human species and, as Knight, Studdert-Kennedy and Hurford [1] argued, the symbolic adventure began in its fullness. Actually, with the evolutionary emergence of language, communication expanded its range of opportunities in an exponential manner, although it retained the nonverbal roots in its architecture. As Deacon [2] pointed out, thanks to language human species became a symbolic species, since language enabled to generate and share meanings, to develop abstract ways of thinking, to grasp the other's mind, as well as to participate plans and goals. As a result, human beings began to question about the sense of life and death, to produce rituals, to invent first magic and religions and then philosophy and science, to give a hierarchical architecture to social order, and the like.

Within this evolutionary perspective, meaning is actually a complex matter, insofar as linguistic abilities have not cancelled the previous nonverbal (or extra-linguistic) competences; rather, they have rooted in the nonverbal ground. Consequently, linguistic meaning is always associated with extra-linguistic (or, nonverbal) components. Its semantic compositionality does not only concern linguistic features but also nonverbal ones. Meaning is patterned in nature. Without patterns meaning may not be meaning anymore; rather, it might be a chaotic and ungraspable aggregate which does not mean anything. Without patterns any communicative interaction becomes anarchic, disorganized and purposeless, by nature unforeseeable.

Therefore, as Anolli [3] highlighted, meaning turns out to be the local outcome of a large and consistent multiplicity of distinctive semantic facets, some of which are apparent and immediately understandable, while others are latent and concealed. The meaning design of a word, an utterance, a gesture, or whatever else is not obvious and plain in its entirety; rather, given a contingent situation between communicators, it always displays some hidden elements to be detected through an inferential way. As a result, meaning is not given once and for all and for any circumstance; instead, it should be recognized and defined each time within a specific situation.

The present chapter aims at facing this complex subject by developing a course through three subsequent steps. First, the meaning complexity will be deepened considering different theoretical standpoints: the truth-conditional semantics (meaning as plain reference), the structural semantics (meaning as mere linguistic value), and the cognitive semantics (meaning as cognitive pattern). Second, the dilemma between variability and stability of meaning will be examined. Obviously, meaning is a flexible and contingent matter, insofar as it is subjected to a wide range of semantic phenomena like the defeasibility of semantic traits, fuzzy boundaries, the radial categorization, the semantic gradualness and polysemy, context dependence, and so on. Within this domain modal meaning turns out to be the contingent outcome of inferential processes, ruled out by the principle of semantic and pragmatic synchrony. However, at the same time, meaning displays stability since without stability it is ungraspable. Meaning is coded in some way and follows at least some standard features to be taken by default. Presumptive meanings basically depend on context regularity and communicative formats. Third, on this platform it will be worth analysing the compositionality of meaning in its different versions. Particularly, the feature semantics, the extended prototype theory, and the type-pattern framework will be focused.

So, my aim in this chapter is to show how the type-pattern concept, proposed by Magnusson [4-6] for a wide range of interactions and events, is also very useful for semantic analysis and understanding. Within the communicative sequence of exchanges between interlocutors, there seems to be some chances to initiate a new path to detect, recognize, and interpret meaning in an empirical way, adhering to the contingent situation in a given cultural system.

2.2 Meaning as complexity

Meaning is, at the same time, a marvellous and dreadful matter. The starting point of this challenge is that meaning is neither totally intelligible nor totally unintelligible. As Bohr [quoted from Morin, 7] persuasively illustrated, you have to kill a dog to obtain the whole information included in it. Till it is alive, you have not its complete information. Similarly, it is impossible to gain the entirety of meaning hold in a word or in an utterance or in a gesture. Of course, the meaning of a number, like "two", is apparently self-evident. "Two" means "one plus one" and it seems that such necessary truth incorporates the whole meaning of "two". However, also in this case – an elementary semantic item – "two" does not always mean exactly "two" but could mean less or more than "two". For instance, if you say "two" with a very low pitch and with a sad and disappointed expression for receiving something much less of what you expected, you would very likely mean "just two". Conversely, if you exclaim "TWO!" with a high pitch and a happy smile for getting more than the one only gift you expected, you would very likely mean "really two!". In another situation, to the question "What time is it?", the answer "It is two o'clock" could mean "right two".

In each of these instances the literal meaning of "two" is always the same but at a subjective (experiential) layer the meaning of "two" is quite different for it could mean much less or much more than two or elsewhere exactly two. In the linguistic domain the attention of scholars has often been focused on the literal meaning, as if the linguistic level were able to exhaust the totality of meaning.

As Sapir [8] pointed out, never a plain word like "horse" can be pronounced without some kind of prosodic melody and vocal variation in pitch profile that, unavoidably, modifies, and in some circumstances deeply modifies, the meaning of the word in matter. On these nonverbal aspects of meaning we will come back later. At the moment, it is worthwhile to highlight that there is an enormous range of ambiguities in natural language, requiring at least a one-to-many correspondence between the lexical item and its meanings. Paraphrasing the words of Cruchfield, it is rarely, if ever, the case that the appropriate notion of meaning is extracted from the communicative interaction itself using minimally biased procedures. Briefly stated, meanings are usually guessed and then verified [quoted from Solé and Goodwin, 9, p. 20].

Meaning cannot be considered as an univocal, closed, and fixed entity, atomic in nature, universally shared and invariable in time. It has not a discrete structure, defined by clear-cut boundaries. Rather, meaning should be interpreted as a mental and cultural scheme, endowed with a high flexibility and adaptability to the different contingent situations through communicative exchanges.

Historically, philosophy and logic, linguistics and semiotics, sociology, anthropology and psychology coped with the challenges of meaning. Furthermore, phonology, syntax, semantics, and pragmatics are areas each with their own generative capacities in defining the meaning structure. As Jackendoff [10, 11] underlines, there are correspondences across phonological, syntactic, and semantic representations, but such correspondences may be partial and not one-to-one. Also Levinson [12] points out that the correspondence rules between these representations are not deterministic in nature.

As a complex and a multidimensional subject, not reducible to a single component by definition, meaning should be thought of as a relation between *expression, representation,* and *referent*, as it is highlighted in the following semiotic triangle (see figure 2.1):

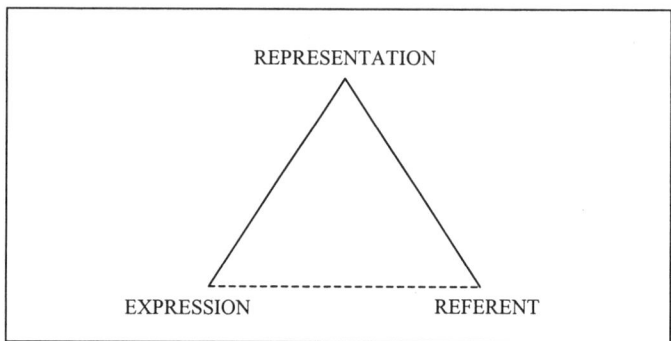

Figure 2.1 Semiotic triangle (adapted from Ogden and Richards, [13])

In such a diagram, derived from the one proposed by Ogden and Richards [13], *expression* is meant as every sign able to generate a meaning between the interlocutors (i.e. an utterance, a word, a gesture, and the like). In turn, *representation* should be considered as a mental schematic image extracted from all the modes of experience, and indicates the manner (or way) in which an expression designates its referent. It is a mediating term, insofar as individuals understand a referent through the mental representation of a given expression. Last, *referent* means the object, the event or something else in a (real or possible) world.

According to this point of view, *meaning* may be defined in a threefold manner: (a) the meaning of an expression is the state of things to which the expression refers; (b) meaning is the relation that each linguistic item entails with all the other elements; (c) meaning is the mental image that connects an expression to the correspondent referent. On this ground, as Violi [14] sharply argued, three main theoretical approaches for meaning analysis were developed: referential or truth-conditional semantics, structural semantics, and cognitive semantics.

2.2.1 Meaning as plain reference

In the truth-conditional semantics, starting with Frege, Russell, Carnap, and Tarski and running through to the more recent theories of Montague, Hintikka, Barwise, etc., the relationship between language and world has been deepened, insofar as the meaning of a sentence would consist in saying something about a given state of things that could be true or false in a (real or possible) world. Therefore, the meaning of a sentence is essentially given by its *truth conditions*. More precisely, understanding a sentence about a certain state of things means understanding in what conditions and circumstances such state of things would be true, independently from its reality. As Wittgenstein [15] stated in his Proposition 4.024: "To understand a proposition means to know what it is the case, if it true. (One can therefore understand it without knowing whether it is true or not)".

Frege [16] first introduced the basic distinction between *sense* (*Sinn*) and *reference* (*Bedeutung*). Sense is the way through which we can grasp the reference connected with a certain expression. Sense thus is able to mediate the relation between language and the world. However, according to Frege, sense is not a psychological and subjective process but a "common property of many people and so is not a part or a mode of the individual mind" [16, p.59].

Reformulating the Frege's notion of sense, Carnap [17] proposed the idea of *intension* to resolve the so-called "opaque or non-truth-conditional contexts". Such contexts are generated by verbs of propositional attitude like *to believe that p, to hope that p*, and so on, in which the truth value of the completive clause following verbs does not depend on referring to an actual state of affairs but on the mental attitude of the speaker. To overtake this difficulty, Carnap developed the viewpoint of *possible world*. If I say *The king of France is tall*, we are able to grasp the sense of this utterance even though everybody knows that nowadays there is not any kingdom in France. Its meaning is not given by what it designates in the actual world but it is an *intension*, that is, a function to a possible world in which a kingdom would exist in France and the king would be tall. The *extension* of a sentence is what it refers to, and gives the truth conditions on whose ground it might be taken as true (or false). The intension of a word or a sentence is a function which fixes its extension in every possible world.

Going on with this theoretical framework, Montague [18] founded his formal analysis of language. According to him, there is no difference between natural language and formal language, and semantics should be considered as a meta-mathematics that interprets syntax. Montague conceives syntax and semantics as having a parallel construction, as each syntactic category has a corresponding semantic type and, likely, each syntactic rule has a corresponding semantic rule which attributes intension to the linguistic expression. So, according to Montague, syntax and semantics are characterized by isomorphism, since the syntax of a language is closely linked to its semantics.

To put in a nutshell, denying any attention to flesh and blood individuals and confining the meaning's study to the formal logic, the truth-conditional point of view turned out to be referential and anti-psychological in nature. In such perspective, meaning was designed as an independent affair from the subjective mind, and as a matter of fact it was regarded as an objective and absolute entity. However, this standpoint was not without a set of logical and semantic difficulties. Herein I will limit to mention only some of them.

First, the notion of meaning itself remains unconsidered, insofar as the analysis of the mental representation has been disregarded. Without any mental representation, meaning, intended as a logical and mathematical construct which serves to define truth conditions, becomes an empty formula, unable to explain elementary linguistic processes. For instance, according to Montague's semantic model, the intensions of simple expressions are determined only in terms of their logical type. In such a way, it is possible to distinguish between the intension of a transitive verb from that of an intransitive one (as in *Peter leaps* and *Peter loves his mother*) but it is impossible to discern the intensions within a given category, such as transitive verbs. So, we cannot distinguish the meaning between *Peter loves his mother* and *Peter hits his mother*, as these two sentences have the same logical type of intension. Therefore, truth conditional semantics, which focuses on truth conditions, is not in the position to actually define them.

Second, this prevalence of formal semantics and the lack of reference to mental representation lead to misleading analysis in linguistic semantics. For instance, within the field of quantifiers, in formal semantics there is no difference between the quantifiers *each, every*, and *all* as they are represented by the universal quantifier. However, in linguistic semantics they originate significant differences as it shows in the following sentences:

1a. *All the men lifted the car.*
1b. ?? *Every man lifted the car.*
1c. ?? *Each man lifted the car.*

The sentences (1b) and (1c) sound odd since the use of *every* and *each* implies a distributive meaning, while in (1a) the use of *all* entails a collective meaning.

Third, within the case of lexical substitution, while the truth conditions remain the same, there is a change in the point of view with which the statement is said. See, for instance, the following couple of sentences:

2a. *The cat is under the chair.*
2b. *The chair is over the cat.*

In such a case, the truth conditions are the same in both sentences but the meaning is quite different, as the difference of the subjective point of view entails a different mental orientation of speakers toward the contingent situation in (2a) and (2b).

Summing up, the truth-conditional theory of meaning appears to be explicitly abstract and formal, without any attention to subjective aspects. The notion of truth condition has been developed within a totally objective viewpoint, insofar as a sentence turns out to be true or false independently of our recognition of it as such. Meaning is conceived as an objective entity disconnected to the mental processes which make the linguistic understanding possible. As Lakoff [19] pointed out, the truth-conditional theory assumes a "God's eye" standpoint to see and grasp the meaning in its absolute and objective nature.

2.2.2   Meaning as mere linguistic value

de Saussure [20], Hjelmslev [21] and other scholars of the structural linguistics advanced the hypothesis that language may be considered as an autonomous network of mutually interdependent relations within which linguistic items exist by virtue of each other, independently from any outside determination. Thanks to its autonomy, structural semantics conceives meaning as a biunivocal combination of signifier (i.e., the acoustic image) and signified (i.e., the mental image). The inseparable link between signifier and signified assures the autonomy of meaning from any possible adulteration coming from the mental and psychological field.

What does meaning mean according to de Saussure? In his latest writings meaning is *value*, that is, the possibility for each lexical item to be compared and contrasted to any other in the linguistic system. The starting point is given by the consideration according to which "in a language there are only differences, and no positive terms" [20, p. 118]. Thus, the meaning of *apple* is not given by a set of its features (i.e., what it is, described in positive terms); rather, it is only given by the comparison with all the other linguistic items within a certain language. *Apple* is what it is, insofar as no one other linguistic item takes its own position within a certain natural language. Consequently, meaning is generated by the intra-linguistic negative relations of a given word with one other, and consists of the set of differences which exist between that word (i.e., *apple*) and all the other words of a given natural language.

For the structural semantics, the meaning of a word is defined in a positional differential negative way. Meaning is put totally within the boundaries of a linguistic system, and there is no need to do any reference to an extra-linguistic world and to any conceptual and mental representation. Meaning is designed only by the position of a word in the linguistic system. As a consequence, the autonomy of semantics implies an anti-referential and anti-psychological approach. Concerning this, Hjelmslev [21] formulated the *principle of immanence*, according to which semantics aims at an immanent understanding of language as a specific self-sufficient system, looking for consistency and regularity inside language rather than outside of it.

Nevertheless, the structural semantics turned out to be invalidated by its intrinsic circularity. If all linguistic items are defined on the ground of the relations between them, how can such relations be defined without referring to the items themselves? As De Mauro [22] highlighted, we define the terms thanks to the relations, but the relations cannot be defined without having defined the terms. Knowing all the system of linguistic relations existing between a linguistic entry and each other entries does not generate any meaning. Knowing that *zeffo* is the opposite of *zoffo*, a pejorative of *zaffo*, and the superlative of *ziffo* does not enable anybody to know the meaning of *zeffo* at all.

2.2.3 Meaning as cognitive pattern

Around the eighties, in an anti-Chomskian position, a group of scholars – among others I would like to mention Fillmore [23, 24], Jackendoff [25, 26], Lakoff [19], Talmy [27] – gave rise to the so-called *cognitive semantics*. Rather than a unitary theory, it is a family of theories which share some common principles and assumptions. Generally speaking, these scholars were unsatisfied with a viewpoint of meaning as an objective, discrete, absolute entity just as it was developed by the traditional semantics in both formal and structural design. On this ground, they set up a network – although loose, by nature – of semantic principles useful to grasp the character of meaning. Thus, they suggested a new design of meaning as the outcome of mental processes and social interactions.

First, in the cognitive semantics understanding meaning involves understanding the way in which individuals communicate each other. Meanings are neither abstract entities as in formal and logical semantics, nor intra-linguistic relations as in structural semantics. Rather, they are items of conceptual and mental networks. So, semantics and understanding are two sides of the same coin.

In particular, Fillmore [28] advanced the distinction between a semantics of understanding (*U-semantics*) and a truth semantics (*T-semantics*). The former is interested in understand the relations between linguistic statements, their context of use, and the processes of their interpretation; conversely, the latter is based on truth judgments. In turn, Jackendoff [26], even more radical in his position, assumes that, to understand the meaning of a word or an utterance, we have to grasp the relations between that word (or utterance) and the corresponding concept.

Consequently, any semantic model should be endowed with psychological plausibility, insofar as it should be able to conform to actual processes of interpretation and linguistic communication, as well as to adopt experimental methods to verify its statements. As a further consequence, within the cognitive standpoint, semantics looses its autonomy, as it turns out to be impossible to study the semantic aspects of language and communication in isolation from other cognitive abilities. It is enough to think of the categorization processes which involve both linguistic and conceptual competences.

The non-autonomy of semantics concerns both cognitive and cultural layers. The meaning of a word, an utterance or a gesture cannot be disconnected from our experience of the world, which is physical, mental, social, and cultural. Even without falling in the relativistic approach of Sapir and Whorf, nowadays there is much evidence of the deep influence of culture on any natural language, concerning the lexical entries, the grammar, the contextualization indices and the like, as Gumperz and Levinson [29] have strongly underlined.

Second, the cognitive semantics broadens the meaning's notion. Meaning cannot be designed only by the dictionary knowledge but should take into account the encyclopaedic knowledge at disposal to an individual. Dictionary knowledge is the circumscribed set of linguistic features and components of a word which it is possible to find in a dictionary, while encyclopaedic knowledge is the general collection of factual knowledge, extracted from the daily experience. In this sense, it is impossible to discern on principle what is intrinsically linguistic and what is not, as well as to distinguish between what is essential in defining the meaning of a word or an utterance and what is not. By nature, meaning is "opened up" to encompass all our encyclopaedic knowledge. As a consequence, meaning cannot be disconnected by our experience, culturally mediated and psychologically situated.

Third, according to the cognitive semantics linguistic meanings cannot be isolated and detached from their conceptual correspondences. Yet, there are different theoretical positions on this issue and still nowadays there is not agreement among scholars. According to Fillmore [23], meaning and concept are two different domains, as the information processing and the conceptual system are general and abstract in nature, while linguistic frames turn out to be more specific and detailed in describing categories and individual relations to a contingent situation. Conversely, Jackendoff [26, 11] holds up that the semantic structure coincides with the conceptual one, insofar as the former is a subset of the latter. The meaning of a word is conceivable as a part of the conceptual system, connected in the long-term memory to a phonological circuit and to a syntactic structure.

Fourth, cognitive semantics refuses the externalist position of the truth-conditional standpoint, according to which meanings are externally connected to states of the world through devices that are extrinsic to speakers. At the same time, it rejects the structural approach, according to which meanings are generated only within the linguistic domain. Generally following a phenomenological point of view, cognitive semantics argues that language interacts with perception, cognition, reasoning, and emotion (for instance, see Jackendoff [26]). Eco [30] has already associated linguistic meaning and perceptual meaning, insofar as perceptual aspects are the link enabling the mapping of language onto the world.

Summing up, cognitive semantics endorses a referential and psychological notion of meaning, widening the theoretical boundaries of its comprehension, and offering new possibilities to deepen its empirical understanding.

2.2.4   Toward a unified theory of meaning

As we have seen, truth-conditional, structural and cognitive semantics are in conflict with each other in defining meaning. Each of them has focused its attention on particular facets of meaning. Nonetheless, it is worth deepening the opportunity to put together some facets encompassed in them, actually developing a framework that can match a unified theory of meaning. Herein I intend to point out three basic aspects of the meaning design: (a) the referential facet, (b) the inferential facet, (c) the differential facet.

Referential facet – The referential facet of meaning entails the need to foresee a relationship between meaning and reality. Reference is a necessary condition to generate the meaning of a word, an utterance or a gesture. Putnam [31] argued that meanings are not in the head but depend on references in the environment. Meaning is always the meaning *of* something, and there cannot be the meaning of anything that does not exist somewhere. Even the meaning of nothing is an actual meaning. Without any kind of reference the risk is to collapse in a solipsistic abyss where there is no room for meaning.

Needless to say that reference should not be conceived as an absolute and objective entity, externally defined and independent from speakers. Rather, it should be intended as an entity which designs a given content of experience referring to a specific reality. The connection between meaning and reality is not immediate and direct but normally mediated by the personal experience. In turn, experience constantly and intrinsically is shaped by the referring culture that defines beliefs, ways of thought, values, behavioural, social and moral standards, as well as practices and rituals. To put in a nutshell, meanings are the outcome of a cultural activity generated by everybody who feels and goes through a set of events, who participates each other in creating symbols and mental representations of such events, and who shares with other people the conventional devices to form new meanings in an endless journey.

Inferential facet – The inferential facet of meaning concerns how meanings are mentally organized. First of all, meanings have links with concepts, although meanings and concepts are different each other. They are correlated and interdependent but distinguished. Thus, semantics should not be confused with "conceptual structure"; the semantics of a language is a language-specific phenomenon, and the system of correspondences between language and thought is not, by nature, isomorphic. Consider, for instance, the so-called "lexical gap", that is, the phenomenon in which a given concept does not have its direct equivalent in the lexical system but it is necessary to resort to a circumlocution. This issue is quite recurring in the translation of specific utterances or words from a natural language into another.

Likewise, in the opposite case, we may consider the condition in which a speaker knows a given word but is confused about its meaning, or, alternatively, he does not even have it. Such a condition, called "conceptual ignorance", is often found in the case of scientific words or utterances, as, for instance, for the notion of imaginary number: you can have the meaning of "number" and "imaginary" but not the concept of "imaginary number".

Furthermore, in case of polysemy, it does not exist an equivalent equation between a word and the corresponding concept, as different concepts match one word only (relationship "one-to-many"). Take, for instance, the word *bank*: it has different conceptual equivalents as (a) a business that keeps and lends money and provides other financial services, (b) a land along the side of a river or lake, (c) a large pile of earth, sand, snow etc., (d) the money in a gambling game that people can win as in *break the bank*, (e) a slope made at a bend in a road to make it safer for cars to go around. It happens the reverse with synonymy, where different linguistic items – as *car, automobile, machine* – correspond to the same concept (relationship "many-to-one").

Moreover, the inferential aspect of meaning resorts also to the mental activity of inference. Meanings are not given once and for all in their plain nature. They should be intended and interpreted by interlocutors through a set of linguistic and non-linguistic cues. Grice [32] gave prominence to the distinction between "what is said", "what is meant", and "what is presupposed". The transition from "what is said" to "what is meant" involves many mental operations of inference, in particular of abduction. Concerning this, Grice [32] introduced the notion of *conversational implicature* to explain the gap between what is literally said and what is conventionally implicated by speakers. In turn, Levinson [12] widened this standpoint with the theory of *generalized conversational implicature*, that is, a preferred interpretation of a given utterance, and a default inference able to immediately grasp the presumptive meanings of such utterance.

Differential facet – The differential facet of meaning involves that language, as any other communication system, participates in defining the meaning of a word or an utterance. The semantic organization of an utterance or discourse binds the mental representations which are combined with its speech. The expressive modes of accentuation or mitigation or else inhibition, the contribution coming from hedges or modifiers, the linear order of words in an utterance, and the like effectively contribute in specifying the meaning toward a given sense direction rather than another one. de Saussure was right in taking a language as a system of differences. Such system, insofar as it enables an unlimited set of comparison actions, may generate linguistic variations in meanings.

2.3   Variability and stability of meaning

As we have seen, the complexity of the meaning design is given by the difficulty to grasp and confine it in a circumscribed room. Meaning never repeats itself. A twice-said utterance has not the same meaning of the first-said one, as in any case it arises semantic hidden nuances. Repetition itself intrinsically brings a new meaning. By definition, a semantic clone is impossible. From this standpoint, meaning seems to have the same disease of being: as soon as you grasp a meaning of something, it changes and fades away to leave room for new meanings. Consequently, meaning design seems to be rather slippery and evasive in nature, since it displays a certain number of hidden elements.

On the other side, meaning appears to be eternal and unchangeable. The meaning of *dog* always is the meaning of *dog*, and never will it change in the meaning of *cat*, at least in a (real or possible) world where dogs and cats are animals intrinsically different in their nature. Similarly, it is easy to find regularity, recurrence, and standardization of many kinds of pragmatic inferences, as Levinson [12] highlights. From this standpoint, opposite to previous, meaning design turns out to be rather enduring and well-founded.

Consequently, meaning appears to be struggled between contingency and fixedness. From time to time, the meaning's pendulum swings to contingency and variability to turn back to stability and steadiness, and vice versa. This twofold nature of meaning makes it a theoretical and empirical challenge for scholars belonging to different disciplines. At the same time, it is graspable and ungraspable, as in any case we can grasp it only partially. How to tackle this challenge?

2.3.1   Meaning variability

de Saussure had already considered meaning evolution in the course of time, and differentiated between the synchronic and diachronic levels of a natural language. But it is not necessary to resort to a long temporal period to see the meaning variability – and it is actually a large variability – of a word or an idiom. Many communicative phenomena are implicated in this process.

2.3.1.1 Defeasibility of semantic traits

Following Cruse [33] and Violi [14], we firstly take into consideration the *defeasibility of semantic traits*. Putnam [34] had already suggested that it is not possible to determine semantic definitional features for natural categories or for artefacts. For instance, if we say that cats have four legs and a tail, how can we manage with a cat without a tail and with only three legs? Is it still a cat or not? Recently, it has been underlined by Geeraerts [35], Kleiber [36], and Violi [14] that the *typical properties* of a meaning are practically all subject to the possibility of cancellation, without changing the meaning itself.

We briefly reaffirm that typical features are those that can be recognized by the diagnostic test of the adversative *but*. For instance, consider the following pair of statements:

3a. ?? *It is a bird but it flies.*
3b. *It is a bird but it does not fly.*

There is a semantic anomaly in (3a) but not in (3b). Within this perspective, for instance, in the meaning of *bird* there are typical features – and therefore cancellable or defeasible – like flying ability (there are birds that do not fly, like ostriches), feathers (there are birds without feathers, like penguins), wings (there are birds without wings, like kiwis), as Geeraerts [35] reminds. But even the *essential properties*, that is, those properties which are shared by every member of a category, can be cancelled in extraordinary situations. For example, in the past the whale was considered a fish, because it lives in the sea, while now is considered a mammal: in this case the essential property "fish" has been cancelled and substituted by "mammal".

The possibility of cancelling semantic traits is based on the *conventional nature* of meaning as a historically and culturally defined entity, and entails the overcoming of every ontological and natural conception of meaning. As for being conventional, it can also be negotiated, modified, and culturally transformed.

2.3.1.2 Fuzziness of meaning

Even the folk psychology assumption that meanings have clear-cut boundaries as a discrete semantic unit has been criticised. After several studies, among which those worth mentioning are particularly the ones proposed by Labov [37], and Lakoff [38, 39], it is already recognised that many meanings are characterised by *fuzzy boundaries*. An utterance is fuzzy if it has the property of referential opacity. For instance, a lecture could be *not bad*, a girl may be *rather pretty*, and John may have *many friends*. In all these cases qualifiers and quantifiers enable to carve the meaning of an expression more or less intensively and with a certain semantic shape. Within this perspective, according to Zadeh [40] and Zhang [41] among others, meaning hinges on a *fuzzy set*, that is, a class of communicative units with a continuum of grades of membership.

The same linguistic process is reduplicated with *hedges* which render a reading fuzzy. For instance, the statement:

4a. *It is three o'clock.*

is temporally precise, but it becomes fuzzy when combined with *around*, as in:

4b. *It is around three o'clock.*

Hedges like *about, almost, technically speaking* or *so to speak*, behave in the same way as *around*. Also in the attributive clauses such as *John is clever, Mary is tall*, the hedges *very* and *somewhat* modify the degree of fuzziness. In particular, *very* in *John is very clever* pushes the degree of meaning upwards; while *somewhat* in *John is somewhat clever* pushes the semantic value of *clever* downwards.

Additionally, a word can have a meaning with fuzzy boundaries. In a classic study by Labov [37], based on the analysis of words referring to material artefacts like *bowl*, *cup*, *mug*, and *dish*, which compose the semantic field of "domestic containers for food and drink", the data showed that the meaning of these words varied noticeably for what it concerns the presence and relevance of some perceptual features like depth, breadth, height, presence of a handle and the like, as shown in figure 2.2. As things deviate progressively from a standard type, we enter a semantic vagueness zone, where the same object could be, in turn, a bowl, a mug or a glass. The borderline between them is not clear-cut, but is undetermined and graded. It seems like a continuum more than a fair delimitation.

Figure 2.2 Series of cup-like objects (adapted from Labov, [37])

Semantic fuzziness phenomena were studied in depth within the prototypical framework of meaning, proposed, among other scholars, by Givòn [42], Kleiber [36], Posner [43], and Rosch [44, 45]. Lakoff [38, 39], for instance, had already underlined the fuzzy nature of the semantic boundaries of meaning, considering the different position of a few members along the ranking of a category membership like *bird-likeness*, starting from robins and eagles to chickens and ducks and further on to penguins, ostriches, and pelicans. According to the prototype theory, even in its recently "extended" version advanced by Kleiber [36], and Geeraerts [35, 46], meaning in many circumstances does not symbolise a discrete and unitary category with clear-cut and closed boundaries, but represents a salient features pattern on the base of which we operate by inference and by partial similarity judgements.

In the field of semantic vagueness, it is worth mentioning the *family resemblance* phenomenon, underlined by Wittgenstein [47]. For instance, the meaning of *game* is not univocal but it spreads over a multiplicity of semantic subsets, not always related to each other, as in Wittgenstein's words:

Consider for example the proceedings that we call "games". I mean board-games, card-games, ball-games, Olympic Games, and so on. What is common to them all? – Don't say: "There must be something common, or they would not be called 'games'" – but look and see whether there is anything common to all. – For if you look at them you will not see something that is common to all, but similarities, relationships, and a whole series of them at that. To repeat: don't think, but look! – Look for example at board-games, with their multifarious relationships. Now pass to card-games; here you find many correspondences with the first group, but many common features drop out, and others appear. When we pass next to ball-games, much that is common is retained, but much is lost. – Are they all 'amusing'? Compare chess with noughts and crosses. Or is there always winning and losing, or competition between players? Think of patience. In ball-games there is winning and losing; but when a child throws his ball at the wall and catches it again, this features has disappeared. Look at the parts played by skill and luck; and at the difference between skill in chess and skill in tennis. Think now of games like ring-a-ring-a-roses; here is the element of amusement, but how many other characteristics features have disappeared! And we can go through the many, many other groups of games in the same way; we can see how similarities crop up and disappear. And the result of this examination is: we see a complicated network of similarities overlapping and criss-crossing: sometimes overall similarities, sometimes similarities of detail. [47]

From this point of view the meaning of *game* is not described by a complex of common and necessary features but by a partial similarity shared by at least two or more game types. In this case, members of a specific category are connected to each other without the presence of common properties. Fuzzy boundaries and family resemblance enable meanings to adapt to each speaker and situation and to reach a very high flexibility.

2.3.1.3 Radial categories and semantic polysemy

Endorsing this theoretical perspective, Lakoff [19] has given an accurate analysis of the linguistic categorisation system of Dyirbal language. In this Australian indigenous language there are only four lexical categories: *bayi, balan, balam, bala*, each one comprising totally heterogeneous meanings that cannot be described by referring to the classic categorisation principles. For instance, the *bayi* category contains these items: men, kangaroos, possums, bats, most snakes and fishes, the moon, storms, rainbows, boomerangs etc. The *balan* category includes: women, dogs, most birds, some snakes and fishes, the sun and stars, fire, water etc. Lakoff [19] underlines that these categories are neither arbitrary nor random but they are regulated by a set of local similarities in terms of Dyirbal myths and beliefs. Therefore, we have to understand and manage complex categories made up by successive chains of items linked by local similarities. They can branch out along the so-called *radial categories*, that is, categories "where there is a central case and conventionalised variations on it which cannot be predicted by general rules" [19, p. 84].

Semantic fuzziness and vagueness phenomena like family resemblance and radial categories are neither isolated nor extraordinary, but they are related to the wider field of *polysemy*. The polysemic word refers to a number of different meanings, semantically related to each other, each one, however, having its own autonomy. In the semantic polysemy a word takes different semantic layers. For instance, the Italian adjective *fresco* that corresponds approximately to the English word *fresh*, entails three different meanings along three different levels of sense, as Violi [14] reminds:

a) temporal semantic layer ("new, recent, just given": for instance, *it is fresh news, it is a fresh vegetable*),
b) positive state semantic layer ("pure, uncontaminated, in optimal conditions": for instance, *it is fresh fruit, it is fresh fish, fresh mountain air*),
c) caloric semantic layer ("not hot": for instance, *this room is fresh, fresh air this morning*).

As we can see, there is a partial overlapping area between (a) and (b) and between (b) and (c) but not between (a) and (c). In this example, because of the plurality of different meanings that partially overlap, *fresh* constitutes a polysemic category and cannot have a single prototype, because a central case is not expected. As such, polysemy provides for a basic meaning which includes different courses of meaning.

2.3.1.4 Meaning gradualness

The semantic variability is further strengthened by the *semantic gradualness* phenomenon, according to which the semantic traits (or features) of a word do not share the same semantic weight and value. In particular, Violi [14] deepened the distinction between *essential properties* (common to every member of a category) and *typical properties* (distinctive and specific of only some members of a category, which can increase their representativity and characterize them by other members of the same category). For Cruse [33] the essential properties are *criterion traits* that cannot be cancelled without negotiating the meaning of the word. For instance, for the *bird* category the essential features are only two: (a) being oviparous; (b) having a beak. All the other features are merely typical and can be cancelled without creating semantic modifications. A bird that cannot fly, like an ostrich or a penguin, is nevertheless a bird. The salience of typical properties is strictly connected to a given culture.

Generally speaking, meanings are largely based on gradable or continuous criteria rather than all-or-nothing distinctions. Even in the case of words that, according to Sperber and Wilson [48], express "absolute" (or "well-defined") concepts like *bold* or *dead*, they are gradable in English as in other natural languages. Thus *completely dead, clearly dead, quite dead, nearly dead, almost dead, not quite dead, very dead, not very dead, hardly dead* are scalar modifiers or intensifiers of *dead*. But, according to Thibault [49], the semantic variability of the word *dead* is also present in utterances like *John is dead up top* which does not mean that John is brain-dead but rather that he is stupid or dull. In this perspective *dead* can designate a biological condition, states of mind, moods, and attitudes towards someone or something.

2.3.1.5 The issue of literal meaning

The semantic gradualness enables to overcome the distinction between the *literal* and the non-literal meaning of a word or an utterance. According to the standard semantic theory, the former concerns the linguistic meaning as the combination of meanings of single words, conceived as the outcome of linguistic operations including the phonological, the lexical, and the syntactic ones. It is the basic (primary) meaning of a sentence, i.e. the plain, immediate and unproblematic meaning of a sentence (so-called "sentence meaning"). As a consequence, it has unconditional priority. Within this perspective, literal meaning is an abstraction, grounded on the hypothesis that words are like "meaning containers", which are context-free (that is, they remain unchanged regardless of context of use). They are also sufficient to convey the sense of speech, that is, the "conduit metaphor", according to which "ideas are conducted from one inner mind to another, transported in small compartments by the train of speech", as Gibbs [50] has pointed out.

On the contrary, the *figurative (or non-literal) meaning* is derived from the literal one and can be discovered by resorting to semantic substitution mechanisms (i.e. when non-literal meaning takes the place of the literal one, as in the metaphoric expression, for example, *Surgeons are butchers*). As a result, people can reach a translate and symbolic meaning, used in figurative speech by means of tropes of "speech figures", like metaphor, metonymy, hyperbole, oxymora, and so on.

This standard theory is also shared by Grice [32] when he proposed the dual logic involved in conversation: the *logic of language* which concerns literal meaning (sentence meaning), and the *logic of conversation* which applies to the pragmatic rules used by people to infer ("implicate") what a speaker intends to convey (utterance meaning). "Conversational implicatures" require additional cognitive effort to go beyond the literal meaning of an utterance in order to grasp the speaker's "intended meaning".

However, such a distinction between literal and figurative meaning is not unproblematic and the notion of literal meaning has become a subject of theoretical revision upheld by the work of Gibbs [50] and Glucksberg [51]. The standard logic of literal meaning follows a three-stage model:

a) *Derive the literal meaning of an utterance.*
b) *Test the derived literal meaning against the context of the utterance.*
c) *If the literal meaning makes sense, accept that meaning as the utterance meaning, that is, the speaker's intended meaning. If it does not make sense, then seek an alternative, non-literal meaning that does make sense in the context* [Glucksberg, 51, p. 10].

This standard model entails some testable implications. First, literal meaning is primary and basic, obvious and context-free (unproblematic). Second, literal meaning has unconditional priority, and it will always be derived first; only when it is "defective" can non-literal meaning be attempted. Third, literal meaning is derived automatically, generated easily by the linguistic input (without conscious control), while non-literal meaning is derived only optionally and requires additional cognitive effort. However, none of these statements has been verified empirically; on the contrary, the opposite has been verified, as Glucksberg [51] has highlighted.

Above all, literal meaning is not exclusively the outcome of linguistic decoding, based on linguistic operations (i.e. phonological, lexical, and syntactic ones) but requires a semantic interpretation. The utterance *Cats are animals* could be taken as granted and universally fixed in its literal meaning in any situation, independently from any context. However, the literal interpretation of this utterance is rather different if it is pronounced during a natural science lesson focusing on the distinction between animals and plants, or if it is said as an answer to the comment *Our Pussy went on caterwauling last night*.

As we have already seen, context dependence especially concerns logical connectives, quantifiers (like *some, few, many,* and so on), deictic terms, qualitative adjectives, and pronouns. As Horman [52] underlines, there is a great semantic difference of literal meaning, for instance, of *a few* in: *A few people in the kitchen* (four or five people) and in *A few people in the stadium* (several thousand of people). As we have seen, the fact that words have a graded and gradable meaning inevitably requires reference to the context in order to be able to interpret correctly the semantic value of the literal meaning as well. A plain linguistic decoding is not sufficient to interpret the literal meaning of an utterance.

Likewise, given that meaning (the literal one included) depends upon context, both literal and figurative meaning have the same time of comprehension, as it results from the researches of Onishi and Murphy [53], and Pynte, Besson, Robichon, and Poli [54]. It is also unnecessary to understand literal meaning before proceeding to derive the non-literal meaning. The interpretation of both these kinds of meaning is immediate, and follows the same time curve of computation, because they both show a parallel cognitive processing and activate the same inference mechanisms, as McElree and Nordlie [55] have shown in their research.

Consequently, the determination of so-called "literal meaning" is already the outcome of a choice of a certain interpretation among many other possible ones, all legitimate. The literal meaning of *The cat is on the mat* depends on the basic assumptions about such an utterance (for instance, in this case we do not refer to a floating mat; see next paragraph). Such assumptions are not semantic in their nature but they belong to our *knowledge encyclopaedia*, since they are derived from our experience within the culture of reference. Besides, these assumptions are not fixed, since each assumption entails other assumptions along an associative chain without end.

Within this perspective, determining the literal meaning of every word or sentence is an impossible communicative operation. Each utterance offers an indefinite range of opportunities, among which the addressee has to choose the one that he/she considers more appropriate and effective to the context and communicative interaction. In this respect, the so-called "literal meaning" is one of such possibilities.

Actually, what people above all are interested in is understanding the speaker's communicative intention, which can be conveyed by any kind of utterance and language. They do not proceed to a philological study in order to discover the literal meaning, discriminating it from the figurative one. Instead, they are ready to grasp immediately what a speaker intends to communicate and, on that account, they are able to understand the variations, and also the nuances, of the meaning of an utterance.

2.3.1.6 Context dependence and semantic assumptions

Finally, the meaning design of a word or an utterance or a gesture does not hinge so much upon a universal, abstract and fixed semantic system but it is strictly connected with the *context*. We cannot figure out a meaning isolated from the context or without a context. No meaning is totally foreseeable or definable a priori, because it depends on the context in a contingent way. Due to this context dependence, the meaning of a word, an utterance or a gesture varies each time, being subject to the nonce conditions of a certain situation. For this reason, in different contexts the same message may receive a different interpretation. Besides, it may be a basic ambiguity between a given communicative intention by the speaker and the ascription of another intention to him/her by the recipient [van Rooy, 56].

In particular, the meaning of any utterance, word or gesture cannot be expressed and grasped in a totally explicit way but it always entails some implicit aspects. Practically, it is impossible to enunciate all the features of any meaning because we take for granted many things in speaking and in interpreting the utterances of others. Such things are given as "presupposed" and often they are entailed by the appropriateness condition of the sentence itself. For instance, if I say that Peter has stopped drinking, I presuppose that Peter was used drinking before since the verb *to stop* implies a specific behaviour in the *previous* time.

On this subject Searle [57] introduced the notion of *background assumptions* as the totality of things taken for granted by the interlocutors in a given communicative exchange. For example,

> *Suppose I go into the restaurant and order a meal. Suppose I say, speaking literally, Bring me a steak with fried potatoes. [...] I take it for granted that they will not deliver the meal to my house, or to my place of work. I take it for granted that the steak will not be encased in concrete, or petrified. It will not be stuffed into my pockets or spread over my head. But none of these assumptions was made explicit in the literal utterance.* [Searle, 57, p. 180].

Though not explicitly said, those assumptions contribute in a basic way to determining the meaning of the utterance. Such condition is binding not only for utterances but also for single words. For instance, Searle [57] analyses the word *cut* in sentences such as *Bill cut the grass* and *Sally cut the cake*. The word *cut* is not equivocal, yet it projects a quite different meaning in the two situations because of the differences in the respective background assumptions. It is obvious that grass is cut in a certain way, and cakes in another way.

Besides background assumptions, the *circumstantial assumptions* concern the specific conditions of a given context, the communicative intention of the speaker, as well as the intention ascription by the recipient. People's interpretations of their own and other people's expressions are not necessarily stable or constant over a period of time, but they may change as the context changes. For instance, the semantic features of *book* radically change according to the reference contexts, as in the following examples:

5a. *Peter is reading the book for the exam with attention* (*book* as an object of study);

5b. *Mary has lost the book that George gave her as a present* (*book* as a souvenir in an inattentive and affective context);

5c. *Paul, flown into a rage, has thrown the book against the glass of the window and broken it* (*book* as a blunt tool in an anger context).

In each of these occurrences the context calls attention to some specific properties of the meaning and, at the same time, it "narcotises" other semantic traits, which can be activated in a different circumstance.

The communicative phenomenon herein described is also involved in the so-called *contextual resemanticization* analysed by Violi [14]. In such a case, a speaker can assign specific semantic traits to something that does not possess them of its own, but that obtains them thanks to a specific contingent situation. For instance, we may call *chair* a table, an empty chest, a pile of books, if there are no free chairs, and we seat down on one of these items. Even we may say: "*Please, don't take my seat*". In this process the meaning of a word takes a double semantic valence: the table remains a table, but it performs the general function of a chair (that is, it permits the action of "sitting"). The contextual resemanticization stresses the great plasticity and high flexibility of meaning, allowing a wide range in its use as the result of accurate processes of semantic adjustment.

2.3.1.7 Meaning as inferential outcome

Semantic variability and plasticity entail that, to understand each other, communicators necessarily have to resort to some inferential processes. Meaning design is not an immediate and fully evident datum, univocally correspondent to a real object or event, simply to be produced by a speaker and simply recovered by an addressee. Similarly, meaning design is not an obvious and apparent entity, ready to be recognized. Rather, it is created between two or more communicators in a dynamic way, and then it displays a more or less large number of hidden components to be detected. Moreover, meaning is referred to as a mental and cultural pattern that involves an inference process from the interlocutors, since it shows a specific point of view about reality. It does not only say something; it also points out and indexes how to intend what is said. In this way, meaning implies a *semantic opacity* residue that needs to be elaborated and interpreted starting from some communicative cues and indices conveyed by the speaker.

Particularly, words, utterances, gestures, and other nonverbal signals are to be intended as communicative cues from which communicators can proceed to make suitable and opportune inferences through logical implication, analogy and similarity processes. Aristotle already defined the *sign* (τό σημεῖον) as "a demonstrative premise which is necessary or generally accepted. That which coexist with something else, or before or after whose happening something else has happened, is a sign of that something's having happened or being" (*First analytic*, II, 27; 70a, 7). A classic example is given by the hypothetical enthymeme: "if she has milk, then she has given birth to a new-born child". Subsequently, the Stoics distinguished between "referring signs" (for instance, "where there is smoke, there is fire"), and "indicating signs" (for instance, "body movements are signs of the soul").

Within this perspective, meaning design is not constituted by a fixed system of univocal correspondences between expression and content, but by a set of possible inferences that have different probability degrees of accomplishment. In particular, from a realistic point of view, the meaning of a word, an utterance or a gesture is not to be considered as determined and established in a precise and definitive way by its necessary and sufficient components, because it does not refer to a metaphysical and abstract reality. Conversely, we have to conceive meaning as the semantic expression of our *experience*. Many different factors come into play here, since experience is a complex structure, made up at the same time of sensorial and perceptual, cognitive and emotional, inter-subjective and cultural processes, embedded and interconnected mutually with each other.

Experience is an affair to be analyzed, detected, and interpreted. Linguistic semantics and, more in general, communication are essentially based on our experience of the world, and, consequently, they will be influenced and guided by perceptual, cognitive and emotional constraints which control and manage the interaction with reality. Therefore, meaning entails a remarkable amount of variability in order to fit and express in the right way the continuous flow and the great variety of our human experience.

On one side, this semantic flexibility is at the basis of the *meaning plasticity* that enables speakers to use these meanings in a pliable way, according to their communicative intentions. In this way, we can observe a process of continuous remodelling of meanings in order to adapt them to referring contexts. Meaning is not a closed and univocal, fixed and hard pattern, but it refers to a mental and cultural pattern with a high degree of adaptability to the contingent situations of interlocutors. Within fairly wide limits, meaning can be stretched, expanded or reduced according to the expectancies, beliefs and goals systems of communicators. Essentially, it has a very wide degree of freedom and an opening value that allows a set of its possible and different expressions and interpretations, although such a set is neither undetermined nor chaotic nor even random. In theory and in practice, on that account it is always possible to re-define and re-negotiate meanings in communicative interaction.

On the other side, this semantic variability enables to explain in a relevant way the phenomena and processes of default communication and miscommunication, reaching as far as processes of communicative distortion and pathology. Semantic variability concerns not only what is communicated but also what is said [Reboul, 58]. Consequently, lexical and semantic ambiguities are common; sometimes, conversations are characterised by incomprehension and misunderstanding as well as confusion phenomena. Communicative games often appear and they make the conversation more interesting and intriguing.

2.3.1.8 Modal meaning and semantic-pragmatic synchrony

A last (but not least) notion about meaning variability concerns the *modal meaning*, which summarizes many aspects examined till now in this chapter. To grasp this concept, it is worth starting from the consideration that senders are able to arrange a set of different signalling systems to communicate and make public their communicative intention. Besides language that remains the most powerful, flexible and stable communicational medium, exclusive to the human species, there are several other communicational devices to show their own communicative design, like the paralinguistic (or supra-segmental), the face and gestures system, the gaze, the proxemic and the aptic, as well as the chronemic.

Among others, Anolli [3] argued that each of these communicative systems bears its contribution and participates in defining the meaning of a communicative act in an autonomous way. Such multiplicity enhances the freedom degrees of speakers to manifest and calibrate his/her own communicative intentions as related to the situation. However, the generative capacity of each signalling system should be connected to produce a global and unitary communicative action, with a more or less high consistency degree.

Meaning is not connected with a unique and exclusive signalling system but is generated by the network of semantic and pragmatic connections between different systems. Such a process is ruled out by the so-called *principle of semantic and pragmatic synchrony*, set out by Anolli [3], according to which meaning, whatever it may be, is originated by a non-random combination of different portions of meaning, each of whom produced by a given signalling system. Thus, the meaning of a word, an utterance or a gesture hinges upon its relations to every piece of meaning arising out of each signalling system within the same totality. It has been supposed by Anolli [3] that such semantic and pragmatic synchrony process is ruled out by a general device, dubbed "central communicative processor".

Modal meaning is the standard outcome of the semantic and pragmatic synchrony process, that is, the prevailing and recursive meaning throughout conventionally given situations within a certain cultural community. As Anolli [59] argued, modal meaning is the preferred (or default) one, regularly predominating in a given set of contexts. However, it is neither necessary nor automatic; rather, in certain situations it may be a subject of negotiation between communicators.

2.3.2 Meaning stability

The semantic variability processes taken into consideration in the previous paragraph, if assumed exclusively, risk leading to a perspective of absence of communication and mutual comprehension. In themselves, taken singularly, they would generate a communicative disordered and chaotic situation. We would be compelled to live in a tower of Babel.

Actually, semantic variability phenomena are compensated, completed and balanced by *semantic stability* processes, which make possible and explain the probabilities of order and regularity in the meaning exchange. So, meaning design comes to be a quite complex set of patterns in which the contingent and momentary components are combined with the more enduring and well-grounded ones. Besides, such components of stability are at the base of message intelligibility conditions and of mutual understanding between the communicators. Competence is presumed of that meaning which is considered as shared inside a specific community of participants. In this sense we have to resume the notion of "code" but in a new perspective related to the traditional one.

Semantic stability involves some kind of *convention* between interlocutors, because of their sharing the same cultural belonging. As culture is a mediation system which supplies people with a grid of categories, symbols, values, practices, and mental representations which enable them to read and interpret reality, it also provides the learning and sharing processes of signification and signalling systems. Such processes are to be considered as the outcome of a long, complex and sometimes hard route to obtain consent and devise conventions between interlocutors (*conventionalisation process*). On such a route the *agreement* on how something must be done or said is more significant than what is really done or said.

2.3.2.1 Some more about code

Speaking about meaning regularity and stability as connected with context regularity and stability involves, as a consequence, the opportunity of speaking about the *code* notion under a new light. Some inferential frameworks of communication, in particular the relevance perspective proposed by Sperber and Wilson [48], are opposed to the communicative theory of code and have concluded that it is also possible to communicate without resorting to a code. In its wide theoretic sense, a communicational code is an organised set of rules, which enables communicators to associate in a biunivocal manner elements of one system with elements of another system. Referring to a classic example, the verbal code in language enables a competent speaker to associate biunivocally elements of the phonological system (specific sound combinations) with elements of the semantic system (specific mental images corresponding to these sound combinations).

In a traditional standard perspective, referring, for instance, to the mathematical model of Shannon and Weaver [60], the code is conceived and formulated effectively as a mathematical construct and as a normative cognitive ideal, in which the biunivocal correspondence between the elements of the two systems is practically perfect and automatic. In this way the code, by itself, could deal with and resolve every case of communicative indefiniteness and ambiguousness, as well as implicitness and semantic vagueness phenomena. According to such a framework, communication becomes a simple, immediate and automatic process of message encoding (ciphering) and decoding (deciphering).

Concerning this *strong version of code theory*, Sperber and Wilson have correctly argued that it is untenable on a theoretical and practical level, since a perfect code simply does not exist and never will exist. No code is free of faults, interference, noises, and deviations. Nevertheless, it could be dangerous (perhaps, too dangerous!) to assume that communication can exist without any kind of code.

"Communication without code exists", according to the famous example of the two prisoners of different languages who, breaking stones back to back without seeing each other, succeed in communicating through the rhythm of their hammer strokes [Sperber and Wilson, 48, p.50]. Actually, through the recognisable and shared rhythm of their hammer strokes, the two prisoners generate a local process of conventionalisation, which allows them to convey intentions and meanings. Without some kind of communicative stability, created by sharing a set of regularities and a system of correspondences between the signs and the standard context of use, communication becomes impossible, since it would be totally unforeseeable, confusing and disordered. By nature, in communicative interaction we have to expect some kind of patterns.

Therefore, we have to speak about a "code". However, the "code" herein underlined should be intended as a limited communicative device that institutes general correspondences between one system of elements and another one. It is to be supposed a *weak version of code theory*, as a necessary but non-sufficient condition in order to carry out communicative exchanges. It needs to be integrated by the interlocutors with accurate inference processes of what is communicated. According to this perspective, the code (whichever code) is not able to "disambiguate" and manage all the semantic combinations and correspondences enclosed in a communicative act.

Such a weak theory of code seems to be particularly profitable, since it is consistent either with communicative processes (in the case of communicative exchange success) or with miscommunication phenomena (in the case of deviations and difficulties or even failure of communicative exchange). In particular, this weak theory of code does not entail a fixed semiotic system, but it presupposes a variable system in terms of power and efficacy referring to different binds and opportunities given by a specific communicative situation.

The more a "code" is powerful and "effective", the better it can define a correspondence system and impose semantic constraints on the interlocutors. If they want to communicate something with other people, they are not totally free to invent words and expressions whenever and however they like, but they have to keep to a shared and sharable system of meanings, even if variations and deviations from it can be expected. This system is usually provided by the natural language created in each cultural community. But even in the extreme case of the two prisoners who use hammer strokes in order to communicate, meaning segmentation is connected with rhythm variations and intensity of strokes that need to be created, recognised, and shared by the prisoners.

2.3.2.2 Presumptive meanings

Levinson [12], interested in understanding and explaining regularity in communication, proposed the notion of *presumptive meanings*, that is, preferred (or default) interpretations which are carried by the structure of utterances, given the structure of the language. Such preferred interpretations exist and have a life of their own. For this reason, he proposed a three-layered theory, as, in addition to the layers of "sentence meaning" and "speaker meaning" already grounded in the extant literature, he added a third layer dubbed "utterance meaning". In particular, Levinson distinguished between (a) the *sentence-type meaning* (i.e., the ideal, abstract meaning, defined by a precise set of truth conditions), (b) the *utterance-type meaning* (i.e., the presumptive meaning or preferred interpretation of an utterance via a systematic pragmatic inference based on general expectations about how language is normally used), (c) the *utterance-token meaning* (i.e., the local meaning via a nonce inference within a given context and communicative situation by actual recipients).

Utterance-type meanings are expressed through *generalized conversational implicature*, that is, a default inference, driven by general heuristics, binding in any context unless there are unusual specific context assumptions that defeat it. Such inference is grounded essentially upon three different heuristics:

a) heuristic I: *what isn't said, isn't* (given the assertion: *There's a blue pyramid on the red cube*, licensed inferences are, for instance: "There is not a cone on the red cube", or "There is not a red pyramid on the red cube");

b) heuristic II: *what is simply described is stereotypically exemplified* (given the same assertion, licensed inferences are, for instance: "The pyramid is a stereotypical one, on a square, rather than a hexagonal base", or "The pyramid is directly supported by the cube");

c) heuristic III: *what's said in an abnormal way, isn't normal; or, marked message indicates marked situation* (given the assertion *The blue cuboid block is supported by the red cube*, licensed inferences are, for instance: "The blue block is not, strictly, a cube", or "The blue block is not centrally or stably supported by the red cube").

Within this platform Levinson defined three pragmatic principles to grasp communicative interaction and speech:

1) *Q-principle*
Speaker's maxim: Do not provide a statement that is informationally weaker than your knowledge of the world allows, unless providing an informationally stronger statement would contravene the I-principle. Specifically, select the informationally strongest paradigmatic alternate that is consistent with the facts.
Recipient's corollary: Take it that the speaker made the strongest statement consistent with what he knows.

2) *I-principle*
Speaker's maxim: the maxim of Minimization. "Say as little as necessary"; that is, produce the minimal linguistic information sufficient to achieve your communicational ends (bearing Q in mind).
Recipient's corollary: the Enrichment Rule. Amplify the informational content of the speaker's utterance, by finding the most *specific* interpretation, up to what you judge to be the speaker's intended point, unless the speaker has broken the maxim of Minimization by using a marked or prolix expression.

3) *M-principle*
Speaker's maxim: Indicate an abnormal, non-stereotypical situation by using marked expressions that contrast with those you would use to describe the corresponding normal, stereotypical situation.
Recipient's corollary: What is said in an abnormal way indicates an abnormal situation, or marked messages indicate marked situations.

To sum up, Levinson tries to illustrate the meaning stability resorting to a middle course between semantics and pragmatics, and foreseeing a general heuristic device, able to systematically guarantee preferred interpretations and standard inferences. However, such logical explication, based upon a huge number of linguistic phenomena, does not allow the local understanding of a contingent communicational situation. It does not even seem to respect the semantic variations and changes on an experimental basis. To gain a factual comprehension of meaning from a psychological standpoint, it is worth analyzing the connection between meaning and context as an interesting and effective path to detect the hidden design of meaning.

2.3.2.3 Meaning stability as context regularity

A conventionalisation process presupposes the active participation of the communicators, as well as rules, practices, values, and meanings negotiation and sharing, although they may be local and temporary. It ends in working out a set of what Bruner calls *communicative formats* [61, 62], each of which is made of a structured sequence of interactive (verbal and non-verbal) exchanges, which allows communicators to reach a joint aim, follow the same procedures and rule systems, as well as share the meaning of what they are going to say or to do. Many communicative formats show a high and strong regularity structure, such as the greeting exchange, the call for apologies, a university exam, a political debate, and the like. These cases can be called *standard (or default) formats*, and are based on recognising and accepting a shared system of rules and patterns. Usually, words and other communicative signs are "anchored" to a default format that makes their meaning foreseeable and definable. By the way, it is worth remarking the strong similarity between the concept of format and that of pattern, previous advanced.

In particular, communicative formats oscillate from *re-production processes* to *production processes*. This oscillating motion is analogous to the one proposed by Bourdieu [63, 64] for cultural practices. On the one hand, given the nature of re-production processes, communicative formats tend towards repetition and recurrence in an almost stereotypical way, by creating proper "communicative routines" (obviously articulated in sub-routines), and also by establishing a continuity with semantic and communicative past conventions. These recurring and reduplicating processes are at the base of meaning stability and regularity. They are grounded on *context regularity*, as, if it is true that contexts show a great deal of variability and unpredictability, then it is also true that in most cases contexts are structured and regular forms in our everyday experience of the world. On this platform, individuals build and share their scripts with reference to specific situations.

Standard context is the context that presents a high routine regularity in the repetition of interactions, sequence of events and communicative exchanges. In such a way, we can assume that *context regularity is equivalent to meaning regularity*. No communicative act, like an utterance, a gesture and so on, exists without being context related, since it is always indexed in a standard context of use. The meaning of such a communicative act is given by the mental representation of standard context regularity. On the other hand, thanks to production processes, communicative formats are neither totally constrained nor completely determined by the past and by context regularity, but they expect and produce variations and deviations as an effect of contingent conditions and novel unpredictable aspects that every communicative situation potentially brings on itself.

Context regularity is the outcome of a historical and cultural process, not a logical necessity, and the past neither determines nor constrains the present, although the former steers the latter. In this way, contextual variations may always, in theory and in practice, take place related to the *hic et nunc* situation. Given this double process of re-production and production, regularity and variation are two essential constituents of meaning, reciprocally presupposed and implied. Without regularity there is no awareness of variation and vice versa. That is, *variation in itself does not deny regularity, but demands it*. As the standard communicative format is regular and stable, it contains in itself a range of unpredictability and interpretability conditions of meaning, as well as a set of applicability norms of communicative practices, since it provides the signification and indexing criteria.

2.4   The meaning compositionality

By nature, meaning design is not a homogeneous and univocal representation of reality but has an intrinsically composite character. Such hybrid theory of meaning entails that many aspects of meaning should be explained resorting to different layers and components of communication involving cognitive principles, knowledge factors, subjective experiences, and interactional principles, and no doubt much besides. Grice [65] was essentially correct in thinking of meaning as a composite notion. The full meaning of an utterance may only be captured by considering different kinds of content: what is said, what is conventionally implicated, and what is presupposed.

Such perspective of the heterogeneous nature marked a basilar advance in the theory of meaning. To tell the truth, Frege [16] first had already introduced *the principle of compositionality*, according to which the meaning of a complex expression is a function of the meanings of its parts and its mode of composition. The meaning of each semantic item can be analyzed by a set of meaning components or properties of a more general order. However, the compositionality analysis has followed different courses ending in opposite outcomes, as we are going to show in the following section. Specifically, we will see three distinguishing paths: (a) semantic segmentation via analytic features; (b) semantic segmentation via prototype; (c) semantic segmentation via type-pattern.

2.4.1   Semantic segmentation via analytic features

Feature semantics is a theoretical model grounded on these two assumptions: (a) the semantic features on which the decomposition is based are a set of necessary and sufficient conditions (NSCs) for the definition of meaning; (b) these features constitute a finite list of primitive items. Widely spread and common, compatible with Frege's formulation of meaning as composed by characteristic notes, such a perspective became popular especially thanks to the model of Katz and Fodor [66]. According to the feature semantics, linguistic terms as *man, woman, boy,* and *girl* may be defined by the following NSCs:

Man	= ANIMATE & HUMAN & MALE & ADULT
Woman	= ANIMATE & HUMAN & NON MALE & ADULT
Boy	= ANIMATE & HUMAN & MALE & NON ADULT
Girl	= ANIMATE & HUMAN & NON MALE & NON ADULT

Feature semantics entails some important consequences, as:
a) no feature can be defeasible, being all necessary conditions;
b) no other feature can be added, being also sufficient conditions;
c) all the features have the same semantic value; as a consequence, the model is non-hierarchical and "democratic";
d) meaning, being the outcome of the composition of its features, is never gradual but has clear-cut boundaries; as a consequence, it is fully compatible with Boolean binary (or two-value) logic.

On that account, to define the hidden design of meaning, feature semantics foresees a basic distinction between dictionary knowledge and encyclopaedic knowledge. The former is fundamental for the meaning definition, while the latter consists of accessory and derivative knowledge referring to factual and subjective aspects. Moreover, the key features of meaning are *analytic properties*, which are non-defeasible and unchangeable, necessary in nature, able to define the category membership in positive.

To put in a nutshell, feature semantics is a molecular theory, as there are meaning dependencies but restricted to smaller parts in an unidirectional way. Analytic properties should be intended as primitives and atomic units, through which meaning is composed once for all and for everybody in the same manner. However, such theory is substantially untenable nowadays, because it directly knocks against the linguistic and communicative phenomena of semantic variability examined in the previous paragraphs (see 2.3.1).

2.4.2   Semantic segmentation via prototype

Within the categorization process, *prototype* represents a key notion to explain the horizontal organization of a given category. In the *standard theory*, advanced by Rosch [67, 45], prototype was defined as the best representative and the best case of category membership. In such a way, categories are no more defined by a set of necessary and sufficient properties but in a global and synthetic manner, as prototypes constitute the focal points around which the whole category is organized. Moreover, the category membership is ruled out by the resemblance degree of other members to prototypes; then, the category itself is characterized not by clear-cut boundaries but fuzzy ones.

However, the standard theory of prototype turned out to be invalidated by the conceptual equivalence between *category representativity* and *category membership*. Actually, they are two distinct concepts, as one thing is representativity (that is, to possess the typical features of a category) and another thing is membership (that is, to define the criteria through which an item can be accepted as a member of a certain category or not).

To overcome this issue, Givón [42], Kleiber [36], Violi [14] and other scholars have changed the notion of prototype and have developed the so-called *extended theory of prototype*. Within this new point of view, prototype is no more an actual exemplar (or token) of a category but it is a mental construct, insofar as it has become the exemplar with the most significant properties.

Prototype does no longer represent the horizontal structure of a category. It is the set of *prototypical effects*, that is, the salient properties which distinguish a category from each other. Consequently, we have to discriminate between *category prototypicality* and *meaning typicality*. The former concerns the possess of larger (or smaller) number of prototypical effects, while the latter regards the notion of average value, insofar as the prototypic eagle is not a special kind of eagle but the one that, better than others, possesses the average values of properties typical of its category. Thus, meaning typicality refers to the regularity of situations, and enables to recognize the salient properties which characterize a given meaning.

How such meaning typicality is built up? According to Violi [14], it is worth distinguishing between *essential properties* and *typical properties*. The first ones are the common features for all the members of a certain category, as, for instance, being oviparous and having a beak for the natural category of *bird*. Essential properties, as such, provide us with a negative membership criterion, as they allow to exclude all exemplars that do not possess such properties. For instance, those animals which, jointly, are not oviparous and do not have a beak, cannot belong to the category of *bird*. Albeit they are, by nature, conventional, essential properties have a strong semantic thickness and, as a result, they are resistant over time. For instance, as noted above, in the case of whale, the discovery that, although living in the sea, it is not a fish but a mammal led to erase the property "fish" and to replace it with the property "mammal". That means that there is not any natural ontology, able to permanently fix the essential properties but only cultural criteria, able to define a given category from time to time.

Conversely, typical properties are the additional and specific properties which add semantic portions to a word or an utterance. By definition, they are defeasible and do not determine membership. For instance, as previous mentioned, in the meaning of *bird* a set of features are typical like flying ability (there are birds that do not fly, like ostriches), feathers (there are birds without feathers, like penguins), and wings (there are birds without wings, like kiwis).

However, semantic segmentation via prototype is quite difficult and exacting, as for each linguistic item it should be carry out a deep linguistic analysis to find the essential and typical properties and to detect the hidden design of meaning. Such analysis has been well done for the item *bird* by Geeraerts [35] as exemplary study, but it should be repeated for each other word. We may question whether this way might be covered for natural kinds of words (like *cat, dog*, and so on) and, especially, for abstract and cultural kinds of words (like *liberty, justice, love*, and so on). For these latter, which are the essential properties and the typical ones? As a matter of fact, their meaning changes by changing the referring culture. Provided that semantic segmentation via prototype is achievable and tenable on theoretical basis uniquely for the linguistic domain, it is quite unfeasible on an empirical level. Furthermore, such kind of segmentation is unviable for the analysis and interpretation of non-verbal aspects which, as we have considered previously in deepening the principle of semantic and pragmatic synchrony, concur in an essential way to define meaning of a word, an utterance or a gesture. Summing up, semantic segmentation via prototype is confined only to the linguistic aspects of meaning.

2.4.3 Meaning compositionality via Type-pattern

Another way to analyze meaning compositionality consists in detecting the semantic patterns through which it is composed in an all-inclusive way. The issue is to find regularity in the flow of experiential events. We have already seen that, given the cultural and conventional origin of meaning, context regularity is a basic premise for meaning regularity. Preferred (or default) interpretation is grounded on this experiential platform. In such a way, the detection of meaning components is an *empirical* matter, insofar as, if we have at our disposal a research device able to find regularities in the flow of events, we can detect the essential features of an expression, as well as the typical ones. Furthermore, in such a way it is possible to cope with and overtake an actual difficulty of meaning compositionality. As Dekker and van Rooy [68] argued, we are not able to systematically determine the semantic content of a sentence in a compositional way based on its syntactic structure, without making reference to the attitudes of speakers and hearers.

In particular, the goal is to ascertain the similarity of the semantic design in the stream of events. Similarity is not given by explicit criteria, as in the explicit definitions of identity like those valuable for triangles (i.e. closed figures having three angles, or internal angles that sum to 180° and so on). Similarity is given by comparable patterns which, jointly, have these properties: (a) the patterns have an analogous number of components; (b) the components organization assumes a corresponding shape; (c) the patterns are recursive in nature. From this standpoint, it is not necessary that components involve simple binary truth values; rather, they can have graded degrees to match themselves.

To obtain the semantic patterns of modal meaning, the *Type-pattern* (T-pattern) model, recently advanced by Magnusson [69, 4, 5, 6], seems to be a very important and useful device, as, being empirically operationalized by a specific software dubbed THEME, is strictly adhering to each situation to be analyzed and interpreted (for an explanation of THEME and its rationale see Magnusson, chapter 1 of this book). As a starting pointing, we may assume that, as we have previously seen, in any case the design of meaning includes some hidden elements, due to the huge complexity of the meaning itself. We may also assume that these hidden elements are not at random; rather, they are organized by means of a rather consistent network of real-time relations in some way, although such organization is not immediately manifest.

The T-patterns definition entails to abstract some of these relations to create an algorithm for the detection of hidden semantic patterns of a word, an utterance, or a gesture. Over the repeated occurrences of a particular T-pattern in a given communicative interaction, its semantic components occur in the same order each time and by respecting in a relatively invariant manner the consecutive time distances.

By means of the THEME procedure, it is possible to ascertain both the variable and stable components of meaning design, given a contingent situation of communication. As a matter of fact, the modal meaning of an utterance or a gesture may be detected by observing regularities and similarities in the stream of events, as the empirical detection of systematic and well-founded connections between certain occurrences and other ones enables to find out how communicators communicate each other in a foreseeable and intelligible way within a given circumstance or comparable circumstances. At the same time, it is possible also to recognize how the detection of T-patterns is adhering to the semantic variability in a specific communicative situation. Within this domain the T-patterns procedure is viable and tenable in every kind of semantic process, starting from the fuzzy boundaries of an utterance or a gaze and the semantic gradualness till to radial categories, semantic polysemy and literal vs. non-literal meaning.

The detection of T-patterns enables to appreciate the hidden design of meaning encompassed in an utterance or in a nonverbal item not generally and in an abstract way but locally and in a contingent manner. The attention is focused on the local management of meaning, as each moment communicators have the opportunity of organizing, regulating, managing and monitoring their communicative interaction. They have the strategic possibility of choice between different semantic routes. As a matter of fact, the definition of T-patterns is properly the detection of such routes as a basic premise for their understanding and interpretation. Different instances of THEME application regarding the detection of hidden patterns of meaning are shown in the following chapters of the book.

2.5   Conclusion

Meaning design is a complex affair both at a given moment (synchronically) and in the sequence of real-time interactions (diachronically). The creation of the new T-pattern model with corresponding detection algorithms enables to reach more relevant insights into the hidden folds of meaning both synchronically and diachronically. Obviously, besides an interdisciplinary collaboration, such new line of study demands further steps both at a theoretical and at an experimental level in the linguistic and extra-linguistic domains of meaning.

2.6   References

[1]   C. Knight, M. Studdert-Kennedy, and J. R. Hurford, *The evolutionary emergence of language: Social function and the origins of linguistic form.* Cambridge: Harvard University Press, 2000.

[2]   T. W. Deacon, *The symbolic species: The co-evolution of language and the human brain.* New York: Norton, 1997.

[3]   L. Anolli, MaCHT – Miscommunication as Chance Theory: Towards a unitary theory of communication and miscommunication, in *Say not to say: New perspectives on miscommunication,* L. Anolli, R. Ciceri, and G. Riva, Eds. Amsterdam: IOS Press, 2002, pp. 3-43.

[4]   M. S. Magnusson, [2000], Discovering hidden time patterns in behaviour: T-Patterns and their detection, *Behavior Research Methods, Instruments and Computers* **32**(1), (2000) 93-110.

[5]   M. S. Magnusson, Analyzing complex real-time streams of behaviour: Repeated patterns in behaviour and DNA, in *L'éthologie appliquée aujourd'hui, Vol. 3, Ethologie humaine*, C. Baudoin, Ed. Paris: Levallois-Perret, 2003, pp. 25-36.

[6]   M. S. Magnusson, Repeated patterns in behaviour and other biological phenomena, in *Evolution of communication systems: A comparative approach*, D. K. Oller and U. Griebel, Eds. Cambridge: The MIT Press, 2004, pp. 111-128.

[7]   E. Morin, Le dèfi de la complexitè, *Chiméres* **5/6** (1988) 1-18.

[8]   E. Sapir, *Language*. New York: Harcourt, Brace & Wall, 1921.

[9]   R. Solé and B. Goodwin, *Signs of life: How complexity pervades biology*. New York: Basic Books, 2000.

[10] R. Jackendoff, *The architecture of the language faculty*. Cambridge: The MIT Press, 1997.

[11] R. Jackendoff, *Foundations of language*. Oxford: Oxford University Press, 2002.

[12] S. C. Levinson, *Presumptive meanings: The theory of generalized conversational implicature*. Cambridge: The MIT Press, 2000.

[13] C. K. Ogden and I. A. Richards, *The meaning of meaning*. London: Routledge and Keegan Paul, 1923.

[14] P. Violi, *Meaning and experience*. Bloomington: Indiana University Press, 2001.

[15] L. Wittgenstein, *Tractatus Logico Philosophicus*. London: Routledge and Kegan, 1922.

[16] G. Frege, Uber sinn und bedeutung, *Zeitschrift fur Philosophie und philosophsiche kritik* **100** (1892) 25-50.

[17] R. Carnap, *Meaning and necessity*. Chicago: University of Chicago Press, 1947.

[18] R. Montague, *Formal philosophy*. Yale: Yale University Press, 1974.

[19] G. Lakoff, *Women, fire, and dangerous things: What categories reveal about the mind*. Chicago: University of Chicago Press, 1987.

[20] F. de Saussure, *Cours de linguistique gènèrale*. Paris: Payot, 1916.

[21] L. Hjemslev, *Omkring sprotgeoriens grundlasggelse*. København: Munskgaard, 1943.

[22] T. De Mauro, *Introduzione alla semantica*. Bari: Laterza, 1965.

[23] C. J. Fillmore, Frame semantics and the nature of language, *Annals of the New York Academy of Sciences: Conference on the Origin and Development of Language and Speech* **280** (1976) 20-32.

[24] C. J. Fillmore, Frame semantics in the linguistic society of Korea, in *Linguistic in the morning calm*, The linguistic society of Korea, Ed. Seoul: Hanshin, 1982, pp. 111-137.

[25] R. Jackendoff, *Semantics and cognition*. Cambridge: The MIT Press, 1983.

[26] R. Jackendoff, *Language of the mind: Essays on mental representation*. Cambridge: The MIT Press, 1992.

[27] L. Talmy, How language structures space, in *Spatial orientation: Theory, research, and application* H. Pick and L. P. Acredolo, Eds. New York: Plenum Press, 1983, pp.225-282.

[28] C. Fillmore, Frames and the semantics of understanding, *Quaderni di Semantica* **62** (1985) 222-253.

[29] J. J. Gumperz and S. C. Levinson, *Rethinking linguistic relativity*. New York: Cambridge University Press, 1996.

[30] U. Eco, *A theory of semiotics*. Bloomington: Indiana University Press, 1976.

[31] H. Putnam, Meaning and reference, *Journal of Philosophy* **70** (1973) 699-711.

[32] H. P. Grice, Logic and conversation, in *Syntax and Semantics: Vol. 3, Speech Acts*, P. Cole and J. L. Morgan, Eds. New York: Academic Press, 1975, pp.41-58.

[33] D. A. Cruse, *Lexical semantics*. Cambridge: Cambridge University Press, 1986.

[34] H. Putnam, The meaning of «meaning», in *Mind, language and reality. Philosophical papers, volume 2*, H. Putnam, Ed. New York: Cambridge University Press, 1975, pp. 215-271.

[35] D. Geeraerts, Prospects and problems of prototype theory, *Linguistics* **27**(4), (1989) 587-612.

[36] G. Kleiber, *La sémantique du prototype. Catégories et sens lexical*. Paris: PUF, 1990.

[37] W. Labov, The boundaries of language and their meaning, in *New ways of analyzing variations in English*, C. N. Bailey and R. Shuy, Eds. Georgetown: Georgetown University Press, 1973, pp. 340-373.

[38] G. Lakoff, Linguistic and natural logic, in *Semantics of natural language*, D. Davidson and G. Harman, Eds. Dordrecht: Reidel, 1972, pp. 545-665.

[39] G. Lakoff, Hedges, a study in meaning criteria and the logic of fuzzy concepts, *Journal of Philosophical Logic* **2** (1973) 458-508.

[40] A. Zadeh, Fuzzy sets, *Information and control* **8** (1965) 338-353.

[41] Q. Zhang, Fuzziness-vagueness-generality-ambiguity, *Journal of Pragmatics* **29** (1998) 13-31.

[42] T. Givòn, Prototypes: Between Plato and Wittgenstein, in *Noun classes and categorization*, C. Craig, Ed. Amsterdam: John Benjamins, 1986, pp. 77-102.

[43] M. Posner, *Empirical studies of prototypes*, in *Noun classes and categorization*, C. Craig, Ed. Amsterdam: John Benjamin, 1986, pp. 53-61.

[44]   E. Rosch, Linguistic relativity, in *Human communication: Theoretical perspectives*, A. Silverstein, Ed. New York: Halsted Press, 1974, pp. 95-121.

[45]   E. Rosch, Colour categorization, in *Cognition and categorization*, E. Rosch and B. B. Lloyd, Eds. Hillsdale: Erlbaum, 1978, pp. 27-48.

[46]   D. Geeraerts, Polisemy and prototypically, *Cognitive Linguistics* **3**(2), (1992) 219-223.

[47]   L. Wittgenstein, *Philosophische untersuchungen*. Frankfurt am Main: Suhrkamp, 1958.

[48]   D. Sperber and D. Wilson, *Relevance: Communication and cognition*, Oxford: Oxford University Press, 1986.

[49]   P. J. Thibault, Communicating and interpreting relevance through discourse negotiation: An alternative to relevance theory - A reply to Franken, *Journal of Pragmatics* **31**(4), (1999) 557-594.

[50]   R. W. Gibbs, *Intentions in the experience of meaning*. Cambridge: Cambridge University Press, 1999.

[51]   S. Glucksberg, *Understanding figurative language: From metaphors to idioms*. New York: Oxford University Press, 2001.

[52]   H. Horman, The calculating listener or how many are einige, mehrere and ein paar (some, several and a few), in *Meaning, use, and interpretation of language*, R. Bauerke, C. Schwarze, and A. van Strechan, Eds. 1983, pp. 221-234.

[53]   K. H. Onishi and G. L. Murphy, Metaphoric reference: When metaphors are not understood as literal expressions, *Memory and Cognition* **21** (1993) 763-772.

[54]   J. Pynte, M. Besson, F. H. Robichon, and J. Poli, The time course of metaphor comprehension: An event related potential study, *Brain and Language* **55** (1996) 293-316.

[55]   B. Mc Elree and J. Nordlie, Literal and figurative interpretations are computed in parallel, *Psychonomic Bulletin and Review* **6** (1999) 486-494.

[56]   R. van Rooy, Evolution of conventional meaning and conversational principles, *Synthese (Knowledge, Rationality and Action)***139** (2004) 331-336.

[57]   J. Searle, *The rediscovery of the mind*. Cambridge: The MIT Press, 1992.

[58]   A. Reboul, Semantic transparency, semantic opacity, states of affairs, mental states and speech acts, in *Say not to say: New perspectives on miscommunication*, L. Anolli, R. Ciceri, and G. Riva, Eds. Amsterdam: IOS Press, 2002, pp. 45-72

[59]   L. Anolli, Significato modale e comunicazione non verbale, *Giornale Italiano di Psicologia* **3** (2003) 453-484.

[60]   C. E. Shannon and W. Weaver, *The mathematical theory of communication*. Urbana: Illinois University Press, 1949.

[61]   J. Bruner, *Actual minds, possible worlds*. Cambridge: Harvard University Press, 1986.

[62]   J. Bruner, *Acts of meaning*. Cambridge: Harvard University Press, 1990.

[63]   P. Bourdieu, *Outline of a theory of practice*. Cambridge: Cambridge University Press, 1977.

[64]   P. Bourdieu, *The logic of practice*. Stanford: Stanford University Press, 1990.

[65]   H. P. Grice, *Logic and conversation*. William James Lectures, Harvard: Harvard University Press, 1967.

[66]   J. J. Katz and A. Fodor, The structure of a semantic theory, *Language* **39** (1963) 170-210.

[67]   E. Rosch, Human categorization, in *Advances in cross-cultural psychology, volume 1*, N. Warren, Ed. London: Academic Press, 1977, pp. 1-49.

[68]   P. Dekker and R. van Rooy, Bi-directional Optimality Theory: An application of game theory, *Journal of Semantics* **17** (2000) 217-242.

[69]   M. S. Magnusson, Hidden real-time patterns in intra- and inter-individual behaviour: Description and Detection, *European Journal of Psychological Assessment* **12** (1996) 112-123.

The Hidden Structure of Interaction
L. Anolli et al. (Eds.)
IOS Press, 2005

3. Microanalysis of T-Patterns. Analysis of Symmetry/Asymmetry in Social Interaction

M. Teresa ANGUERA

Abstract. This chapter analyses the relationships between the structure of data gathered from a recorded of an interactive situation and the temporal patterns (T-patterns) obtained through use of the THEME software. Various simulated interactive situations are presented, along with hypothetical data that invite reflection; an initial micro-analytic study that enables the structure of the T-patterns to be better understood is carried out also. Each of the aspects addressed in the microanalysis requires further, more specific studies. As at least two interacting subjects are involved in every social interaction, the analysis of symmetry and asymmetry relationships is particularly relevant; it has to be considered the classical concept and its adaptation to the T-patterns also.

Analysis of the T-pattern structure is argued to be of special interest, the relationship between the characteristics of the codes that comprise the recording (with real or simulated data) and the patterns obtained being taken into account.

Keywords: Nonverbal social interaction; symmetry/asymmetry relationship; T-pattern microanalysis; simulated interactive situations.

Contents

3.1 Introduction

Social interaction is a complex phenomenon for various reasons. The most important of these are the inevitable multiplicity of individuals involved (dyadic, triadic, tetradic, etc. interaction), the diversity of existing interactive structures, the effect of the context and interactive content, and both inter- and intra-session permanence and changeability, among many others. As was pointed out 25 years ago by Cairns [1] and Lamb, Suomi and Stephenson [2], the study of social interaction is undoubtedly difficult from a methodological point of view, and in this regard the contribution of Sackett [3, 4] to observational methodology proved decisive at that time.

The assumptions underlying social interaction may be considered as a basic perspective for the study of social relationships, although there is no unified theory for the study of such processes [5, 6]. Although some authors [1] argue that the social interaction is a broad discipline in which several different methodologies may be applied, the present chapter refers solely to social interaction that is produced spontaneously and in a non-restrictive context; consequently, it adopts the approach of observational methodology [7].

However, there are many specific questions that may be researched in the context of social interaction, as the latter constitutes an extensive framework from which varied elements may be selected. Among the various aspects studied in recent years, there are some issues of clear interest as the search for interactive patterns by means of lag sequential analysis [8-10], the detection of interactive intensity through the analysis of polar coordinates [4, 11-13], the improved understanding of the symmetrical (or asymmetrical) nature of the participative relationship using *log-linear* or *logit* analysis [9, 14], and the incorporation of the temporal dimension in macro form into social care programs [15].

One of the specific questions that is proving to be highly fruitful, and which constitutes the *leitmotif* of the present chapter, is the study of the hidden structures underlying an interactive situation, in other words, the way in which temporal patterns are able to reveal those aspects of social interaction which are not immediately observable. Every interactive flow is governed by behavioural structures of varying stability that can be visualized by obtaining temporal patterns (T-patterns). These temporal patterns, detected by means of the powerful algorithm of the THEME software, developed by Dr. Magnus S. Magnusson (University of Iceland, Reykjavík), constitute the object of the present study.

Given the relevance of T-patterns in terms of their appearance, structure, modifiability, aggregation of sub-patterns, effect of temporal units considered, etc. this chapter focuses on T-patterns microanalysis, with special emphasis on the analysis of their symmetry/asymmetry.

3.2 Analysis of social interaction by means of T-patterns

When, in the 1980s, observational methodology became more widely developed as a discipline it also became clear that the detection of temporal patterns would play an important role. As Bakeman & Gottman [16] stated in their study of interaction, "We believe that great conceptual clarity can be obtained by thinking about temporal patterning, and we believe that anyone who has collected observational data over time and ignores time is missing an opportunity" (p. 201).

In any observational study, and naturally in those dealing with social interaction, the observation instrument, whether this is category system or field format, or a combination of the two [7], has to be developed in accordance with the research objective, the corresponding codes being defined in the process. Once this important stage of the process has been completed, the recording can begin; although the recording stage faces a number of difficulties regarding notational decisions [17], in recent decades it has benefited greatly from the computerized coding that is possible once the recordings have been digitalized [18]. Moreover, it should be remembered that there are many computer programs that enable temporal recording in conventional units of time, whether these are general programs, such as the Excel spreadsheet, or more specific tools such as some of the data types of the SDIS-GSEQ [8], CODEX [19], THEMECODER [20] or THE OBSERVER [21], among many others.

The data gathered through the recording of an interactive situation are subjected to a quality control in order to filter out potential errors and, provided this control is passed, they are then analyzed in accordance with the corresponding observational design. Among many possible statistical analyses, whether conventional or not, the present chapter is concerned exclusively with the detection of temporal patterns.

Over the last twenty years the progressive possibilities opened up by the THEME software [22-29] have made what was once impossible a reality. Although, given the numerous research reports that have used this program in recent years, it may seem unnecessary to restate its possibilities it is worth reiterating that the THEME constitutes a powerful research tool. Indeed it's able to explore behavioural structures in detail by revealing stronger connections between successive recorded behaviours than would be expected by chance; the *critical interval* is the key concept which enables the admissible temporal distances between successive identical or similar occurrences to be delimited in order to consider the existence of a temporal pattern. Obtaining T-patterns is of great importance both theoretically and empirically, and deriving their algorithm has involved the development of new and powerful analytic techniques based on probability theory and, more specifically, the binomial distribution [26].

Obtaining T-patterns proves to be extraordinarily productive and fruitful in the study of any of the multiple facets or fields of social interaction's application, for example, in situations concerning non-verbal behaviour [30] or those where the focus is on proxemic behaviour, as in the case of sport [31-34]; however, as recent research has shown [27, 35] it is equally useful in many other areas, even when their field of action is not restricted to this area of social interaction.

3.3 The T-pattern as product of analysis and research datum: Micro-analytic variability in its development

As Duncan [36] points out, THEME patterns are not in themselves the results, rather these patterns provide the information necessary to formulate structures which must then be fitted and consolidated on the basis of the temporal patterns obtained.

The example proposed by Magnusson [26, p. 25] in Figure 3.1 has been chosen as the starting point for the microanalysis. If we consider solely codes a and b, and naturally the same applies if we only consider codes c and d (if we are interested in taking them all into account the distribution must be considered as multinomial, which is beyond the scope of the present chapter), it can be seen that episodes of a occur at 2 and 24 and those of b at 4 and 26. The probability of the occurrence of b is $p(b) = N_b/N_T = 2/31 = .129$, and $p(\sim b) = 1 - p(b) = 1 - 0.129 = .87$.

Following Magnusson [27, Appendix A and Appendix B] we then check to see if any significant patterns are detected between a and b, whether these are free or fast T-patterns:

In the free T-pattern the critical interval is (2,2) and its length is $d = d_2 - d_1 + 1 = 1$, giving $p = 1 - \Sigma\text{binomial} (2, i, 1-0.87^1) = 1 - 0.9831 = .0169$ (where $i = 0 \dots N_{ab} -1$). This is significant at the level $p = .05$.

In the fast T-pattern the critical interval is (0,2) and its length is d = d_2 – d_1 + 1 = 3, giving p = 1 – Σbinomial (2, i, 1-0.87^3) = 1 – 0.7484 = 0.25 (where i = 0 … N_{ab} -1). This is not significant at the level p = .05. This is shown graphically in Figure 3.1.

Although this approach does not consider a multinomial distribution it is nevertheless possible to check for the hypothetical presence of temporal patterns between any of the pairs of codes. Thus, if we want to check between b and c we know that episodes of b occur at 4 and 26 and those of c at 7 and 28. The probability of the occurrence of b is $p(b)$ = N_b/N_T=2/31=0.129, and $p(\sim b)$ = 1-$p(b)$ = 1-0.129 = 0.87. In order to detect if there is a free T-pattern we delimit the critical interval, which is (2,3) and of length d = d_2 – d_1 + 1 = 2, giving p = 1 – Σbinomial (2, i, 1-0.87^2) = 1 – 0.9424 = 0. 0576 (where i = 0 … N_{ab} -1). A free T-pattern, not significant at the level p = .05, is detected.

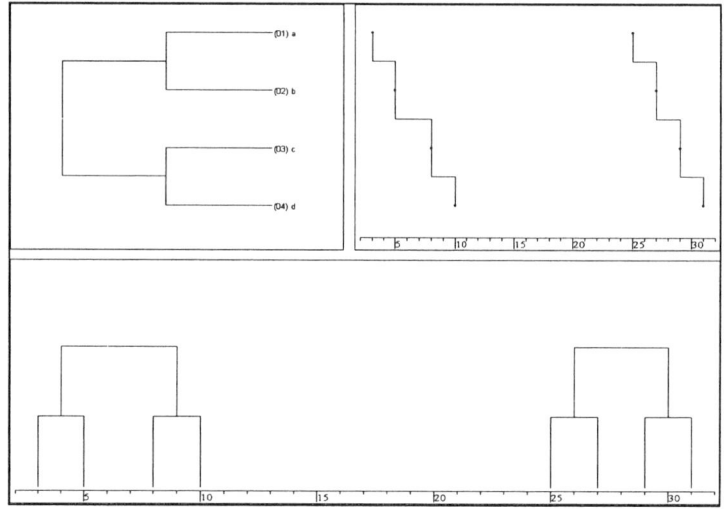

Figure 3.1 Graphical representation of the pattern obtained with the data from the example proposed by Magnusson (2000, p. 95, in Figure 1). The possible binary trees are the one shown ((ab)(cd)), along with ((a(bc))d), (a(b(cd)) and ((ab)c)d), the significance level being p = .05 (no T-pattern with a significance level of p = .005 is obtained).

If we check between b and d the episodes of b occur at times 4 and 26, and those of d at 9 and 30. The probability of the occurrence of b is $p(b)$ = N_b/N_T = 2/31 = 0.129, and $p(\sim b)$ = 1-$p(b)$ = 1-0.129 = 0.87. In order to detect if there is a free T-pattern we delimit the critical interval, which is (4,5) and of length d = d_2 – d_1 + 1 = 2, giving p = 1 – Σbinomial (2, i, 1-0.87^2) = 1 – 0.9424 = 0. 0576 (where i = 0 … N_{ab} -1). A free T-pattern, not significant at the level p = .05, is detected.

Is this significance related to the structure of the tree obtained using THEME? Indeed it is, for if, in the example of Figure 3.1, we obtain the graphical representation of the T-pattern obtained using THEME at a significance level of p = .04 then the single four-branch pattern is transformed into two binary patterns (ab) and (cd); this indicates that the connection between the two binary patterns is weaker than that between their respective components (a and b on the one hand, and c and d on the other).

Given the effect of the critical interval it is worth considering whether microanalysis of the T-pattern would provide a better understanding of the different aspects affecting it.

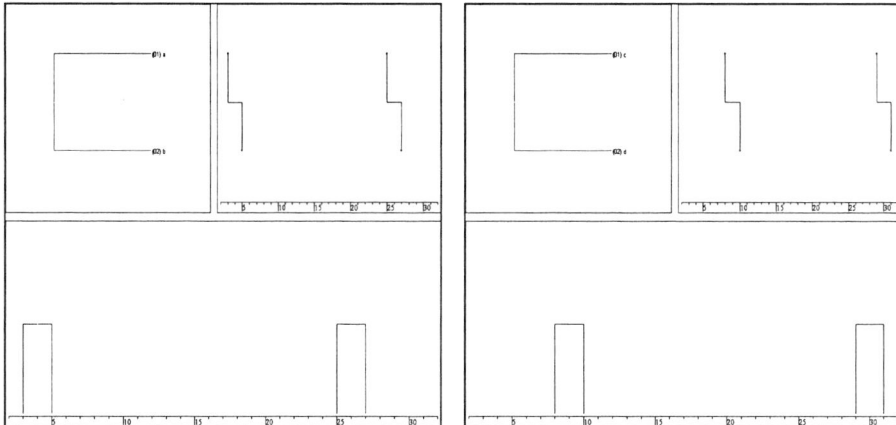

Figure 3.2 Graphical representation of the binary patterns obtained with the data from the example proposed by Magnusson (2000, p. 95, in Figure 1) and with the significance level set at $p = .04$. The binary trees obtained are (ab) and (cd), which are sub-patterns of that shown in Figure 3.1.

As the present chapter forms part of the book's theoretical section, it does not seek to carry out an empirical study or take any of psychology's theoretical frameworks as a reference point. However, it does aim to analyze how temporal patterns behave at the micro-analytic level in particular cases, without any attempt at generalization being made. Different subsequent studies with real data would be able to develop specifically the various aspects that are here only suggested.

3.3.1 Microanalysis according to the unequal duration of behavioural episodes

Let us consider an interactive situation involving the actors *s1, s2, s3, sf* and *sg*, who participate on a turn-taking basis. Consequently, our proposed starting point is a schematic observation instrument (coding system) which will be adopted as the operational basis of simulated data (Table 3.1).

Category Table

ACTOR	BE	ACTIVITY	VERBALBEHAVIOR
s1	b	a1	v1
s2	e	a2	v2
s3		a3	v3
sf			
sg			

Table 3.1 Observation instrument

Table 3.2 shows the recording and illustrates the uniform separation between the turn-taking of the interacting subjects, *s1* and *s2*. Figure 3.3 presents the graphical representation of the only T-pattern obtained using THEME, with a significance level of $p = .05$.

Data name	T	Event
Episode1	1	.
Episode1	100	s1
Episode1	200	sg
Episode1	300	s2
Episode1	400	sg
Episode1	500	s1
Episode1	600	sg
Episode1	700	s2
Episode1	800	sg
Episode1	900	s3
Episode1	1000	s1
Episode1	1100	sg
Episode1	1200	s2
Episode1	1300	&

Table 3.2 Recording of the turn-taking interactive situation

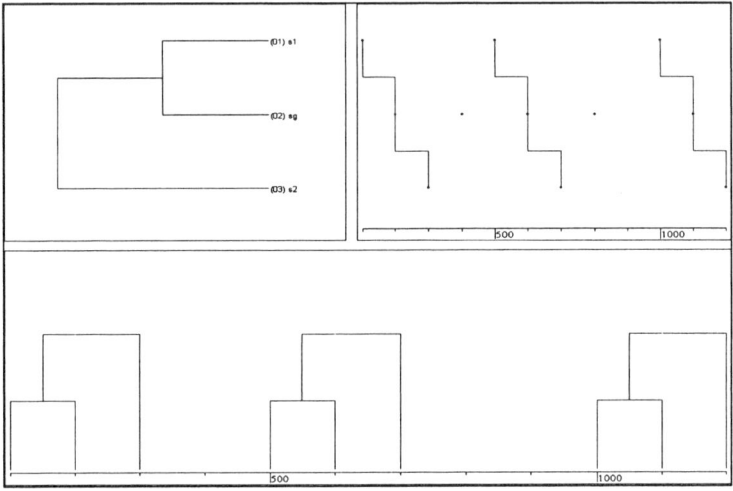

Figure 3.3 Graphical representation of the only primary pattern found with the data from Table 3.2, with p = .05. The only tree obtained is ((s1 sg) s2).

Now let us modify the data of the previous recording in order to observe the effect on the T-pattern. If the duration of the behavioural episodes s1, sg and s2 increases homogeneously the T-pattern is not altered, as can be seen when the duration is doubled (Table 3.2 and Figure 3.4) and tripled (Table 3.3 and Figure 3.5.). However, the same does not occur when the duration of the behavioural episodes is modified irregularly, which is to be expected given that the structure of the T-pattern is developed according to time.

As can be seen in Table 3.4 and Figure 3.6, the only T-pattern obtained (s1 sg) is modified. In this case, the duration of s1 and s2 is, progressively, 100, 200 and 300 time units in each one of the successive episodes.

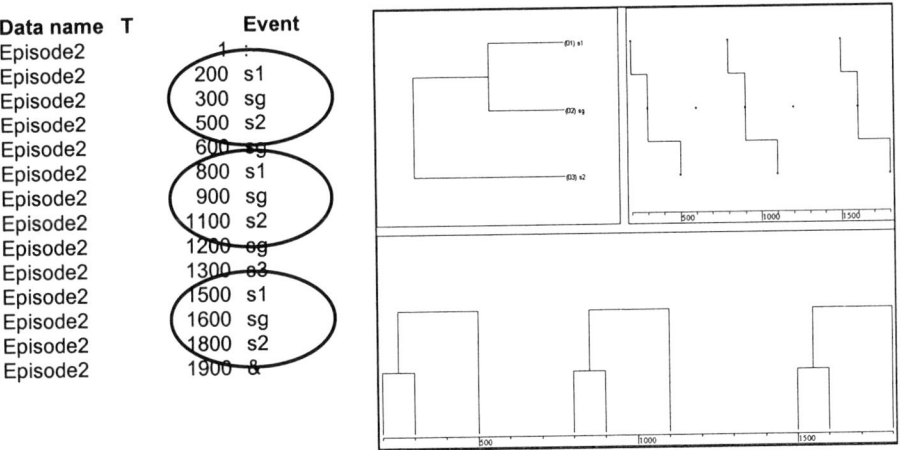

Data name	T	Event
Episode2	1	:
Episode2	200	s1
Episode2	300	sg
Episode2	500	s2
Episode2	600	sg
Episode2	800	s1
Episode2	900	sg
Episode2	1100	s2
Episode2	1200	sg
Episode2	1300	s3
Episode2	1500	s1
Episode2	1600	sg
Episode2	1800	s2
Episode2	1900	&

Table 3.2 and Figure 3.4 Doubling the duration of the episodes of s1, sg and s2, and the nature of the T-pattern obtained ((s1 sg) s2)

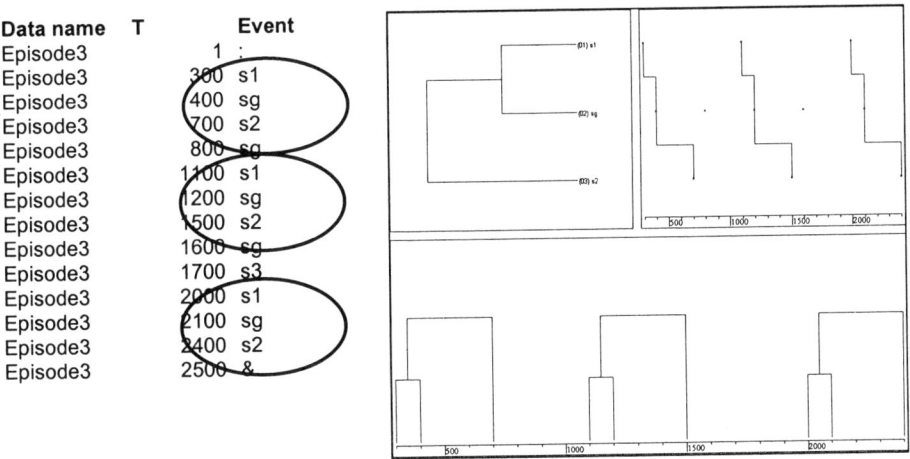

Data name	T	Event
Episode3	1	:
Episode3	300	s1
Episode3	400	sg
Episode3	700	s2
Episode3	800	sg
Episode3	1100	s1
Episode3	1200	sg
Episode3	1500	s2
Episode3	1600	sg
Episode3	1700	s3
Episode3	2000	s1
Episode3	2100	sg
Episode3	2400	s2
Episode3	2500	&

Table 3.3 and Figure 3.5 Tripling the duration of the episodes of s1, sg and s2, and the nature of the T-pattern obtained ((s1 sg) s2)

3.3.2 Microanalysis of the T-patterns according to the recording of their duration (begin/end) and/or only beginning and/or only end.

The THEME software includes, by default, an observation instrument criterion: BE (*begin-end*). This is logical because the common aim of detecting temporal patterns requires markers that delimit the beginning and end of each behavioural episode.

Therefore, we are interested in knowing whether the T-patterns vary when the relationship and the order of the codes are maintained but only the beginning rather than the duration of each action is recorded. Using the observation instrument from Table 3.1, hypothetical data that produce the single pattern shown in Figure 3.7, are proposed.

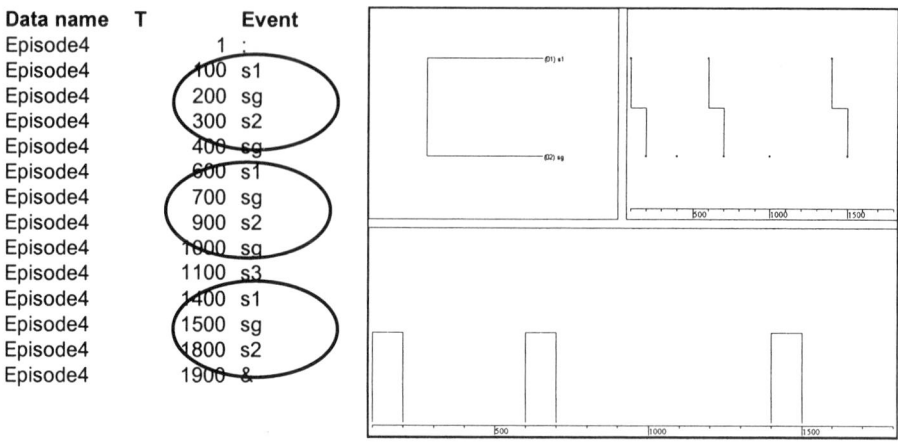

Data name	T	Event
Episode4	1	:
Episode4	100	s1
Episode4	200	sg
Episode4	300	s2
Episode4	400	sg
Episode4	600	s1
Episode4	700	sg
Episode4	900	s2
Episode4	1000	sg
Episode4	1100	s3
Episode4	1400	s1
Episode4	1500	sg
Episode4	1800	s2
Episode4	1900	&

Table 3.4 and Figure 3.6 Non-homogeneous modification of the duration of episodes of s1, sg and s2, and alteration of the previously obtained T-pattern, which now has the structure (s1 sg).

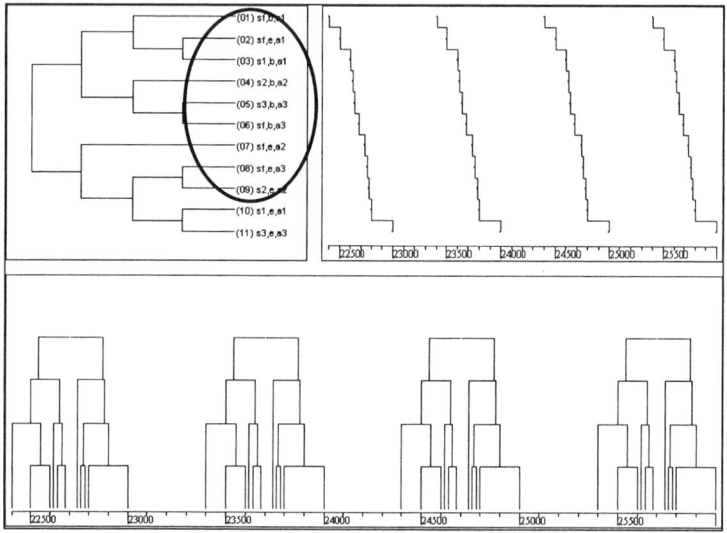

Figure 3.7 T-pattern obtained from a recording in which the beginning and end of each behavioural episode is recorded

The recording has been modified by eliminating the configurations corresponding to the end of each action; it can be seen in the resulting pattern that the configurations including the beginning of the action are maintained, except for *sf,b,a1*, and the new configuration *sf,b,a2* appears. The graphical structure of the pattern is also modified, as illustrated in Figure 3.8.

The recording corresponding to Figure 3.7 is then also modified by eliminating the configurations concerning the beginning of each action (Figure 3.9). Comparing the two T-patterns it can be seen that all the code configurations which include the end are maintained, the sole exception being that of the code *sf,e,a1*. Once again, the graphical structure of the pattern is modified.

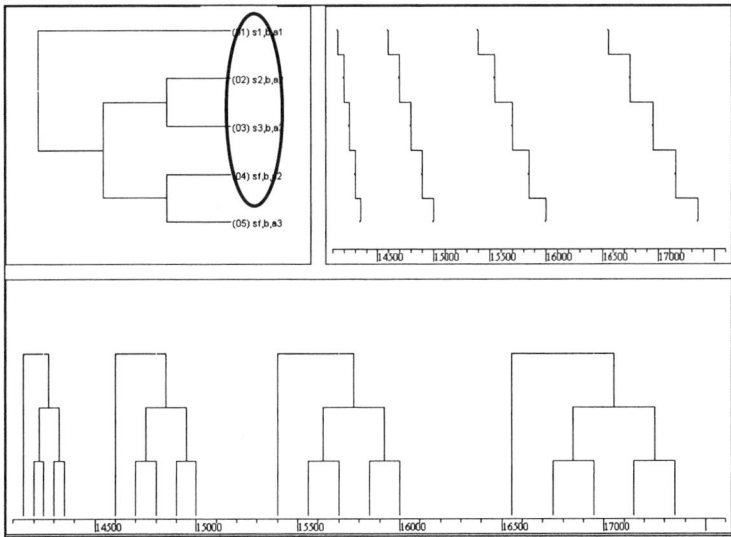

Figure 3.8 T-pattern obtained from the recording corresponding to Figure 3.7 in which the ends of each behavioural episode have been eliminated.

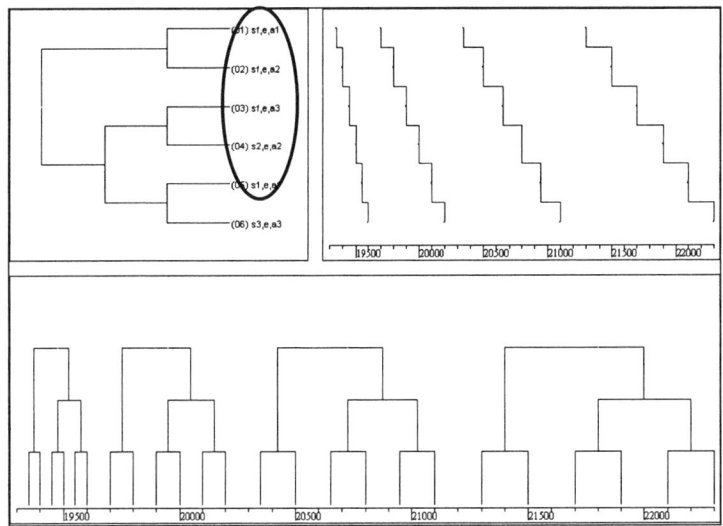

Figure 3.9 T-pattern obtained from the recording corresponding to Figure 3.7 in which the beginning of each behavioural episode has been eliminated.

As a single T-pattern is obtained the structures shown in Figures 3.8 and 3.9 are comparable. If all the configurations forming part of these two T-patterns had been identical a second example would have been used to check this finding further. However, as they were not identical (Figure 3.8) the decision to record solely the beginning or the end of behavioural episodes should not be taken lightly, bearing in mind that this may alter the T-pattern(s).

3.3.3   Variability of the T-patterns according to temporality (units of time assigned to each code)

Section 3.3.1. dealt with the duration's effect those codes of *a priori* interest (the interacting subjects s1 and s2). In this section we are interested in knowing the margin of variability and constancy of the behavioural patterns, in other words, the sensitivity of the temporal pattern(s) with respect to the modifications produced in the recording.

Figure 3.10 shows the graphical representation of a T-pattern in which the same recording has been carried out in four successive blocks, but where the number of time units has been modified, this increasing regularly. This example considers a separation between codes of the same block that is identical to the duration in frames of each behaviour and which, respectively, is 50, 100, 150 and 200 in each of the four successive recording blocks. The upper left window (Figure 3.10) shows the pattern obtained, while the upper right and lower windows show the progressively increasing distances in the four patterns.

In this case, the difference in duration of the actions recorded in the successive episodes is constant across the four patterns. However, we can see below what happens when the variability between the different episodes is not constant (Figure 3.11).

Taking into account the recorded configurations of each episodes considered in the two cases (Table 3.5) and comparing the structures obtained (Figure 3.10, on the one hand, and Figures 3.11(a) and 3.11(b) on the other) it can be seen that the only primary pattern that disappears as such in 3.11(a) and 3.11(b) is precisely (sg,b sg,e), which is situated at the end of each episode (sub-stage of maximum difference between the time units), and that part the t-pattern's structure is modified.

Obviously, this is a hypothetical case, which is also particular and, therefore, not generalizable. However, it is worth noting both that the T-patterns appear to be highly versatile with respect to temporality, and that the recordings in which the distribution of time units in the successive episodes is irregular and different maintain the same structure.

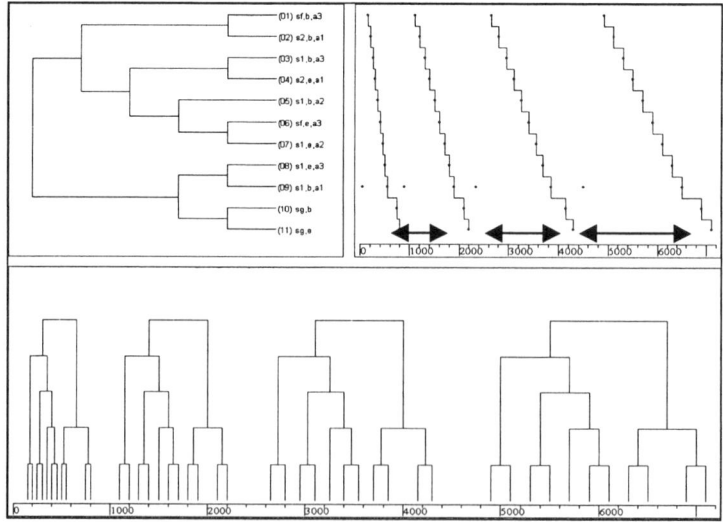

Figure 3.10 T-pattern with regular temporal differentiation and a significance level of p = .0001. The structure obtained is (((sf,b,a3 s2,b,a1)((s1,b,a3 s2,e,a1)(s1,b,a2 (sf,e,a3 s1,e,a2)))((s1,e,a3 s1,b,a1) (sg,b sg,e)))

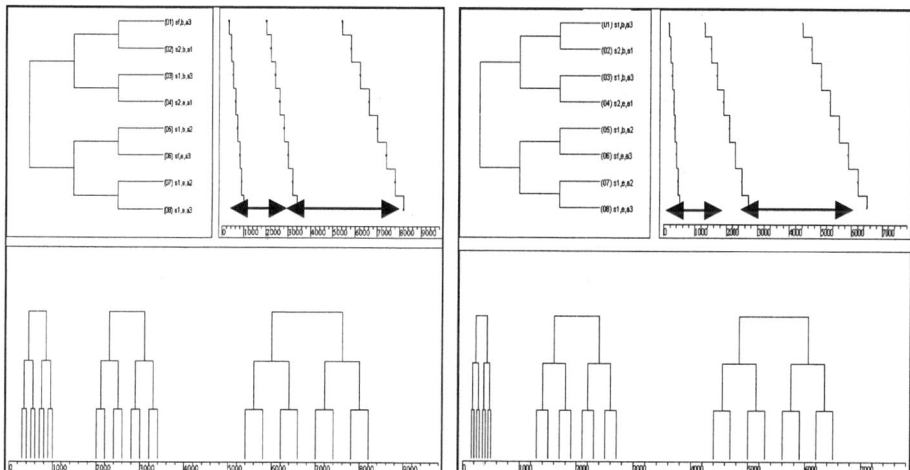

Figures 3.11(a) and 3.11(b) Graphical representation of the T-pattern corresponding to the same recorded configurations (simulated data that gave rise to the T-pattern in Figure 3.10), with a temporal differentiation corresponding to an arithmetical progression of durations in the three successive episodes (100, 200 and 400 time units) in Figure 3.11(a), and with an irregular differentiation of 50, 200 and 300 time units in Figure 11(b). Significance is $p = .001$, and the tree structure is identical in (a) and (b): (((sf,b,a3 s2,b,a1)(s1,b,a3 s2,e,a1))((s1,b,a2 sf,e,a3)(s1,e,a2 s1,e,a3))).

Data name	T	Event
Episode5	1 :	
Episode5		s1,b,a1
Episode5		s1,e,a1
Episode5		sf,b,a3
Episode5		s2,b,a1
Episode5		s1,b,a3
Episode5		s2,e,a1
Episode5		s1,b,a2
Episode5		sf,e,a3
Episode5		s1,e,a2
Episode5		s1,e,a3
Episode5		s1,b,a1
Episode5		s1,e,a1
Episode5		sg,b
Episode5		sg,e
Episode6		s1,b,a1
Episode6	...	...

Table 3.5 Recording configurations corresponding to each of the episodes giving rise to the T-patterns in Figures 3.10 and 3.11. The time units are not shown in column T as they are different in the two cases.

3.3.4   Microanalysis according to the repeatability of behavioural sequences through the aggregation of progressively incomplete blocks of data from initially identical episodes

The detection of T-patterns is inextricably linked to the repeatability of homogeneous behaviours. Although at times these may be identical, on most occasions it is more correct to refer to a similar 'core' surrounded by 'layers' of varying degrees of malleability, and it is within this wide range of possible cases that the T-pattern occupies an important place, its special mission being the detection of stable structures, no matter how hidden they are by the overlap with other behaviours, individuals or contextual features.

The previous figures have illustrated the simulation of consecutive interactive episodes, either identical ones (Figures 3.3, 3.7, 3.8 and 3.9) or those modified in certain aspects (Figures 3.4, 3.5, 3.6, 3.10, 3.11(a) and 3.11(b)). In the present section the aim is to consider a question of fundamental importance in the detection of hidden behaviour patterns, namely, on what aspects does the consistency of the various behaviours enacted depend. Although there are undoubtedly many such aspects, the attention will focus on the key role played by temporality.

In order to illustrate this point, let us use a hypothetical recording made with the observation instrument from Table 3.1. The recording comprises three episodes beginning with that indicated in Table 3.6 and separated from one another by the code *sg*; each one of the successive episodes (2nd and 3rd) omits the first piece of recorded data (see 2nd row of Table 3.7). Figure 3.12 shows the only T-pattern obtained, with a significance level of *p*=.001 and the structure (((s3,b,a1,v1 s1,b,a2,v2)(s2,b,a2,v2 s3,b,a2,v2))((s1,b,a3,v3 s2,b,a3,v3)(s3,b,a3,v3 sg))). The temporal pattern is not affected by the modification of the 2nd and 3rd episodes as indicated.

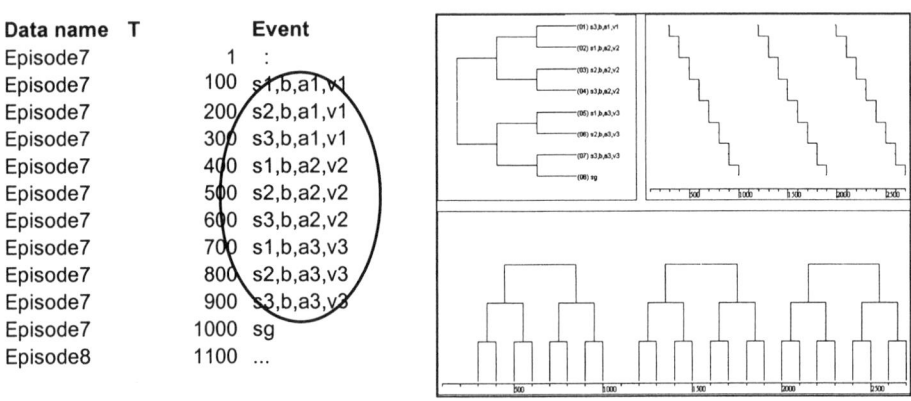

Data name	T	Event
Episode7	1	:
Episode7	100	s1,b,a1,v1
Episode7	200	s2,b,a1,v1
Episode7	300	s3,b,a1,v1
Episode7	400	s1,b,a2,v2
Episode7	500	s2,b,a2,v2
Episode7	600	s3,b,a2,v2
Episode7	700	s1,b,a3,v3
Episode7	800	s2,b,a3,v3
Episode7	900	s3,b,a3,v3
Episode7	1000	sg
Episode8	1100	...

Table 3.6 and **Figure 3.12** First episode of a hypothetical recording used as a module into which subsequent modifications are introduced (in this case, omission of the episode's first piece of data) (Table 3.6), and the graphical representation of the only T-pattern obtained (Figure 3.12).

Table 3.7 proposes various recording characteristics. Obviously, there are a very high number of possible modification profiles, which could be applied regularly to all the episodes or in a different way to each one of them: eliminate data (code configurations) randomly or systematically, introduce new codes, change the order of the codes, etc. Here, for the purposes of illustration, some of these modifications are shown in order to see the effect on the structure of the T-pattern.

3.4   Symmetry/asymmetry in T-patterns

In every interactive situation the issue of symmetry must be considered from various perspectives: roles of the interacting subjects, initiative taken, uni- or bi-directional effect between the interacting subjects, crossed situations in cases of *n* (>2) interacting subjects

Characteristics of the recording	Structure of the T-pattern
3 identical episodes (reference recording)	((((s3,b,a1,v1 s1,b,a2,v2)(s2,b,a2,v2 s3,b,a2,v2))((s1,b,a3,v3 s2,b,a3,v3)(s3,b,a3,v3 sg))) (Significance p = .005)
2nd and 3rd episodes omit the first piece of recorded data	((((s3,b,a1,v1 s1,b,a2,v2)(s2,b,a2,v2 s3,b,a2,v2))((s1,b,a3,v3 s2,b,a3,v3)(s3,b,a3,v3 sg))) (Significance p = .005)
2nd and 3rd episodes omit the first and last recorded data	((s3,b,a1,v1 s1,b,a2,v2)((s2,b,a2,v2 s3,b,a2,v2)(s1,b,a3,v3 s2,b,a3,v3))) (Significance p = .005)
2nd and 3rd episodes omit the first two recorded data	((((s3,b,a1,v1 s1,b,a2,v2)(s2,b,a2,v2 s3,b,a2,v2))((s1,b,a3,v3 s2,b,a3,v3)(s3,b,a3,v3 sg))) (Significance p = .005)
2nd and 3rd episodes omit the first two and last two recorded data	(s2,b,a3,v3 (s3,b,a3,v3 sg)) (Significance p = .05)
2nd and 3rd episodes omit the first three recorded data	((s1,b,a2,v2 (s2,b,a2,v2 s3,b,a2,v2))((s1,b,a3,v3 s2,b,a3,v3)(s3,b,a3,v3 sg))) (Significance p=.005)
2nd and 3rd episodes omit the first three and the last three recorded data	((s1,b,a2,v2 s2,b,a2,v2)(s3,b,a2,v2 s1,b,a3,v3)) (Significance p = .005)
2nd and 3rd episodes omit the first four recorded data	((s2,b,a2,v2 (s3,b,a2,v2 s1,b,a3,v3))(s2,b,a3,v3 (s3,b,a3,v3 sg))) (Significance p = .005)

Table 3.7 Relationship between recording characteristics and the structure of the only T-pattern obtained in each case.

(triadic, tetradic, pentadic interaction, etc.), dissonance between the interaction and the activity performed, temporal symmetry of interactive interventions, etc.

As the aim of this chapter is to discuss key issues consideration should also be given to a certain 'isomorphism' between the nature of each interactive situation, reflected in the recording, and the possible symmetry of the T-patterns; it should, of course, be remembered that there are syntactic rules which determine the appearance of T-patterns, as in the vertical reading of the pattern (upper left window), and this has a bearing on the issue of symmetry.

Symmetry has been studied from within various disciplines, including mathematics, physics, philosophy and law, and has been of interest from the time of Aristotle to the present day. As Van Fraassen [37] points out, the symmetries of time, space and movement determine the structure of modern science. However, very little research has addressed, from the empirical perspective, the issue of 'interactive symmetry' or, from a more conceptual angle, a 'symmetry in interactive models'; although this situation invites researchers to adopt a novel approach to the area it also places them in a somewhat lonely and challenging position due to the lack of prior reference points.

There are three basic kinds of symmetry: central, axial and mirror (Figure 3.13).

In what is an exploratory discussion the approach here presented merely seeks T-patterns that correspond to one or more types of symmetry, and reflects upon the possible correspondence with interactive symmetry. Furthermore, it offers an opportunity to study whether the breakdown of sub-patterns is also governed by one of the types of symmetry. Let us turn once again to the observation instrument from Table 3.1.

Firstly, it should be borne in mind that although a dyadic interaction (and, therefore, an n-adic one) may be symmetrical (or asymmetrical) according to various criteria, the initiative in interactive intervention is unquestionable. Does symmetrical initiative (in a real or simulated situation) correspond to a symmetrical T-pattern? What is understood by a symmetrical T-pattern? What different kinds of symmetry may be reflected in a T-pattern?

The simplest case would be that of central symmetry, which appears in primary patterns corresponding to situations that refer merely to the beginning and end of a given action. In this case, axial and mirror symmetry would also be present. Figure 3.14 shows an example. Its structure is (s1,b,a1   s1,e,a1), although it is not in itself an interactive situation (as it corresponds to the beginning and end of the activity *a1* carried out by participant *s1*).

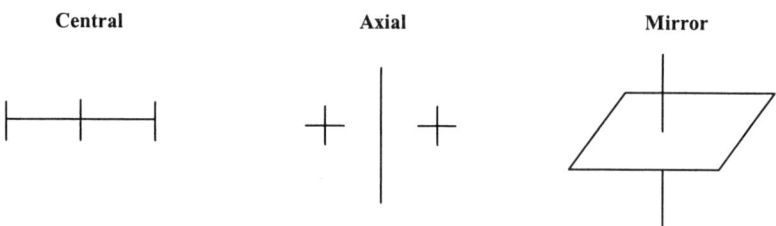

| Central | Axial | Mirror |

Figure 3.13 Basic kinds of symmetry

With several interacting subjects the approach is repeated for each one of them. Figure 3.15 illustrates a case of *n*-adic interaction.

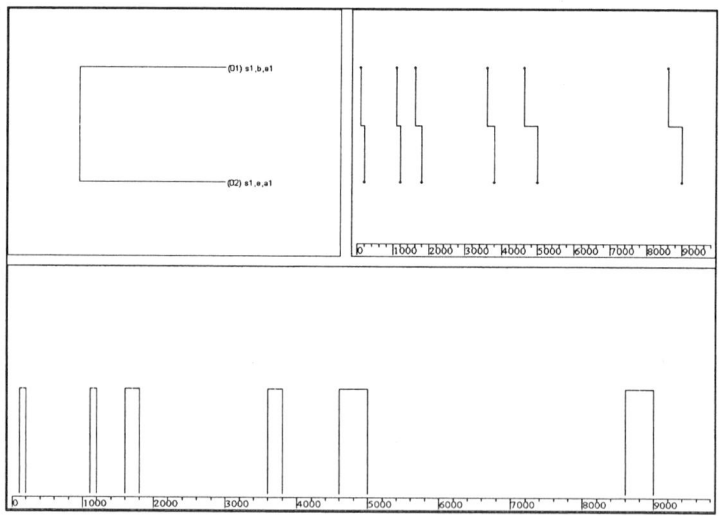

Figure 3.14 T-pattern showing central symmetry, with the structure (s1,b,a1 s1,e,a1) and significance level of *p* = .005.

Axial symmetry is reflected in the graphical representation of the dendogram corresponding to the T-pattern, its structure being irrelevant. An example is shown in Figure 3.16. Mirror symmetry is revealed in the interactive structure of the code configurations, regardless of the graphical representation of the dendogram (Figure 3.17).

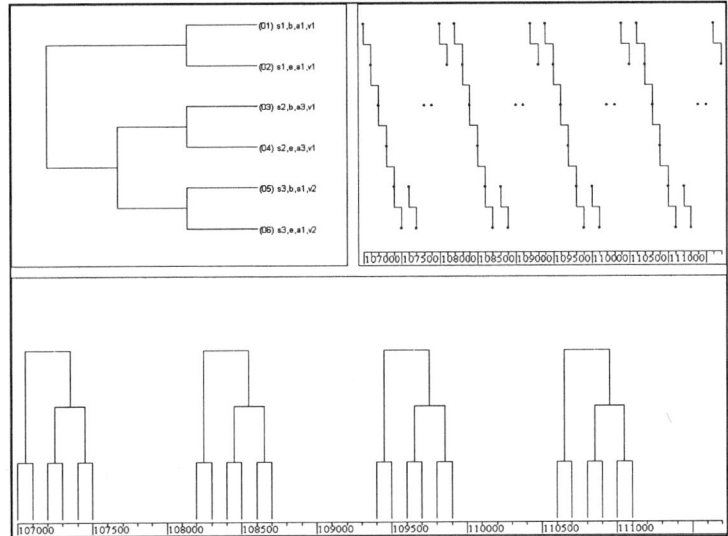

Figure 3.15 Asymmetric T-pattern (see Figure 3.21) corresponding to a triadic central symmetry at the primary level, with the structure ((s1,b,a1,v1 s1,e,a1,v1)((s2,b,a3,v1 s2,e,a3,v1)(s3,b,a1,v2 s3,e,a1,v2))) and significance p = .005.

Mirror symmetry does not imply a correspondence with axial symmetry. Figure 3.17 shows a T-pattern corresponding to mirror symmetry, with the structure (s2,e,a3,v1 ((((s2,e,a3 s3,b,a1) s3,b,a1,v2 (s3,e,a1,v2 (s3,e,a1 s2,b,a3))) s2,b,a3,v1)), although graphically it does not appear as symmetrical. Inversely, Figure 3.18 shows a case of axial symmetry that also does not correspond to interactive symmetry, as the structure of the T-pattern is (((s2,b,a3,v1 s2,e,a3,v1) (s3,b,a1,v2 s3,e,a1,v2)) ((s1,b,a1,v1 s1,e,a1,v1) (s1,b,a2 s1,e,a2))).

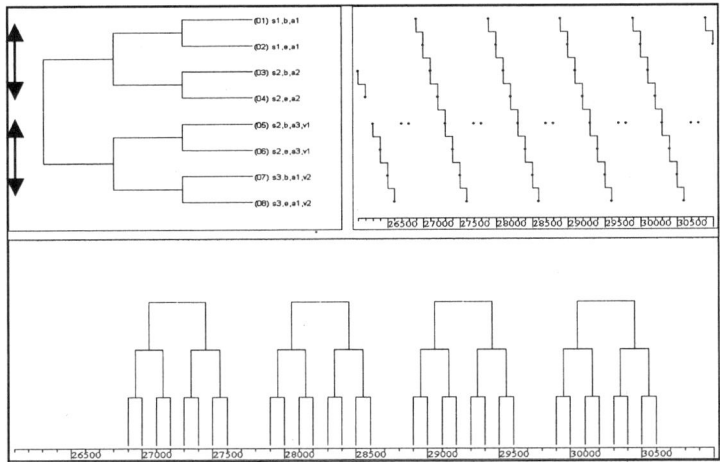

Figure 3.16 T-pattern showing axial symmetry in a triadic interaction, with the structure (s1,b,a1 s1,e,a1) and level of significance p = .005. The dendogram is symmetrical with respect to one axis.

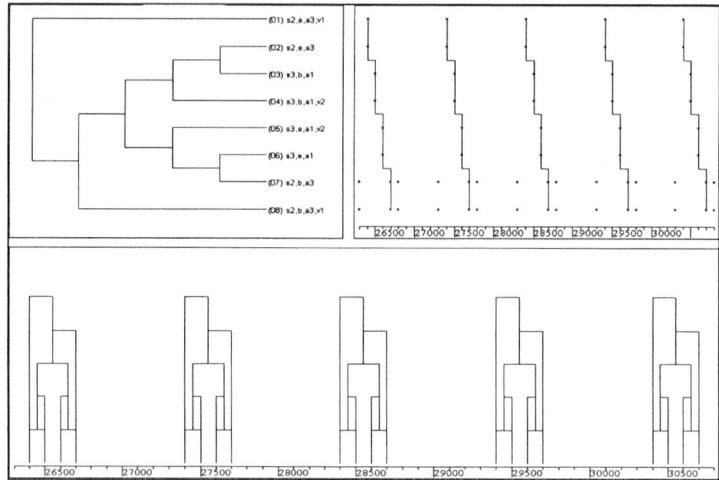

Figure 3.17 Mirror symmetry in the T-pattern with the structure (s2,e,a3,v1 ((((s2,e,a3 s3,b,a1) s3,b,a1,v2)(s3,e,a1,v2 (s3,e,a1 s2,b,a3))) s2,b,a3,v1)) and significance *p* = .005.

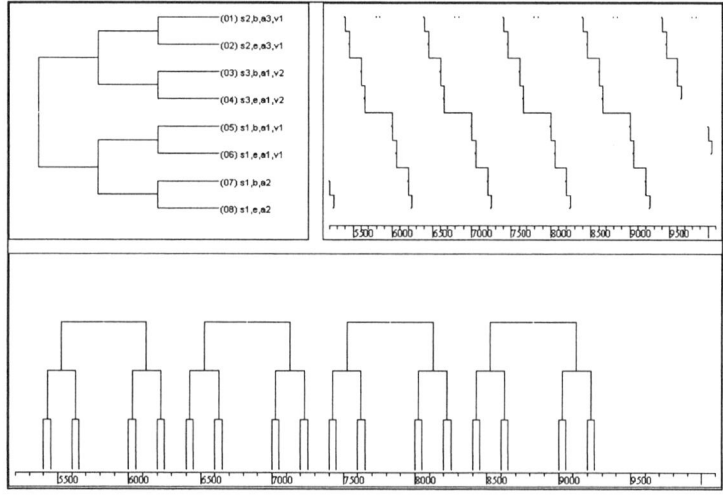

Figure 3.18 Axial, but not mirror, symmetry in (b), giving the T-pattern (((s2,b,a3,v1 s2,e,a3,v1) (s3,b,a1,v2 s3,e,a1,v2)) ((s1,b,a1,v1 s1,e,a1,v1) (s1,b,a2 s1,e,a2))) and with level of significance *p* = .005.

Another possibility is that there is mirror symmetry and that the interacting subjects participate with identical "weight" in the T-pattern but with asymmetrical initiative, as illustrated in Figure 3.19.

In asymmetrical T-patterns different prototypes may also appear, whether at the graphical or structural level, and these illustrate the wide range of possible cases which may arise. The present chapter only considers some of these, this issue requiring further, more specific study.

One of the most characteristic is asymmetry with repeatability of sub-patterns (primary, secondary, tertiary, etc.). Figure 3.20 shows the repeatability of primary and secondary sub-patterns, which may be graphical or structural.

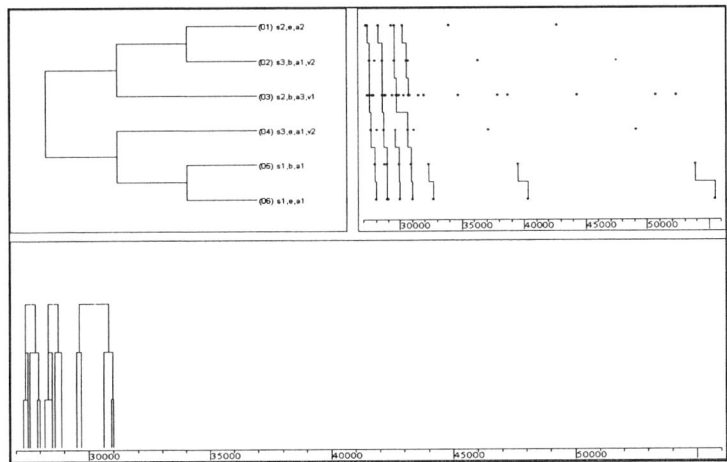

Figure 3.19 T-pattern with axial symmetry and rotational structure between the interacting subjects *s2* and *s3*, as well as identical interactive 'weight' of the three participants; however, there is no symmetrical interactive structure (mirror symmetry), it being (((s2,e,a2 s3,b,a1,v2) s2,b,a3,v1) (s3,e,a1,v2 (s1,b,a1 s1,e,a1))), with level of significance *p* = .005.

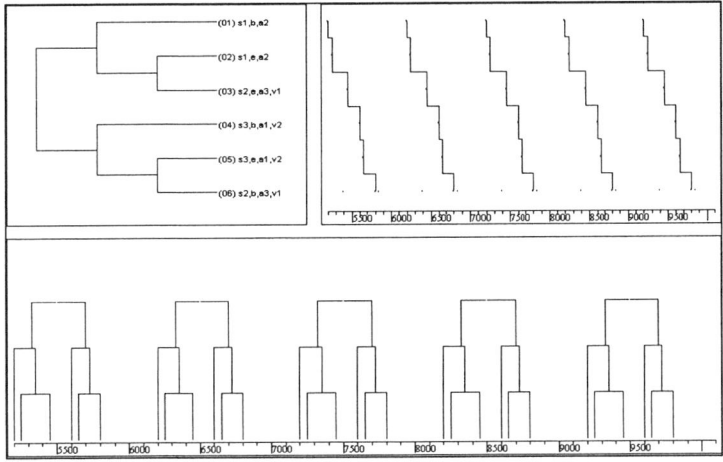

Figure 3.20 Asymmetrical pattern with graphical repeatability of primary and secondary sub-patterns.

Figure 3.21 presents a T-pattern (identical to Figure 3.15) showing axial symmetry but which, however, is comprised of primary patterns with central symmetry, implying a formal repeatability as it corresponds to the different interacting subjects.

Finally, there are also T-patterns which show asymmetry with irregular sub-patterns, as can be seen in Figure 3.22.

These T-patterns constitute the majority of cases and analysis of their structure enables us to determine the nature of the interactive situation which they reflect. The study of symmetry/asymmetry in T-patterns is a highly suggestive field and its detailed development may lead not only to the identification, but also to the analysis of prototypes and pattern categories, in a given area and from a specific theoretical perspective, that enable us to understand better how a temporal pattern is broken down into sub-patterns, or how different patterns become integrated into wider structures.

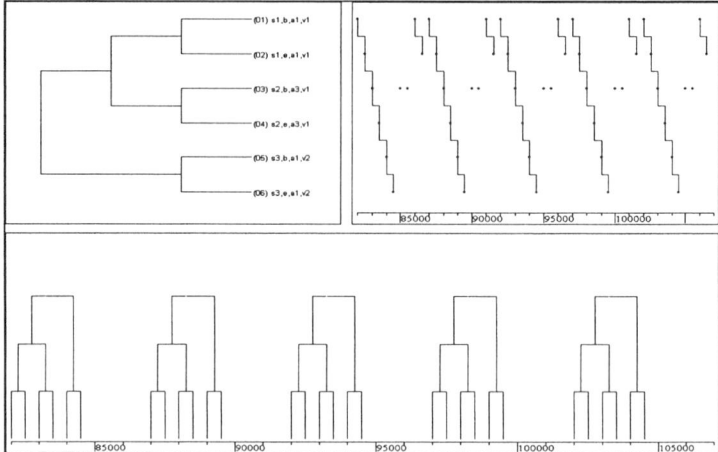

Figure 3.21 T-pattern with axial symmetry and formal repeatability (corresponding to the three interacting subjects), with the structure (((s1,b,a1,v1 s1,e,a1,v1)(s2,b,a3,v1 s2,e,a3,v1))(s3,b,a1,v2 s3,e,a1,v2)) and level of significance $p = .005$.

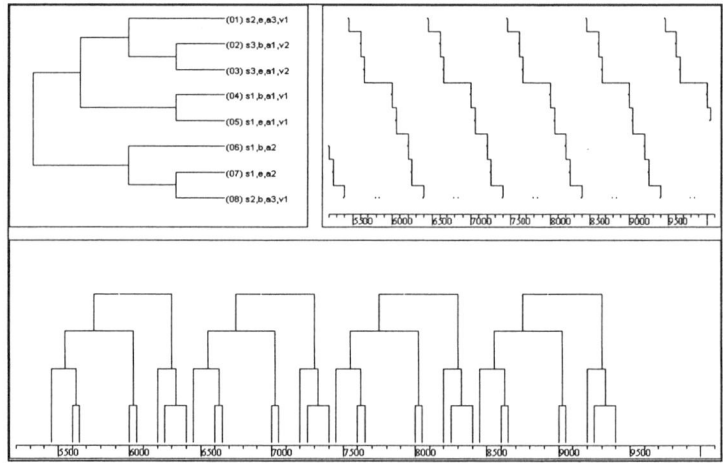

Figure 3.22 Asymmetrical temporal pattern that does not fit any prototype.

3.5   Conclusions

This chapter has aimed to draw attention to a number of questions.

Firstly, the enormous wealth of information contained within every interactive situation and the great power of the THEME software in detecting hidden patterns, which are then visualized and analyzed through knowledge of their structure.

Secondly, the great versatility of T-patterns, which are subject to multiple recording contingencies such as the duration of behaviours in each episode and/or the type of recording, the aggregation of progressively incomplete blocks of data from initially identical episodes, etc.

Thirdly, it has been suggested that there is an 'isomorphism' between the symmetry/asymmetry which arises in each interactive situation and the T-patterns obtained.

This chapter has only sought to make an initial approach to each of these aspects on the basis of examples using simulated data. Naturally, more specific research is now required in order to provide a more detailed understanding of the field.

3.6 References

[1]   R. B. Cairns, *The analysis of social interactions: Methods, issues, and illustrations.* Hillsdale: Lawrence Erlbaum Associates, 1979.

[2]   M. E. Lamb, S. J. Suomi, and G. R. Stephenson, *Social interaction analysis. Methodological Issues.* Madison: The University of Wisconsin Press, 1979.

[3]   G. P. Sackett, *Observing behavior (Vol. 2): Data collection and analysis methods.* Baltimore: University of Park Press, 1978.

[4]   G. P. Sackett, The lag sequential analysis of contingency and cyclicity in behavioral interaction research, in *Handbook of Infant Development*, J. D. Osofsky, Ed. New York: Wiley, 1979, pp. 623-649.

[5]   C. Santoyo, *Contexto e interacción social. Bases conceptuales y metodológicas.* Barcelona: P.P.U., 1994.

[6]   C. Santoyo, Behavioral assessment of social interactions in natural settings, *European Journal of Psychological Assessment* 12 (2), (1996) 124-131.

[7]   M. T. Anguera, Observational methods (general), in *Encyclopedia of Psychological Assessment, VOL. 2*, R. Fernández-Ballesteros, Ed. London: Sage, 2003, pp. 632-637.

[8]   R. Bakeman and V. Quera, *Analyzing interaction: sequential analysis with SDIS and GSEQ.* New York: Cambridge University Press, 1995.

[9]   J. C. Tójar, Classroom interaction evaluation through sequential analysis of observational data, *European Journal of Psychological Assessment* 12 (2), (1996) 132-139.

[10]   A. Hernández Mendo and M. T. Anguera, Behavioral structure in sociomotor sports: Roller-Hockey, *Quality & Quantity. International Journal of Methodology* 36 (2002) 347-378.

[11]   M. T. Anguera and G. K. Jonsson, Detection of real-time patterns in sports: Interactions in football. Paper presented at the *Third Meeting of the European Research Group on "Methodology for the analysis of social interaction"*. Milan: Catholic University of Milan, 2002.

[12]   C. Lago and M. T. Anguera, Use of the polar coordinates technique to study interactions between professional soccer players, *Revista Portuguesa de Ciências do Desporto* 2 (4), (2002) 21-40.

[13]   M. T. Anguera, C. Santoyo, and M. C. Espinosa, Evaluating links intensity in social networks in a school context through observational designs, in *People, environmental action and urban sustainability*, R. García Mira, J. M. Sabucedo Cameselle, and J. Romay Martínez, Eds. Göttingen: Hogrefe & Huber, 2003, pp. 281-292.

[14]   P. Sánchez-Algarra and M. T. Anguera, The collapsability theorem in log-linear analysis of categorical data: an application in program evaluation, *Quality & Quantity. International Journal of Methodology* 31 (2), (1997) 199-206.

[15]   P. Sánchez-Algarra and M. T. Anguera, Time management in the cost evaluation of limited resource programs, *Quality & Quantity. International Journal of Methodology*, in press.

[16]   R. Bakeman and J. M. Gottman, *Observing interaction. Introduction to sequential analysis*, 2nd ed. Cambridge: Cambridge University Press, 1986.

[17]   C. Izquierdo and M. T. Anguera, The role of the morphokinetic notational system in the observation of movement, in *Oralité et Gestualité. Interactions et comportements multimodaux dans la communication*, Ch. Cavé, I. Guaïtella, and S. Santi, Eds. Paris: L'Harmattan, 2001, pp. 385-389.

[18]   M. T. Anguera, A. Blanco, J. L. Losada, T. Ardá, O. Camerino, J. Castellano, A. Hernández Mendo, and G.K. Jonsson, Match & player analysis in soccer: Computer coding and analytic possibilities, *International Journal of Computer Science in Sport* 2 (1), (2003) 118-121.

[19]   A. Hernández-Mendo, M. T. Anguera, and M. A. Bermúdez-Rivera, Software for recording observational files, *Behavior Research Methods, Instruments & Computers* 32 (3), (2000) 436-445.

[20]   Pattern Vision, *THEME Coder* (software), 2001. Retrieved January 15, 2002, from http://www.patternvision.com.

[21]   L. P. J. J. Noldus, The Observer: A software system for collection and analysis of observational data. *Behavior Research Methods, Instruments & Computers* **23** (1991) 415-429.

[22]   M. S. Magnusson, Le Temps et les patterns syntaxiques du comportement humain: Modèle, méthode et programme THEME, in *Revue des Conditions de Travail*, Les actes du Premier Colloque National d'Ergonomie Scolaire, Université de Lille, 19-20 mars, 1987. Marseille: Octares, 1988, pp. 284-314.

[23]   M. S. Magnusson, Structure syntaxique et rythmes comportamentaux: Sur la détection de rythmes cachés, *Science Technical Animal Laboratoire* **14** (2), (1989) 143-147.

[24]   M. S. Magnusson, *THEME user's manual: With notes on theory, model and pattern detection method.* Reykjavik: University of Iceland, 1993.

[25]   M. S. Magnusson, Hidden real-time patterns in intra- and inter-individual behavior, *European Journal of Psychological Assessment* **12** (2), (1996) 112-123.

[26]   M. S. Magnusson, Discovering hidden time patterns in behavior: T-patterns and their detection, *Behavior Research Methods, Instruments & Computers* **32** (1), (2000) 93-110.

[27]   M. S. Magnusson, Analyzing complex real-time streams of behavior: Repeated patterns in behavior and DNA, in *L'Éthologie Appliquée Aujourd'hui. Vol. 3, Éthologie Humaine*, C. Baudoin, Ed. France : Levallois-Perret, 2003.

[28]   M. S. Magnusson and J. Beaudichon, Détection de 'marqueurs' dans la comunication référentielle entre enfants, in *Conversation, Interaction et Fonctionement Cognitif* , J. Bernicot, J. Caron-Parque and A. Trognon, Ed. Nancy: Presse Universitaire de Nancy, 1997 pp. 315-335.

[29]   H. Montagner, M. S. Magnusson, C. Casagrande, A. Restoin, J. P. Bel, P. N. M. Hoang, V. Ruiz, S. Delcourt, G. Gauffier, and B. Epoulet, Une nouvelle méthode pour l'étude des organisateurs de comportement et systèmes d'interaction du jeune enfant, *Psychiatrie de l'Enfant* **33** (2), (1990) 391-456.

[30]   S. G. Chinnici, M. Crippa, A. Agliati, and L. Anolli, Nonverbal Communication of Emotions: Analysis of Behavioral Patterns in Children. Poster presented at the *Measuring Behavior 2002, 4ᵗʰ International Conference on Methods and Techniques in Behavioral Research.* Amsterdam, 2002.

[31]   A. Borrie, G. K. Jonsson, and M. S. Magnusson, Application of T-pattern detection and analysis in sports research, *Metodología de las Ciencias del Comportamiento* **3** (2), (2001) 215-226.

[32]   A. Borrie, G. K. Jonson and M. S. Magnusson, Temporal pattern analysis and its applicability in sport: An explanation and exemplar data, *Journal of Sports Sciences* **20** (2002) 845-852.

[33]   M. T. Anguera and G. K. Jonsson, Detection of real time patterns in sport: Interactions in football, *International Journal of Computer Science in Sport* **2** (2), (2003) 118-121.

[34]   G. K. Jonsson, S. H. Bjarkadottir, B. Gislason, A. Borrie, and M. S. Magnusson, Detection of real-time patterns in sports: interactions in football, in *L'éthologie appliqué aujourd'hui, Vol.3*, C. Baudoin, Ed. Paris: Editions ED, 2003 pp. 37-45.

[35]   K. Hirschenhauser, D. Frigerio, K. Grammer and M. S. Magnusson, Monthly patterns of testosterone and behavior in prospective fathers. *Hormones Behavior* **42** (2002) 172-181.

[36]   S. Duncan, Using THEME to analyze interaction structure and strategy. Paper presented at *Measuring Behavior 2002, 4ᵗʰ International Conference on Methods and Techniques in Behavioral Research.* Amsterdam, 2002.

[37]   B. C. Van Fraassen, *Laws and Symmetry.* Oxford: Clarendon Press, 1991.

SECTION II

HIDDEN PATTERNS IN NEURONAL AND PHYSIOLOGICAL ACTIVITY

> *A search for T-patterns is considered successful when considerably more and/or longer T-patterns are found in the original data than in any of its randomized versions. How much difference is required may depend on various factors, such as external validation and the type of research.*

Magnusson, 2000

Finding regular temporal patterns that links environmental events with internal and not visible, changes in the human body (e.g. neuronal activation and communication, or hormonal level) may help understanding the hidden functioning of human beings. In this sections are presented two chapters whose main aim is to detect physiological temporal patterns, using THEME.

More in detail, the studies presented try to identify some temporal regularity between the internal human process and their external occurrences.

The focus of chapter 4, by NICOL, KENDRICK and MAGNUSSON, are some complex sequences of neuronal activity, at the level of both synaptic transmission and action potential generation amongst simultaneously sampled multiple neurons.

It is more than 40 years since the first observations on temporal sequencing of the activities of simultaneously sampled multiple neurons were published. Since then, such interactions have been linked to perceptual cognition, whereby the combined features of a complex stimulus come to be associated by the synchronisation of the activities of neurons responsive to one or more of those features. The most widely accepted theory of the physiology of memory formation, that of Donald Hebb, is also based upon the occurrence of such interactions in a memory system – *"When an axon of cell A is near enough to excite B and repeatedly or persistently takes part in firing it, some growth process or metabolic change takes place in one or both cells such that A's efficiency, as one of the cells firing B, is increased"*. Certain experimental models provide evidence that memory formation may adhere to hebbian principles. For this reason, and because spike-timing is of such theoretical importance, analysis of temporal sequencing in multiple neuronal activity, using such techniques as T-pattern analysis, may be of great value in understanding the mechanisms whereby neuronal networks encode sensory information.

Authors collected data from the olfactory bulb of anaesthetised rats that were exposed to different odorous stimuli and conducted a T-pattern analysis with the THEME software: many patterns were identified in all of the data, both pre- and during odour presentation. All the patterns detected were categorised in terms of their association with inhalation or exhalation, or both breathing-related events and analysed using *ANOVA*. Patterns distribution resulted very different between pre-stimulus activity and activity during stimulus, both in number of patterns and in occurrences. In particular a higher number of patterns involving both onset of inhalation and onset of exhalation, and those involving only onset of inhalation were recognized during stimulus presentation than in pre-stimulus activity. Conversely, such a difference was not found for patterns involving onset of exhalation but not onset of inhalation. It seems that the sequences of neuronal firing are especially associated with inhalation, particularly when the inhaled air is carrying odour information.

The main conclusion of the chapter is that the identified sequences may have a functional relevance: according to the authors, "neuronal activity involves precise sequences of discharge that are related both to ventilatory activity and to odour information".

The goal of Chapter 5 by HIRSCHENAHAUESER and FRIGERIO was the research of regular internal pattern of hormones and behaviour in men. Especially, authors investigated the relationship between Testosterone level, Progesterone level and sexual behaviour in adult men.

Testosterone and Progesterone levels were assessed from saliva samples collected from twenty-seven adult males over a period of ninety days, while sexual events were registered through daily questionnaires. In addition, other males' life history traits, such as being paired, were assessed. This evaluation allowed to separate the sample in two broad groups: "wannabe fathers" and "not wannabe fathers".

Time-patterns involving testosterone, sexual activity, and monthly (i.e. 28-day full-moon) intervals were observed among wannabe fathers, but not in singles or those of the paired men who did not have a wish for children with their current partner. This study demonstrated that the detection of non-random THEME patterns may be regarded as a measure of the interaction between hormones and behaviour or of the co-occurrence with an environmental parameter.

Further, the authors compared the patterns of men's testosterone and progesterone obtained using conventional approaches with the ones detected by THEME analyses. The results suggest that THEME may become a more general tool for studying real-time response patterns in behavioural endocrinology.

The Hidden Structure of Interaction
L. Anolli et al. (Eds.)
IOS Press, 2005

4. Communication within a Neural Network

Alister U. NICOL, Keith M. KENDRICK,
Magnus S. MAGNUSSON

Abstract. Recent observations of complex sequences of neuronal activity, at the level of both synaptic transmission and action potential generation amongst simultaneously sampled multiple neurons, have demonstrated that such patterns can occur spontaneously in the brain. Using multielectrode array (MEA) technology we have sampled simultaneously from a large number of neurons (typically >100 neurons), across a large area (>2mm^2) of the olfactory bulb in anaesthetised rats. Here also we find complex sequences in neuronal firing. Connections in these sequences may traverse the entire area populated by the sampled neurons. Most notably, these studies have demonstrated functional significance in such sequences of neuronal activity; in the olfactory bulb precise sequences of discharge are related both to ventilatory activity and to odour information. Indeed, both the number of occurrences and the variety of neuronal sequences appear to reflect stimulus quality.

Keywords: Olfactory bulb; electrophysiology; neuron; neuronal sequence; encoding; odour.

Contents

4.1   Introduction

It is more than 40 years since the first observations on temporal sequencing of the activities of simultaneously sampled multiple neurons were published [1]. Since then such interactions have been linked to perceptual cognition, namely "the binding problem" [2], whereby the combined features of a complex stimulus come to be associated by the synchronisation of the activities of neurons responsive to one or more of those features. The most widely accepted theory of the physiology of memory formation, that of Donald Hebb [3], is also based upon the occurrence of such interactions in a memory system – *"When an axon of cell A is near enough to excite B and repeatedly or persistently takes part in firing it, some growth process or metabolic change takes place in one or both cells such that A's efficiency, as one of the cells firing B, is increased"*. Through this process, Hebb postulated that a cell assembly would be formed (the *Hebbian* cell assembly) which would constitute *"the simplest instance of a representative process... the firing of the efferent cell is more likely to follow the lead of the afferent cell"*. It is interesting to note that James [4] proposed similar principles underlying memory formation – *"When two elementary brain-processes have been active together or in immediate succession, one of them, on recurring, tends to propagate its excitement into the other... The tendency is proportionate to the intensity of the excitement and to the number of times it has occurred"*. Even according to Aristotle [5], *"Acts of recollection, as they occur in experience, are due to the fact that one thought has by nature another that succeeds it in regular order"*.

Certain experimental models provide evidence that memory formation may adhere to hebbian principles. Long-term potentiation (LTP) is a physiological process that has been studied extensively since it was first described by Bliss & Lomo [6]. In LTP, pre- and postsynaptic elements in a neural pathway are driven into synchronised activity by repeated electrical stimulation of the pre-synaptic elements, thereby fulfilling the first of Hebb's principles – neuron A repeatedly activates neuron B through the synaptic connection between the two elements. Subsequently, the efficiency of A in firing B is increased, and thus is formed a simple hebbian assembly. In this paradigm, a large number of neuron A's activate a large number of neuron B's (i.e. there is little noise in the system), and the enhanced efficiency of transmission from one to the other manifests in the increased amplitude of the field potential generated when a single pulse is delivered to the pre-synaptic elements. However, evidence for such a process occurring in a functioning memory system remains elusive. Often comparisons between the experimental model (LTP) and memory formation in the functioning system assume that activation of a postsynaptic neuron may be reliably predicted by activation of an afferent pre-synaptic neuron. However, in a system where a postsynaptic neuron may receive many inputs from many afferent neurons, activation by the input from a single afferent neuron may have little impact relative to ongoing activation by the large number of other neurons. For this reason, and because spike-timing is of such theoretical importance, analysis of temporal sequencing in multiple neuronal activity, using such techniques as T-pattern analysis, may be of great value in understanding the mechanisms whereby neuronal networks encode sensory information.

4.2   Neuronal encoding of odour information in the olfactory bulb

Behavioural paradigms underpinning studies of the neurobiology of olfactory learning and memory are considered particularly robust [7] and considerable progress has been made in establishing the neural substrates and pathways involved [8-10]. Much of the encoding takes place at the level of the olfactory bulb (OB), the primary cortical projection area for olfactory input and an area that is entirely given over to processing this information [11]. The area has been confirmed as playing an important role in olfactory memory formation and for this reason understanding the processes involved in encoding olfactory information is of great importance to understanding the neuronal mechanisms of learning and memory. Olfactory receptor neurons in the olfactory epithelium in the nasal cavity project to mitral cells in glomeruli in the OB [11]. Optical imaging studies demonstrate that different odorants elicit spatially defined patterns of glomerular activity in the olfactory bulb [12, 13]. The quality of an olfactory stimulus is encoded by the specific combination of glomeruli activated by a given odorant. Gaining access to the olfactory bulb with a multiple electrode array (MEA) allows in vivo electrophysiological monitoring of neurons over a relatively large area of cortex. This makes possible the study of spatiotemporal patterns of activation across, and interactions between a large number of simultaneously sampled and widely dispersed neurons in this area.

Data currently being analysed by T-pattern analysis [14, 15] with the THEME software (see www.patternvision.com & www.noldus.com) have been collected from the olfactory bulb of anaesthetised rats (25% urethane, intraperitoneal, 1.5g per kg body weight). Using an MEA of either 30 or 48 electrodes advanced laterally into the OB (see Fig. 4.1A), action potentials (spikes) were sampled from mitral layer OB neurons across an area of approximately 2.3mm^2 using a 100 channel laboratory interface (Cyberkinetics Inc., USA). Typically, spikes were sampled from approximately 60 – 70% of electrodes. After completion of recordings, off-line discrimination of spikes from individual neurons was performed using a PCA (principle components analysis) sorting algorithm developed specifically for these data allowing discrimination of activity from multiple neurons at each active electrode (Horton PM, http://www.sussex.ac.uk/Users/pmh20). Typically, spikes were sampled simultaneously from > 100 neurons across the entire MEA. Times of occurrence of spikes generated by individual neurons were stored as events coded with the identity of the neuron and its location on the MEA. Also stored were events marking onset of expiration and onset of inspiration in the breathing cycle to allow this data to be related to patterns identified in the neural data. The data stored in this way are suitable for analysis by THEME. Separate data files were generated for activity preceding and during presentation of odour stimuli to the rat over a number of trials using different odours at various concentrations.

4.3   Spatiotemporal patterns in olfactory bulb neuronal activity

Event types entered into the T-pattern analysis were times of occurrence of spikes from individual neurons, and times of onset of inhalation and exhalation in the breathing cycle. A minimum of 15 repetitions with a significance level of $p < .005$ was required for recognition of a pattern.

Many patterns were identified in all of the data, both pre- and during odour presentation (see Fig. 4.2): as many as 3949 different patterns of neuronal firing sequence were identified in a single 10s period of sampling, with patterns repeating as frequently as 480 times during that period. Patterns included as many as nine event types. In all data sets, the number of patterns detected greatly exceeded that found when the data were randomised ($p < .001$), i.e. when all events occurring in the data were located randomly in the observation period. This was so across all pattern lengths. By plotting temporal sequences of neuronal firing in two dimensions, it can be seen that an individual pattern may span a large part of the area covered by the MEA (an example plot of such a sequence is shown in Fig 4.1A, another is presented in chapter 1 of this book).

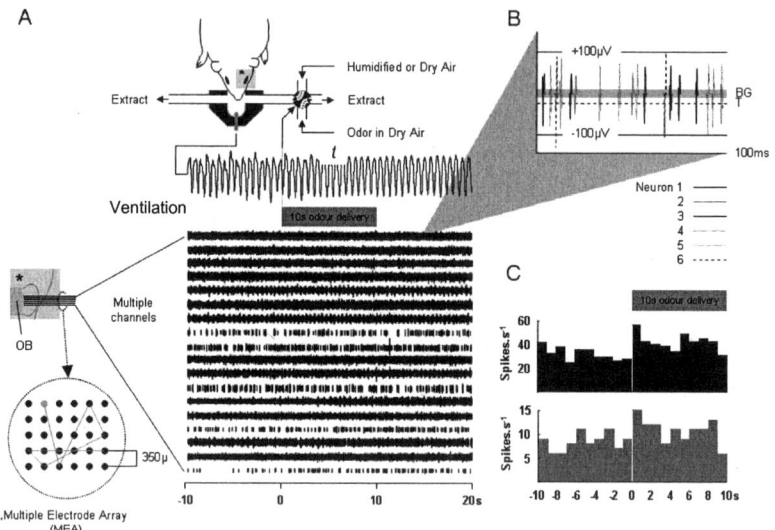

Figure 4.1 *Recordings from OB during odour presentations.* (*A*) Neuronal activity (action potentials, shown, and local field potentials) was sampled from electrodes in a microelectrode array (MEA) positioned in the olfactory bulb (OB). Microelectrode arrays comprised either 30 electrodes (6×5, 350μm separation, illustrated) or 48 electrodes (6×8, 250μm separation). An example two-dimensional plot of a sequence of neuronal discharges (grey line) is superimposed on the diagram of a 30 electrode MEA, commencing at the electrode denoted by the grey circle. Craniotomy and removal of the left eye permitted lateral access to the OB through the left orbit (inset*). During surgery and recordings, humidified air was supplied to the rat through a mask over the nose. A thermistor was used to record air temperature in the mask and so monitor breathing. Shortly (~30s) before delivery of an odour stimulus, the air to the mask was switched to dry air. Odours, carried as saturated vapours in nitrogen gas (odourless), were mixed in various concentrations with dry air, and were delivered for 10s to the rat via the mask. Onset of odour delivery (t) was precisely timed to mid-expiration. Neuronal activity was recorded for a period spanning 10s before odour onset to 10s after odour offset. In the recordings shown, spikes were detected in 18 of 30 channels. (*B*) Spikes were detected when a triggering threshold (T) was crossed by the recorded signal from each electrode. The threshold was set at $\geq 2 \times$ the background noise level (BG). A 100ms section of the upper spike train has been expanded to show times of occurrence of discriminated spikes. Two of the neurons, identified by the solid black and solid grey spikes, responded to the presentation of 5.4×10^{-4} M amyl acetate. The responses of these neurons to the presentation of this odour are represented (*C*) by the black and grey histograms respectively, representing the firing rates of the two neurons over a period spanning 10s before to 10s after stimulus onset.

The activities of approximately 25% of the neurons were involved in patterns that included breathing-related events. Patterns were categorised in terms of their being associated with one or other, or both breathing-related events and analysed using *ANOVA*. The distribution of patterns between pre-stimulus activity and activity during stimulus presentation varied significantly across the three categories of breathing-related pattern, both in terms of the number of different patterns detected ($F_{2,29} = 7.25$, $p < .05$) and the number of occurrences of patterns ($F_{2,29} = 7.12$, $p < .05$). The number of patterns involving one or other of the breathing-related events (onset of inhalation or onset of exhalation) was greater during odour presentation than before (59% : 41%). The difference between pre-stimulus activity and that during stimulus presentation was most marked for patterns involving both event types (62% : 38%) or those involving the onset of inhalation but not onset of exhalation (67% : 33%) (Fig. 4.3). The number of patterns detected similarly reflected stimulus presence or absence. The numbers of patterns involving both onset of inhalation and onset of exhalation, and those involving onset of inhalation but not onset of exhalation were greater during stimulus presentation than in pre-stimulus activity (66% :

34%). For patterns involving onset of exhalation but not onset of inhalation, there was little difference between pre-stimulus activity and activity during stimulus presentation either in terms of number of different patterns or number of occurrences of patterns (see Fig. 4.3). The implication of these findings is that sequences of neuronal firing are associated with inhalation, particularly when the inhaled air is carrying odour information.

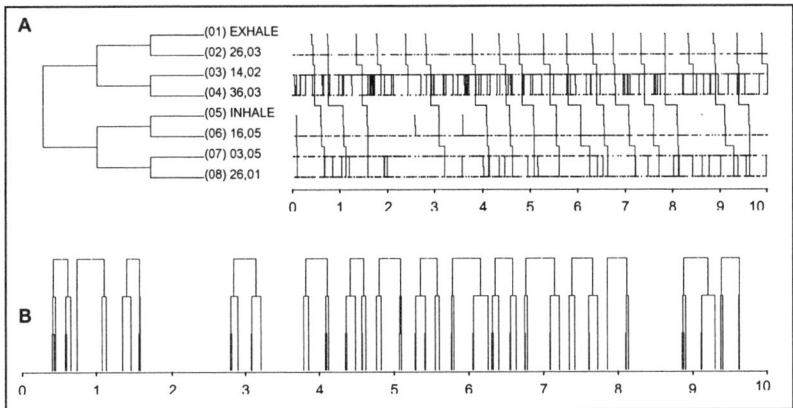

Figure 4.2 *Breathing-related sequence of neuronal discharge.* This sequence shown in A, detected in activity recorded during odour presentation, involved eight event types, including both markers of breathing – onset of exhale and onset of inhale (events 01 and 05 in the sequence). The first of the two comma-separated numbers annotating the neuronal events (spikes) indicates the position of the neuron sampled using a 5×6 electrode array (i.e. 03 = row 0, column 3). The second number indicates the identity of an individual neuron sampled on the given electrode. Sequences involving both breathing markers, and those involving onset of inhalation but not onset of exhalation, were more numerous during odour presentation than in pre-stimulus activity. Occurrences of events associated with this T-pattern, and connections between them, are plotted to the right of their labels over the 10s period of recording. Complete occurrences of the sequence shown in A are plotted in B.

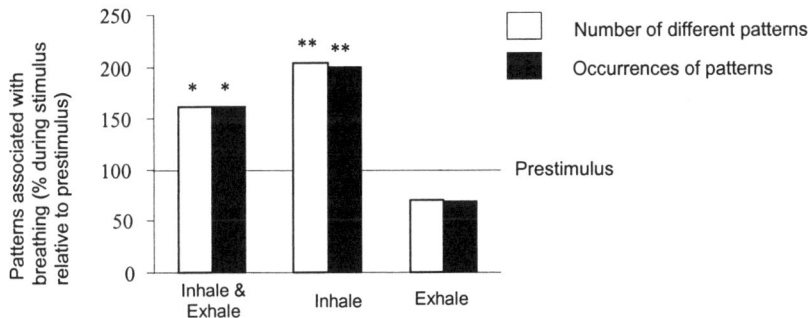

Figure 4.3 *Odour-related change in neural sequences associated with breathing.* The number of different patterns associated with both the start of inhalation and the start of exhalation, and also the number of patterns associated exclusively with the start of inhalation increased significantly between pre-stimulus activity and activity during stimulus presentation (*ANOVA*: *$p < .05$, ** $p < .01$). This was the case also for the number of occurrences of patterns. There was no such distinction in either measure between pre-stimulus activity and activity during stimulus presentation for patterns involving onset of exhalation but not onset of inhalation. Here the number of different patterns and the number of occurrences of patterns detected in activity during stimulus presentation are expressed relative to the corresponding numbers in pre-stimulus activity (100% representing no change).

4.4   Discussion

Precise sequences in spontaneous cortical neuronal activity were recently identified both in an isolated tissue preparation and *in vivo* [16]. These patterns were found both in intracellularly recorded postsynaptic potentials, reflecting release of discrete quantities of neurotransmitter, and in extracellularly recorded neuronal action potentials (spikes). Here we show that such sequences occur across large areas of the two-dimensional network of mitral neurons in the olfactory bulb, with functional connections spanning in some cases the entire area sampled by the MEA (>2mm).

This perhaps is less remarkable given a recent account of anatomical connections ("short axons") spanning many mitral cells across the olfactory bulb [17]. Most notable in our findings is that these sequences, whilst present in spontaneous neuronal activity, have functional relevance. Presentation of an odour stimulus increases both the variety of sequences detected, and the number of patterns generated amongst the neurons. These increases are selective for sequences of neuronal firing that are associated with the onset of inhalation. Included amongst these sequences are those associated with both onset of inhalation and onset of exhalation, but not those associated exclusively with onset of exhalation. Thus stimulus quality is represented in the richness of neuronal sequencing in mitral cell activity.

These findings are consistent with other recent observations of neuronal activation in phase with breathing using *in vivo* optical imaging techniques [13] or electrophysiological techniques [18], the latter study demonstrating that mitral cell membrane potential fluctuations, and therefore likelihood of discharge, occur in phase with ventilatory rhythm. However, here we have shown that neuronal activity involves precise sequences of discharge that are related both to ventilatory activity and to odour information.

4.5   References

[1]   J. S. Griffith and G. Horn, Functional coupling between cells in the visual cortex of the unrestrained cat, *Nature* **199** (1963) 893-895.
[2]   A. K. Engel, P. R. Roelfsema, P. Fries, M. Brecht, and W. Singer, Binding and response selection in the temporal domain - a new paradigm for neurobiological research, *Theory in biosciences*, **116** (1997) 196-221.
[3]   D. O. Hebb, *The organisation of behaviour.* New York: Wiley, 1949.
[4]   W. James, *The principles of psychology.* New York: Holt, 1890 (Reprinted, Bristol: Thoemmes Press, 1999).
[5]   Aristotle, (350BC), On memory and reminiscence, in J. Barnes, (trans.) *Complete works of Aristotle.* Princeton: Princeton University Press, 1984.
[6]   T. Bliss and T. Lomo, Long-lasting potentiation of synaptic transmission in the dentate area of the anesthetized rabbit following stimulation of the perforant path, *The journal of physiology* **232** (1973) 331-341
[7]   J. J. Bolhuis and E. M. MacPhail, A critique of the neuroecology of learning & memory, *Trends in cognitive science* **5** (2001) 426-433.
[8]   K. M. Kendrick, F. Levy, and E. B. Keverne, Changes in the sensory processing of olfactory signals induced by birth in sheep, *Science* **256** (1992) 883-886.
[9]   A. P. C. Da Costa, K. D. Broad, and K. M. Kendrick, Olfactory memory and maternal behaviour-induced changes in c-fos and zif/268 mRNA expression in the sheep brain, *Molecular brain research* **46** (1997) 63-76.
[10]   K. M. Kendrick, R. Guevara-Guzman, J. Zorrilla, M. R. Hinton, K. D. Broad, M. Mimmack, and S. Ohkura, Formation of olfactory memories mediated by nitric oxide, *Nature* **388** (1997) 670-674.
[11]   K. Mori, H. Nagau, and Y. Yoshihara, The olfactory bulb: coding and processing of odor molecule information, *Science* **286** (1999) 711-715.
[12]   B. A. Johnson, S. L. Ho, Z. Xu, J. S. Yihan, S. Yip, E. E. Hingco, and M. Leon, Functional mapping of the rat olfactory bulb using diverse odorants reveals modular responses to functional groups and hydrocarbon structural features, *The journal of comparative neurology* **449** (2002) 180-194.

[13]   H. Spors and A. Grinvald, Spatio-temporal dynamics of odor representations in the mammalian olfactory bulb, *Neuron* **34** (2002) 301-315.

[14]   M. S. Magnusson, Discovering hidden time patterns in behavior: T-patterns and their detection, *Behavior, research, methods: Instruments and computers* **32** (2000) 93-110.

[15]   M. S. Magnusson, Repeated patterns in behavior and other biological phenomena, in *Evolution of communication systems: A comparative approach (Vienna series in theoretical biology)*, D. K. Oller and U. Griebel, Eds. Cambridge: MIT Press, 2004, pp. 111-128.

[16]   I. Ikegaya, G. Aaron, R. Cossart, D. Aronov, I. Lampl, D. Ferster, and R. Yuste, Synfire chains and cortical songs: temporal modules of cortical activity, *Science* **304** (2004) 559-564.

[17]   J. L. Aungst, P. M. Heyward, A. C. Puche, S. V. Karnup, A. Hayar, G. Szabo, and M. T. Shipley, Centre-surround inhibition among olfactory bulb glomeruli, *Nature* **426** (2003) 623-629.

[18]   T. W. Margrie and A. T. Schaefer, Theta oscillation coupled spike latencies yield computational vigour in a mammalian sensory system, *The journal of physiology* **546** (2002) 363-374.

5. Hidden Patterns of Male Sex Hormones and Behaviour Vary with Life History

Katharina HIRSCHENHAUSER, Didone FRIGERIO

Abstract. Androgens regulate sperm production, the expression of secondary sex characters and behavior in males and also vice versa, androgens are modulated by the male's interactions with his social environment. In search for a regular internal "cycle" of hormones and behavior in men, the individual time patterns of salivary testosterone and progesterone of adult healthy men, self-reported behavior and their co-occurrence with regular weekly or monthly intervals were studied. Twenty-seven volunteer males (mean age 33 ± 1 years) collected daily morning saliva over a period of 90 days. Evening questionnaires provided daily information on sexual activities, pairbond-specific behavior and life habits. From the saliva, testosterone and progesterone levels were determined using enzyme immunoassay. To detect events in which increases of testosterone were associated with sexual activity and at the same time controlling for regular internal patterns in men, data were analysed using THEME. The social context of the occurrence of specific pattern combinations was elaborated using parameters from the men's self-reported life history profiles. Time-patterns involving testosterone, sexual activity, and monthly (i.e. 28-day full-moon) intervals were observed among wannabe fathers, but not in singles or those of the paired men who did not have a wish for children with their current partner. The presented data, furthermore, suggested progesterone as a male sex steroid found in large amplitudes in saliva and seemingly of gonadal origin. Co-occurrences of progesterone and sexual activity were particularly observed in "unexpected" or "secret" episodes. Moreover, the parallel nature of individual testosterone and progesterone fluctuations decreased with sexual experience. Using THEME, time-patterns involving progesterone and monthly intervals occurred in "wannabe fathers" but not in singles, similar to the observed testosterone patterns. We compared the patterns of men's testosterone and progesterone using conventional approaches with THEME analyses. This study demonstrated that the detection of non-random THEME patterns may be regarded as a measure of the interaction between hormones and behavior or of the co-occurrence with an environmental parameter. Therefore, THEME analyses to express real-time response patterns may be an emerging general tool also in behavioural endocrinology.

Keywords: Real-time-patterns; THEME; sexual behaviour; human males; testosterone; progesterone; saliva; hormone behaviour interaction.

Contents

5.1   Introduction

In contrast to the well-known hormonal base of the menstrual cycle in women [1], a regular internal pattern of hormones and behavior in men, for example on a monthly base, has to our knowledge not been studied. The existence of a male "cycle" in terms of hormones and behavior may be considered for a number of reasons. Testosterone (T) plays a role in erectile function, sexual behavior and mood, which may vary from day to day [2], [3, 4] or across the days of a week [5, 6]. Furthermore, unconscious auto-ejaculations during phases of sexual inactivity are common. Finally, physical welfare, concentration, mood and aggressive as well as sexual motivation may vary noticeably in men [7, 8], as observed throughout the female monthly cycle [9-11]. Alternatively, men may be responsive to the hormonal fluctuations and sexual responsivity of their wives [11] rather than exhibiting a regular internal cycle themselves [12]. Observations from a number of species (including the human male) point at the adaptive value for a (monogamous) male to be hormonally and behaviourally responsive to his partner's fecundity phases [13-16].

We will present a study that was conducted to examine regular patterns of T and sexual behavior on a daily base over a three months period in healthy adult men. As a consequence a large database on the interactions between T and sexual activity has been accumulated. Peak levels of T were expected in response to sexual activity [8, 17]. Analyses focused on three major questions: (a) whether the males' T peaks anticipated or followed periods of sexual activity, (b) the social context of the observed interaction patterns, and (c) a potential involvement of regular environmental parameters in the observed time-patterns, which included weekly and monthly intervals [18]. The rates of co-occurrences between T or progesterone (P) peaks and sexual activity were compared with regard to social context and life histories of the candidates.

5.1.1   Social modulation of androgens

Androgens play major roles in the conserved vertebrate reproductive axis (i.e. hypothalamus-pituitary-gonads). T, in particular, is essential for spermatogenesis, the maintenance of the genital tract, and the development secondary sexual characters in male vertebrates, including the human male. Early behavioural endocrinology studies in normal human males were focused predominantly on the effects of androgens on sexual activity [19, 20]. Beard growth rate was then observed to increase in anticipation of sexual activity [21], which along with the development of non-invasive saliva assays [22-25] paved the way to study the role of the social environment and of behavior as short-term modulators of T [26-29]. In sum, T was observed to influence and, reversibly, be modulated by sexual interest, arousal and enjoyment [17]. Also paternal investment plays a role. From avian studies we know that T may be regarded as the physiological mediator of the trade-off between investing in male-male aggressiveness or in paternal care [30, 31]. Decreased T levels in response to paternal investment were observed in monogamous fishes, birds and mammals [32-35]. In humans too, the T of new fathers was observed to decrease in response to the birth of their infants [16].

5.1.2   Progesterone in male vertebrates

We will also present and discuss the results of measuring P in the human males' saliva. P is a gestagen known for its role in the female cycle. It induces female sexual behavior and regulates receptivity in intact female mammals [36]. Furthermore, it plays an important role in the priming of maternal behavior [37]. Although less prominent than androgens, P is produced in large quantities in the male testes, as well as in the adrenals [38, 39]. In birds sex-specific differences were reflected in the seasonal timing of P fluctuations rather than in the amplitudes [38, 40]. In free-living Greylag geese P was higher in unpaired than in paired males throughout the year, in fall the male singletons' P was even double that of all females [41]. The P molecule (C_{21}) is an obligate precursor of androgens (C_{19}), as well as of glucocorticoids (C_{18}). However, this does not explain why male gonads produce (and also excrete) relatively high amounts of P. Thus, its function in male sexual behavior remained an open issue so far. In male rats, mice and lizards copulatory behavior is only expressed when both, T and P act in conjunction, which is facilitated by sexual experience [42]. Studies in male rats suggested that P induces social tolerance [43]. The presented P patterns may add to postulate it as another "male sex hormone" and to unravel its interactions with the social environment.

5.1.3 The hidden structure of hormone-behavior interactions

The novel approach we have used to statistically process the interaction between hormones and behavior was the detection of hidden real time patterns using THEME [44, 45]. THEME detects and analyzes repeated non-random time-patterns hidden within complex real-time records. Each time-pattern is a repeated chain of a set of behavioural events characterized by fixed event order and/or co-occurrence. Time distances (≥ 0) between the consecutive events are significantly similar in all occurrences of the chain [44, 45]. In our context, an important aspect of this pattern type is that its definition does not rely on cyclical organization, i.e. the full pattern and/or its components may or may not occur in a cyclical fashion. This method allows processing the repeated measures of a large number of variables per individual. Because it simultaneously takes into account the sequence and the relative timing of events, it enabled us to translate and reduce the accumulation of data into new operational units to be compared between social categories. Thus, in our example, THEME depicted those hormone peaks that were specifically co-occurring with one or more behavioural events over the sampling period, rather than processing all hormone peaks observed in that individual. The pattern characteristics we took into further analyses were (1) the complexity of interaction patterns, (2) the proportion of all time patterns that involved a significant interaction between a T or P peak and a behavioural event (e. g. sexual activity), (3) the sequence of the co-occurring events (i.e. was the behavior observed prior to the hormonal response, or was a hormone peak observed prior to the behavior), and (4) the frequency of occurrence of the most complex pattern. In short, the method as applied in this study may be regarded as a way to reduce the number of variables and process it as individual characters of repeatedly measured time patterns.

One disadvantage of using this approach is that some of the information may get lost. To set up using THEME, the original data have to be translated into temporal events along a time axis, for example, the days with occurrences of peak concentrations in the saliva. With regard to continuous variables such as the salivary hormone concentrations from 90 consecutive days, information may get lost. We chose peaks rather than troughs because the focus of this study was on T responses to sexual activity. For the days between two peaks, however, the only measure processed was the interval between two peak events, while the fine-scale of eventual hormone fluctuations was not taken into account. This is a major disparity to using conventional correlation coefficients. The benefits of applying the hidden time-pattern analysis to study hormone-behavior interactions, however, outweigh this gap by far.

5.2   Study subjects and methods

Twenty-seven adult, anonymous and volunteer males collected daily morning saliva samples for a period of 90 days using salivette devices (Sarstedt). Each candidate was provided with a sampling package, which included 90 salivettes labeled for each day, 90 "daily questionnaires" to be completed every evening and a singular "general questionnaire" to be filled in once. At distribution of the sampling packages, the candidates randomly drew a number, and were thereafter treated anonymously. The anonymity of the candidates was an essential feature to communicate at this point. Self-reported male sexual activity rates are likely to be overrated or spurious. Additionally, it seems that almost everyone ever sampled wanted to have a lot of T [46]. Therefore, we pointed out to the candidates that we were interested in studying the days in which they felt stronger or weaker, and not who was the "superman" as compared to the others. Mean age of the candidates was 33 ± 1 years (ranging from 23 to 47 years). We included men from various professions (workers, employees, students, and professors) and from different environments, eighteen candidates lived in urban settings (Vienna, Austria and Bergamo, Italy), and eight lived in a rural environment (Austria; hometown with less than 5000 inhabitants).

5.2.1   Hormone sampling

The mode of saliva collection was introduced to the males. To standardize variation due to daytime [12, 47] and to avoid contamination of the samples by food, drink or toothpaste, saliva was collected every morning right after waking up. Candidates stored the samples at their houses at $-20°C$ until further processing. All of them started their sampling periods between May and June 1998 to minimize the potential effects of season on T patterns [48].

Immunoreactive T and P equivalents were assayed from a total of 2190 saliva samples by enzyme immunoassay (EIA) following the methods as outlined in Hirschenhauser et al. ([18] for T; [41] for P).

5.2.1.1 Gonadal origin of progesterone

In male vertebrates the source of P may be gonadal or extra-gonadal. In addition, P is an obligate precursor for both, T, an androgen secreted from the hypothalamus-pituitary-gonads axis, and cortisol, a glucocorticoid secreted from the hypothalamus-pituitary-adrenals stress axis. To clarify the origin of the salivary P measures, we recruited another nine men (mean age 42 ± 4 years) to collect daily morning saliva for seven days. From each of these samples, we assayed T, P and cortisol equivalents. The results clearly indicated that the P levels measured in the saliva were correlated with the gonadal T levels, rather than with the adrenal glucocorticoid levels (Figure 5.1). We are, therefore, confident that the observed P patterns were secreted by the gonads.

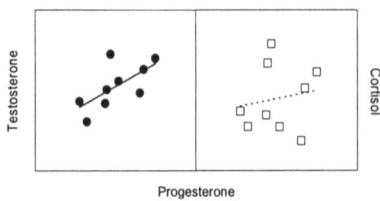

Figure 5.1 Men's salivary progesterone levels were correlated with testosterone (left panel: $r_s = 0.7$, $p < 0.05$) but not with cortisol (right panel: $r_s = 0.6$, NS). Individual median levels in ng steroid per ml saliva are shown ($N = 9$).

5.2.2   Behavior sampling

Self-reports of each day's eventual sexual activities (including masturbation) were recorded using a "daily questionnaire" to be completed every evening. Furthermore, the candidates were asked whether sexual activity occurred with a familiar partner, and had to indicate the intensity of the sexual activity by intuitively placing a mark along a scale of 50mm, where "0" represented low intensity and "50" indicated very intensive sexual activity. As environmental parameters, weekends and full moon intervals were coded post-hoc by the authors. Daily behavioural events, as well as the environmental parameters were then analyzed for their co-occurrence with T and P peaks.

A singular "general questionnaire" was collected to assess information on the males' life history traits, such as being paired, the pairbond duration, whether they were fathers already, whether they had the wish to have children with their current partner ("wannabe fathers") or "not with this partner", on sharing the household, polygynous mating strategy (men who had reported sex with more than one partner during the 6 months preceding the sampling period), and on their sexual history (up to 5, up to 10, or more than 10 previous sexual partners). The life history traits were used as social categories for the elaboration of the social context of the occurrence of non-random hormone-behaviour patterns.

5.2.2.1 Hormone-behavior interactions: conventional approach

To underline the benefits of using THEME to analyze hidden real-time patterns we also demonstrate how far we could get by analyzing the data with conventional analyses of variance and correlation statistics. Because we had to deal with a large number of variables sampled repeatedly over a 90-day period we were restricted to calculate with derived measures of individual variability, such as individual mean hormone levels, the individual maximum amplitude observed, or the individual coefficient of variation throughout all days sampled. Using these measures one may conclude about the hormonal status of some general demographic and life history prototypes.

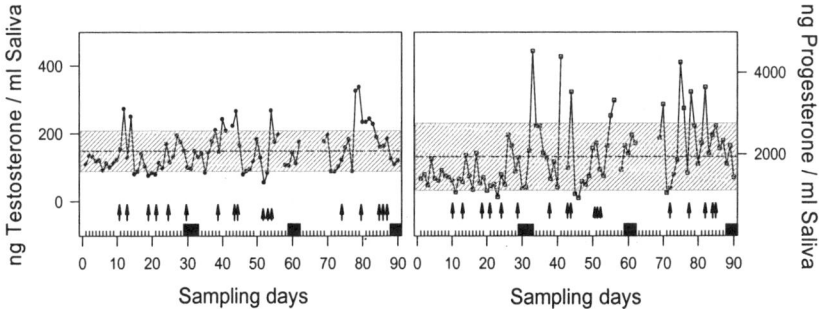

Figure 5.2 Example of one individual's testosterone and progesterone patterns over the 90-day sampling period. Shaded areas represent the individual mean ± standard deviation. Peaks were defined as testosterone and progesterone levels greater than or equal to the individual mean plus standard deviation. Arrows indicate days with reported sexual activity of intensity greater than 35 and black bars are the menstruation periods of the female partner.

5.2.2.2 Hormone-behavior interactions: Time-patterns

Days with peak occurrences were recoded from all hormonal and behavioural variables, and thereby between-males variation of amplitudes was not subject of the subsequent analyses.

A peak was defined as a T or P level $\geq$ individual mean + standard deviation [49] (Figure 5.2) and as sexual activities of intensities greater than 35 (data above the third quartile).

To perform THEME-analyses on the repeated measurements of each individual the number of actors was one in this study. A minimum of three repeated pattern occurrences throughout the 90 days sampled and a $p < .05$ significance level were specified. THEME identified time periods when, for example, T peaks and sexual activity co-occurred. The detection of a non-random time-pattern may, thus, be regarded as a measure of the interaction between T and sexual behavior or of the co-occurrence with an environmental parameter. From the numerous detected non-random time-patterns per individual the "frequency of occurrence" (N occurrences divided by the total duration of the sampling period) of each male's most complex pattern within the 90 days was derived. The frequency of occurrence was compared between those 22 candidates in whom THEME detected patterns involving both, hormonal and behavioural variables.

5.2.3 Social and environmental context of observed testosterone- and time-patterns

To compare an estimate of the individual degree of hormonal responsivity to a specific behavior, the proportion (%) of all time-patterns that involved a significant interaction between the focal questioned hormone-behavior interactions was determined per individual. In order to elaborate a possible prevalent direction of the interaction, time-patterns ranking the T peak before the behavior were distinguished from those ranking the behavioural event before the T peak. To compare observed time-patterns that involved regular environmental parameters, the number of detected time-patterns that involved weekly intervals (i.e. Saturdays) and monthly intervals (i.e. the 28-days intervals between full moons) were determined per individual and compared between life history categories.

Number of individuals may vary among the different analyses because the "daily questionnaires" of five candidates were not returned and thus, missing, and two "general questionnaires" were incomplete. Therefore, time-patterns involving hormones and behavior were available from 22 males; comparisons between different social categories could be performed among 21 males, and comparisons between children-related parameters among 20 males. Phenologies and "environmental parameters", such as weekly or monthly intervals, were independent of the number of returned daily questionnaires and, therefore, available from 27 males. Means ± standard errors were used for all descriptives. To control for the possibly confounding effects of season, sampling time, age [24, 48], and pairbond duration, Spearman's rank correlations were employed. Temporal sequences of the observed interactions between T and behavior were compared using Wilcoxon tests matched for individuals. The comparisons between social categories were performed using Mann-Whitney U tests. All probabilities were two-tailed.

5.3   Results and Discussion

5.3.1   Phenology of hormone patterns

5.3.1.1 Testosterone

On average 86 of the 90 requested daily morning saliva samples were delivered ($N= 27$). Amplitudes of the observed individual T fluctuations varied to a high extent over the sampling period (1100 ± 100 ng/ml) with a mean coefficient of variation of 50%. However, the T variation observed in this data set was not due to effects of season, sampling time, age or pairbond duration [18]. Thus, although not ideal, these data reflect daily patterns of morning T levels in 27 healthy men monitored over a three months period.

5.3.1.2 Progesterone

Also the amplitudes of the observed individual P fluctuations varied to a high extent over the sampling period (4400 ± 500 ng/ml) with a mean coefficient of variation of 45%. Remarkably the amplitudes of the salivary P levels were on average 4-times those of the T amplitudes measured from the same samples (Figure 5.2). As with T, the P variation observed in this data set was not confounded by season, sampling time, age or pairbond duration.

5.3.2 Hormone-behavior interactions: Conventional approach

5.3.2.1 Social context of testosterone and sexual behavior

The comparison of simple mean T levels and of individual coefficients of variation did not yield any difference between the assessed life history profiles. However, the individual T peaks of men from rural environments were generally larger than of men living in urban settings. There were no differences between the individual T amplitudes due to any of the other social categories.

A general interaction of T with parameters in a direct sexual context was observed. For example, in the seven men who reported sexual activity with an unfamiliar partner salivary T of the next morning was on average 25 ± 14 % (ranging from –30 to 230 %) higher than their individual average levels. Even more amplified, T amplitudes of the six candidates who reported sexual activities with more than one partner within the preceding 24 hours were on average 120 ± 29 % (ranging from –20 to 360 %) larger than their individual average T levels.

In rural towns anonymity is missing and communicative interactions are more limited to the available actors. The large T peaks we found among rural inhabitants may reflect a strong sensitivity to, for example, sexual, territorial or competitive stimuli. The fact that urban men had lower T peaks is plausible in the light of the anonymity, hyper-stimulation (from advertisement walls to fashion style), and higher physical densities that men in urban settings have to cope with. As men living in urban settings are permanently exposed to these stimuli, their responsivity was probably more saturated than in the countryside men. Imagine a woman passing by in short skirt and skinny top on a hot summer day. If this took place in a rural village, it would provoke a clear response among the men of any age. If the same lady was walking along the streets of a big city, it would not necessarily be extraordinary or provoking, because in cities this simply happens more often.

Surprisingly, we did not find higher T levels in singles than in married men, which have been suggested in the literature [50]. However, Booth & Dabbs had shown in this long-term study that high T levels were prerequisites of the life history rather than being modulated by the men's social environment. Although such results are of interest, they simply deal with the characters of one variable, i.e. T levels, not taking into account the potential modulators of the focal variable. We will present in chapter 5.3.3. how different the THEME approach worked.

5.3.2.2 Social context of progesterone and sexual behavior

Although human males' P was not necessarily predicted with a direct sexual context, we observed some curious P responses to "unexpected" sexual activities. For example, if the men reported sexual activity with an unfamiliar partner, salivary P of the next morning was on average 40 ± 19 % higher than their individual average levels (ranging from –20 to 300 %). Moreover, in cases where they reported sex with more than one partner within the preceding 24 hours, P peaks were on average 50 ± 23 % of their individual average level (ranging from –50 to 350 %).

As with the T data, comparing simple mean P levels did not show any differences between the assessed life history profiles. However, the individual P variability (coefficients of variation) was higher in singles than in paired men, and the P peaks of men who had rated their relationship as "unofficial" (secret partner) were larger than those of men with official commitment to their relationship .

Human males' P was indeed involved in sexual behavior, which matched the results from rats [42]. Although this was observed particularly in "unexpected" or "secret" episodes, so far, we had found no effect of sexual experience, and a direct measure of "social tolerance" was not provided by our questionnaires. At this point drawing a consensus from our results would have been highly speculative. Yet, we were puzzled by the unknown degree of interaction between T and P levels. Therefore, we assembled individual correlation coefficients between each male's T and P levels over the total sampling period. In 82% of all males the T-P correlation coefficients were significant. Comparisons between life history parameters revealed that the parallel nature of the T and P fluctuations was decreasing with sexual history. Men who had reported to have known more than ten previous sexual partners had on average correlation coefficients of 0.2 ($\pm$ .06) as compared to an average of 0.6 ($\pm$ .04) among those men who reported up to ten previous sexual partners. Thus, there may be potential insights in focusing on the interaction between male T and P levels, rather than analyzing each hormone per se.

5.3.3   Hormone-behavior interactions: Time-patterns

5.3.3.1 Testosterone

Structure of time-patterns involving testosterone. THEME detected a total of 1641 non-random time-pattern combinations that involved T (75 $\pm$ 16 per individual, $N = 22$). The percentages of all detected time-patterns involving T (*diversity*) occurred more frequently in "wannabe fathers" than in those males who had no partner or did not want to have children with their current partner. No variation of the time-pattern diversity was observed due to any of the other investigated social categories. This pattern will return in the following steps of analyses, as we are yet going to filter out those time-patterns which involved T peaks specifically related to intense sexual activity, rather than elaborating any event combination ever observed.

THEME detected a large variety of numbers of co-occurring events in the most complex time-pattern (with a range of 3 to 28 events; *complexity*). However, none of the assessed social categories explained any of the observed time-pattern complexities. In the majority of candidates (19 from 22 males) the most complex patterns occurred with a frequency of .03, i.e. three times throughout the sampling period (Figure 5.3).

Social context of time-patterns involving testosterone. An interaction between T and sexual activity was detected in 75% of all time-patterns that involved T (59 $\pm$ 13 per individual; total number = 1238). The proportions of all time-patterns that involved T and sexual activity were not different between singles and paired men, and also not between non-fathers and fathers. However, the specific interactions between T and sexual activity were more frequent among "wannabe fathers" as compared with men who had no partner or did not want to have children with their current partner (Figure 5.4AC).

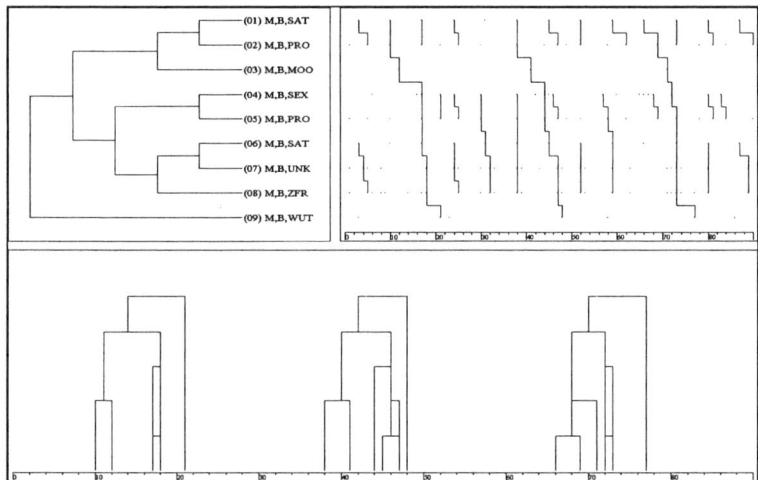

Figure 5.3 Example of a complex time-pattern involving nine event types with a monthly frequency of occurrence (i.e. three times during the sampled 90 days). Upper left panel shows how the pattern was detected level by level. Upper right panel gives the occurrence times of each event type as a series of points. The lines connecting the occurrence times show, how the pattern has been gradually built up. Lower panel visualizes the frequency of occurrence along the total sampling period.

To elucidate the temporal sequence of the observed interactions, the proportions of all observed time-patterns that involved the morning T peak preceding a behavioral event during the day were compared with those that involved the behavior reported from the day preceding a next morning's T peak (for an example see Figure 5.2) in all candidates. Interactions between sexual activity and T were observed at equal rates in either direction [18]. Therefore, the presented time-patterns were not to be regarded as interactions with one prevalent direction, but rather represented a high degree of a two-way type of interaction between sexual behavior and T levels in all males sampled.

Environmental modulation of time-patterns involving testosterone. Time-patterns involving T and weekly intervals (i.e. Saturdays) were observed in 89% of all males. THEME, furthermore, detected time-patterns involving T and monthly intervals (i.e. the 28 days period of full moon phases) in 15 of 27 males, ranging from one to 15 pattern combinations per individual. Because this interval echoes the average length of the female cycle, we expected to find this interaction in paired rather than in unpaired men. Surprisingly, the observed variation of male monthly time-patterns could not be explained by being paired or not (Fig. 5.5A). However, as already observed for the interaction with sexual activity, also the T peaks interacting with monthly intervals occurred significantly more frequent in "wannabe father" as compared to those men who had no partner or did not want to have children with their current partner (Figure 5.5C). There was no difference between the occurrences of monthly T patterns of non-fathers or fathers and also not due to any of the other investigated life history parameters.

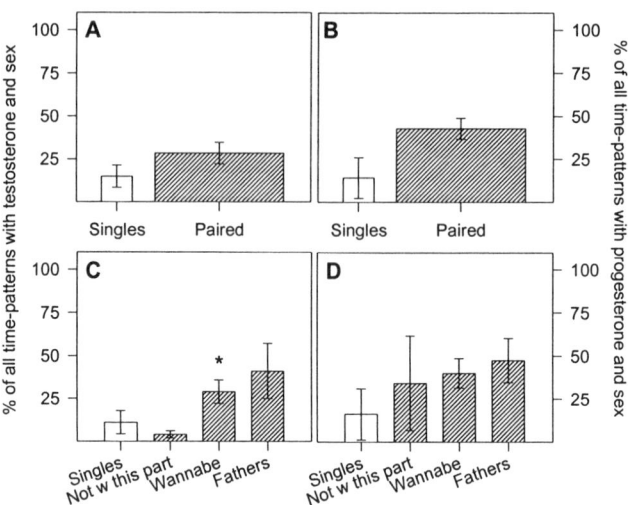

Figure 5.4 Proportion of all time-patterns involving (A) testosterone (T) or (B) progesterone (P) and sexual activity occurred at equal rates in singles and in paired men. (C) "Wannabe fathers" showed a larger proportion of time-patterns that involved T and sexual activity (in either sequence) than singles or those who did not have the wish to have children with their current partner. This was not the case with (D) the proportion of time-patterns involving P and sexual activity. Asterisk indicates a significant effect ($p < 0.05$).

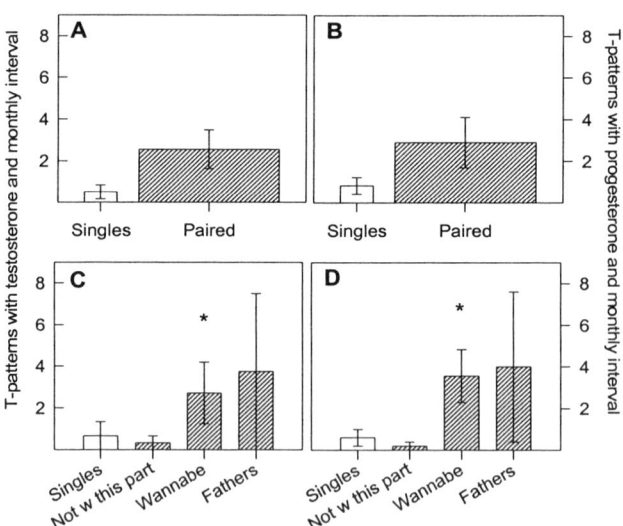

Figure 5.5 The number of detected time-patterns that involved A) testosterone (T) peaks or B) progesterone (P) peaks at monthly intervals per individual. The differences between singles and paired men were not significant. In "wannabe fathers" THEME detected more time-patterns that involved C) T and D) P at monthly intervals than in singles or those who did not wish to have children with their current partner. Asterisks indicate significant effects ($p < .05$).

5.3.3.2 Progesterone

Structure of time-patterns involving progesterone. THEME detected a total of 1895 non-random time-pattern combinations that involved P (86 ± 18 per individual, $N = 22$), which was an even larger number than with the time-patterns involving T. The percentages of all time-patterns involving P increased with the men's commitment to the relationship, with single men at the lower end and wannabe fathers and fathers at the upper end. However, this was less pronounced than with T. Interestingly, we observed a higher proportion of time-patterns with P among monogamous ("faithful") men than among polygynous men. In contrast, the P diversity was equal in singles and paired men as we had already observed with the time-patterns involving T.

Social context of time-patterns involving progesterone. An interaction between P and sexual activity was detected in 66% of all time-patterns that involved P (59 ± 12 per individual; total number = 1247). The proportions of all time-patterns that involved P and sexual activity did not differ between singles and paired men, and also not with regard to wannabe fathers (Figure 5.4BD). Monogamous ("faithful") men had a higher degree of interaction between P peaks and sexual activity than the three men who had sex with more than one partner during the six months preceding the sampling period ("polygynous"), however, this result was flawed by the very small sample size. Sexual history, rural or urban living, and shared or own household had no effects on the proportion of time-patterns with P and sex.

Environmental modulation of time-patterns involving progesterone. Varying numbers of time-patterns with P peaks at weekly intervals (i.e. Saturdays) were observed in 82% of all males. Time-patterns involving P peaks at monthly intervals were detected in 15 of the 27 candidates, with a range from one to 22 pattern combinations per individual. As with the T and monthly interval patterns, also the P and monthly intervals patterns were not simply due to being paired or not (Figure 5.5B), but were clearly more frequent among wannabe fathers than in singles or those men who did not wish to have children with their current partner (Figure 5.5D). None of the other investigated life history parameters had an effect on the occurrence of P peaks at monthly intervals.

5.4   Conclusions

5.4.1   Facultative potential for monthly patterns of hormones and sexual behavior

The social context of androgen fluctuations is not a new concept in non-human behavioral endocrinology [6, 30, 34, and 51]. However, studies on the social modulation of T response patterns in human males suffer from the complexity of social interactions and from the ethical restriction of designing controlled studies in our own species. Here, the application of THEME analyses [44, 45] resulted in time-patterns that may be regarded as measures of the co-occurrence of T with sexual behavior. Such time-patterns also provide information on the temporal sequence of the parameters involved. Dabbs and Mohammed [28] found that sexual activity affected T more than initial T affected sexual activity, where saliva samples had been collected immediately before and after sexual activity. In this study, on a daily morning base, no prevalent direction of the relationship between T peaks and sexual behavior was detected, rather there seems to have been a high degree of mutual interaction.

The existence of a regular cycle of hormones and sexual behavior in human males was an open question so far and the results of this study did not support the hypothesis. The known peak of sexual intercourse in couples around weekends [5] was reflected in the presently observed co-occurrences of sexual activity and T with weekends. This does not point at a male cycle in any parameter, but rather at the males' hormonal responsiveness to sexual activities. With regard to a potential male responsiveness to the 28-days interval of the female's menstrual cycle, one would expect to observe such response patterns in paired men rather than in singletons. Our results, however, did not confirm this prediction. The occurrences of observed time-patterns that involved T at monthly intervals differed due to the reproductive context of and commitment to the males' relationship to a regular partner, rather than to being paired per se. In specific, the wish to have children with a current partner explained both, the observed degree of interaction between T and sexual activity, as well as the occurrence of monthly intervals in the males' T fluctuations. Thus, men who had revealed a reproductive context to the sexual activities with their partners showed different T response patterns than men who reported sexual activities without commitment to reproduction.

As 75% of all time-patterns involved an interaction between T and sexual activity one may argue that these similarly emerging pictures are to be regarded as simple artifacts of a higher diversity of time-patterns in general. However, there was no similar result observed with time-patterns that involved T and weekly intervals or with the frequency of occurrence. Furthermore, an effect of using oral contraceptives, which affects the regularity of the female's 28-days period, may be excluded from this study, because its use was only reported in two cases. We also controlled for a possible effect of sharing the household with a partner, but there was no difference in any of the parameters between paired men living in shared households versus paired men living in own (single) households. Therefore, the observed patterns between T and sex, and the monthly interval of these interactions in "wannabe fathers" may point at the males' facultative hormonal and behavioral responsiveness to their female partner's cycle. We suggest that our results reflected the indirect responses of "wannabe fathers" to their female partners' regular monthly cycles, rather than internal male rhythms. However, we want to clearly point out that the speculation that men who have no wish to have a family with their current partner might remain hormonally and psychologically unresponsive to their partner's fertility phase seems not trustworthy. This is by no means an option for contraception, and it also does not solve the causality of unsuccessful trials to have a baby or shift it to the male side.

5.4.2 Progesterone as another male sex steroid

Both, T and P characteristically co-occurred with sexual activity in a large proportion of the sampled men, which suggests regarding P as another male sexual steroid. Particularly, P-responses were involved in "unexpected" or "secret" episodes. P is an obligate precursor for T, found in up to 10-fold larger amplitudes than the T in saliva (Figure 5.2), and the levels of both were positively correlated in our sample (in 82% of all males sampled). We, furthermore, explored whether life history parameters would explain any of the observed variation of the degree of correlatedness. Fascinatingly, the males' sexual history had an effect on the parallel nature of the T and P fluctuations, with those men who had reported more than ten previous sexual partners at the lower end. This gave a first indication that sexual experience may be involved in human males' P, as was postulated for rats before [43]. It remains open to test the social component of human males' T-P-interactions in further detail. However, using THEME, an effect of social categories was only found for the interaction between T and sexual activity, with larger proportions in wannabe fathers than in singles. The detected time-patterns involving P and sexual activity did not vary due to any of the presently investigated life-history parameters (Figure 5.4CD). We concluded that, although P peaks were co-occurring with sexual activities in more than thousand time-patterns, no social component was related with it.

On the other side, the occurrence of time-patterns involving P peaks at monthly intervals was clearly increasing with the males' commitment to their current relationship. Thus, without including sexual activity events the P patterns were matching the observed time-patterns involving T at monthly intervals (Figure 5.5). At this point it is important to mention that the 28-day full moon intervals did not have to indicate that the sexual activities were peaking exactly in those full moon nights. The interval simply worked as a Zeitgeber, we may as well have detected regular events at half moon, or new moon, for example. The same applies for Saturdays that were used as Zeitgebers for a possible weekly interval in hormones and behavior. The curiously large proportions of candidates with regular weekly patterns of T (89%) and P (82%) were not necessarily representing the "Saturday night fever". The weekly interval may as well have indicated that it was, for example, Tuesday or Friday evenings or mornings. Which day of the week ever, the men in our sample seemed to have rather regular life-styles, at least concerning their sexual lives.

5.4.3 *"It takes two to tango": future directions*

Alternatively, the candidates' wives may have been the ones living at a regular pace, and the male patterns we measured would then reflect the men's responsivity to their partner's pace. The current study exclusively sampled the male side. However, this probably represented only half of the picture and including the female side into a follow-up study should be the logical next step from here. As "it takes two to tango" it would be most exciting to investigate the "within-pair" patterns of hormones and behavior by monitoring the female partner's cycle and asking her details in daily questionnaires simultaneously with what we had asked from the men in the current study.

The concept that males may potentially respond and adapt to their partners' hormonal and fecundity phases, has been proposed before. In small mammals rapid, but long-lasting oxytocin increases were found in both partners during pair formation [13, 14]. In a socially monogamous bird the within-pair T co-variation between the male and the female partners' seasonal levels was reflecting the pair's reproductive success [15]. Human males' T was shown to correspond with the partner's sexual responsivity scores [11]. Recently, Storey et al. [16] reported that T of expectant fathers was specifically related to the women's hormone levels, rather than to the time before birth. Taken together, these phenomena are based on mechanisms associated with social monogamy, including affiliation, paternal care and pair bonding. The males' wish for children with a specific partner, which led to the distinction of "wannabe fathers" in this study, may be regarded as one possible approach to express the intensity and the subjective perception of a pair bond in human males. One might even speculate that "wannabe fathers" had to invest into mate-guarding more intensively and therefore, were responding more specifically to their partners' behavior than, for example, men who had a sexual partner but were not willing to invest into parental care with this partner. This "mate-guarding hypothesis" among human males remains one more exciting field for future research.

5.5   Acknowledgements

We are especially thankful to the 27 volunteers who provided the saliva samples and behavioral data. F. Schachinger contributed to creating the questionnaires. The KLF Grünau, two anonymous sponsors and the Vienna local board (H.C. Ehald) provided financial support. We acknowledge the technical expertise of E. Möstl, A. Kuchar-Schulz,

H. Spendier and M. Stark from the Institute for Biochemistry at the Veterinary University of Vienna and thank for the lab space. Furthermore, we thank L.A. Carneiro, N.J. Cook, H. Fuchs, K. Grammer, A. Hirschenhauser, A. Jütte, K. Kotrschal, M.S. Magnusson, R.F. Oliveira, M. Ortobelli, A. Ros, and B. Valoti for their assistance. K. Wynne-Edwards provided very helpful comments on an earlier draft of the manuscript. KH was supported by a post-doctoral grant from the Fundação para a Sciência e a Tecnología (FCT: PRAXIS XXI/BPD/20142/99).

5.6   References

[1]   S. H. Van Goozen, V. M. Wiegant, E. Endert, F. A. Helmond, and N. E. Van de Poll, Psychoendocrinological assessment of the menstrual cycle: the relationship between hormones, sexuality, and mood, *Archives of Sexual Behavior* **26** (1997) 359-382.

[2]   C. Carani, J. Bancroft, A. Granata, G. Del Rio, and P. Marrana, Testosterone and erectile function, nocturnal penile tumescence and rigidity, and erectile response to visual erotic stimuli in hypogonadal and eugonadal men, *Psychoneuroendocrinology* **17** (1992) 647-654.

[3]   T. Mulligan and B. Schmitt, Testosterone for erectile failure, *Journal of General Internal Medicine* **8** (1993) 517-521.

[4]   R. A. Anderson, C. W. Martin, A. W. Kung, D. Everington, T. C. Pun, K. C. Tan, J. Bancroft, K. Sundaram, A. J. Moo-Young, and D. T. Baird, 7Alpha-methyl-19-nortestosterone maintains sexual behavior and mood in hypogonadal men, *Journal of Clinical Endocrinology & Metabolism* **84** (1999) 3556-3562.

[5]   J. D. Palmer, J. R. Udry, and N. M. Morris, Diurnal and weekly, but no lunar rhythms in humans copulation, *Archives of Sexual Behavior* **7** (1982) 157-173.

[6]   K. Wallen, Sex and context: hormones and primate sexual motivation, *Hormones and Behavior* **40** (2001) 339-357.

[7]   J. K. Van Niekerk, F. A. Huppert, and J. Herbert, Salivary cortisol and DHEA: association with measures of cognition and well-being in normal older men, and effects of three months of DHEA supplementation, *Psychoneuroendocrinology* **26** (2001) 591-612.

[8]   M. Zitzmann and E. Nieschlag, Testosterone levels in healthy men and the relation to behavioural and physical characteristics: facts and constructs, *European Journal of Endocrinology* **144** (2001) 183-197.

[9]   P. Schreiner-Engel, R. C. Sciavi, H. Smith, and D. White, Sexual arousability and the menstrual cycle, *Psychosomatic Medicine* **43** (1981) 199-214.

[10]   J. W. Kemnitz, J. R. Gibber, K. A. Lindsay, and S. G. Eisele, Effects of ovarian hormones on eating behaviors, body weight, and glucoregulation in rhesus monkeys, *Hormones and Behavior* **23** (1989) 235-250.

[11]   H. Persky, H. I. Lief., D. Strauss, W. R. Miller, and C. P. O'Brien, Plasma testosterone level and sexual behavior of couples, *Archives of Sexual Behavior* **7** (1978) 157-173.

[12]   P. H. Rowe, G. A. Lincoln, P. A. Racey, J. Lehane, M. J. Stephenson, J. C. Shenton, and T. D. Glover, Temporal variations of testosterone levels in the peripheral blood plasma of men, *Journal of Endocrinology* **61** (1974) 63-73.

[13]   C. S. Carter, J. R. Williams, D. M. Witt, and T. R. Insel, Oxytocin and social bonding, *Annals of the New York Academy of Sciences* **12** (1992) 204-211.

[14]   R. Barth, B. Wallner, J. Dittami, and D. Schrams, Oxytocin as a means or end to pair bonding: data from guinea pigs, *Advances in Ethology* **32** (1997) 58.

[15]   K. Hirschenhauser, E. Möstl, and K. Kotrschal, Within-pair testosterone co-variation and reproductive output in Greylag geese (*Anser anser*), *Ibis* **141** (1999) 577-586.

[16]   A. E. Storey, J. C. Walsh, R. L. Quinton, and K. E. Wynne-Edwards, Hormonal correlates of paternal responsiveness in new and expectant fathers, *Evolution and Human Behavior* **21** (2000) 79-95.

[17]   G. M. Alexander and B. B. Sherwin, The association between testosterone, sexual arousal, and selective attention for erotic stimuli in men, *Hormones and Behavior* **25** (1991) 367-381.

[18]   K. Hirschenhauser, D. Frigerio, K. Grammer, and M. S. Magnusson, Monthly patterns of testosterone and behavior in prospective fathers, *Hormones and Behavior* **42** (2002) 172-181.

[19]   W. A. Brown, P. M. Monti, and D. P. Corriveau, Serum testosterone and sexual activity and interest in men, *Archives of Sexual Behavior* **7** (1970) 97-103.

[20]   C. A. Fox, A. A. Ismail, D. N. Love, K. E. Kirkham, and J. A. Loraine, Studies on the relationship between plasma testosterone levels and human sexual activity, *Journal of Endocrinology* **52** (1972) 51-58.

[21]   Anonymous, Effects of sexual activity on beard growth in man, *Nature* **226** (1970) 869-870.
[22]   R. F. Walker, D. W. Wallace, G. F. Read, and D. Riad-Fahmy, Assessment of testicular function by radioimmunoassay of testosterone in saliva, *International Journal of Andrology* **3** (1980) 105-120.
[23]   K. Howard, M. Kane, A. Madden, J. P. Gosling, and P. F. Fottrell, Direct solid-phase enzymeimmunoassay of testosterone in saliva, *Clinical Chemistry* **35** (1989) 2044-2047.
[24]   J. M. Dabbs, Salivary testosterone measurements: reliability across hours, days, and weeks, *Physiology & Behavior* **48** (1990) 83-86.
[25]   J. Archer, S. S. Birring, and F. C. W. Wu, The association between testosterone and aggression among young men: empirical findings and a meta-analysis, *Aggressive Behavior* **24** (1998) 411-420.
[26]   J. M. Graham and C. Desjardins, Classical conditioning: induction of LH and testosterone secretion in anticipation of sexual activity, *Science* **210** (1980) 1039-1041.
[27]   D. H. Hellhammer, W. Hubert, and T. Schürmeyer, Changes in saliva testosterone after psychological stimulation in men, *Psychoneuroendocrinology* **10** (1985) 77-81.
[28]   J. M. Dabbs and S. Mohammed, Male and female salivary testosterone concentrations before and after sexual activity, *Physiology & Behavior* **52** (1990) 195-197.
[29]   G. S. Stoléru, A. Ennaji, A. Cournot, and A. Spira, LH pulsatile secretion and testosterone blood levels are influenced by sexual arousal in human males, *Psychoneuroendocrinology* **18** (1993) 205-218.
[30]   J. C. Wingfield, R. M. Hegner, A. M. Dufty Jr., and G. F. Ball, The "challenge hypothesis": theoretical implications for patterns of testosterone secretion, mating systems, and breeding strategies, *American Naturalist* **136** (1990) 829-846.
[31]   E. D. Ketterson and V. Nolan Jr., Hormones and life histories: an integrative approach, *American Naturalist* **140** (1992) S33-S62.
[32]   R. E. Brown, Hormonal and experimental factors influencing parental behaviour in male rodents: An integrative approach, *Behavioral Processes* **30** (1993) 1-28.
[33]   K. Wynne-Edwards, Hormonal changes in mammalian fathers, *Hormones and Behavior* **40** (2001) 139-145.
[34]   K. Hirschenhauser and R. F. Oliveira, Social modulation of androgens in male vertebrates: meta-analyses of the "challenge hypothesis", *Animal Behaviour* (2005) in press.
[35]   C. S. Carter, Neuroendocrinology of sexual behavior in the female, in *Behavioral Endocrinology*, J. B. Becker, S. M. Breedlove, and D. Crews, Eds. London: MIT Press, 1993, pp. 71-95.
[36]   Rosenblatt J. Hormone-behavior relations in the regulation of parental behaviour, in *Behavioral Endocrinology*, J. B. Becker, S. M. Breedlove, and D. Crews, Eds. London: MIT Press, 1993, pp. 219-259.
[37]   A. Dawson, Plasma gonadal steroid levels in wild starlings (*Sturnus vulgaris*) during the annual cycle and in relation to the stages of breeding, *General and Comparative Endocrinology* **49** (1983) 289-294.
[38]   D. M. Witt, L. J. Young, and D. Crews, Progesterone modulation of androgen-dependent sexual behavior in male rats, *Physiology & Behavior* **57** (1995) 307-313.
[39]   R. S. Donham, Annual cycle of plasma luteinizing hormone and sex hormones in male and female mallards (*Anas platyrhynchos*), *Biology of Reproduction* **21** (1979) 1273-1285.
[40]   K. Hirschenhauser, E. Möstl, and K. Kotrschal, Seasonal patterns of sex steroids determined from feces of free-living greylag geese (*Anser anser*), *General and Comparative Endocrinology* **114** (1999) 67-79.
[41]   D. M. Witt, G. Gao, and J. D. Caldwell, Testosterone and sexual experience alter levels of plasma membrane binding sites for progesterone in the male rat brain, *Hormone and Metabolic Research*, **35** (2003) 69-75.
[42]   D. M. Witt and P. A. Mitrani, Sex differences in plasma membrane responses following progesterone stimulation, *Hormones and Behavior* **39** (2001) 354.
[43]   M. S. Magnusson, Hidden real-time patterns in intra- and inter-individual behavior: description and detection, *European Journal of Psychological Assessment* **12** (1996) 112-123.
[44]   M. S. Magnusson, Discovering hidden time patterns in behavior: T-patterns and their detection, *Behavior Research Methods, Instruments, & Computers* **32** (2000) 93-110.
[45]   J. Dabbs, *Heroes, Rogues, and Lovers. Testosterone and Behavior.* New York. McGraw-Hill, 2000.
[46]   E. Nieschlag and A. A. Ismail, Diurnal variations of plasma testosterone in normal and pathological conditions as measured by the technique of competitive protein binding, *Journal of Endocrinology*, **46** (1970) 3-4.
[47]   J. M. Dabbs, Age and seasonal variation in serum testosterone concentration among men, *Chronobiology International* **7** (1990) 245-249.
[48]   H. E. Edwards, C. J. Reburn, and K. E. Wynne-Edwards, Daily patterns of pituitary prolactin secretion and their role in regulating maternal serum progesterone concentrations across pregnancy in the Djungarian hamster (*Phodopus campbelli*), *Biology of Reproduction* **52** (1995) 814-823.

[49]   A. Booth and J. Dabbs, Testosterone and men's marriages, *Social Forces* **72** (1993) 463-477.
[50]   R. F. Oliveira, Of fish and men: a comparative approach to androgens and social dominance, *Behavioral Brain Sciences* **21** (1998) 383-384.

SECTION III

HIDDEN PATTERNS IN COURTSHIP INTERACTION

The detection of hidden recurrent action patterns and probabilistic social interaction sequences, in natural or relatively unconstrained settings, is a common goal of ethological research and of human interaction research, such as the analysis of turn taking.

Magnusson, 2000

Courtship behaviour is a complex sequence of actions that depends on both participants: complex trigger patterns are involved in the various stages of courtship behaviour where each of the partners may perform a specific sequence of routines, each in turn triggered by the body language of the other partner.

Given the complexity of the recurrent action patterns, the detection of hidden interaction sequences in courtship is a common goal of ethological and human interaction research. For this reason, courtship analysis is the main focus of this section. On one side, the chapter by Sakaguchi, Jonsson and Hasegawa investigated interaction between mixed-sex human dyad. On the other side, the chapter written by Arthur JR. and Magnusson presented the microanalysis of the *Drosophila* courtship behaviour.

Chapter 6, by ARTHUR JR. and MAGNUSSON, investigated the courtship behaviour displayed by a *fruitless* mutant (*fru^1*), a courtship mutant of *Drosophila melanogaster*, towards mature males and virgin females. The approach used in the chapter is characterized by two major features.

First, data were collected at temporal and spatial resolutions that revealed actions invisible to the unaided eye. Second, the THEME program was used to detect hidden structures from courtship behaviour data. In particular, the authors investigated the following three issues: Are there differences in how *fru^1* males court mature virgin wild-type females compared with how they court mature wild-type males? How does the courtship of a mature virgin wild-type female by male carrying *fru^1* mutation differ from that of a wild-type male?

The findings suggested that there is this little interaction among the patterns derived from the *fru^1* males and the mature virgin wild-type females and even less among *fru^1* males and mature wild-type males, but there was more interaction among patterns derived from mature wild-type males and mature virgin wild-type females.

Further, these data suggest that this research approach may provide a new and deeper insight into the interaction and contribution of each partner in a dyad. The next steps would be the development of quantitative methods to measure the complexity of the patterns and to compare them.

Chapter 7, written by SAKAGUCHI, JONSSON and HASEGAWA, focused on the movement synchrony in mixed-sex dyads during initial interpersonal attraction.

Particularly, the chapter discusses the use of THEME to detect *movement synchrony*, the gestalt-like perception of movement rhythmicity or coordination.

In a waiting room situation, the authors videotaped initial interaction of unacquainted mixed-sex dyads, and investigated whether movement synchrony between a dyad related with the formation of interpersonal attraction. Participants' behaviour in the first and last minutes of initial 10-minute interaction was coded frame by frame. Both interactants' movements were considered and coded according to seven categories: (1) looking at the partner, (2) nodding, (3) other head movements; two categories of hand and arm movements, i.e. (4) gestures, (5) auto manipulation; touching one's body or clothes, (6) leg movements, and (7) trunk movements.

Movement synchrony measures calculated from the coded data related with a participant's interest in the partner more strongly in the first minute than in the last minute. However, the relationships were mostly explained by the increase of movement frequency.

A movement synchrony measure that remained to be a significant signal was the repetitiveness of behaviour time-sequences. A dyad with a male participant interested in the partner decreased the repetitiveness of movement synchrony in the first minute. On the other hand, a dyad with a female participant who reported frequent sexual approaches by male strangers showed increase in the repetitiveness of movement synchrony.

These data suggest that such behavioural characteristics of frequently approached women tend to be interpreted as a courtship-like signal by male strangers. Only among dyads with frequently picked up women, the increase of female self-synchrony patterns positively correlated with male interest in her, circumstantially supporting the explanation.

Authors also concluded that movement synchrony may be considered as a courtship-like communication signal during rapid interactions, as it shows interest formation between first-met dyads: the movement of male participants gave the timing to form synchronous patterns, while the female respond giving a higher or a lower level of repetition or complexity.

6. Microanalysis of *Drosophila* Courtship Behaviour

Benjamin I. ARTHUR, JR., Magnus S. MAGNUSSON

Abstract. We investigated the temporal structures of behavioural interactions. Our approach is characterized by two major features: data were collected at high temporal and spatial resolutions that revealed acts invisible to the unaided eye and patterns were detected in the collected data using THEME. We investigated courtship displayed by a *fruitless* mutant (*fru¹*) male, a courtship mutant of *Drosophila melanogaster*, towards mature males and virgin females compared with wild-type males. Novel elements of behaviour revealed at high temporal and spatial resolution were used to augment the repertoire of elements. We showed that frequency of an element was not a reliable indicator of its involvement in patterns. Our findings reveal behaviour structures not apparent to the unaided observer: that *fru¹* males interact little with their courtees when courting both wild-type females and males; wild-type females contribute more elements to the common pattern when being courted by *fru¹* males; wild-type males interact more with females during courtship. The contribution of elements made by wild-type female to the common pattern does not change whether the partner is *fru¹* male or wild-type male. The co-occurrence of specific pairs of elements, one from each partner, hints at a putative syntax of communication underlying these interactions.

Keywords: *Drosophila melanogaster*; courtship behaviour; behavioural patterns; video-recording.

Contents

6.1   Introduction

We are interested in how genes control behaviour. For this, we study courtship behaviour of the fruitfly *Drosophila melanogaster* in which it is a well established social interaction behaviour paradigm. This fruitfly also has the best developed molecular genetics of any metozoan. The behaviour of males during courtship has been characterized as consisting of eight steps (orientation following, tapping, wing extension, circling, licking, attempted copulation, copulation) but not much is known about the females [1, 2]. The fruitfly is relatively easy to maintain and has a short generation time. Although it has a simple nervous system (approx. 10^5 neurons) and small genome (4 pairs of chromosomes), the fruitfly is able to display complex behaviours [3].

The measure of courtship has been the courtship index (CI) defined as the fraction of the courtship period during which a courter performed courtship towards the courtee. Thus, only a number was used to describe the whole observation period. To augument the presentation of behaviour, another parameter the wing extension index (WEI) was introduced to be used in addition to CI. These two numbers were used to describe the entire observation [1,2, and 4]. There have been efforts to fit the kinetics of mating to second order reaction kinetics [5] and others have applied sophisticated methods like multivariate courtship profile [6]. Whereas these methods summarize and clarify the given data they impose rather than reveal intrinsic structures in the behaviour.

Behaviour is inherently a multidimensional and fraught with nonlinearities: even small changes that may be statistically insignificant could result in massive changes in phenomena. This renders classical statistics methods effective in revealing some salient features. In this chapter, we collected data at high temporal and spatial resolution to capture micro-scale activity observable during courtship behaviour by male carrying a mutant allele of the *fruitless* gene (*fru^1*). Males carrying this *fruitless* allele court females and also display aberrant behaviour by courting mature males [7-9]. The THEME program was used to detect hidden structures from courtship behaviour data [10, 11]. We investigated the following three issues: Are there differences in how *fru^1* males court mature virgin wild-type females compared with how they court mature wild-type males? How does the courtship of a mature virgin wild-type female by male carrying *fru^1* mutation differ from how a wild-type male does it?

The detected patterns indicate that there was little interaction between the *fru^1* males and the mature virgin wild-type females and even less between *fru^1* males and mature wild-type males, but there was more interaction among patterns derived from mature wild-type males and mature virgin wild-type females during courtship.

6.2   Experimental procedures

6.2.1   Fly stocks

The *D. melanogaster* flies used in this study are of the wild-type Canton S (CS) strain and mutants carrying an allele of the *fruitless* mutation (*fru^1*) [7,9]. The flies were raised on a cornmeal/agar/molasses/yeast medium at 25°C on a 12:12 L:D cycle. The flies were sexed and the naive males and virgin females were isolated within two hours after eclosion under cold anaesthesia (4°C). The males were kept individually in test tubes until the recording. The mature males and females flies used for the recording were 4-5 days old. Mutant males used in the assays were homozyous for *fru^1*.

6.2.2   Video-recording

A male and a female fly were transferred, by aspiration, into a cylindrical chamber of a mating wheel. Each chamber had dimensions of 0.8 cm diameter and 0.5 cm height. There were four such chambers on each wheel. A 5-min episode (or until copulation in the case of the mature virgins) was recorded for each pair with a Sony Hi8 video/audio camera. The recordings were performed at 25°C and at 75% humidity.

6.2.3   Coding of the behaviour

The videotape recordings were first converted from Hi8 video to digital video. The digital video was compressed (~ 90% compression: From 1GB to 60MB) and converted into MPEG 1 files (29.97 frames per second) using Cleaner 6 software (Discreet, New York, NY). The data were analyzed frame by frame (30 frames per second) using an interactive multimedia program. The beginning and ending of every behaviour was systematically registered for the male and female of each pair to a 1/30 of a second resolution. At this time resolution, we discovered novel behaviour elements that were invisible to the unaided eye [Arthur et. al., in prep].This coded data were then imported into THEME (Noldus, Netherlands) and further processed for pattern detection and analyses. Conditions for the analyses of the courtship data from *fru*[l] males paired with mature virgin wild-type females and with mature wild-type males and also for the mature wild-type virgins paired with mature wild-type males the minimum occurrences were set at 5 and the maximum search level was 3. The significance level was set at $p = .005$ and Excluded Frequent ET's at 1.5 (i.e. frequency threshold above which patterns involving certain event types are rejected). Mean number of patterns obtained under these conditions are: 106 for real data and 12 for the randomized data for the dyad of mature virgin wild-type females and *fru*[l] males and 68 for real data and 5 for randomized data for the dyad of mature wild-type male and *fru*[l] male; for dyad of mature virgin wild-type female and mature wild-type male the real data gave 531 and the randomized 3 [11]. The behaviour elements coded for are the following:

Female behaviour elements
Abdotwist: a twisting of the abdomen sideways and downwards. *Kicking:* applying tarsi forcefully against partner. *Ovipositor extrusion:* telescoping extension of ovipositor. *Wiggle:* Wagging of abdomen and wings in opposite directions. *Wingflutter:* left and right flicks in succession.

Male behaviour elements
Orientation: Fly is facing the partner, and may involve little motion such as turning to keep facing the partner, leaning over or no motion. *Following:* locomotion in directed pursuit of a partner. *Tapping:* touching partner with tarsi of prothoracic forelegs. *Fencing:* face-to-face and engaged in sparring with prothoracic forelegs. *Wing extension:* wing stretched out away (i.e. perpendicular to the head abdomen axis) from the body biased to the left or right. *Circling:* a sideways skid along a semi-circular path around a partner. *Licking:* proboscis contact with partner. *Abdominal bending (Abdobend):* abdominal curling under thorax towards the head direction. *Attempted copulation:* abdominal curling directed towards a partner. *Copulation:* sustained genital connection between male and female.

Common behaviour elements
Abdominal vibration: vertical up and down movement of the abdomen. *Decamp:* an evasive jump away from partner, usually involving a somersault. *Grooming:* rubbing of tarsi together, forelegs, midlegs or hindlegs. *Standing:* Absence of locomotion with no

indication of activity directed towards the partner. *Still:* no detectable movement of any body parts during standing. *Walking (walk):* locomotion that is not directed towards courting the partner. *Wing Flicks:* brief spasmic movement of wings to and from the antero-posterior axis of the body in rapid succession. *Wing Scissoring:* both wings moved away from and back to the body in a rapid scissor-like manner. *Wing Spread:* Both wings are stretched out away from the body to give a wide V-shape forming an angle of at least 90 degrees that is bisected by the anterior to posterior axis of the fly.

6.3   Results

6.3.1   Novel behaviour elements

We set a criterion that any continuous action that had a beginning and ending that was clearly observable at the temporal resolution of 30 frames per second fit our definition of behaviour element. The new behaviour elements: fencing, abdominal vibration, wiggle, wingflutter, wing flicks, wing scissoring and wing spread were by thus found (See section 6.2.3 for descriptions). The high spatial resolution and sub-second temporal resolution enabled us to observe such fast action behaviour elements.

6.3.2   Frequencies of individual behaviour elements

The mature wild-type male displays orientation and following elements during the courting of a mature virgin wild-type female significantly more often than fru^1 male courting a mature virgin wild-type female or mature wild-type male. This wild-type male also grooms, walks and stands significantly less often when courting mature virgin wild-type females than fru^1 males courting either mature wild-type males or mature virgin wild-type females (Table 6.1.A). There was no fencing observed for mature wild-type males. The only significant difference between how fru^1 males courted mature wild-type males and mature virgin wild-type females is that fru^1 males displayed more fencing when they courted the mature wild-type males (Table 6.1.A).

Mature virgin wild-type females kicked significantly more often when courted by mature wild-type males than by fru^1 males (Table 6.1.B). The experiment consisted of three dyads; a mature virgin wild-type female paired with a mature wild-type male; fru^1 male paired with either a mature virgin wild-type female or a mature wild-type male. One-way ANOVA revealed significant differences among the three dyads in 7 out of the 14 behaviour categories: male orientation ($F_{2,14}$ = 5.82, p = .017); male following ($F_{2,14}$ = 5.9, p = .016); male fencing ($F_{2,14}$ = 8.034, p = .006); male grooming ($F_{2,14}$ = 14.2, p = .0007); male walk ($F_{2,14}$ = 13.75, p = .0008); male standing ($F_{2,14}$ = 8.96, p = .004); female kick ($F_{1,9}$ = 8.33, p = .02). Subsequent application of unplanned Tukey-Kramer tests uncovered the significance of differences among the members dyads within each category (see Table 6.1 A & B) The differences among the three dyads in the remaining seven categories of behaviour elements were found not to be significant (p > .05) [12]. Noteworthy is that the reference to male behaviour in the dyad consisting of the mature wild-type male and fru^1 male is intended for the fru^1 male.

	orientation	following	tapping	fencing	wing extension	wing flicks	licking	grooming	walking	standing
♂f vs ♂	5.6 ± 1.7	7.0 ± 0.7	14.4 ± 2.9	5.4* ± 1.86	8.2 ± 3.3	4 ± 1.9	9.2 ± 2.6	10 ± 1.3	40.8 ± 7.6	28 ± 4.1
♂f vs ♀	5.2 ± 2.5	6.4 ± 1.3	15.4 ± 6.0	0.2 ± 0.2	16.6 ± 9.9	13.8± 8.6	11 ± 3.9	10 ± 1.6	58.6 ± 8.4	33.2 ± 4.8
♂ vs ♀	19.8* ± 5.8	24.2* ± 7.0	26.8 ± 10.3	0.0 ± 0.0	31.6 ± 9.54	19 ± 8.4	12.2 ± 5.8	1.6* ± 0.75	8.4* ± 3.5	8.6* ± 4.13

♂f is *fruitless* mutant male, ♂ is wild-type mature male, ♀ is mature virgin wild-type female. * -implies statistically significant difference from other entries in row.

Table 6.1.A Frequency of display of behaviour elements by *fruitless* mutant male as courter.

	wing flicks		kicking		decamp		grooming	
♀ vs ♂f	0.2	± 0.2	0.2	± 0.2	2.2	± 0.37	5.4	± 0.9
♀ vs ♂	8.0*	± 5.4	3.2*	± 1	2.8	± 0.9	5.4	± 1.4

♂f is *fruitless* mutant male, ♂ is wild-type mature male, ♀ is mature virgin wild-type female. * -implies statistically significant difference from other entries in row.

Table 6.1.B Frequency of display of behaviour elements by mature virgin wild-type female as courtee.

6.3.3   Which behaviour elements are most involved in patterns ?

To determine the contribution of a behaviour element to the patterns, we expressed the number of patterns in which that particular element occurred as a ratio of the total number of patterns generated for each dyad. We reported the mean of these ratios for every group (See Table 6.2 A & B). One-way ANOVA tests revealed significant differences among the groups for the behaviours: orientation by fru^1 male ($F_{2,14} = 8.2, p = .006$); following by fru^1 male ($F_{2,14} = 4.8, p = .03$); decamping by fru^1 male ($F_{2,14} = 4, p = .046$); fencing by fru^1 male ($F_{2,14} = 6.75, p = .01$) [12].

	orientation	following	tapping	fencing	wing extension	wing flicks	licking	grooming	walking	standing	abdobend	decamp
♂f vs ♂	0.07	0.16	0.27	0.02	0.04	0.01	0.13	0.03	0.39	0.27	0.01	0.03
♂f vs ♀	0.04	0.10	0.16	0.00	0.14	0.05	0.15	0.06	0.24	0.08	0.00	0.09*
♂ vs ♀	0.44	0.49	0.18	0.00	0.17	0.04	0.11	0.00	0.11	0.08	0.08	0.00

♂f is *fruitless* mutant male, ♂ is wild-type mature male, ♀ is mature virgin wild-type female. * -implies statistically significant difference from other entries in row.

Table 6.2.A Occurrence of individual elements as fractions of total number of patterns detected from *fruitless* mutant male courter (mean of individual ratios).

	wing flicks	kicking	decamp	grooming	Standing	walking
♂ vs ♂f	0.01	0.00	0.00	0.03	0.10	0.20
♀ vs ♂f	0.00	0.00	0.00	0.01	0.40	0.42
♀ vs ♂	0.01	0.03	0.00	0.01	0.15	0.42

♂f is *fruitless* mutant male, ♂ is wild-type mature male, ♀ is mature virgin wild-type female.

Table 6.2.B Occurrence of individual elements as fractions of total number of patterns detected from mature virgin wild-type female (mean of individual ratios).

6.3.4   Characteristic interactions within patterns of each dyad group

Patterns obtained within each dyad group were aligned to each other to construct a pattern that is common within each dyad group. This gave an idea of how the elements of the courter and courtee interact with each other. The *fru*[1] male and mature wild-type male dyad group shows for the common pattern that: i) elements of *fru*[1] male are not interspersed with those of the mature wild-type male. ii) there is only one element contributed by mature male (Fig. 6.1A). The *fru*[1] male and mature virgin wild-type female dyad group shows for the common pattern that: i) elements from *fru*[1] male and mature virgin wild-type female do not intermingle ii) mature virgin wild-type female contributes about a third of the elements of the pattern (Fig. 6.1B). Finally, the mature wild-type male and mature virgin wild-type female dyad groups show that for the common pattern: i) the elements of the female are widely distributed among the male's; ii) female contributes about a third of the elements of the pattern; iii) there are characteristic pairings of elements, with one from the male and the other from the female, in each case (Fig. 6.2).

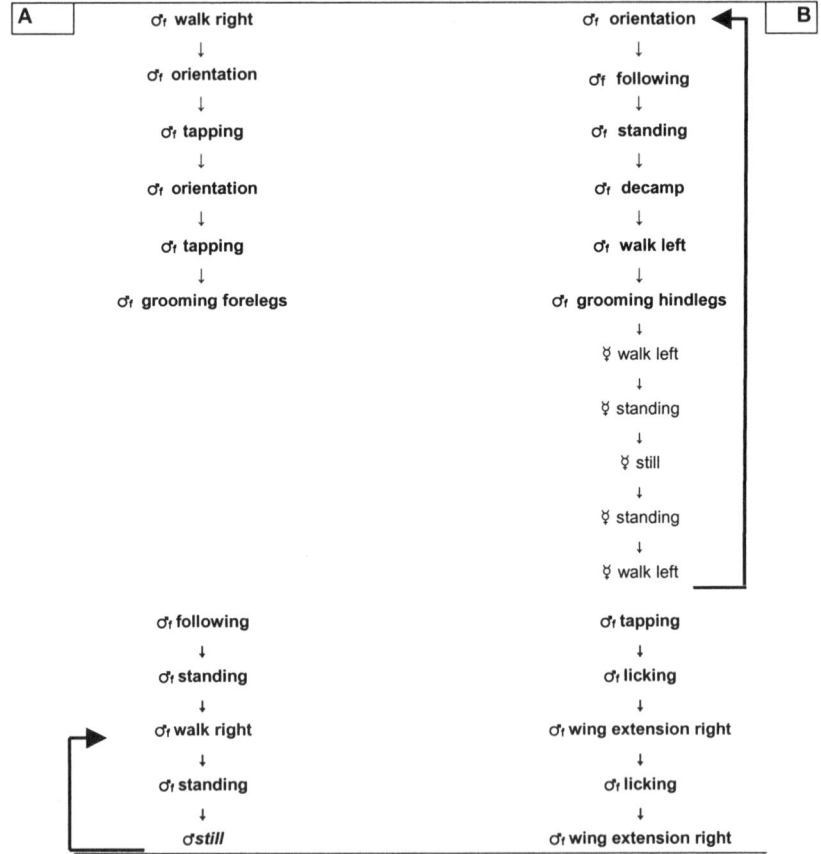

♂₁ is *fruitless* mutant male with elements in bold print, ♂ is wild-type mature male with elements in bold italics, ☿ is mature virgin wild-type female with elements in normal print.

Figure 6.1 Common patterns derived from aligning and selecting the overlapping pattern that occur in each dyad within a pairing group with *fruitless* mutant male as a courter A. Pairing of *fruitless* mutant male and a mature wild-type male B. Pairing of *fru*[1] mutant male with mature virgin wild-type female.

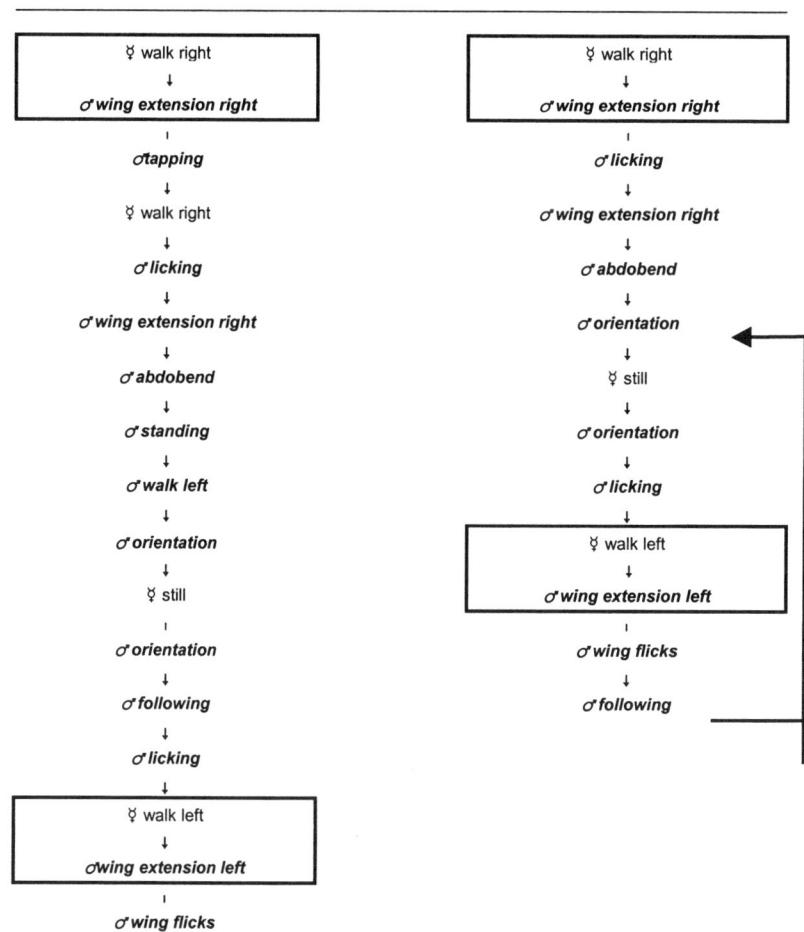

♂₁ is *fruitless* mutant male with elements in bold print, ♂ is wild-type mature male with elements in bold italics, ♀ is mature virgin wild-type female with elements in normal print. Two elements, one from each partner that appear always appear together are enclosed in the rectangles.

Figure 6.2 Common patterns derived from aligning and selecting the overlapping pattern that occur in each dyad within a pairing group of mature virgin wild-type female and mature wild-type male.

6.4   Discussion

Our approach enabled us to discover novel micro-behaviours that are invisible to the unaided eye at normal temporal resolution. We showed that high frequency of a behaviour element is no guarantee that it would contribute to a pattern. Furthermore, the analysis using THEME revealed some structures of the courtship behaviour architecture that were not apparent to the observer: It appears that *fru¹* males did not interact with their partners in sustained activity that was long enough to generate an integrated pattern (i.e. there was total segregation of the elements contributed by each partner to the common pattern for the dyad group). A similar result was obtained using nonlinear methods to extract salient components from the same data set [13]. This suggests that courtship display of *fru¹* male depends less on cues from the partner. Thus *fru^l* males require only a short trigger to initiate the male courtship program. The *fru^l* male displayed courtship behaviour similarly towards wild-type female or male partners, except that the females contributed more elements to the common pattern. Wild-type females contribute equally (i.e. about a third of elements) when courted by *fru^l* males or by wild-type males, but there is more interaction and wider distribution between the elements from wild-type males and females in a pattern (i.e. better integration). Characteristic pairings of some elements displayed by the dyad of wild-type male and female are suggestive of a type of syntax used in the communication.

Our findings show that this approach provides a new and deeper insight into the interaction and contribution of each partner in a dyad. The next steps would be to develop quantitative methods to compare patterns on basis of length and diversity of elements that compose the patterns, to develop a measure of complexity of the patterns and to decipher the grammar of a putative syntax. This would provide an even more detailed account of the courtship behaviour and a basis for comparison between different dyad groups.

6.5   References

[1]   J. C. Hall, The mating of a fly, *Science* **264** (1994) 1702-1714.

[2]   R. J. Greenspan and J. F. Ferveur, Courtship in *Drosophila, Annual Review of Genetics* **34** (2000) 205-232.

[3]   B. S. Baker, B. J. Taylor, and J. C. Hall, Are complex behaviors specified by dedicated regulatory genes? Reasoning from *Drosophila, Cell* **105** (2001) 13-24.

[4]   B. J. Taylor, A. Villella, L. C. Ryner, B. S. Baker, and J. C. Hall, Behavioral and neurobiological implication of sex-determining factors in *Drosophila, Developmental Genetics* **15** (1994) 275-296.

[5]   H. B. Dowse, J. M. Ringo, and K. M. Barton, A model describing the kinetics of mating in *Drosophila, Journal of Theoretical Biology* **121**(2), (1986) 173-183.

[6]   T. A. Markov and S. J. Hanson, Multivariate analysis of courtship in *Drosophila, Proceedings of the National Academy of Sciences of the United States of America* **78** (1981) 430-434.

[7]   D. A. Gailey and J. C. Hall, Behavior and cytogenetics of *fruitless* in *Drosophila melanogaster*: different courtship defects caused by separate, closely linked lesions, *Genetics* **121** (1989) 773-785.

[8]   L. C. Ryner, S. F. Goodwin, D. H. Castrillon, A. Anand, A. Villella, B. Baker, J. C. Hall, B. J. Taylor, and S. A. Wasserman, Control of male sexual behavior and sexual orientation in *Drosophila* by the *fruitless* gene, *Cell* **87** (1996) 1079-1089.

[9]   A. Villella, D. A. Gailey, B. Berward, S. Ohshima, P. T. Barnes, *et al.*, Extended reproductive roles of the *fruitless* gene in *Drosophila melanogaster* revealed by behavioral analysis of new *fru* mutants, *Genetics* **147** (1997) 1107-1130.

[10]   M. S. Magnusson, Hidden real-time patterns in intra- and inter-individual behavior: description and detection, *European Journal of Psychological Assessment* **12**(2), (1996) 112-123.

[11]   M. S. Magnusson, Discovering hidden time patterns in behavior: T-patterns and their detection, *Behavior Research Methods, Instruments and Computers* **32**(1), (2000) 93-110.

[12]   R. R. Sokal and F. Rohlf, *Biometry*, 3rd ed. New York: W. H. Freeman, 1995.

[13]   B. I. Arthur and R. Stoop, *Drosophila m.* – where normal males tend to be female, and supermachos are *fruitless, Nonlinear sensors and sensory processing: Proceedings of* NOLTA *2004*, 2004.

7. Initial Interpersonal Attraction and Movement Synchrony in Mixed-Sex Dyads

Kikue SAKAGUCHI, Gudberg K. JONSSON,
Toshikazu HASEGAWA

Abstract. Rhythmic synchronization phenomena in interpersonal communication are classified into two, based on its temporal aspect and behavioural form similarity aspect. We focus on the temporal aspect, *movement synchrony*, the gestalt-like perception of movement rhythmicity or coordination. With the aid of THEME, we aim to describe it based on statistical definition of objective behavioural data. Behavioural synchronization phenomena can also be conceptualised according to the number of actors involved in synchrony (*self-synchrony* and *interactional synchrony*). In a waiting room situation, we unobtrusively videotaped initial interaction of unacquainted mixed-sex dyads, and investigated whether movement synchrony between a dyad related with the formation of interpersonal attraction. Participants' behaviour in the first and last minutes of initial 10-minute interaction was coded frame by frame. Movement synchrony measures calculated from it related with a participant's interest in the partner more strongly in the first minute than in the last minute. However, the relationships were mostly explained by the increase of movement frequency. A movement synchrony measure that remained to be a significant signal was the repetitiveness of behaviour time-sequences. A dyad with a male participant interested in the partner decreased the repetitiveness of movement synchrony in the first minute. On the other hand, a dyad with a female participant who reported frequent sexual approaches by male strangers showed increase in the repetitiveness of movement synchrony. It suggested that such behavioural characteristics of frequently approached women tend to be interpreted as a courtship-like signal by male strangers. Only among dyads with frequently picked up women, the increase of female self-synchrony patterns positively correlated with male interest in her, circumstantially supporting the explanation.

Keywords: Movement synchrony; interpersonal attraction; rhythm; sexual approach

Contents

7.1   Introduction

7.1.1   Movement synchrony: one definition of rhythmic behavioural synchrony

From the pioneering work of Condon and Ogston [1], the importance of movement timing matching in smooth, friendly communication has been suggested among behavioural scientists, and efforts have been made to empirically describe phenomenon and explore its significance in interpersonal communication. Condon and Ogston filmed natural dyadic interaction, examined the films frame by frame, and coded points when the movement direction and speed of each body part changed. The work impressively demonstrated that in communication, etic segmentations of articulated speech correspond with changes of direction and speed of interactants' body parts. Such matching of movements was observed to occur with small time-lag (less than 50 ms [2]), suggesting its unconscious, automatic formation.

Condon and Ogston [1] revealed that bodily "dance" of interactants is inherent in normal communication, and the main point of the described phenomenon was the precise matching of movement timing within individual (*self-synchrony*) and inter-individuals (*interactional synchrony*). However, their coding method was extraordinary time consuming, and simplified method of it may lead to a spurious conclusion [3]. Even when coding is correctly applied, there was difficulty in describing statistically meaningful differences in forming behavioural synchronization. Bernieri and his colleagues relied on raters' perception instead, and explored the relationship between behavioural synchrony phenomena and rapport among interactants [4-6]. Raters viewed interaction clips and rated the degree of (a) simultaneous movement, (b) tempo similarity, (c) coordination/smoothness, and (d) posture similarity, as synchrony variables. The results revealed that raters were not able to discriminate among detailed aspects of temporal synchronization, but the distinctive aspects were *movement synchrony* (a, b, c) and *posture similarity* (d). Posture similarity does not concern with temporal aspects of behaviour so much, but movement synchrony refers to general impression of tempo coordination or entrainment between interactants.

Grammer, Kruck, and Magnusson [7] coded the beginnings and endings of interactants' behaviour catalogued from past ethological research, and analyzed time-patterns of them using THEME. The method defined the rhythmicity of interaction as repeated patterns of time structure of categorized movement, as *hierarchically patterned synchronization*. Patterns are characterized by similar time intervals between their components, and larger patterns are built up of smaller ones [8, 9]. This definition is similar to movement synchrony defined by Bernieri and his colleagues, in the respect that definition of interaction rhythmicity is based on gestalt perception of movement time structure, not solely on strict coincidence of movement timing.

However, some differences in synchronization phenomena covered by movement synchrony and hierarchically patterned synchronization should be noted. The definition by Grammer et al. [7] did not include which behavioural event types should constitute synchronous patterns, but because THEME searches for patterns using elaborate behavioural categorization adopted by the authors, the categorization necessarily affected what kind of patterns were detected. And also, they analyzed 10-minute interaction as a whole. Therefore time ranges of repeated behaviour patterns were broad, and detected patterns should have been differed from gestalt perception of movement rhythmicity occurring in short time spans. In this study, we modify rhythmic synchrony definition by Grammer et al., and use the patterns detected, using THEME, as objective measurement of movement synchrony. The targets for analyses are the first and last minutes of 10-minute interaction, 1-minute each. Behavioural categorization adopted is broader seven categories instead of 83 categories used in the previous study.

7.1.2 Does rhythmic synchrony indicate positive affection between first-met dyad?

Independent from the type of synchronization, the higher degree of synchronization is generally regarded to be a sign of higher degree of mutual rapport, involvement, and togetherness [10, 11]. However, the meaning of temporal aspect of behavioural synchronization in mutual rapport may change according to the degree of acquaintanceship. The formation of interest between opposite-sex interactants should also be considered with that prospect in mind.

Animals of many species and people in many cultures use dance in courtship. Coordination of rhythmical tempo [12, 13], and the repetition of *ritualized* (patterned) behaviour sequences [14] are regarded to be important aspects of it, functioning as mutual assessment process of coordination.

Perper [15] observed opposite-sex approaches in public places like bars, parties, trains, and so on. Intimacy developed in the sequence - approach, talk, turn, touch, synchronize, and it took from 15 minutes to over 3 hours. The synchronization reported by Perper seems to refer to the simultaneous and similar movement of interactants, thus containing both temporal and form aspects of synchronization. With regard to interaction between intimate couples, Weisfeld and Stack [16] reported that happily married couples tended to synchronize with in timing of expressing the same emotions, though they did not show baseline data comparative to it.

Does rhythmic synchrony play a significant role in initial interaction between first-met couples? The initial assessment of attractiveness and degree of interest in the first-met partner are reported to occur in a very short time span [17, 18], and such difference in affection may appear in behavioural synchrony. Bernieri et al. [6] filmed interaction between unacquainted mixed-sex dyads, and examined the relationships between movement synchrony and posture similarity in the second minute from the start of interaction, and rapport perceived by interactants. Both kinds of interactional synchrony positively correlated with the rapport reported by females but not with the rapport reported by males. Bernieri et al. concluded that this was because women are superior to men at nonverbal behaviour perception, and more attended to interactional synchrony phenomena as the socioemotional status of the interaction.

Grammer et al. [7] examined the relationship between hierarchically patterned synchronization in the first 10-minute interaction and participants' reported interest in the opposite sex partner. They also found positive relationships with regard to female interest, not with regard to male interest. They associated the phenomena with the initiation of courtship with subtle female signals, sometimes reported on opposite-sex approaches in public places [15, 19, for a review, see 20]. Therefore, they assumed that women interested in a male partner manipulated synchronization behaviour.

Caution should be taken to regard the rhythmic synchrony as a sign of rapport or affection in initial interaction between first-met dyads. In comparison of the first and third minutes of mother-infant interaction, Bernieri et al. [5] found difference in the development of movement synchrony between true mother-infant dyads and unrelated, first-met mother-infant dyads. In the interaction of true mother-infant dyads, movement synchrony increased as the time passed. On the other hand, in the interaction of first-met mother-infant dyads, movement synchrony decreased as the time passed, to the degree of baseline, random occurrence. The result indicates that synchronization development in time series may differ according to the depth of relationship between interactants.

Another suggestion to caution the interpretation of rhythmic synchrony as the manifestation of positive affection comes from the work by Warner, Malloy, Schneider, Knoth and Wilder [21]. They did not measure nonverbal behavioural data, but analyzed rhythmicity of 40-minutes interaction as the cyclicity of vocal activity, using spectral analysis. As demonstrated by the work of Condon and his colleagues [1, 2, 22, 23], vocal activity should be tightly linked with interactants' movement. Warner et al. reported the curvilinear relationship between rhythmicity of interaction and the positive affect between interactants rated by observers. That is, the rated positive affect was the highest when rhythmicity level was intermediate, and was lower when rhythmicity level was very low or high. Therefore, as it was probably the case, in the first minute interaction of first-met mother-infant dyads in Bernieri et al. [5], high movement synchrony in initial interaction of unacquainted dyads may contain the dimension of nervousness manifestation, rather than an active solicitation signal. In the current study, we contrast the first and last minutes of 10-minute interaction of first-met dyads, and explore the development of movement synchrony in time series.

7.1.3   The aim of current research

The previous study of Grammer et al. [7] found positive correlation between hierarchically patterned synchronization and female interest in the male partner. However, questions whether women controlled interactional synchrony as a courtship signal and, whether they used male partner's movement as a "Zeitgeber (exogenous stimulus to give timing to start rhythm)," were left not fully answered.

To explore whether movement synchrony, in an initial opposite-sex encounter, has the function of a female courtship signal, the frequency of women's experiences of having been a target for picking up is considered as an independent factor. Frequently picked up women are reported to have characteristic personality traits such as unrestricted sociosexuality, high extraversion and openness (submitted) [24], and high self-monitoring (submitted) [25]. These personality traits are known to associate with the differences in nonverbal communication style. Especially, self-monitoring concerns with the tendency to strongly control one's expressions of emotion, responding to the keenly perceived needs of social environment. One possible strong cause for that some women experience frequent sexual approaches by strangers is, they emit courtship like movement signals though they may not mean or be aware of it [23]. Therefore, if high movement synchrony is a female solicitation signal in general, and if it is true in many populations, as was suggested concerning other subtle movement signals [26], dyads with frequently picked up women are expected to form more movement synchrony.

As mentioned before, the first and last minutes of the first 10-minute interaction of unacquainted mixed-sex couples are analyzed for movement synchrony using THEME. To identify the contribution of each sex's movement, measures of self-synchrony (time-patterns formed by only one individual) are calculated and their impact on interpersonal communication is examined.

7.2   Method

7.2.1   Overview

Interaction of unacquainted 47 mixed-sex couples was videotaped unobtrusively for 10-minute. After the interaction session, participants answered a questionnaire that assessed their interest in the partner, and the frequency of approaches by strangers they had experienced in daily lives. Recorded interaction was coded into beginnings and endings of categorized behaviour in time series, and their time-patterns were detected with THEME. Relationships between the measures of movement synchrony, interest in the partner, and the frequency of women's having been picked up were analyzed.

7.2.2 Participants

Forty-seven female (mean age 21.6 years, age range 19-24 years) and 47 male (mean age 20.6 years, age range 18-27 years) undergraduate and graduate students from universities in Tokyo, Japan, volunteered for "an experiment on communication with strangers". Male and female strangers were selected randomly to form 47 mixed-sex dyads. Age differences between the two participants of a dyad ranged from –6 to 6 (female age minus male age; M = 1.04). As the formation of rhythmic synchrony is timing-sensitive and assumed to be beyond conscious control, we informed participants about the video recording in recruitment, rather than relying on deception. Participants were given a small gift for their participation.

7.2.3 Setting and equipment

The observation room was 4.2 m long, and 2.8 m wide (Figure 7.1). The participants were seated approximately 1.3 m from each other, with an angle of 120 degrees between them. A pinhole surveillance camera (measuring 3.5 × 3.5 cm) was used to monitor the interactions between participants. The camera was mounted about 1.3 m above the floor in ductwork in the corner of the room. A colour television monitor and recording devices were placed in another room and were concealed from the participants.

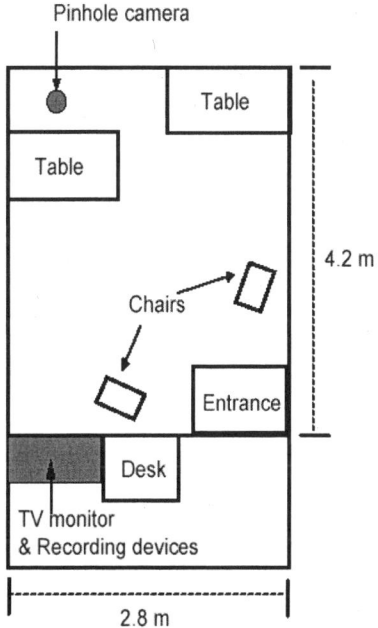

Figure 7.1 Floor plan of the observation room.

7.2.4   Procedures

A female researcher escorted one male and one female participant into the observation room. The researcher briefly introduced them to each other, but no instructions were made to encourage conversation. Then the researcher left the room to "continue setting up the experiment" creating a waiting room situation. This is a standard dyadic interaction paradigm in studies of unstructured interaction between unacquainted dyads [27]. A research assistant in the adjacent monitor room activated the video recording devices and a stopwatch, and the interaction of the dyad was recorded for 10 minutes. After five minutes, the researcher entered the observation room to explain a further delay and asked the participants to wait a little longer. When the 10-minute observation period ended, the researcher returned to the room. Each participant was taken into a separate room and filled out a questionnaire. The researcher then informed them that the experiment had been completed and debriefed the participants. The researcher also asked them for permission to use the videotape for analysis. All participants gave their permission.

7.2.5   Nonverbal behaviour data

Video-recorded data of the interactions of the 47 pairs were converted into digital *avi* files, 25 frames/s, on a Windows OS personal computer. The beginnings and endings of categorized movements for each participant, during the first and last minutes of the 10-minute interaction were coded frame by frame using special multimedia software (Video Coder for THEME, Beta version).

A catalogue of 83 categories of nonverbal behaviour adopted by Grammer et al. [7] was considered to be too detailed classification for the purpose of measuring rhythmic synchrony in this study. Therefore, we used broader categories. First, movements were categorized depending on the main body parts that acted (head, hand, leg, trunk). Second, categories of major nonverbal behaviour that are often studied by themselves were included. Consequently, the following seven categories were used to code behaviour: three categories of head movement i. e. (1) looking at the partner, (2) nodding, (3) other head movements; two categories of hand and arm movements, i.e. (4) gestures, (5) automanipulation; touching one's body or clothes, (6) leg movements, and (7) trunk movements. Coded beginning and end points on video frames were the *raw data points* of movement occurrences.

The reliability and robustness of behaviour coding based on the broader 7-category system was tested. Four one-minute time periods, randomly chosen from the entire dataset, were used for testing. Pearson correlations were calculated between the coded data of a trained researcher and an independent coder who was untrained about detailed discrimination criteria of the coding system. High reliabilities were observed for looking at the partner, gestures, manipulation, and leg movements ($r = .83 \sim .97$, n = 4). Correlations in the other three categories did not reach .80. Disagreement was caused mostly by confusion between nodding and other head movements, and there were differences in response to the criterion for detecting trunk movements. Correlations including all categories were moderately high ($r = .78$, n = 4), and the data coded by the researcher were used in the subsequent analyses. The standard deviation of frame differences between matched events coded by two raters was 15 frames. This rather large discrepancy was derived from the difference and limit of the personal computer's processing parameters.

THEME analyzed time-patterns of coded behaviour (T-*patterns*). Patterns were formed automatically (bottom-up) from coded events, based on the repeated appearance of behavioural sequences with a significantly similar time structure, for example, the end of the male looking at the partner followed the beginning of female nodding with a four second interval. If this behaviour sequence appeared more than twice in the one-minute observation period, it was detected as one kind of T-pattern (Figure 7.2). Each dyad formed many different patterns, each of which was repeated a certain number of times. The average repetition times for one kind of pattern can be calculated. The other measures, pattern length and pattern level, represent the complexity of the pattern cluster. Behavioural measures used in this study were as follows:

1. Number of raw data points (conventional movement frequency)
2. Number of different patterns (variability of T-patterns)
3. Average pattern length (complexity of T-patterns)
4. Average pattern level (complexity of T-patterns)
5. Average pattern repetition

T-pattern measures (2) – (5) were used to describe the quality of dyadic interaction from the aspect of movement synchrony. To attend to rhythmic aspects of gestalt-like movement patterns, contents of behaviour event types were disregarded in subsequent analyses.

Both self-synchrony (time-patterns of movements within an individual) and interaction synchrony were included to describe the characteristics of the interaction as a whole. Subsequently, to examine an individual's contribution to form rhythmicity of interaction, (2) the number of different patterns formed by each participant, outside the interactional synchrony was calculated.

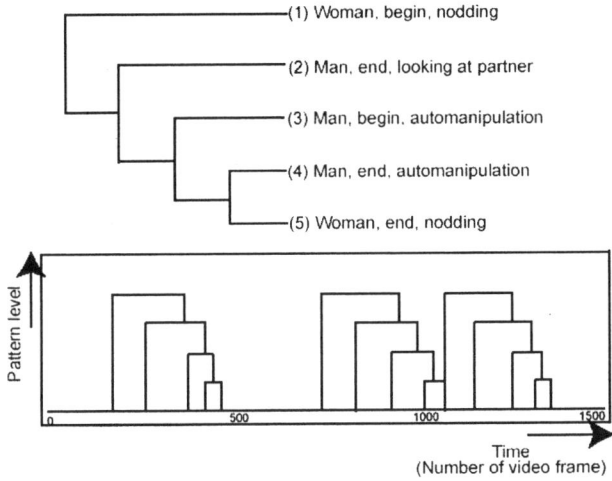

Figure 7.2 Upper: the inner structure of a T-pattern. Lower: time distribution of a repeated pattern. Example of one kind of pattern repeated three times, that is, the *number of different patterns* is one. *Pattern length* is five; one cluster contains five elements of movement. *Pattern level* is four; one cluster contains four nodes.

7.2.6 Questionnaire data

7.2.6.1 Interest in the partner participant

Participants answered questions about their degree of interest in the partner participant using 7-point Likert scales (1 = very unlikely, 7 = very likely). Interest was assessed by rating the following statements: (1) "I would give my telephone number to the partner if asked for it," and (2) "I would go out for lunch or dinner with the partner if asked". The Spearman rank correlation coefficient between these two items was .60 for women (N = 47, $p < .0001$), and .63 for men (N = 47, $p < .0001$). The two items were summed to form one composite score of *interest in the partner*, with a possible range of 2 to 14. The interest scores of both sexes were sufficiently variable (women: range 2-12, Mdn = 8.0; men: range 3-14, Mdn = 10.0). Female interest in the partner was independent of male interest in her (ρ = -.17, ns).

Estimation of the partner participant's interest in themselves was also rated on a 7-point scale: (1) "The partner would give his/her telephone number if I asked for it," and (2) "The partner would agree to go out for lunch or dinner with me if I asked." The Spearman rank correlation between the two items was .66 for women (N = 47, p < .0001), and .53 for men (n = 46 because of missing data, p = .0001). The two items were summed to form one composite score of *estimated interest of the partner*.

7.2.6.2 Frequency of being a target for picking up

Female participants answered a question about the frequency of (1) being approached or followed by strangers with apparent sexual intentions when walking in the street (being a target for picking up) since entering high school (i.e., after 15 years of age); (2) being a target for picking up before entering high school. Participants responded using a five-point scale (1 = never; 2 = 1-2 times; 3 = 3-5 times; 4 = 6-9 times; 5 = more than 10 times). They were asked about their experiences in these two periods of life to assess internal consistency within individuals. Participants reported that most of the sexual approaches were heterosexual.

Scores on both items did not correlate significantly with participants' age (p > .65, N = 47, Spearman rank, two-tailed; this condition was also applied to subsequent correlation analyses). This may look strange, but the effect of individual differences in the frequency of being approached is much stronger than the effect of age at participation [24]. Therefore it is plausible that we failed to find significant correlations in this age range and sample size of participants. The frequency scores of two periods of life significantly correlated with each other (ρ = .58, p < .0001), and a composite score of the two items were used in subsequent analyses as the frequency of being a target for picking up (possible score range: 2-10). Two subgroups of women were made based on this composite score; *rarely picked-up women*, with a score range of 2-4, n = 22, and *frequently picked-up women*, with a score range of 5–10, n = 25. In the last analysis, correlations between a participant's interest in the partner and behavioural measures in dyads were contrasted between dyads with two subgroups of women.

7.3   Results

7.3.1   Descriptive statistics of behaviour data

Among 47 dyads, the number of raw data points (measure 1) ranged from 14 to 160 (M = 119.1) in the first minute and from 22 to 153 (M = 112.1) in the last minute. From these, THEME found different time-patterns (2) ranging from 1 to 436 (M = 126.6) in the first minute and from 2 to 566 (M = 138.2) in the last minute. The number of patterns can be larger than the number of raw data points, because the same data point can belong to different T-patterns. The average pattern length (3) within a dyad ranged from 2.0 to 7.1 (M = 4.75) in the first minute and from 2.0 to 8.8 (M = 4.88) in the last minute. The average pattern level (4) ranged from 1.0 to 4.2 (M = 2.81) in the first minute and from 1.0 to 4.5 (M = 2.80) in the last minute. Average pattern repetitions (5) ranged from 2.0 to 4.0 (M = 2.63) in the first minute and from 2.0 to 3.4 (M = 2.69) in the last minute.

	1.	2.	3.	4.	5.
1. Number of raw data points	--	.84***	.68***	.72***	-.34*
2. Number of different patterns	--	--	.87***	.88***	-.53***
3. Average pattern length	--	--	--	.98***	-.41**
4. Average pattern level	--	--	--	--	-.45**
5. Average pattern repetition	--	--	--	--	--

Table 7.1 Intercorrelations between behaviour data, the first minute (N = 47) *Spearman rank, $p < .05$, **$p < .01$, ***$p < .0001$.

As is shown in Table 7.1, these behaviour data were strongly intercorrelated with each other. Though detected time-patterns were non-random patterns statistically calculated with THEME, if number of raw data points (conventional movement frequency) strongly correlated with movement synchrony measures, there is a possibility that movement synchrony was a redundant explaining factor in this interactional situation. Therefore, in subsequent analyses, partial correlations controlling the number of raw data points were also considered.

7.3.2 Movement frequency and interest in the partner

Correlations between the number of raw data points (measure 1) of a dyad in each observation period, the frequency of a woman's being a target for picking up and interest in the partner were calculated. The frequency of being a target for picking up did not significantly correlate with the number of raw data points. Female interest in the partner and male interest in the partner both significantly positively correlated with the number of raw data points in the first minute (female interest, $\rho = .32$, $p = .03$; male interest, $\rho = .29$, $p = .05$), but not with the number of raw data points in the last minute ($ps > .30$).

To explore the movement frequency of which sex more reflected the interest of a participant, the number of raw data points of female movements and that of male movements were separately examined for correlations with the interest of a participant. The only significant correlation found from eight possible combinations (2 observation periods × data points of 2 sexes × interest of 2 sexes) was raw data points of male participants in the first minute and male interest ($\rho = .33$, $p = .02$). The number of raw data points of either sex had no significant correlations with the frequency of a woman's being a target for picking up.

To summarize these results is; the interest of a participant was more apparent in the behaviour at the very beginning of an interaction, and male interest more directly related to his movement frequency.

7.3.3 Movement synchrony measures, the frequency of having been a target for picking up and interest in the partner

Correlations between movement synchrony measures (measures 2-5) of a dyad, the frequency of a woman's having been a target for picking up and interest in the partner were calculated. As is shown in Table 7.2, in the first minute of an interaction, both female interest and male interest correlated with movement synchrony measures. More numerous kinds, more complex, and less repeated time-patterns indicated higher interest of participants. On the other hand, dyads with frequently picked up women tended to form more repeated behavioural time-patterns.

	Female picked up	Female interest	Male interest
2. Number of different patterns	-.05	.23	.33*
3. Average pattern length	-.04	.25†	.27†
4. Average pattern level	-.06	.29*	.32*
5. Average pattern repetition	.28†	-.21	-.38**

Table 7.2: Correlations between movement synchrony measures and questionnaire data, the first minute (N = 47). †Spearman rank, $p < .10$, *Spearman rank, $p < .05$, **$p < .01$.

In the last minute of a 10-minute interaction, no significant correlations were found at the 10% significance level. As described in the preceding section, the interest of a participant was revealed to be more apparent in behaviour at the very beginning of an interaction.

7.3.4   Partial correlations of movement synchrony measures and questionnaire data

To explore the significance of movement synchrony measures besides the effect of mere movement frequency, correlations between synchrony measures and questionnaire data, statistically controlling for the number of raw data points were calculated.

Note the decrease of absolute values of correlation coefficients concerning interest of a participant in the partner. On the other hand, with regard to the frequency of female experiences of having been a target for picking up, changes of coefficient values were minor. Correlations remained significant after controlling for movement frequency were the one between pattern repetition and the frequency of a woman's having been picked up, and the one between pattern repetition and male interest in the partner. As is the same with zero-order correlations, no significant correlations were found in the last minute of a 10-minute interaction.

	Female picked up	Female interest	Male interest
2. Number of different patterns	-.06	-.07	.17
3. Average pattern length	-.04	.05	.11
4. Average pattern level	-.07	.09	.16
5. Average pattern repetition	.30*	-.12	-.32*

Table 7.3 Partial correlations between movement synchrony measures and questionnaire data, the first minute (N = 47) *Spearman rank, $p < .05$.

The results indicate that the relationship between the complexity of movement synchrony and interest of a participant in the partner in the first minute was basically derived from the effect of frequent movement. A movement synchrony measure that was likely to have a function as a nonverbal signal beyond movement frequency was the average pattern repetition. That is, dyads with frequently picked-up women developed more repeated manneristic behaviour sequences, and higher male interest in the partner related with the reduced repetition of manneristic behaviour sequences.

7.3.5   Self-synchrony and a participant's interest in the partner

Movement synchrony measures considered so far included both self-synchrony and interactional synchrony. To examine behavioural characteristics of each sex independent of the interactive behaviour of the two, self-synchrony of each sex that was not included in interactional synchrony was considered. In the whole sample (N = 47), the number of different behavioural patterns (measure 2) within each sex did not have a significant correlation with the frequency of a woman's being a target for picking up, nor with a participant's interest in the partner.

Consequently, correlations between the number of self-synchrony patterns and interest in the partner were contrasted between the two subgroups based on the frequency of a woman's being a target for picking up (Table 7.4).

Self-synchrony	Female interest	Male interest	Female interest	Male interest
	Rarely picked up (n = 22)		*Frequently picked up* (n = 25)	
	The first minute			
Female patterns	-.06	-.19	.01	.49*
Male patterns	.37†	.30	.09	.07
	The last minute			
Female patterns	-.05	-.15	-.04	.36†
Male patterns	-.08	-.17	.05	-.07

Table 7.4 Correlations between self-synchrony within one sex and interest in the partner. †Spearman rank, $p < .10$, *Spearman rank, $p < .05$.

There was a trend of a positive correlation between self-synchrony within a man and female interest in him, in dyads with rarely picked-up women, in the first minute of the interaction. On the other hand, in dyads with frequently picked-up women, positive correlations were found between self-synchrony within a woman and male interest in her, though the correlation was somewhat weaker in the last minute of the observation period.

The results indicated that synchronization of female behaviour correlated positively with male interest in the woman, among dyads with frequently picked-up women. And such sex roles tended to reverse in dyads with rarely picked up women. Then, did interest of a participant precede self-synchrony of the opposite-sex partner, or was it the other way around? There is indirect evidence to reject the former possibility: That is, both sexes were bad estimators of the partner's interest in themselves (Spearman's rank correlations between a participant's interest in the partner and the partner's estimation of it: $ps > .24$, N = 47, for female estimation and male estimation), so it is rather unlikely that a participant sympathized with the partner's attention and its physical response appeared on higher self-synchronous behaviour. When the other way around is more likely, the interpretation is that among dyads with frequently picked up women, a woman's self-synchronous movement attracted male interest in her, but it did not occur among dyads with rarely picked up women.

7.4   Discussion

We explored the relationship of initial attraction between an unacquainted mixed-sex dyad and their behavioural signals, from the perspective of movement synchrony. The results demonstrated that the relationships were stronger at the very beginning of interaction, and much weaker at the latter stage of interaction. In the first minute, male interest in the partner as well as female interest related with higher movement synchrony.

This may look contradict to the results of the previous study [7], that reported more complex hierarchically patterned synchronization in the initial 10-minute related only with female interest, not with male interest. However, our coding method restricted time ranges for analyses to short, and this seems to have enabled to capture movement synchrony phenomenon at very the beginning of interaction and its significance to the interpersonal attraction formation. Some studies reported that in interaction of unacquainted dyads, movement signals are heightened in the first one or two minutes [5, 17, 28], and settle down in the latter minutes. The current study suggested the function of the initial signaling as an interpersonal assessment and interest formation phase. In this phase, complexity of movement synchrony (i.e. pattern length and pattern level) was rather a secondary product of movement frequency, and a pattern repetition was a more significant measure (Table 7.3).

With regard to differences in nonverbal signals between frequently picked up and rarely picked up women, only among dyads with frequently picked up women, were positive correlations found between female self-synchrony and male interest in her (Table 7.4). Are there any possible behavioural characteristics among frequently picked up women that might have brought about such relationship? That is the high pattern repetition of movement synchrony among dyads with frequently picked up women (Table 7.3). Note that such increased repetitiveness of behavioural patterns was not explainable by the mere increase of movement frequency, implying that it is subtle but may have the special significance as a communication signal. As behavioural ecological study suggests, high repetitiveness of manneristic behavioural sequences is one important aspect of courtship signals [14]. Therefore, it is plausible to hypothesize that frequently picked up women, who possibly have personality characteristics of unrestricted sociosexuality and high self-monitoring (submitted) [24, 25], tend to unconsciously make more repeated rhythmically synchronous movement in an initial interaction with a male stranger, and as such synchronous movement increases, a man gets interested in her. Another, but not mutually exclusive possibility is that frequently picked up women tend to react sensitively to the stressful situation with a male stranger, that was the cause of high repetitiveness of movement synchrony, and they tend to make patterns more when they unconsciously perceive the partner's interest in them. The examination of relationships between the personality traits and repetitive movement synchrony in a similar experimental setting will test the hypotheses.

Then, what is the function of reduced pattern repetition among dyads with men who were highly interested in the female partners? Our idea is that reduced repetitiveness of movement synchrony is a manifestation of a male drive to initiate patterns; a man moved more with increased interest in the partner (7.3.2), resulting in a more diversity of formed patterns (Table 7.2). This assumption concerns the hypothesis that a man may act as a zeitgeber (who gives the timing to form synchronous patterns) and a woman follows it and makes synchronous patterns more repetitive (this study) and more complicated [7]. Analysis of hierarchically patterned synchrony in interaction with allocation of speaker/listener roles (unpublished data) gives collateral evidence: The public self-consciousness of a *listener* positively correlated with the complexity of synchrony, but with regard to a *speaker*, negative correlations with the repetitiveness and interactiveness were observed in a certain situation. In summary, an unobtrusive, observational experimental design left causal association concerning movement synchrony unresolved but has raised many interesting questions to deal with in further studies in this area. The current study underlines the importance of using advanced methods and tools, such as THEME, to study movement synchrony phenomena objectively. Movement synchrony may have significance as a courtship-like communication signal in quick interpersonal assessment and interest formation between first-met dyads, and the movement of male participants was also actively involved in such relationship.

7.5   References

[1]   W. S. Condon and W. D. Ogston, Sound film analysis of normal and pathological behavior patterns, *Journal of nervous and mental disease* **143** (1966) 338-347.

[2]   W. S. Condon, Cultural microrhythms, in *Interaction Rhythms: Periodicity in Communicative Behavior*, M. Davis, ed. New York: Human Sciences Press, 1982, pp. 53-77.

[3]   J. B. Gatewood and R. Rosenwein, Interactional synchrony: Genuine or spurious? A critique of recent research, *Journal of nonverbal behavior* **6** (1981) 12-29.

[4]   F. J. Bernieri, Coordinated movement and rapport in teacher-student interactions, *Journal of nonverbal behavior* **12** (1988) 120-138.

[5]   F. J. Bernieri, J. S. Reznick, and R. Rosenthal, Synchrony, pseudosynchrony, and dissynchrony: Measuring the entertainment process in mother-infant interactions, *Journal of personality and social psychology* **54** (1988) 243-253.

[6]   F. J. Bernieri, J. M. Davis, R. Rosenthal, and C.R. Knee, Interactional synchrony and rapport: Measuring synchrony in displays devoid of sound and facial affect, *Personality and social psychology bulletin* **20** (1994) 303-311.

[7]   K. Grammer, K. B. Kruck, and M. S. Magnusson, The courtship dance: Patterns of nonverbal synchronization in opposit-sex encounters, *Journal of nonverbal behavior* **22** (1998) 3-29.

[8]   M. S. Magnusson, Hidden real-time patterns in intra- and inter-individual behavior: Description and detection, *European journal of psychological assessment* **12** (1996) 112-123.

[9]   M. S. Magnusson, Discovering hidden time patterns in behavior: T-patterns and their detection, *Behavior, research, methods, instruments and computers* **32** (2000) 93-110.

[10]   T. L. Chartrand and J. A. Bargh, The chameleon effect: The perception-behavior link and social interaction, *Journal of personality and social psychology* **76** (1999) 893-910.

[11]   H. S. Friedman, M. R. DiMatteo, and A. Taranta, A study of the relationship between individual differences in nonverbal expressiveness and factors of personality and social interaction, *Journal of research in personality* **14** (1980) 351-364.

[12]   I. Eibl-Eibesfeldt, *Human Ethology*. New York: Aldine De Gruyter, 1989.

[13]   H. E. Fisher, *Anatomy of Love: A Natural History of Mating, Marriage, and Why We Stray*. New York: Ballantine, 1992.

[14]   J. R. Krebs and R. Dawkins, Animal signals: Mind-reading and manipulation, in: Behavioural ecology. An evolutionary approach, in *Behavioral ecology: An evolutionary approach, 2nd ed.*, J. R. Krebs, N. B. Davies, Eds. Oxford: Blackwell, 1984, pp. 380-402.

[15]   T. Perper, *Sex Signals: The Biology of Love*. Philadelphia: ISI Press, 1985.

[16]   C. C. Weisfeld, M. A. Stack, When I look into your eyes, *Psychology, Evolution & Gender* **4** (2002) 125-147.

[17]   K. Grammer, *Signal der Liebe: Die biologischen Gesetze der Partnerschaft*. Hamburg: Hoffmann und Campe Verlag, 1993.

[18]   P. J. Locher, R. Unger, P. Sociedade, and J. Wahl, At first glance: Accessibility of the physical attractiveness stereotype, *Sex Roles* **28** (1993) 729-743.

[19]   M. M. Moore, Nonverbal courtship patterns in women: Context and consequences, *Ethology and sociobiology* **6** (1985) 237-247.

[20]   M. M. Moore, Nonverbal courtship patterns in women: Rejection signaling. An empirical investigation, *Semiotica* **118** (1998) 201-214.

[21]   R. M. Warner, D. Malloy, K. Schneider, R. Knoth, and B. Wilder, Rhythmic organization of social interaction and observer ratings of positive affect and involvement, *Journal of nonverbal behavior* **11** (1987) 57-74.

[22]   W. S. Condon and W. D. Ogston, A segmentation of behavior, *Journal of psychiatric research* **5** (1967) 221-235.

[23]   W. S. Condon and L. W. Sander, Neonate movement is synchronized with adult speech. Integrated participation and language acquisition, *Science* **183** (1974) 99-101.

[24]   K. Sakaguchi and T. Hasegawa, Personality correlates with the frequency of being a target for unexpected approaches by strangers, (submitted).

[25]   K. Sakaguchi and T. Hasegawa, Predictors of unexpected approaches by strangers: With impression ratings of natural gait, (submitted).

[26]   K. Grammer, H. Honda, A. Schmitt, and A. Juette, Fuzziness of nonverbal courtship communication. Unblurred by motion energy detection, *Journal of personality and social psychology* **77** (1999) 487-508.

[27]   W. Ickes, V. Bissonnette, S. Garcia, and L. L. Stinson, Implementing and using the dyadic interaction paradigm, in *Review of Personality and Social Psychology: Volume 11, Research Methods in Personality and Social Psychology*, C. Hendrick and M. Clark, Eds. Newbury Park: Sage, 1990, pp. 16-44.
[28]   K. Grammer, K. Kruck, A. Juette, and B. Fink, Non-verbal behavior as courtship signals: the role of control and choice in selecting partners, *Evolution and human behavior* **21** (2000) 371-390.

HIDDEN PATTERNS IN NON-VERBAL COMMUNICATION WITHIN THERAPEUTIC CONVERSATION

Only about 8% of all psychological research is based on any kind of observation. A fraction of that is programmatic research. And, a fraction of that is sequential in its thinking.
Possibly, the still relatively limited offer of domain-specific methods and tools is a part of the explanation. In any case, seems that useful types of hidden patterns in behavior need to be formally defined and methods adapted or created for their detection.

Magnusson, 2000

Everyday interaction depends on a subtle relationship between what we express in words and what we convey through numerous forms of non-verbal communication. For this reason, non verbal communication, both of the patient and the therapist, is considered as an important aspect of the therapeutic process. In particular, non verbal cues play a critical role in the patient-therapist relationship and in the final outcome of the intervention.

To deepen these points this section includes four chapters concerning the analysis of non verbal communicative interactions in therapeutic settings through the use of THEME program. These contributions focused on the detection of real-time behavioural patterns and on their use as possible indexes to gain a higher level of awareness about how the therapy is going on.

In chapter 8 BLANCHET, BATT, TROGNON, and MASSE analyzed an interactive sequence between therapist and patient, extracted from a psychoanalytically oriented psychotherapeutic session. The authors observed and analyzed the verbal and nonverbal behaviour during communicative exchanges that encouraged patient to change his/her thinking about the cause of his/her symptoms. Identifying specific interactive conditions that occur when an insight is produced could be a very important element to improve the efficacy of the psychotherapeutic practice. The results show that therapeutic interventions first result in a deconstruction of the patient's initial point of view, followed by reinforcement of the patient's new point of view by means of confirmation. In this phase of reconstruction, the patient is led to reinterpret his symptoms along the lines encouraged by the therapist. In particular, the analysis of temporal patterns shows that (a) the deconstruction phase involves many non-verbal signs associated with challenges to the patient's statements, and (b) that certain themes in the patient's discourse are regularly associated, throughout the sequence, with gestures and hand movements that might constitute these themes' gestural signature.

Chapter 9, by HAYNAL-REYMOND, JONSSON, and MAGNUSSON, investigated the non verbal communication of suicidal patients. Many suicide patients are thought to disclose their intentions to their significant others (particularly in nonverbal ways), who too often fail to grasp these hints. Therefore, the authors studied patients' and doctor's facial behaviours and their interactive behavioural patterns, in order to get a better understanding on how they communicate at a nonverbal level. They hypothesized that, by correlating these variables with the patients' future suicide behaviour outcome, could be a very important index for improving the reliability of prediction and to make clinicians aware of them. The research analyzed video-recorded psychiatric interviews of patients admitted to the Geneva University Hospitals after a suicide attempt. After each interview the psychiatrist was asked to assess suicide risk on a 4-point scale. Facial expression was coded using Ekman and Friesen's "Facial Action Coding System" (FACS), and therapist interactive communication using THEME. Results indicate that non verbal communication of the therapist differed during the interview depending on the patient's tendency to repeat a suicide attempt: 81.8 to 90.9 % of the patients were correctly distinguished on the basis of the therapist-patient non verbal communication. Written predictions, instead, were not reliable: only 22.7 % of the patients were correctly classified. This could indicate that therapist had an accurate perception of risk, but lacked awareness.

Chapter 10, written by MERTEN and SCHWAB, investigated the differences between the facial expressions displayed by participants in psychotherapeutic situations and other dyadic common situations. Facial behaviour was coded using EMFACS (Emotional Facial Coding System). In particular, authors wanted to demonstrate the usefulness of the detection of Emotional Process Patterns (EPP) using THEME. E.P.P. contain information about emotional self-regulatory processes and about the quality of the relationship-regulation in social interactions. The results presented provided evidence that EPP are valid and useful indicators of individual and interactive emotional processes. In "everyday"-situations EPP are indicators of sex typical styles of relationship regulation and could be used as indicators for the severity of a mental disturbance. EPP are also substantial indicators of therapeutic processes and can be used as good predictors of therapeutic outcome. As predicted therapeutic outcome was worse if this involvement of the therapist on the level of spontaneous emotional behavior was high.

The last chapter of the section, 11, by RIVA, ZURLONI, and ANOLLI, linked therapeutic process and non verbal communication to computer-mediated communication, in particular to Virtual Reality. The current study was intended to describe patients' communicative style in a psychological treatment supported by Virtual Reality (VR). For this purpose, authors analyzed patients' non verbal communication during a therapeutic session while interacting with the therapist before and after VR exposure: patients were treated according to the Experiential-Cognitive Therapy (ECT), a new treatment protocol that integrates the use of VR with the traditional CBT (Cognitive-Behavioural treatment) strategy. 12 women affected by Panic Disorder with Agoraphobia were video-recorded; using THEME, a number of non-verbal indexes were considered to detect real-time behaviour patterns. The effect of VR on non-verbal communication was verified comparing PRE-VR and POST-VR conditions. All the T-patterns taken during the PRE-VR format have some interesting traits in common: the high level of emotional arousal seems to be strengthened by a continuous repetition of hand movements (i.e., "touching hairs") and trunk movements ("turn trunk") along many observed periods [43]. On the contrary, observed T-patterns during POST-VR condition show an increase of level complexity and of the ability of co-regulating different behavioral items. On one side, the present results indicate a reduced level of emotional arousal in POST-VR. On the other, the presence of different items expressing posture changing ("shoulder forward" and "trunk forward") and the frequent temporal sequences regarding smile items seem to outline an increase of the level of engagement of the subjects. This suggests the presence of a higher variety of bodily gestures that could be interpreted as a signal of self-control and of an increased ability in organizing conversational flow by the patients.

8. Language and Behaviour Patterns in a Therapeutic Interaction Sequence

Alain BLANCHET, Martine BATT,
Alain TROGNON, Laurence MASSE

Abstract. The goal of this study is to describe an interaction sequence between a therapist and a patient. This sequence is extracted from a psychoanalytically oriented psychotherapeutic session that was filmed and transcribed. The selected sequence meets a specific criterion: to observe and analyze verbal and non-verbal dialogue in a series of patient-therapist exchanges that encourage the patient to change his thinking about the cause of his symptoms. We seek to specify the interactive conditions under which a form is insight is produced that we consider the key and driving factor in all psychotherapy. Two types of analysis were conducted: a hierarchical semantic analysis and an analysis of temporal behaviour patterns using the THEME program. The results show that therapeutic interventions first result in a deconstruction of the patient's initial point of view, followed by reinforcement of the patient's new point of view by means of confirmation. In this phase of reconstruction, the patient is led to reinterpret his symptoms along the lines encouraged by the therapist. The analysis of temporal patterns shows that (a) the deconstruction phase involves many non-verbal signs associated with challenges to the patient's statements, and (b) that certain themes in the patient's discourse are regularly associated, throughout the sequence, with gestures and hand movements that might constitute these themes' gestural signature. Therapeutic influence, far from being ineffable and based on therapists' impenetrable charisma, derives from concrete actions and an interactional approach that can be described and used in the psychotherapeutic training of university students.

Keywords: Psychotherapy; language; behaviour pattern; THEME.

Contents

8.1   Introduction

Since the famous "cigarette scene," which describes in great detail a short sequence from a psychological interview between a therapist and his patient [1], few similar studies have been conducted until the present time. Is this because the author demonstrated the limitations of this type of study by addressing the problem of the level of observation and analysis of short interactive sequences? Or is it because the psychological interview seemed so complex that any precise description risked being reductive and therefore not generalisable? We have nevertheless decided to apply the techniques of language and behavioural analysis to a brief sequence from a psychoanalytically oriented psychotherapeutic interview. There currently seems to be a wide range of psychotherapeutic situations and therapeutic theories and within the same approach, practice seems to depend more on the therapist's personality than on any dogma or clinical manual [2]. In this landscape of undefined contours, we wanted to observe and describe how a therapist interacts with his patient. We believe that this interaction, which consists of encouraging a patient to change his viewpoint and discourse about a subject of direct concern to him, is the paradigm for all psychotherapy. We also think that psychotherapy is defined less by theory or the practice of this theory by patients and therapists than by the actions taken jointly by the therapist and patient. The common thread linking all psychotherapies may therefore reside in the similarity of concrete language and behavioural actions, even rituals, carried out in part or full by every psychotherapist. In our view, this perspective justifies the highly detailed analytical work that must be conducted to understand these various psychotherapeutic behaviours.

8.2   The therapeutic interaction

8.2.1   Evaluation of psychotherapies

Psychotherapeutic practices are observed in all contemporary cultures and they seem to have existed throughout history. They are consubstantial with human anxiety, cultural ritualisations and the existence of treatment practices. In today's environment of hundreds of psychotherapeutic techniques, the evaluation of their efficacy is more important than ever. The many studies conducted over the past 50 years [2] show that overall psychotherapies have little efficacy but are rather effective. The concept of efficacy involves the achievement of a specific goal (for example, the disappearance of a particular symptom), while the concept of effectiveness involves the non-specific effects of the therapy on the patient (for example, improvement in the patient's quality of life). In fact, overall studies or meta-analyses do not take into consideration the many different factors that occur during psychotherapy, which is a highly complex interactive situation. It has already been demonstrated [3] that therapeutic effectiveness is better explained by the relationship the professional establishes with his patient than by the application of a particular technique. These are non-specific factors inherent in any human relationship that allow us to explain the positive effects of any type of therapy. A number of factors characterizing this relationship have already been described [4], including the following: (i) an intense, emotional and trusting relationship with the helper, (ii) the use of a model or explanatory myth that allows the helper to understand the patient's suffering, (iii) the addition of new information and concepts concerning the nature of the patient's problems, their possible origin and possible alternative behaviours, (iv) an awakening of hope in the patient that he can be cured, based on his recognition of the therapist's personal and professional qualities, (v) the patient's experience of improvement, which strengthens his self-confidence and the psychotherapeutic treatment, and (vi) development of the patient's ability to feel and identity his emotions. In a recent publication, Lecomte et al. [5] provide a remarkable summary of this issue. They show that the patient-therapist relationship and the therapist's contribution to the establishment of this relationship is the best criterion for distinguishing between effective and less effective psychotherapy. These results, which demonstrate the importance of the patient-therapist relationship in psychotherapy, lead to recommendations about the training of psychotherapists and the need to conduct research that focuses on the behavioural characteristics of this very special interaction. In fact, any psychotherapy can be described as a sort of conversation that includes specific constraints.

8.2.2 A specific type of conversation

This conversation can be seen as having an asymmetric structure and being fundamentally oriented toward a process of influence.

The conversation's asymmetric structure results from differences between the patient's and therapist's degree of verbosity and nature of discourse. The patient primarily talks about his life, while the therapist listens and occasionally interrupts to reflect back, reorganize and interpret the patient's statements. The therapist therefore responds to the information communicated by the patient in real time. Three components – referential (state of the world), modal (psychological state) and illocutionary (intention to act) – are simultaneously taken into account but the illocutionary component, which represents the speech acts carried out by the patient, is an essential factor in the therapist's analysis of the patient's discourse [6].

The therapist's act of listening is not comparable to a recording of data. Instead, it produces meaningful activity, bringing about the operations of selection, inference and comparison relative to the interview's objectives. The act of listening is similar to diagnostic activity [7] as it seeks to evaluate behavioural changes and patient reactions in response to the therapist's promptings. It is fundamentally a process involving self-reflective awareness [8]. Indeed, the therapist's evaluation of his own interventions and their effects cannot rely solely on the patient's immediate responses, as we shall see. Because listening is driven by objectives, it is guided by prior hypotheses that are either based or not based on a theoretical frame of reference. It is a cognitive behaviour that consists of obtaining clues, producing hypotheses, interpreting these clues and testing the hypotheses by obtaining yet more clues.

During the interview, the psychotherapist constructs a meaningful structure, from which he develops interventions. These interventions convey to the patient an approximate reflection of the psychotherapist's listening techniques. They also help initiate the influence process that will allow the patient to reconsider the meaning he gives to his life and symptoms. This influence process triggers and drives the effects of change observed in patients' representations and behaviours [9]. The process is therefore comprised of factors that constitute the clinician's therapeutic function.

The quality of treatment is primarily based on the therapist's inferential behaviour. This behaviour does not rely on the concept of truth but on the notion of relevance. As a result [10], the efficacy and evolution of a therapeutic interview largely derive from the quality and validity of the therapist's clinical inferences and judgments. But what are the principles on which these therapeutic inferences are based? In other words, which principles distinguish these therapeutic inferences from conversational inferences? According to Labov and Fanshel [6], the therapist's listening behaviour mainly focuses on two phenomena that emerge from the patient's discourse: factual contradictions and emotional expression.

For example, in the case carefully analyzed by these authors, the patient, "Rhoda," presents with anorexia and discusses family problems involving her mother and aunt. Her mother has left the home to live with her other daughter and Rhoda lives her with her aunt (mother's sister), who makes her do all the household chores, including cleaning, shopping, cooking and dishwashing, in addition to her homework. The patient believes her behaviour toward her mother and aunt is irreproachable. For example, she called her mother to ask for help, but states that her mother never offers to help her. She made the same request of her aunt, but she states that her aunt does not give her any concrete help. As for her weight loss, the patient claims that she eats normally, but her weight is actually far from normal. The therapist cannot resolve these contradictions, but he observes them and underscores the importance of the problem by focusing his attention on the patient's verbal inconsistencies. According to Labov and Fanshel [6], this gives rise to the necessity to discover the patient's psychological defenses and the emotional problems that underlie her repeated failure to assert what she believes are her rights.

Emotional expression is largely conveyed by intonation. The authors demonstrate (by analyzing verbalization wavelengths) that the paraverbal system of the patient's discourse reflects an emotional semantics that is often taken into account by the therapist as he develops his understanding of the problem parallel with the patient's own understanding.

This therapeutic function is therefore closely related to the therapist's thought process, which leads the patient to recast his representational systems in a more efficient, and therefore more logical, manner. As a result, it can be demonstrated [11] that the therapist's interventions tend to create new semantic links between the major themes of the patient's discourse. The new verbal construction encouraged by the therapist is therefore essential to the effectiveness of treatment. This new verbal construction, however, cannot be dictated to the patient from the "outside"; the patient must develop his own new representations and conceptions. This change was described as a high point of therapy, during which the patient became more convinced of his beliefs. This heuristic process of an internal reshaping of beliefs is generally called "insight." To our knowledge, there are no studies that attempt to describe the language and behavioural interaction underlying the mechanism of patient insight.

The therapist's verbal and non-verbal interventions are technical tools whose objective is to modify the patient's discourse and, correlatively, his way of thinking. Curiously, there is little clinical and scientific literature that seeks to observe and explain the nature and effect of these interventions, while most case narratives give considerable weight to "the therapist's words, which have the power to cure." The famous study by Birdwhistell [1] discusses the methodological problems inherent in this type of analysis. In particular, it raises the following question: "At what level of description should we conduct the analysis using the defined units? With slow-motion and stop-action techniques, a single moment in time can be captured, following the example of the "cigarette scene" [1].

In this chapter, our objective is to describe the moment in which the patient modifies his representation in response to the therapist's encouraging attitude. We will describe all the language and behavioural processes involved in the development of interactive insight. To conduct this study, we selected an excerpt from a dialogue between a psychoanalyst and his patient – an excerpt that clearly includes a change in the patient's point of view in response to therapeutic interventions.

8.3   Therapeutic interaction sequence

To describe and analyze a therapist-patient interaction leading to a process of therapeutic change, we chose a sequence comprised of nine turns at speaking from a set of videotaped interviews. During this sequence, the patient, responding to the therapist's interventions, is encouraged to radically change his representation of reasons for taking heroin. The selected sequence satisfied several requirements. The sequence had to include a change in the patient's discourse (a statement made by the patient at the beginning of the sequence had to be modified by the same patient by the end of the sequence). This change had to clearly result from the effects of the therapist's interventions. The sequence had to be short so that the analysis could include the relevant verbal and non-verbal elements in the explanation for the observed change.

8.3.1 Analyzed data

The verbal data come from an interview between an experienced psychoanalyst specializing in the treatment of drug addicts and a patient who is a drug addict. The psychoanalytically oriented therapy is conducted face-to-face. The patient, age 30, has been addicted to heroin for several years and is undergoing withdrawal. The psychotherapy's goal is to support the patient during withdrawal and reduce the probability of a relapse. The interaction is excerpted from the third session.

8.3.1.1 Recording context and conditions
The sequence is recorded with the full agreement of the patient and therapist. Two video cameras (Figure 8.1) simultaneously filmed the patient and therapist in such a way that the final videotape shows a wide-angle frontal view of each person, including the tops of the legs. The sequence lasts one minute and 16 seconds.

Figure 8.1 Filmed sequence with two cameras

8.3.1.2 The actual sequence
(P1) Patient: I feel alive to some extent but at the same time, I feel like I've been dead for some time, you know? You see, I mean…
(T1) Clinician: Dead
(P2) Patient: Yeah, yeah, dead because I wasn't alive; it wasn't me who was alive. I was living through heroin. It wasn't me expressing myself, you know?
(T2) Clinician: You said "dead"; you didn't say "hibernating."
(P3) Patient: No, I can't say I was hibernating because somehow through heroin I was also searching for a kind of death.
(T3) Clinician: You think so?
(P4) Patient: Well, yeah, somehow I was…
(T4) Clinician: You thought that.
(P5) Patient: Yeah, it was kind of like self-destruction; at the beginning it was…

(T5) Clinician: You really think so?

(P6) Patient: Oh yeah, to be honest, yeah, to be honest. And then at the beginning, heroin made me feel pretty good; it let me express myself in a certain way.

(T6) Clinician: And then...

(P7) Patient: And then it started to really bother me, you know?

(T7) Clinician: Destruction if...

(P8) Patient: Yeah, no – but then, then, I found that heroin led to my destruction. I couldn't stand it anymore; it made me feel bad; it really bothered me, you know, but unfortunately I needed it to exist.

(T8) Clinician: To exist.

(P9) Patient: Yeah, to exist but at the same time I was showing off.

8.3.1.3 Descriptive analysis of the sequence

In this sequence, the therapist reacts to a statement made by the patient that does not meet the therapeutic objectives. In fact, the main hypothesis underlying this type of therapy is the concept that the patient is treating himself with drugs (self-medication). Psychotherapy can thus focus on the mental suffering that the person is seeking to alleviate with chemical substances. As a result, the therapist cannot allow the patient to say that he is taking drugs to kill himself. At the same time, this representation of death-seeking corresponds to a social stereotype that is not compatible with the therapeutic experience, which consists of saying what one feels. For the therapist, the patient's impression of being dead provides a less satisfactory account of the experience (its role in the subject's background and desires) than the impression of hibernation. The therapist therefore suggests a second version (T2) of the modality associated with taking drugs. The consent of the patient (P3) is indicated by the term "also."

This passage helps us better understand how a patient concept that the therapist believes to be mistaken or incomplete can be changed by suitable therapeutic interventions. All such interventions are geared toward one objective: to modify the patient's version of seeking death through drugs and to make sure he understands that drugs are filling a certain need, allowing him to treat his mental suffering. Treatment involves moving from one semantic framework to another, throwing lifelines likely to be accepted by the patient. These mediations provide the patient with a rationale that is more likely to lead to a favorable outcome. In this excerpt, the therapist's interventions (T1), (T3), (T4) and (T5) first reflect an implicit challenge to the patient's "resistant" point of view, then a logical conclusion (T6) and (T7) that reinforces the patient's modified discourse.

This sequence demonstrates how therapeutic persuasion and influence can change patient representations by:

a) encouraging patient discourse so that the therapist can gain an understanding of the patient's contradictions;

b) confronting the patient with his contradictions;

c) encouraging the patient to change his concepts in line with his own discursive logic.

8.3.2   Analytical method

First, we submitted the therapeutic interaction sequence to a hierarchical structural analysis to demonstrate the construction of the discourse during therapy. This analysis reveals the ways in which the interaction and discourse develop. We will show that the entire interaction is comprised of two complex components. One involves refinement and thematic explication while the other involves reinterpretation and thematic expansion.

Next, we will analyze the sequence using THEME software [12]. We will show how the behaviours of the therapist and patient are composed of meaningful patterns. We will focus on a joint analysis of verbal and non-verbal elements. With this analysis, we wish to demonstrate how the various components of the interaction work together. Verbal and non-verbal sign systems are not independent; an interlocutor uses both registers, verbal and non-verbal, to interpret the meaning of an utterance [13]. Moreover, we assume [14] that many different behavioural patterns will convey the intensity of the patient-therapist relationship.

8.3.2.1. Hierarchical semantic analysis

Analyzing the structural and functional organization of the conversation consists of studying the relationships among speech acts in order to understand the architecture of the resulting discourse. According to the Geneva theory [15], conversations are comprised of three components: the exchange [E], the intervention [I] and the speech act. Simple interventions are distinguished from complex interventions. A simple intervention means that one of the interlocutors speaks and therefore carries out a speech act [16]. A complex intervention includes speech acts, interventions and exchanges; as a result, conversations are analyzed on the basis of complex interventions [17]. An exchange is a linear series of at least two interventions uttered by two different interlocutors.

For example, figure 8.2, a formal diagram of a conversation excerpt, illustrates an initial model for structuring the various components. The diagram shows that during his first statement (P1), speaker P made an assertion, indicated as simple intervention I_{11}, after which speaker T, during his first statement (T1), made a request. T thus opens a first exchange (E_1), one of whose branches is the intervention containing the request and whose second branch is supposed to contain the response to this request. However, the expected response turns out to be complex because it is composed of several turns at speaking; in fact, the response itself generated a request, which waited for a response that also turned out to be complex, etc. One therefore observes that the more the conversation progresses according to this first structuring model, the further it strays from the initial question that awaited a response. The conversation thus progresses according to a retroactive or bottom-up structure. This structure is formally represented by a rightward expansion because, in order to diagram the structure, it is necessary to retrace the path of the conversation to the most dominant feature.

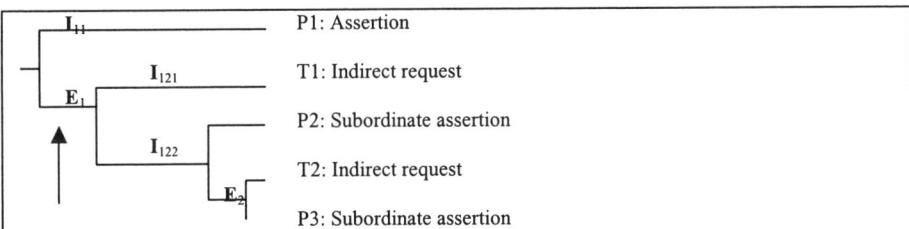

Figure 8.2 Retroactive and bottom-up structure

Figure 8.3 illustrates a second way of structuring the conversational components. On the one hand, exchange E_n makes way for intervention I_{n+1}, but on the other hand, the appropriation of exchange E_n takes place due to intervention I_{n+1}. In other words, the occurrence of component I_{n+1} in the conversation requires a reinterpretation of the previous component, E_n, because it is subordinate to I_{n+1}. The sequence (P8, T8, P9) progresses according to a proactive or top-down hierarchical structure and this structure is formally represented by a leftward expansion.

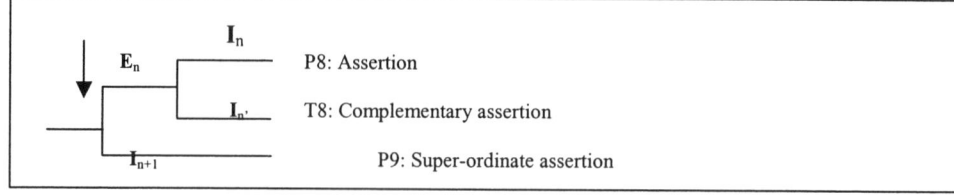

Figure 8.3 Proactive or top-down structure

This analysis illustrates interlocutors' subordinate or subordinating actions during a dialogue. It should be noted that the Geneva School [15] does not provide precise decision-making criteria for distinguishing a subordinating intervention from a subordinate intervention. According to other authors [17], analyzing the property of a speech act to which its successor is linked allows us to define the hierarchical structure of a conversation: *"negotiating the conditions of success for a request finds conversational expression in the appearance of a subordinate exchange"* ([17], p. 212).

8.3.2.2 Analysis of the temporal structure of THEME interactions
The temporal structure of interactions was analyzed using THEME software. It should be recalled that the basic principle underlying this software consists of revealing behavioural patterns in the patient-therapist dialogue as well as patterns in the behaviour of each individual. In the first stage, we selected frequent and obvious language and gestural behaviours that occurred during the sequence. To avoid the stumbling blocks of a microanalysis, such as the one conducted by Birdwhistell [1], we decided to select the most salient language and behavioural elements for encoding. This selection is based on the observable principles of communicative acts. From a language perspective, the selection includes speech actors, the major types of verbs used, key thematic references and different discourse markers. From a gestural perspective, the selection includes eye movements, direction of gaze, movements of the head, hands and fingers, and changes in posture. An encoding table was created for all encodings (Table 8.1).

ACT	B_E	SUJ	ATT	BUT	MOD	TEM	CON	YEU	REG	TET	EXP	MAI	DOI	POS
pa	b	p	cr	mo	o	av	ca	hau	dro	d	sou	ouv	tou	chg
th	e	t	di	vi	n	ap	ad	cli	gau	H	cri	fer	btt	
	:		ds	he	at	pd	op			g			cro	
	&		da	hi	pas	du								
	*				af									

Table 8.1 Encoding table. Legend: ACT: Actors (pa: patient; th: therapist); B-E: Beginning/End (b: beginning; e: end); SUJ: Subject uttered in the proposition (p: patient; t: therapist); ATT: Propositional attitude verb (cr: believe; di: say; ds: desire; da: bother;); MOD: Modalisation (o: yes; n: no; at: attenuation; pas: negation of phrase; af: affirmation); TEM: Modalisation of time (av: before; ap: after; pd: during; durant: for); CON: Connectives (ca: cause; ad: addition; op: opposition); YEU: Eyes (hau: up; cli: blinking); REG: Gaze (dro: right; gau: left); TET: Head (d: right; h: up; g: left); EXP: Expression (sou: smile; cri: tension); MAI: Hands (ouv: open; fer: closed); DOI: Fingers (tou: touching; btt: drumming; cro: crossed); POS: Posture (chg: change).

In the second stage, the beginning and end of the behaviours were encoded on a time scale of 1/25th of a second (Table 8.2). One observes that at 72/25[ths] of a second, the patient begins to raise his eyes, at $73/25^{ths}$ of a second, the therapist begins to blink his eyes, at $93/25^{ths}$ of a second, the therapist stops blinking his eyes, etc.

Time in 1/25th of a second	Events
...	...
72	pa,b,hau
73	th,b,cli
93	th,e,cli
106	pa,e,hau
108	pa,b,cli
110	pa,e,cli
123	pa,b,hau
147	th,b,cli
147	pa,b,vi
148	pa,e,hau
152	pa,e,dro
152	pa,e,tou
154	pa,b,btt
155	pa,b,ouv
...	...

Table 8.2 Table of behavioural and time data

In the third stage, the THEME software analyzed the behavioural and time data. The search for interactive patterns reveals behaviours that tend to occur together in a significant manner. For this analysis, we chose the significance level of $p < .001$.

8.4   Results

The results of the analysis indicate an initial hierarchical structure that conveys the therapist's and patient's speech acts and a second structure comprised of behavioural patterns that illustrate the intense relationship between therapist and patient at this stage, during which the patient's representations are being reshaped.

8.4.1   Hierarchical analysis

Viewed from above, this sequence is an example of embedding, with an upper-level structure comprised of two complex components: a complex constituent α (P1...P6), which gives rise to a subordinating complex constituent β (T6 ... P9). This is illustrated in figure 8.4.

8.4.1.1 Analysis of the sequence's first constituent: α
α is mainly comprised (4 times out of 5) of the clinician's (T) simple interventions and the patient's (P) complex interventions; the two speakers thus construct a series of five successive exchanges. The exchanges succeed one another in a relationship of subordination, with the last exchange, E_5, subordinated to the first, E_1, which can be represented as an embedding of brackets: $\{E_1[E_2[E_3[E_4[E_5\}$.

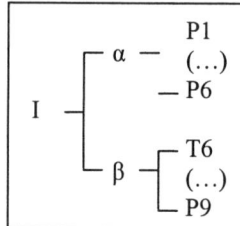

Figure 8.4 The sequence's two complex constituents

Figure 8.5 demonstrates that it is the clinician's implicit challenges [18] – during exchanges E_1, E_2, E_3, E_4, E_5 – that generate the opening of subordinate exchanges. The patient responds to the clinician's use of encouragers, which prevents a closing-off of the dialogue. These encouragers have the opposite effect of signs of agreement, which would have given rise to simple three-part exchanges [15]. As a result, the clinician keeps the dialogue going and due to T1, T2, T3, T4 and T5, the patient is encouraged to:

–   to explain (develop) what he means by, "I feel like I've been dead," arguing (elaborating) his point of view (enunciative justification)

–   explain and reaffirm his initial assertion (illocutionary justification)

–   support his utterance ("because" could, for example, be replaced by "since")

In these three cases, the Geneva School [15] supports an argument-directive act structure in which the argument, of course, is subordinate. It therefore appears that complex constituent α generally shows a rightward expansion (or bottom-up or retroactive) that locally integrates proactive levels (top-down, leftward structural development).

8.4.1.2 Analysis of the second constituent of the sequence: β
The second complex constituent, β, depends on the first series of exchanges. It is initiated by the clinician in T6 by the utterance of "then," a consecutive connective [15]; the second complex constituent β is thus in a subordinating position to the first major constituent α.

In this second part, the interaction allows the semantic contrast of "bad drug ("destruction") *versus* a good drug for self-treatment" to appear explicitly in P8. The connective, "but," in P8g invalidates and rejects the preceding utterances and gives way to a version in which the drug allowed the patient to treat his mental suffering. The strength of the reiteration ("to exist") in T8 leads to an intersubjective construction of this version. It is thus the process of influence (acceptance of the clinician's point of view) and the patient's reinterpretation of his initial discourse (death => to exist and to show off) that brings the exchange to an end. This is illustrated in figure 8.6.

An analysis of the sequence's hierarchical structure shows how the dialogue is conducted by the therapist, who indirectly encourages the patient to explain and justify his initial utterance by means of repetitions that implicitly challenge the patient's arguments. Afterwards, the patient is encouraged to reinterpret his reasons for taking drugs in line with the therapist's theory. The influence mechanism is apparent, but it also relies on non-verbal interactions.

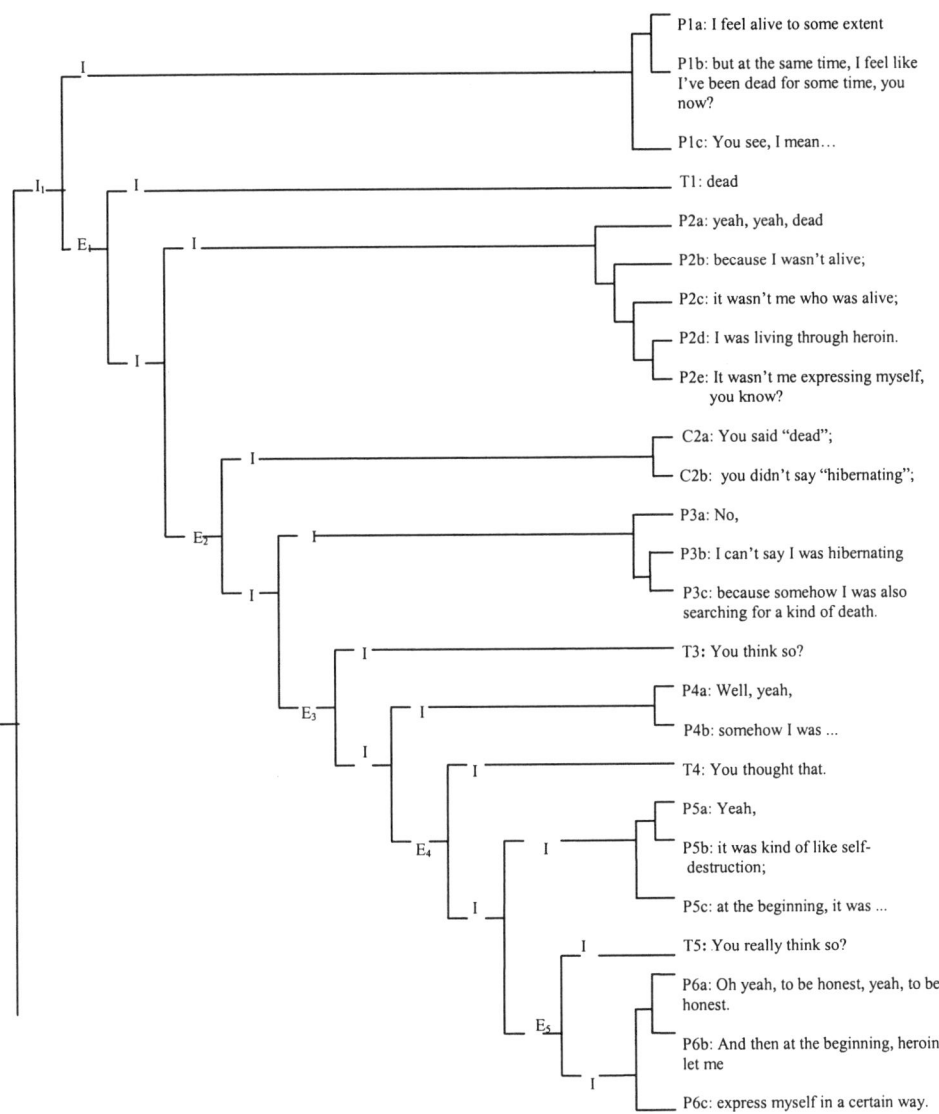

Figure 8.5 Complex constituent α

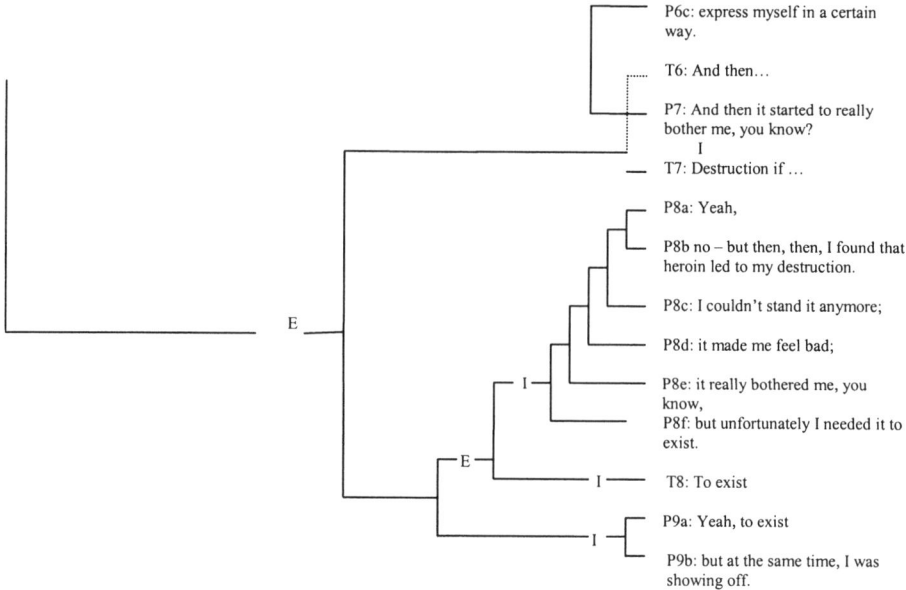

Figure 8.6 Complex constituent β

8.4.1.3. Overall analysis of the sequence

In part α (P1 to P6), the patient-therapist interaction is based on the therapist's indirect challenge to the patient's P1 assertion. In this first part, the therapist encourages the patient to develop a discourse that leads him to contradict his first P1 assertion. The therapist largely proceeds by indirectly challenging the patient's sincerity ("You think so?").

This stage is marked by a conflictual elaboration of the patient's discourse, which produces a deepening of this discourse.

In the second part, β, the exchange initiated by the intervention (T6) – "And then" – creates a collaboration aiming to draw conclusions from the new assertions uttered in the first part, α.

This phase is marked by a collaborative elaboration of the patient's discourse, which produces an expansion of this discourse.

8.4.2. Analysis of behavioural patterns

For this analysis, we are first going to consider the patterns that characterize the patient-therapist exchanges, then the patterns that appear in the patient's discourse. It should be recalled that the exchange includes a conflictual phase and a collaborative phase. The beginning of the collaborative phase (T6) is indicated in the figures illustrating these patterns.

8.4.2.1. Analysis of interactive patient-therapist patterns

The first pattern characterizes the linkage between the patient's discourse and the therapist's interventions. The "you think so" interventions follow the patient's attenuations, such as "to some extent, somehow, to be honest, in a certain way," after which the patient agrees by saying "yeah" (Figure 8.7). It is as if the therapist were stepping into the breach created by the doubt expressed by the patient. This type of pattern only occurs in the first part of the sequence (before the change in the patient's point of view, supported by statements T6, T7 and T8).

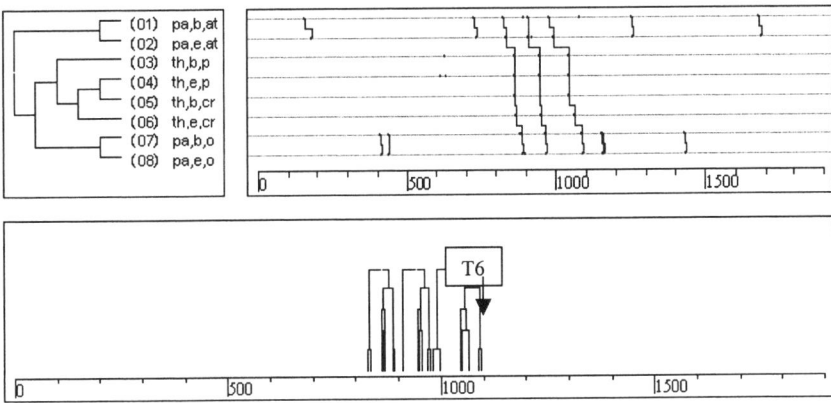

Figure 8.7 Patient's attenuations, therapist's interventions and patient's confirmations

In the following pattern, the patient's attenuations and expressions of doubt are linked with non-verbal signs communicated by the therapist's eye-blinking (Figure 8.8).

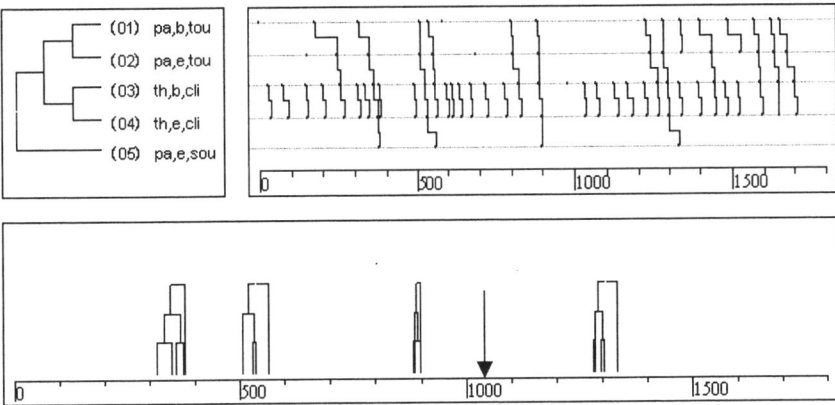

Figure 8.8 The therapist's eye-blinking is associated with the patient's smiles and touching hands

The therapist's eye-blinking is frequently associated with the patient's touching hands, then with his smiles. Through his facial expressions, the therapist expresses a connection with the content of the discourse, which is accompanied by certain patient gestures. The intensity of the relationship is conveyed by meaningful behavioural patterns.

8.4.2.2 Analysis of behavioural patterns in the patient's discourse

The patient's language and gestural behaviours also show special characteristics. Because the sequence revolves around two themes – death and life – we observe that any mention of these two themes is associated with a gesture specific to each one.

In figure 8.9, we observe that the patient discusses death in a complex behavioural pattern. Before bringing up the subject of death, he does not look at the therapist and his head is turned toward the right; after bringing up the subject, he turns his head back toward the right. During his mention of death, he opens his hands, and then crosses his fingers.

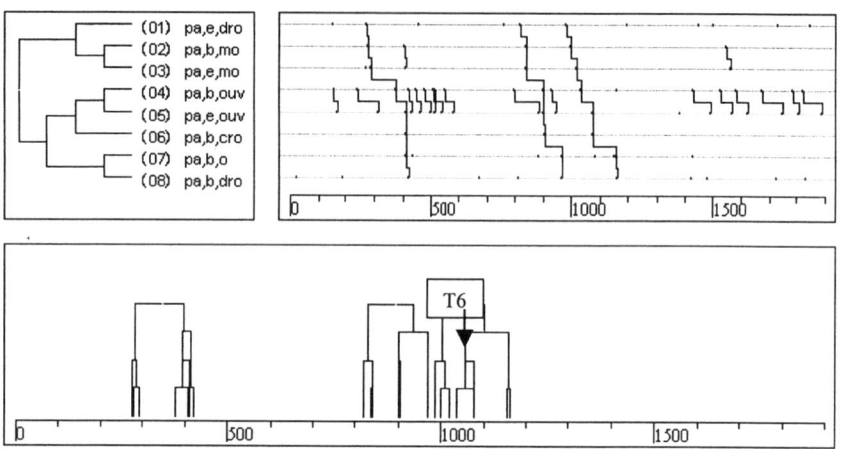

Figure 8.9 The patient stops looking to the right, talks about death, opens his hands, crosses his fingers, says "yeah" and then again looks to the right

In figure 8.10, the patient touches his fingers when he talks about life and does so throughout his discourse. This pattern is very apparent throughout the sequence.

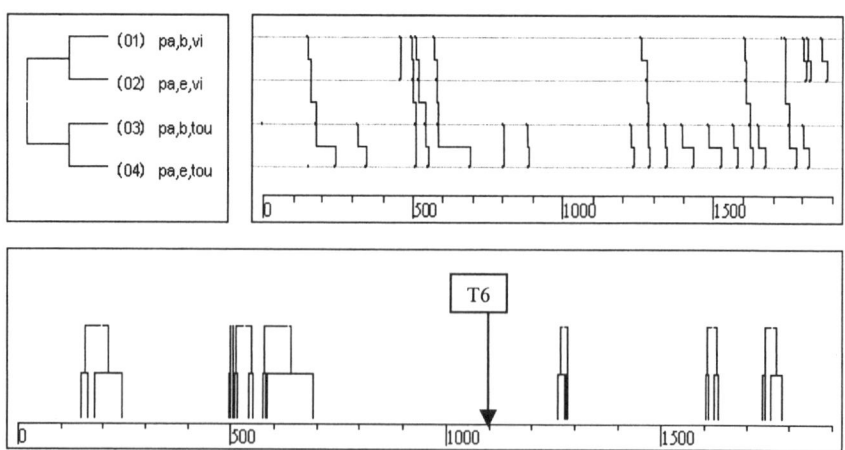

Figure 8.10 The patient talks about life and touches his fingers

In figure 8.11, the patient's discussion of heroin is followed by the same behaviour of touching his fingers as when he talks about life. This observation tends to confirm the implicit analysis of the therapist, who believes the patient takes heroin to live and not to die. In both cases, the patient makes similar movements with his fingers.

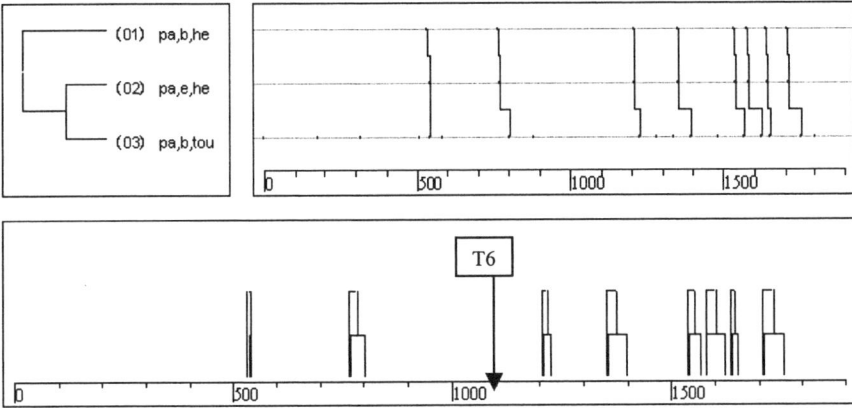

Figure 8.11 The patient talks about heroin and touches his fingers

8.5   Discussion

The goal of this study is to demonstrate the hidden behavioural factors that occurred during a psychotherapeutic exchange. The sequence we selected shows a series of therapeutic interventions that lead the patient to change his discourse. This is a complex interaction that involves verbal exchanges and non-verbal behaviours. Using a hierarchical semantic analysis, we demonstrated that this sequence is comprised of two distinct parts structured around a reversal of the speakers' positions in the dialogue and a modified discourse on the part of the patient.

In the first part of the dialogue, the psychotherapist challenges the patient's initial version, according to which he took heroine because he wanted to die. Two reasons can be proffered to explain the therapist's position: first, the patient's initial version is not compatible with the therapist's psychoanalytical theory and second, the therapist doubts the patient's sincerity. The first part of the sequence consists of the therapist questioning the patient's sincerity by indirectly challenging it. The therapist's successive challenges are gradually integrated into the patient's discourse. The patient uses attenuators that diminish the truth value of his first version. The hierarchical analysis shows that the therapist's challenges construct a retroactive hierarchical structure with the patient in which all the patient's utterances are subordinated to the therapist's utterances. The patient responds to the challenges of the therapist, who initiates the exchanges. Using THEME software, we demonstrated that in this part of the dialogue the therapist structures his speech around the patient's attenuators, as if to base his challenges on the patient's own doubts. We had already demonstrated this type of pattern, which is typical of psychological interviews. In general, interviewers have a tendency to select the attenuated parts of the interviewee's discourse for their use of encouragers and paraphrases [19]. But we also showed that the therapist demonstrates a specific response – eye-blinking – to the patient's body language.

In the second part, the therapist's statements agree with the patient's discourse. The therapist thus reinforces the second version of the patient's discourse, according to which he took heroine to live, to take care of himself, to get better. This part is characterized by a proactive structure in which the therapist's statements are subordinated to the patient's statements. The therapist radically changes his dialogic position in this second part. The dialogue is initiated by the patient and the therapist finds himself in the position of confirming the patient's utterances. The patient initiates the discourse; in psychoanalytic terms, he is the "subject."

The behavioural analysis conducted with THEME software also allows us to understand hidden patterns that characterize the patient's discourse and body language. In particular, the patient's discussion of death is accompanied by a specific head movement. The patient talks about death after turning his head to the right and then again turning his head to the right. The patient gives the impression of seeking this idea elsewhere, far from the therapist's gaze, and then turns elsewhere again, far from the therapist's gaze once more. This thought seems to be located outside the therapeutic session, as if it were not included in the discourse jointly constructed with the therapist. When the patient talks about life, however, he tends to touch his fingers and does so throughout the sequence. This same gesture of touching his fingers accompanies his discussion of heroine. Heroine and life therefore seem to be associated with the same gestural behaviour. The therapist's eye-blinking accompanies, confirms or reinforces this pattern of "life – heroine – hand touching." This observation could account for the accuracy of the therapist's inferences and their basis in the patient's statements and gestures. It is because the therapist pays such close attention to the patient's speech and body language that he can lead the patient to modify his own point of view regarding the causes of his addictive behaviours.

8.6   Conclusions

Psychotherapy is a complex interactive situation based on the asymmetry of the speakers and the therapist's search for specific goals. While research on the efficacy of psychotherapy uses clinical studies to address various psychotherapeutic situations as if they were "soul medicine," few studies examine the properties of the "active ingredients." What are the interactive factors that explain the phenomena of change and influence that are sometimes observed? The research we conducted attempts to answer the following question: How do we encourage individuals to modify the representational system they have constructed of themselves and their lives? The techniques used are never described in psychotherapy manuals; instead, they illustrate the therapist's specific qualities [5]. The therapist's work involves analyzing the patient's discourse and inducing change in patient representations. But this goal can only be achieved if an intense relationship is established between the patient and therapist. The behavioural factors that we demonstrated confirm the existence of this relationship, which mobilizes all the attention and interest of the two individuals.

The microanalysis we conducted on a short sequence of verbal interaction in a therapeutic setting helps us refine our understanding of the therapeutic influence mechanism. This influence comes about through intense communications that concentrates the attention of the two partners. In this relational context, which is sometimes called the "therapeutic alliance," the therapist strives to expand the patient's discourse through explication (retroactive structure) and interpretation (proactive structure). The result of this patient-therapist effort is the joint construction of a discourse that can lead to a better understanding of the patient's life, emotions and experiences. This effort is guided by the therapist, his gestures, facial expressions and verbal interventions. This type of so-called "non-directive" therapy tends to exert all the more influence because it is indirect and the patient perceives it as relatively unintrusive.

This type of study also aims to provide analytical and diagnostic tools for the training of psychotherapists. Unfortunately, new therapists largely receive such training through on-the-job experience. The teaching of therapeutic techniques is a considerable challenge for the future of this type of treatment and for technique-related advances in a field in which human suffering still remains insufficiently alleviated by psychotherapeutic treatment.

8.7   References

[1]   R. L. Birdwhistell, Un exercice de kinésique et de linguistique: la scène de la cigarette, in *La nouvelle communication*, G. Bateson, R. L. Birdwhistell, and. E. Goffman,, Eds. Paris: Seuil, 1981, pp. 160-190.

[2]   P. E. Nathan, S. P. Stuart, and S. L. Dolan, Research on psychotherapy efficacy and effectiveness: between Scylla and Charybdis?, *Psychological Bulletin* **126** (6), (2000) 964-981.

[3]   H. H. Strupp and S. W. Hadley, Specific vs Nonspecific factors in Psychotherapy, *Archives of General Psychiatry* **36** (10), (1979) 1125-1136.

[4]   J. D. Frank and J. B. Frank, *Persuasion and healing*, 3rd ed. Baltimore: The John Hopkins University Press, 1991.

[5]   C. Lecomte, R. Savard, M. S. Drouin, and V. Guillon, Qui sont les psychothérapeutes efficaces? Implications pour la formation en psychologie, *Revue Québecquoise de Psychologie* (2004), (In press).

[6]   W. Labov and D. Fanshel, *Therapeutic discourse*. New York: Academic Press, 1977.

[7]   J. M. Hoc, Les activités mentales de diagnostic, in *Traité de psychologie cognitive*, C. Bonnet, R. Ghiglione, and J. F. Richard, Eds. Paris: Dunod, 1990.

[8]   B. Lamboy, C. Lecomte, and A. Blanchet, La conscience réflexive du psychothérapeute, *Revue Québécoise de Psychologie* (2004) (In press).

[9]   C. Lecomte and M. Alain, Les facteurs communs dans les entretiens thérapeutiques, *Psychologie Français* **35** (3), (1990) 185-193.

[10]   F. Dumont and C. Lecomte, Inferential processes in counseling and psychotherapy: an inquiry into the logical errors that affect diagnostic judgements, *Professional Psychology: Research and Practice* **18** (5), (1987) 433-438.

[11]   A. Blanchet, P. Cocchi, F. Doukhi, and T. Nathan, Interaction thérapeute et patient dans une thérapie ethnopsychanalytique, *Psychologie Française*, **36** (4), (1991) 323-330.

[12]   M. S. Magnusson, Discovering Hidden Patterns in Behaviour: T-patterns and their detection, *Behaviour Research Methods, Instruments and Computers*, **32** (1), (2000) 93-110.

[13]   L. Anolli, *Psicologia della comunicazione*. Bologna: Il Mulino, 2002.

[14]   G. K. Jonsson, Self-esteem, friendship and verbal and non-verbal interaction, in *New Aspects of Human Ethology*, A. Schmitt, K. Atzwanger and K. Grammer, Eds. New York: Plenum Pub Corp, 1997, p. 206.

[15]   E. Roulet, A. Auchlin, J. Moeschler, C. Rubattel, and M. Scheling, *L'articulation du discours en français contemporain*. Berne: Peter Lang, 1985.

[16]   D. Vanderveken, *Mining and speech acts*. Cambridge: Cambridge University Press, 2000.

[17]   R. Ghiglione and A. Trognon, *Où va la pragmatique?* Grenoble: PUG, 1993.

[18]   A. Blanchet, L'interaction thérapeutique, in *Psychothérapies*, T. Nathan, A. Blanchet, S. Ionescu, and N. Zadje, Eds. Paris: O. Jacob, 1998, pp. 97-163.

[19]   A. Blanchet and M. Magnusson, Processus cognitifs et programmation discursive dans l'entretien de recherche, *Psychologie Française* **33** (1-2), (1988) 91-98.

9. Non-Verbal Communication in Doctor-Suicidal Patient Interview

Véronique HAYNAL-REYMOND, Gudberg K. JONSSON,
Magnus S. MAGNUSSON

Abstract. Current techniques of repeated suicide risk assessment are not reliably predictive, and research into new methods is needed. The judgment of clinicians relies partly on nonverbal signs such as facial expressions. If differences in patients and/or interviewer's facial expressions appeared between subjects who were to make subsequent attempts (Repeaters) and those who were not (Non-Repeaters), this could lay the foundations for new ways of prediction.
Fifty-nine patients admitted to the Geneva University Hospitals after a suicide attempt were video-recorded during an interview with a psychiatrist. After the interview, the therapist was asked to assess the suicide risk on a 4-point scale. At 24-months follow-up, we identified 10 Repeaters, who were matched with 11 of the 48 Non-Repeaters, with respect to gender, age, and number of previous suicide attempts. To code the doctor's and patient's facial behaviour, we used Ekman and Friesen's "Facial Action Coding System" (FACS) and we analyzed her behavioural differences with both groups. Results indicated an average activation of all coded units, peri-ocular activation, and duration of her gaze straight at the patient, which were all significantly higher, distinguishing correctly 81.8 to 90.9 % of the patients. By contrast, the doctor's written predictions were erroneous: only 22.7 % of the patients were correctly classified. This fact reflects the doctor's perception of risk, without awareness.
To analyze the structure of the interactive behaviour, we used THEME. Different types of behavioural patterns were found to occur exclusively by either repeaters or non-repeaters and significant differences were found in the complexity of patterns between groups. They give us a sense of the nonverbal communication quality.

Keywords: Suicide attempt; nonverbal behaviour; patient-therapist interaction; suicide risk assessment; T-patterns.

Contents

9.1   Introduction

The incidence of suicide in Switzerland is quite high and at present stands at about 20 per 100.000 inhabitants per year. According to WHO statistics suicide attempts can be multiplied by 10. The risk of reattempt, even frequent reattempt, is high in these patients [1, 2]. The accuracy of suicide reattempt risk assessment therefore plays a crucial role in effective prevention of suicide. However, the limitations of the suicide scales concerning suicide attempts lead most experienced clinicians to trust primarily their own intuition and their personal expertise. *But what is this intuition made of?* It is our belief that clinicians rely heavily on nonverbal signs (i.e., tone of voice, facial expressions, gestures or posture) [3]. Number of studies has shown that dyadic interaction is highly structured and ritualized [4-8]. Many suicide patients are thought to disclose their intentions to their significant others (particularly in nonverbal ways), who too often fail to grasp these hints [9-11]. Therefore, in the present study, we set out to assess suicide risk by exploring this new lead, which is their nonverbal communication and the structure of the interaction. With this in view, we proposed to study patients' and doctor's facial behaviour and their interactive behavioural patterns, in order to get a better understand on how they communicate at a nonverbal level. We hypothesized that, by correlating these variables with the patients' future suicide behaviour outcome, we might have a more direct access to the patients' inner state of mind and suicide intentions, and to the interviewer's perception of such intentions.

9.2   Hypothesis

Our hypotheses are the following:
  1) Differences in repertoire and type of facial expressions, related to emotions and the intensity of interaction would appear between both groups;
  2) The doctor's head and facial behaviour would differ when talking to a future repeater or to a future non-repeater;
  3) We expect to find pattern types occurring exclusively in one group or the other as well as a repertoire of common patterns.

9.3   Method

Video recordings were made of 59 adult suicide patients admitted to the Emergency ward at Geneva University General Hospital. Recordings of patients' who did not speak fluent French, those who were not living in the Geneva area (making them difficult to be traced after two years), and those who were in an acute psychotic state were excluded. A written informed consent was obtained after a thorough explanation of the nature and procedures of the research, in conformity with the procedure set out by the Ethics Committee of the Geneva University Psychiatry Department, according to the latest edition of the Declaration of Helsinki. All patients, after having been examined and attended to, were interviewed by the same experimenter, an experienced psychiatrist who was not aware of the psychiatric diagnosis, the medication and the number of previous attempts. During the interview, two visible video cameras recorded the facial expressions of both doctor and patient. The doctor interviewed each patient during 20 minutes using a standardized questionnaire. The questions concerned first the patient's general physical condition, his/her sensations and emotional status, degree of self-confidence, suicide intentions, and satisfaction with the care provided. The patient was then asked to describe in three words, if he/she so wished, his/her feelings at that moment. After each interview, the doctor rated the patient's suicide risk, (her "written prediction"), on a 4-point scale (no risk, low risk, moderate risk, and high risk).

Twenty four months after the interview we checked the hospital files: 11 patients had been admitted again to one of our Geneva hospitals (the "Repeaters") (one tape was technically unusable) following at least one further attempt since our study; 48 patients had not (the "Non-Repeaters"). We then matched each of the 10 Repeaters against a Non-Repeater of same gender, age and number of preceding suicide attempts (bringing the total to 21 subjects). As FACS coding is time consuming, we selected one question (Question 1) on the possible intention of a further suicide attempt: "Do you think that one day, you will attempt suicide?" ("Suicide topic"), and another (Question 2), not directly related to suicide, on satisfaction with care received: "Could you tell me what you liked and disliked in the care you received here, at the hospital?" ("Care topic"). We assumed that the latter would elicit different emotions (anger?) than the first topic. These two samples were analyzed by four coders qualified to use the "Facial Action Coding System" (FACS) [12] with an inter-coder reliability of 0.82. The coders were blind to who was a Repeater and who was not. FACS is a system for recording all visible movements of facial muscle groups, called action units (AU). Each one of these AUs is given a code number. The direction in which the subject is looking and the tilt of the head are also recorded. The time of onset of each AU, its intensity, any asymmetry (left / right), the time of disappearance, are all taken into account. The AUs can combine to form recognizable configurations which Ekman and Friesen [13] have related to basic emotions such as anger, fear, joy, contempt, surprise and sadness. The intensity of each unit is coded on a 3 to 5 point scale (A to E) depending on the type of AU.

First, we used a two-tailed signed ranks Wilcoxon test [14] for statistical analysis. In order to test the discriminative value of the variables we calculated an *"efficiency value"* (in %), using Belson's criterion. This made it possible to split the sample into two groups, based on a threshold defined by maximized inter-group variance [15]. We then crossed these results with our Repeaters and Non-Repeaters classification in order to see how many Repeaters were above the threshold and how many below [16].

Following the transcription of FACS codes the THEME 5.0 [17, 18] was used to detect and analyze behaviour patterns.

9.4   Results

Our first series of analysis of the doctor's nonverbal behaviour brought to light numerous differences, according to whether the interview was being held with a future Repeater or a Non-Repeater. Three aspects of the doctor's behaviour were significantly more frequent with a future Repeater: i.e., doctor's average activation, peri-ocular muscular activation and gaze direction. By contrast, her written prediction did not show significant differences between groups.

1) Average activation: Here we considered the mean of *all facial, head and eyes* Aus' intensities during one given time segment. This value was significantly higher when the doctor was interacting with a future Repeater, particularly during the "suicide topic" time segment. With this variable, 81.82 % of patients were correctly classified as Non-Repeaters or Repeaters.

2) Peri-ocular muscular activation: This includes all action units of the upper face. However, the result we achieved is mostly a function of the lowering of the eyebrow (as when frowning). When listening to the Repeater during the "suicide topic" time segment, the doctor's peri-ocular region was activated significantly more frequently and with greater

intensity. With a maximum inter-group variance threshold of 0.94, we correctly classified 90.9 % of the patients.

3) Direction of gaze: During the "suicide topic" time segment, the doctor held her eyes on Repeaters' face for a significantly longer time than on Non-Repeaters' faces. Through this variable, we classified correctly 86.4 % of the patients.

4) Analysis of the doctor's "written predictions" showed, by contrast, that the doctor could not predict who was at risk: She rated 14 patients as presenting a moderate risk of reattempt, 7 as high risk (5 of whom were Repeaters), and 1 as low risk (who eventually was a Repeater). In short, here she classified correctly only 22.7% of the patients (5 in 22).

5) Our second series of analysis, that Analysis of T-patterns indicated some differences between repeaters and non-repeaters concerning complexity and frequency of behavioural patterns. On average we find a higher number and frequency of patterns for Repeaters than Non-Repeaters in both questions, but the differences are not significant. The number and frequency of patterns is also higher in Question 2 than Question 1 for both Repeaters and Non-Repeaters, non-significant though. The same is also true for number and frequency of individual and interactive patterns.

Concerning analysis of Question 1 we find Repeaters having significantly higher number of *individual* pattern types than Non-Repeaters (see Figure 9.1). On average the number of individual patterns was also higher for Repeaters in Question 2, but the group difference were not significant.

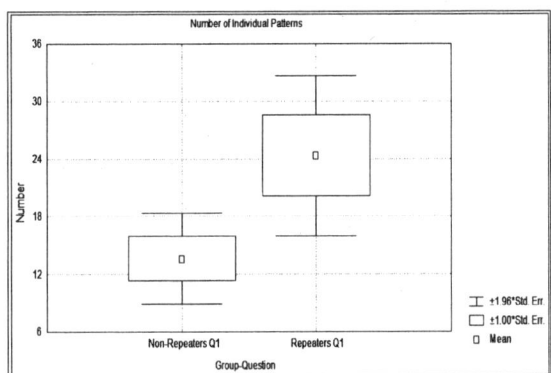

Figure 9.1 Number of Individual patterns detected in Question 1 for groups Non-Repeaters and Repeaters ($t = -2,23$; df = 19; $p < .03$).

Concerning Question 2 we find significant differences between Repeaters and Non-Repeaters on maximum number of pattern occurrences, being higher for Non-Repeaters (see Figure 9.2). On average the maximum number of pattern occurrences is also higher for Non-Repeaters in Question 1, but the group difference was not significant.

Certain complex patterns were found exclusively to be produced either by Repeaters or by Non-Repeaters (see examples 1 and 2 below) and some pattern types, not as complex, were found to occur in both groups (see example 3 below).

Example 1. The following pattern (Figure 9.3), was found to occur in 70% of the Non-Repeaters group for Question 1, not found in the Repeaters group, can be considered as a NVC prototype as it displays the structure of a speaking turn, that is, the ritual that allows the therapist to speak. We see that the patient turns his face and his eyes toward the therapist who sits facing him slightly on the left, then the therapist turns his face and eyes toward the patient (eye contact), then the therapist prepares to speak and eventually speaks.

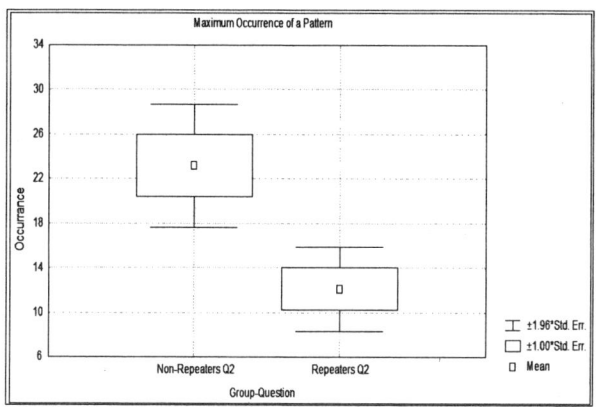

Figure 9.2 Maximum occurrence of a pattern detected in Question 2 for groups Non-Repeaters and Repeaters ($t = 3,17$; df = 19; $p < .004$).

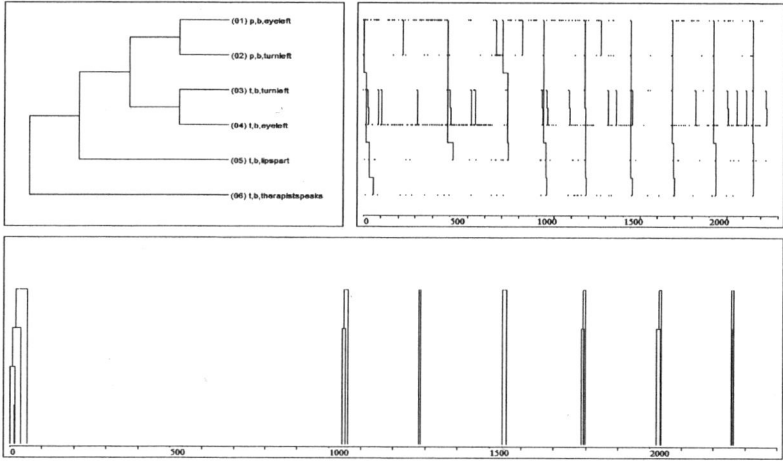

Figure 9.3 Pattern found in the Non-Repeaters group concerning question 1. Events – 1) Patient, begin, eyeleft, 2) Patient, begin, turnleft, 3) Therapist, begin, turnleft, 4) Therapist, begin, eyeleft, 5) Therapist, begin, lipspart, and 6) Therapist, begin, speak.

Example 2. Figure 9.4. displays a T-pattern found exclusively in the Repeaters patients group. The ritualistic pattern describes the therapist lowering her head before speaking, speaking, then turns her face and eyes toward the patient who then begins to speak. At that moment, the therapist closes her eyes, then opens them looking down. Two sub-patterns occur frequently within the larger structure; the therapist begins to speak and then turns toward the patient, and the patient speaks and the therapist closes her eyes.

Example 3. This simple pattern (Figure 9.5) displays a regularity of both parts of the eyebrow being raised. This pattern appears in at least 70% of the files of Repeaters *and* Non-repeaters in Question 1. This facial expression is well known as being highly communicative, its role being to captivate the listener's attention [19]. This simple repeated structure was not detected as part of larger pattern and the events did not form a pattern for neither subject groups in Question 2.

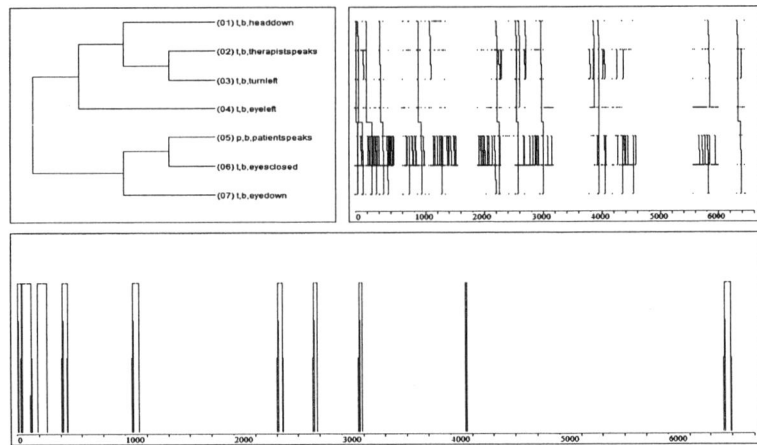

Figure 9.4 Pattern found in the Repeaters group concerning question 1 and 2. Events – 1) Therapist, begin, headdown, 2) Therapist, begin, therapistspeaks, 3) Therapist, begin, turnleft, 4) Therapist, begin, eyeleft, 5) Patient, begin, patientspeaks, 6) Therapist, begin, eyesclosed, and 7) Therapist, begin, eyedown.

9.5   Discussion

In the first series of our findings, the therapist's increase in peri-ocular activity can be considered as a sign of anxiety or preoccupation. Her tendency to look very constantly and carefully at the patient's face could be understood as a way of scrutinizing it during the discussion on the "suicide topic". This particular behaviour could be associated with the interviewer's heightened concern about the patients who, later, actually did repeat a suicide attempt. This attitude was not found when she was talking with "Non-Repeaters". Therefore, her nonverbal attitude could reflect an accurate perception of the suicidal patient's intentions. Apparently, the doctor's perceptions did not lead to a conscious acknowledgement on her part: her written predictions did not help to discriminate between "Non-Repeaters" and "Repeaters". Consequently, she did not prescribe specific safety measures (e.g., hospitalization versus discharge) for some persons of the repeater group. Her perception, as inferred from her nonverbal behaviour, seems to have had no impact on her clinical decision-making.

In the second series of analysis, we present the THEME analysis of patterns, which brings us the following results.

1)   The significantly higher number of individual patterns by Repeaters, joint with the fact that there were also significantly less maximum occurrences of each of these patterns means that the *variety* of patterns was much greater by the Repeaters. This may have given a feeling of unusual communicative style.

2)   The analysis of the numerous individual patterns of the therapist let us understand better the communicative style of the therapist (the same therapist in all interviews)

3)   The analysis of interactive patterns gives us valuable information about the quality and the peculiarities of nonverbal communication in each group. In fact, the most complex and frequent patterns, for all subjects, include mainly eye and head movements. Facial expressions, however, were not found in many patterns, as they are scarcer and more individual. Politeness smiles did not emerge, and further examination of the data may bring an explanation to this. In example 1, what we can clearly observe are eye contacts in the well known ritualized speaking turns. This ritual implies that both partners are willing to look at each other in the eyes in a foreseeable way. As exposed above, we know that by

Repeaters, eye contacts were transcribed, but they aren't found as a part of detected pattern. In example 2, the pattern is unexpected, as it shows the doctor closing quickly her eyes when the patient begins to speak. Does she need to gather her thoughts and/or concentrate on her feelings? Example 3 shows us a very typical communicative pattern, and as such, it is surprising *not* to find it included in a larger interactive pattern, but only isolated, by itself.

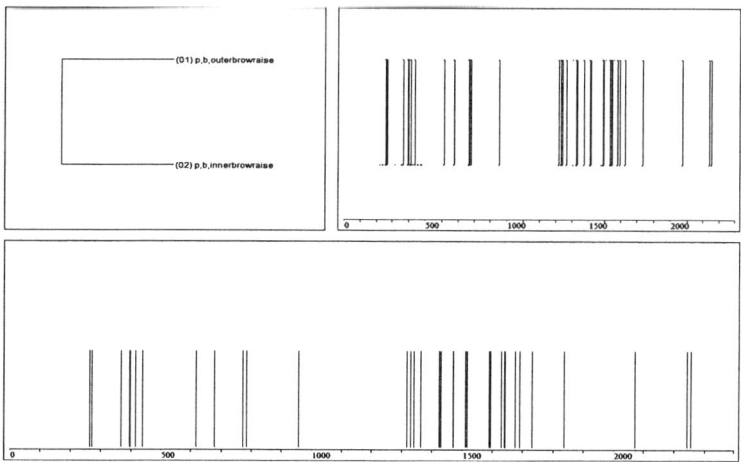

Figure 9.5 Pattern found in over 70% of Repeaters and Non-Repeaters group concerning Question 1. Events – 1) Patient, begin, outerbrowraise and 2) Patient, begin, innerbrowraise. Not found in Question 2.

9.6 Conclusion

We would like to propose three conclusions from the first part of our analysis. First, we can confirm that nonverbal, non-intentional, and non-conscious interaction between patient and therapist does occur. Second, that nonverbal communication could provide important clues regarding the affective state and suicidal tendency of patients, even if they don't verbally disclose their intentions. Third: if the interviewer would give credit to her own reactions, they would influence her decision-making.

Our hypothesis that the THEME analysis would detect the presence of individual as well as interactive patterns could be verified. Here we find patterns that happen exclusively in one group, moreover, some are found in as much as 75% of cases in that group. This thus amounts to a qualitative (but still probabilistic) difference between the groups. Assuming that such patterns can be identified directly by the therapist, it seems that their discovery could eventually facilitate diagnostics in the actual interview situation more than overall group differences in average frequencies of certain elements.

The significant differences between groups concerning occurrences and types of T-patterns give us some clues about the differences in nonverbal communication between groups. For example, we find significantly more individual patterns by Repeaters. In their group, there is a tendency to more *varied* but less frequently occurring patterns. Concerning interactive patterns, their behavioural content differs according to groups. They show the same behavioural elements (head and eye movements with speech) but their configuration is different. This is of interest, knowing the speaking turn rituals described by Duncan and Fiske in 1977 [4]. Looking closely we notice less eye contact in patterns by Repeaters, although we know that they were scrutinized longer by the therapist. It seems therefore that the interaction with Repeaters may have been more disruptive than with the other patients.

These findings about a different "dance" performed in each group will support our efforts to promote body and emotions awareness in the therapists' training as well as in the post-graduate medical workshops. In our ongoing study with other therapists, we will explore in more details the patterns including facial expressions and what they mean.

9.7   Acknowledgments

We own deeply felt thanks to Michael Heller, late Marc Archinard, and Danielle Chevey-Buchs without whom this research wouldn't have been possible. This study was sponsored by the Swiss National Fund for Scientific Research, grant no. 32-33548.92

9.8   References

[1]   V. Granboulan, D. Rabain, M. Basquin, The outcome of adolescent suicide attempts, *Acta Psychiatrica Scandinavia* **91** (1995) 265-270.

[2]   U. Bille-Brahe, A. Kerkhof, D. De Leo, A. Schmidtke, P. Crepet, J. Lönnqvist, K. Michel, E. Salander-Renberg, T. C. Stiles, D. Wasserman, and H. Egebo, A Repetition-Prediction Study on European Parasuicide Populations, *Crisis* **17**(1), (1996) 22-31.

[3]   J. A. Motto, An integrated approach to estimating suicide risk, *Suicide and Life-Threatening Behaviour* **21**(1), (1991) 74-89.

[4]   S. Duncan Jr and D. W. Fiske, *Face-to-Face interaction: research, methods, and theory*. Hillsdale, New Jersey, 1977.

[5]   J. Cosnier and C. Kerbrat-Orecchioni, *Décrire la conversation*. Lyon: Presses Universitaires de Lyon, 1987.

[6]   M. L. Brunel, C. Martiny, and J. Cosnier, Motor mimicry demonstrating empathy: sharing versus exchange mode of communicating, in *ISRE'96*, N. Frijda, ed. Toronto, 1996, pp. 324-327.

[7]   K. Grammer, K. B. Kruck, and M. S. Magnusson, The courtship dance: Patterns of nonverbal synchronization in opposite-sex encounters, *Journal of Nonverbal Behaviour* **22**(1), (1998) 3–29.

[8]   G. K. Jonsson, Self-esteem, friendship and verbal and non-verbal interaction, in *New Aspects of Human Ethology*, A. Schmitt, K. Atzwanger, and K. Grammer, Eds. Plenum Pub Corp, 1997, p. 206.

[9]   K. Hawton, J. Fagg, St. Platt, and M. Hawkins, Factors associated with suicide after parasuicide in young people, *British Medical Journal* **306** (1993) 1641-1644.

[10]   H. Hjelmeland, Verbally expressed intentions of parasuicide: I. Characteristics of patients with various intentions, *Crisis* **16**(4), (1995) 176-180.

[11]   H. Hjelmeland, Verbally expressed intentions of parasuicide: II. Prediction of fatal and nonfatal repetition, *Crisis* **17**(1), (1996) 10-13.

[12]   P. Ekman and W. V. Friesen, *Facial Action Coding System: a technique for the measurement of facial movement*. Palo Alto: Consulting Psychologists Press Inc., 1978.

[13]   W. V. Friesen and P. Ekman, *EMFACS-7*. Unpublished manual, 1984

[14]   S. Siegel and N. J. Castellan Jr, *Nonparametric Statistics for the Behavioural Sciences*. New York: McGraw-Hill International editions, 1988.

[15]   M. Hugues, *Segmentation et typologie*. Paris: Bordas, 1970.

[16]   M. Archinard, V. Haynal-Reymond and M. Heller, Doctor's and patient's facial expressions and suicide reattempt risk assessment, *Journal of Psychiatric research* **34** (2000) 261-262

[17]   M. S. Magnusson, Hidden real-time patterns in intra- and inter-individual behaviour: description and detection, *European Journal of Psychological Assessment* **12**(2), (1996) 112-123.

[18]   M. S. Magnusson, Discovering Hidden Time Patterns in Behaviour: T-patterns and their Detection, *Behaviour Research Methods, Instruments and Computers* **32**(1), (2000) 93-110.

[19]   P. Ekman, About brows: Emotional and conversational signals, in *Human Ethology: Claims and Limits of a New Discipline: Contributions to the Colloquium*, J. Aschoff, M. von Cranach, K. Foppa, W. Lepenies, and D. Ploog, Eds. Cambridge: Cambridge University Press, 1979, pp. 169-202.

The Hidden Structure of Interaction
L. Anolli et al. (Eds.)
IOS Press, 2005

10. Facial Expression Patterns in Common and Psychotherapeutic Situations

Jörg MERTEN, Frank SCHWAB

Abstract. The T-pattern algorithm of Magnusson's was used to find emotional process patterns EPP in facial expressions shown by subjects in different social situations (Common and psychotherapeutic situations). The facial behaviour of the participants was coded using EMFACS (Emotional Facial Coding System). Purpose of the study of common situations was to find indicators for the influence of gender and mental disorder on EPP. 60 dyadic discussions about common political problems were analysed focussing on smiling patterns between subjects. 134 therapy sessions were analysed to find EPP representing psychotherapeutic processes. In the psychotherapeutic situations early indicators of the enactment of maladaptive relationship pattern were searched and related to the emotional quality of the therapeutic relationship and therapeutic outcome. It was shown that the frequency of dyadic EPP in the first session correlated negatively with therapeutic outcome and that they are indicators of conflictous psychotherapeutic processes. The results demonstrate that EPP analysis is a useful tool to identify maladaptive relationship patterns in psychotherapeutic interactions.

Keywords: Emotional process patterns (EEP); facial expression; psychotherapy; gender; mental disorder.

Contents

10.1   Introduction

Several studies investigating the functions of facial expressions of emotions in dyadic interactions demonstrate the importance of facial expressions for the self-regulatory processes and for the relationship-regulation in social interactions [1]. In the realm of mental disorders and psychotherapeutic processes facial-emotional behaviour is a good starting point for the understanding of psychopathological processes taking place in social interactions between patients and their interacting partners [2]. Most clinical disorders can be understood as being based on maladaptive relationship-patterns [3].

The present contribution describes facial-emotional behaviour of different subjects (healthy subjects, subjects suffering from mental disorder, therapists) in dyadic interactions and especially demonstrates the usefulness of the detection of Emotional Process Patterns (EPP) with the aid of Magnusson's algorithm THEME [4].

The results presented are part of the projects of the Analysis of Multi-Channel Spontaneous Behaviour (AMC-SB) in clinical and normal contexts [5]. Besides the analysis of facial behaviour other nonverbal channels are analyzed and combined with multi-channel context-analysis as described in. In the present chapter the focus of the analysis is on "Emotional Process Patterns" EPP as they can be detected in the spontaneous facial-emotional behaviour. Emotional Process Patterns (EPP) can be used to investigate individual and dyadic emotional processes. EPP contain information about emotional self-regulatory processes as well as about the quality of the relationship-regulation in social interactions. In some cases they indicate potential conflicts in the self- or relationship-regulation of patients, which makes them extremely useful to study the psychodynamic backgrounds of spontaneous social interactions not only in the realm of clinical research.

Study 1 investigates the role of EPP in common situations. Are they useful (diagnostic) indicators for the influence of gender and mental disorders in everyday situations?

Study 2 investigates the role of EPP in psychotherapeutic situations. How useful are EPP to analyze the quality of the therapeutic relationship and its effect on therapeutic outcome? First (a) emotional behaviour in the therapeutic relationship is compared to that in everyday relationships. (b) The effect of the implementation of relationship-patterns on therapeutic outcome is studied. Finally a single case study (c) is described to exemplify how EPP indicate intra- and interpersonal conflictive processes in a less successful psychotherapy.

10.2   Method

10.2.1   Coding of facial behaviour

Facial behaviour of all protagonists was measured using EMFACS (Emotional FACS), a technique developed by Friesen and Ekman [6] based on the Facial Action Coding System (FACS, [7]). While FACS comprehensively measures all movements in the face, EMFACS measures only movements which are potentially relevant to emotion. Using a dictionary [6] the measured facial events are interpreted as expressions of the basic emotions of happiness, anger, contempt, disgust, fear, sadness, and surprise or as social smiles (see Figure 10.1). The dictionary also interprets blends and masks from the raw scoring of facial events. Blends are innervations of two of the above mentioned basic emotions from the anhedonic spectrum, which are emitted at the same time. Masks are patterns where a happiness display is used to cover a negative expression. Since the dictionary is restrictive and an interpretation is given only if the coded facial pattern fits one of the listed configurations, a number of facial actions are categorized as non-emotional.

Anger	Disgust	Contempt	Fear	Sadness	Joy	Surprise

Figure 10.1 Examples of facial displays of basic emotions interpreted by the emotional dictionary

10.2.2 M the EMFACS-coding software

A software called M to code digitized video recordings was developed and adapted to the coding of facial behaviour as measured by EMFACS. The two main windows of M (The video-window and the coding-window) are depicted in Figure 10.2. In the background of Figure 10.2 a time-lining software is running that gives the graphical illustration of the codings done on a timeline. This software is called ForM.

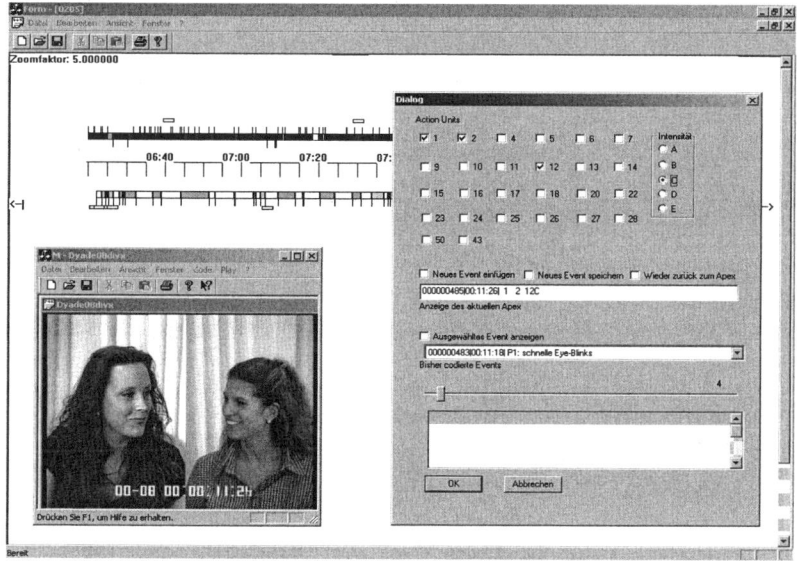

Figure 10.2 Screenshot of the M software

The software M allows fast coding and retrieving of events. A list of coded events can be scrolled through while the corresponding video frames are shown. The same can be done by a slider. Important for the coding of micromomentary behaviour is the possibility to go through the video back and forward frame by frame or in slow motion. The video-window and the coding-window can be sized independently of each other and can be adapted to the needs of the coder. Another important feature is the possibility to synchronize frame numbers and visible video timers. So the time marks of the codings are not only in frames but can be related to timers already mixed in the video.

10.3   EPP of patients and healthy subject in everyday relationships (Study 1)

The following examination focuses on emotional process patterns (EPP) detected with THEME [4] that are consisting of simple forms of smiling. Smiling is an often found facial expression that seems to be prominent in common situations. We differ smiles called "happy felt" (Duchenne Smile) and "happy unfelt" (social smile) and their interactive combinations. Within the THEME detected patterns as EPP one could distinguish different simple interpersonal smiling patterns along their possible functions to express emotional states and/or interaction regulating intent.

1) EPP as an *intimacy implementing* pattern: Both show Duchenne Smiles aligned by a T-pattern. This may signal positive interactive intentions and express enjoyment.

2) EPP as an *appeasement* pattern: Both show social smiles aligned by a T-pattern. These patterns may function as appeasement signals, with no connection to enjoyment

3) EPP as an *intimacy intensifying* pattern: On partner (A) shows a social smile while the other (B) is reacting with a Duchenne Smile. These facial expressions are aligned by a T-pattern and may be understandable as intimacy intensifying signals, with a positive evaluation of the partner by B.

4) EPP as an *intimacy de-intensifying* pattern: On partner (A) shows a Duchenne Smile while the other (B) is reacting with a social smile. These facial expressions are aligned by a T-pattern and may be understandable as an intimacy de-intensifying signaling.

To study facial emotional interactive behaviour we videotaped the facial-emotional behaviour of healthy and non-healthy subjects of both sexes (see video-window in Figure 10.2). The participants discussed political problems for about 20 minutes. The healthy partner was uninformed about the diagnosis of their interlocutor. Dyads were matched in age and education.

The sample consisted of 120 subjects from 60 dyads (see Table 10.1). Two healthy controls one with male subjects (N= 10 dyads) and one with female subjects (N= 10 dyads), a male and a female sample (each with 10 dyads) in which one partner suffered from colitis ulcerosa were videotaped. Two other samples were composed of male subjects only: 10 dyads with one schizophrenic outpatient interacting with a uninformed healthy partner and 10 dyads with a patient suffering from colitis ulcerosa.

	sci	col (m)	lbp	cg (m)	col (f)	cg (f)
N of dyads	10	10	10	10	10	10

sci = dyads with schizophrenic outpatient; col (m) = ...with male colitis ulcerosa patient; lbp = ...with male low back pain patient; cg (m) = male control group; col (f) = ...with female colitis ulcerosa patient; cg (f) = female control group

Table 10.1 Subjects in everyday relationships

Women show more interactive intimacy implementing EPP (both showing Duchenne Smiles) independent of a their status of mental disorder. In healthy male control dyads THEME detects 51 EPP with two Duchenne Smiles. The male dyads with one colitis ulcerosa patient show 30 patterns where a Duchenne Smile followed by the same expression of the partner. In female dyads the sum of these intimacy implementing EPP is significantly higher (U-test of male control and colitis dyads vs. female control and colitis dyads; $p = .000$). The disorder of one interaction partner in the other male dyad samples doesn't seem to have an effect on intimacy implementing EPP (see Table 10.2).

T-pattern	sci	col (m)	lbp	cg (m)	col (f)	cg (f)
intimacy implementing EPP	44	30	44	51	157	158
appeasing EPP	65	60	31	95	7	0
intimacy intensifying EPP	48	51	28	38	33	17
intimacy de-intensifying EPP	44	33	13	14	17	18

sci = dyads with schizophrenic outpatient; col (m) = ..with male colitis ulcerosa patient; lbp = ...with male low back pain patient; cg (m) = male control group; col (f) = ..with female colitis ulcerosa patient; cg (f) = female control Group

Table 10.2 Sum of interactive Smiling-Patterns detected with THEME

Dyads with a severely disturbed partner show more intimacy de-intensifying EPP. In the aggregate this T-pattern is rarely detected (control groups: female: 18; male: 14) mostly it is found in male dyads with an unhealthy interlocutor (sci: 44; col: 33). Men show significantly more appeasing EPP than female dyads independent of an existing disturbance of one partner (U-test of male control and colitis dyads vs. female control and colitis dyads; $p = .000$).

In sum women show more intimacy implementing EPP, while men show more appeasing EPP. While Dyads with a severely disturbed partner *do not* show less intimacy implementing EPP they show more intimacy de-intensifying EPP. This intimacy reducing smiling pattern of answering a Duchenne Smile with a social smile may be the mild or polite kind of rejecting an invitation to intimacy and mutual positive evaluation. This EPP may only be one part of a affective choreography that forms a "dance" (vicious circle) of reduced involvement. These simple event pairs between two persons are a starting point in the analysis of affective choreographies. THEME is detecting a lot of other affective patterns and higher level patterns that are of interest too. What is described here are smiling patterns that gave a hint of how hidden choreographies in interactions can be analyzed and may reveal different choreographies for different dyads (see also Schwab [11]). Sex-differences seem to be a main factor of facial-emotional behaviour. Any diagnosed disturbance may influence those choreographies through a modification of the basic sex typical shape of the facial-emotional interaction-behaviour. As Malatesta and Culver [10] criticized, it would be a serious mistake to generalize from any observation of disturbances made in one sex to the other. If we start to analyze disturbance-specific interactive facial behaviour intimacy implementing EPP don't seem to be a good predictor for the severity of a disturbance. Maybe the healthy partners try to compensate or reinforce the rare Duchenne Smiles of their partners. The intimacy reducing Duchenne Smile – social smile – patterns seem to come along with more severe mental illness. In the following study the emotional quality of the relationship of patients and their therapists is described by EPP.

10.4 EPP of patients and therapists in therapeutic relationships (Study 2)

10.4.1 The therapeutic relationship in contrast to an everyday relationship

In a research project, funded by the German Research Community, 11 experienced therapists of cognitive-behavioural, psychoanalytic, and client-centered theoretical orientation, who treated severely disturbed patients in a brief psychotherapy setting of 15 hours, were videotaped by two cameras. The patients were selected by the therapists as being very severely disturbed, 9 of whom had been treated before without success.

If one compares facial-emotional behaviour in "everyday"-situations and psychotherapeutic situations, one yields the following results: the overall facial emotionality of patients and therapist is reduced when compared to that of healthy subjects in "everyday"-interactions. Joy and disgust are especially displayed less by patients and therapists, while fear and surprise are more often shown by patients in the psychotherapeutic situation. The therapists also show more surprise than subjects in "everyday"-interactions. Patients and therapists often display less contempt than healthy subjects in "everyday"-interactions, but patients show contempt twice as much as therapists. In comparison to "everyday"-interactions simultaneous Duchenne Smiles (indicative of felt happiness) of both patient and therapist are significantly reduced. Healthy subjects in "everyday"-interactions show three times more simultaneous Duchenne Smiles than patients and therapists.

10.4.2 How is the implementation of relationship-patterns tied to therapeutic outcome?

10.4.2.1 Negative emotions, the "Leitaffekt" and therapeutic outcome
The analysis of facial behaviour in therapy-sessions yielded the following results: facial activity in the first session was highly variable across patients and therapists. Patients displayed facial events in a range from 145 to 641 events per session, therapists from 48 to 226. In 10 of the 11 therapies, patients' facial activity was higher than that of their therapists. Taking into account only basic emotions, only 8 patients were more expressive than their therapists. In general, the therapists showed less idiosyncratic facial behaviour, less emotional blends and more "pure" basic emotions than the patients.

Facial behaviour of the therapists did not exhibit any change that could be related to differences in their theoretical orientation (psychodynamic, cognitive-behavioural, humanistic). The variance between therapists of the same theoretical orientation was even higher than that found between the groups of different theoretical orientation. Facial behaviour depends more on individual characteristics and/or dyadic adaptation processes than on theoretical orientation. In dyadic interactions between two healthy persons, the most frequent facial-emotional event was felt happiness. This occurred during therapeutic interaction only in 6 therapists and 5 patients out of a sample of 11. The others showed mainly contempt or disgust and in one dyad anger was the most frequent facial-emotional event. The "Leitaffekt", which is the most predominant and constantly displayed emotion of a subject, was shown in different frequencies. One patient displayed 187 facial events interpreted as disgust during the 50 minutes of the first session but only once expressed felt happiness. These emotions can be considered as indicators of interactive and self-regulatory processes, which is a way of defining transference as a function and could be related to therapeutic outcome. Nevertheless, neither the emotional valence of the "Leitaffekt" of the patient nor its frequency correlated significantly with one of the outcome measures (Perspective of therapist with frequency: $r = .23$, $p = .49$; Patient: $r = .22$, $p = .54$; FBL (Freiburger Beschwerdeliste: $r = .08$, $p = .83$, all 2-tailed).

In line with the above-mentioned results on adaptation [5], therapists whose facial-emotional behaviour responded to the facial control of their patients could be expected to be related to poor therapeutic outcome. Indeed the relative frequency of the "Leitaffekt" of the therapist correlated negatively with therapist's outcome rating which was given usually half a year later ($r = -.63$, $p < .05$, N = 11). Therapists who displayed high amounts of *one single* facial emotion during the first session rated therapeutic outcome as "worse" after the 15th session and this was irrespective of the type of "Leitaffekt" displayed. This could be interpreted as a consequence of the implementation of a maladaptive repetitive pattern which reduces the normal variance of emotionality. This hypothesis is supported by the fact that three *different* negative emotions (anger, contempt and disgust) in the amounts shown by the therapist were positively correlated with his own outcome rating ($r = .81$, $p = .003$,

N = 11) and with the change assessment scores of a questionnaire for symptoms (pre-post differences, $r = .54$, $p = .11$, N = 10). The proportion of felt happiness of patients and negative emotions of therapists correlated with all three outcome measures as depicted in table 10.3. In therapies in which patient expressed many positive emotions and there were only a few negative emotions on behalf of therapist outcome was worse. Successful therapists compensated an excess of positive emotions with their own negative emotions.

	Outcome perspective		
Predictor	*Therapist*	*Patient*	*Combined*
%"Leitaffekt$_T$"	-.63*		
Negative emotions$_T$	+.81*		
Happy felt$_P$/ negative emotions$_T$	-.64*	-.55+	-.76*

Spearman correlations, * $p < .05$, + $p < .10$ %; "Leitaffekt$_T$": relative frequency of most frequent facial emotion ("Leitaffekt"); Happy felt$_P$/negative emotions$_T$: Proportion of patient's happy felt expression and therapist's negative emotions

Table 10.3 Facial-emotional behaviour and therapeutic outcome

10.4.2.2 EPP in the first session and therapeutic outcome

The correlations reported above between frequencies of facial-emotional and therapeutic outcome do not cover the actual implementation of maladaptive relationship-patterns. The actual implementation of maladaptive relationship-patterns takes place on the level of dyadic emotional patterns that describe emotions of patient and therapist as they occur simultaneously or within a short temporal distance. The application of the algorithm of Magnusson revealed that dyadic patterns of Duchenne Smiles (that is, smiles that appear simultaneously or almost simultaneously in the interaction) occurred in nearly all analyzed therapies and that no pattern of negative emotions on behalf of both participants was found. Therefore, motor mimicry of facial-emotional behaviour - as far as it is registered by EMFACS - only takes place in the case of a positive emotion when indicated by a Duchenne Smile. In cases where negative emotions are part of a dyadic pattern, the negative emotion is compensated by a social smile or a Duchenne Smile of the partner. In addition, several therapy-specific patterns describe core psychodynamic conflicts of the patient. An example of a patient with a conflict with attachment and separation is given below. This and other cases are described elsewhere in detail in [2, 8, 9]. Table 10.4 shows the correlations between characteristics of emotional patterns in the first session of different therapies and therapeutic outcome. One major result is that the frequency of dyadic emotional patterns correlates negatively with therapeutic outcome in all three perspectives. Maximum complexity of the patterns - number of elements in a pattern - also correlates negatively in the same manner.

A specific subcategory of emotional patterns is that composed of the appearance of a Duchenne Smile in both interacting partners, which occurs simultaneously. The frequency of simultaneous Duchenne Smiles correlates significantly with therapeutic outcome, namely from the perspective of the therapist (table 10.4).

In addition, we found a curvilinear quadratic relation between the frequency of mutual smiling initiated by the therapist and therapeutic outcome ($p = .038$, $b_2 = -.64$). Therapies in which not even one incident of positive mutual smiling initiated by the therapist is observed were rated on a medium level of outcome. In the therapies in which the process was deteriorated or the patient dropped out more than four incidents of mutual smiling initiated by the therapist were found. The therapies with highest outcome rate lie in between the two above described cases.

	Outcome perspective		
Predictor	Therapist	Patient	Combined
Maximum complexity of patterns	-,69*	-,43	-,68+
# of dyadic patterns	-,58+	-,81*	-,75*
Simultaneous Duchenne Smiles	-.63*		

Complexity of patterns: Number of elements in a pattern Spearman correlations, * $p < .05$, + $p < .10$

Table 10.4 Correlations between EPP in the first therapy session and therapeutic outcome

It can be concluded that the implementation of relationship-patterns is indicated, in general, by high frequencies and high complexity of dyadic patterns and also by the presence of too many patterns of positive emotions from both interacting partners. Furthermore, this kind of implementation is correlated with bad therapeutic outcome.

If the therapist gets involved in the maladaptive relationship-pattern and it is not resolved during the course of treatment, the dreaded pattern will be repeated and further reinforced. This assumption was confirmed by the following results. In therapies with better outcome conflict-indicators augmented to a certain point in treatment and tended to decrease in later sessions. Indicators for bad outcome were high complexity in dyadic relationship-patterns and their predominance in high frequencies in the last session. In these cases therapists were unable to recognize and/or resolve the maladaptive relationship-pattern they were involved in.

10.5   Single case study: EPP in a less successful psychotherapy

One of the 10 psychotherapies analyzed above was used to detect T-patterns in all the 15 sessions. The advantage of the procedure was that also patterns are detected that occur only once in a session, if they also occur in the other sessions. Several patterns were found that demonstrate how intra- and interpersonal conflicts are implemented in the spontaneous facial-emotional behaviour.

10.5.1 Inhibition of the patient's anger by herself and by the therapist

In short the strategy of the therapist can be described as supportive. The patient did avoid to really work on her conflictive problems and also the therapist was not able to change this attitude because he was hampered by feelings of countertransference. Under these circumstances one can expect that a lot of the conflictive issues not dealt with explicitly come up in the spontaneous emotional behaviour. In line with this expectation is the fact that this therapy was one with suboptimal outcome. For a more detailed description of this case please see [2, 9].

Prototypical relationship-patterns were already found when analyzing the first therapy session (Figure 10.3). There was one positive reciprocal pattern of smiling that occurred very often, but was followed in some cases by an anger expression of the therapist. And there was a individual pattern of the patient that indicates the core of her conflict between autonomy and attachment. The first element of the pattern - an anger-expression - was followed by a fear-expression, indicating that the mobilization of the action-tendency of separation immediately induced fears to loose the emotional attachment.

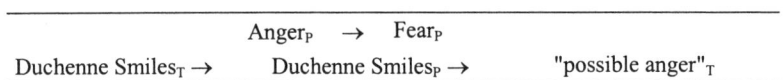

| | Anger$_P$ | → | Fear$_P$ | |
| Duchenne Smiles$_T$ → | Duchenne Smiles$_P$ → | | "possible anger"$_T$ |

Figure 10.3 Patterns in the first session

In the course of this treatment several EPP were found that characterize the psychodynamic of patient and therapist and their kind of relationship regulation. Also in the course of treatment it was the expression of anger on the side of the patient which was crucial. Although the patient showed anger only very seldom, five different T-patterns started with the patient's expression of anger. In one pattern the anger was followed by a expression of joy. This might indicate a positive evaluation of the autonomy-potential of the anger by the patient and/or an interactive compensation of the separating effects of the anger. In line with these interpretations there are two other patterns that demonstrate the ambivalence of anger for the patient. In the first one the anger was followed by fear (as described for the first session) and in the other one the anger was followed by a mixture out of negative emotions also indicating the conflictiveness of the separating power of the anger. But not only the patient inhibited her anger, but also the therapist did as can be seen in two interindividual T-patterns involving the patients anger (Figure 10.4).

Anger$_P$	→	Joy$_P$
Anger$_P$	→	Fear$_P$
Anger$_P$	→	Blends$_P$
Anger$_P$	→	Contempt$_T$
Anger$_P$	→	Blends$_T$

Figure 10.4 EPP involving "anger" (across treatment)

The therapist once responded with contempt and in the second pattern with a mixture out of negative emotions. Especially the expression of contempt signals to the patient that her anger is not evaluated positive by therapist. On the contrary it means to the patient that she has become worthless and that she is in danger to loose the emotional bond to the therapist. That the therapist's contempt-expressions have considerable importance for the patient can be seen in the interindividual EPP starting with the therapist's contempt (Figure 10.5).

Contempt$_T$	→	Joy$_P$
Contempt$_T$	→	Social Smile$_P$
Contempt$_T$	→	Blends$_P$

Figure 10.5 EPP involving "contempt" (across treatment)

At the fist glance this interpretation is contradicted by two other dyadic T-patterns found which start with the therapist's expression of contempt and are followed by a joy-expression in the first case and a social smile in the second case both shown by the patient. These should not be misinterpreted as a positive evaluation of the therapist's contempt but are better understood as compensatory signals to the therapist to reestablish the emotional attachment to the patient.

10.6   Summary

The results presented supply evidence that EPP are valid and useful indicators of individual and interactive emotional processes. In "everyday"-situations EPP are indicators of sex typical styles of relationship regulation and could be used as indicators for the severity of a mental disturbance. What was described here were simple smiling patterns. Sex differences seem to be a main factor of facial-emotional behaviour. Mental disturbances of one interlocutor seemed to influence those sex typical relationship-patterns through modifications of the facial-emotional interaction-behaviour.

EPP are also substantial indicators of therapeutic processes and can be used as good predictors of therapeutic outcome. The frequency of EEP in the first session indicated the amount of the implementation of relationship-patterns and showed to what amount the therapist had become part of the relationship-pattern. As predicted therapeutic outcome was worse if this involvement of the therapist on the level of spontaneous emotional behaviour was high. The quality of EPP across therapy sessions indicate therapeutic (no-) change processes and can be used as explanation for "failures" in therapy as was demonstrated in a single case study.

It has become obvious that the conflicts not only show up in individual patterns but mostly in dyadic patterns which comprise emotional expressions of patient and therapist. This results emphasizes the importance of the analysis of the dyadic behaviour for the understanding of psychotherapeutic processes.

10.7   References

[1]   R. Krause, E. Steimer-Krause, J. Merten, B. Ullrich, Dyadic interaction regulation, emotion and psychopathology, in *Emotions and psychopathology: Theory and* Research, W. F. Flack and J. Laird, Eds. Oxford: Oxford University Press, 1996.

[2]   J. Merten, B. Ullrich, T. Anstadt, R. Krause, and P. Buchheim, Emotional experiencing and facial expression in the psychotherapeutic-process and its relation to treatment outcome. A pilot-study, *Psychotherapy Research* **6**(3), (1996) 198-212.

[3]   R. Krause and J. Merten, Affects, Regulation of Relationship, Transference and Countertransference, *International Forum of Psychoanalysis* **8** (1999) 103-114.

[4]   M. S. Magnusson, Hidden Real-Time Patterns in Intra- and Inter-Individual Behaviour: Description and Detection, *European Journal of Psychological Assessment* Vol. **12** (2), (1996) 112-123.

[5]   J. Merten, Context-analysis of facial-affective behaviour in clinical populations, in *The Human Face: Measurement and Meaning*, M. Katsikitis, Ed. Amsterdam: Kluwer, 2002, pp.131-147.

[6]   W. Friesen and P. Ekman, *EMFACS-7: Emotional Facial Action Coding System,* Version 7. (1984). Unveröffentlicht.

[7]   P. Ekman, and W. V. Friesen, *The facial action coding system (FACS) (A technique for the measurement of facial action)*. Palo Alto, CA: Consulting Psychologists Press, 1978.

[8]   J. Merten, Facial microbehaviour and the emotional quality of the therapeutic relationship, *Psychotherapy Research*, 2004 in press

[9]   J. Merten, *Beziehungsregulation in Psychotherapien. Maladaptive Beziehungsmuster und der therapeutische Prozess*. Stuttgart: Kohlhammer, 2001

[10]   C. Z. Malatesta and C. Culver, Gendered health: Differences between men and women in relation between physical symptoms and emotion expression behaviour, in *Emotion, inhibition and health*, H. C. Traue and J. W. Pennebaker, Eds. Göttingen: Huber & Hogrefe, 1993, pp.116-144.

[11]   F. Schwab, Affektchoreographien. Eine evolutionspsychologische Analyse von Grundformen mimisch-affektiver Interaktionsmuster. Dissertation am FB 5.3 Empirische Humanwissenschaften der Universität des Saarlandes. Berlin: dissertation.d, 2000.

The Hidden Structure of Interaction
L. Anolli et al. (Eds.)
IOS Press, 2005

11.   Patient-Therapist Communication in a Computer Assisted Environment

Giuseppe RIVA, Valentino ZURLONI, Luigi ANOLLI

Abstract. Getting involved in a virtual environment (VE) cannot be only considered a plain process of attention shifting, but it must be regarded as well as a crucial event able to distinguish the actors' communication in a peculiar way. A study is presented herein in order to describe patients' communicative style in a psychological treatment supported by Virtual Reality (VR). In particular, we proposed to understand some basic mechanisms through which VR may be considered as a communicative tool in a therapeutic interaction. To verify the features of patients' communication during VR, the present chapter analyzes whether there are significant differences in non-verbal communicative style of the patients before and after VR exposure. By means of such analysis it should be possible to discover the cognitive and emotional patterns that influence the non-verbal communication adopted by the patients. To reach this goal, we analyse how patients used a number of non-verbal indexes while interacting with the therapist before and after VR exposure. Participants in the present study were 12 women affected by Panic Disorder with Agoraphobia (PDA). Implications of the present findings to the contribution of VR assisted protocol to the study of patient-therapist communication are discussed.

Keywords: patient-therapist communication; non-verbal communication; virtual reality; cognitive-behavioural treatment; panic disorder with agoraphobia.

Contents

11.1   Introduction

11.1.1 Virtual Reality as a communication interface

Virtual reality (VR) can be considered as a leading edge of the computer-mediated communication, whose main characteristic is the full immersion of the human sensorimotor systems into a vivid and global communication experience [1, 2]. As Bricken [3] sketched out, the essence of VR is the inclusive relationship between the participant and the virtual environment (VE), where direct experience of the immersive environment constitutes communication. In this sense, Ellis [4] described VEs as "communication media", while Biocca and Levy [5] argued that VR "is likely to emerge as the next dominant medium, if not the ultimate medium" (p. 9).

According to Schroeder [6], it would be misleading to think of single-user VR systems in this way because "the notion of a communications technology normally implies that two or more people are involved and that the emphasis is placed on the messages that pass between them... it follows that the terms 'communication' and 'medium' should only be used in the context of multi-user VR" (p. 146).

If multi-user VR can be described as a communication technology, how can we define single-user VR? The notion of "information" contained in "information technology" can imply conveying something to a single person rather that an exchange between two or more users. In this sense, it is possible to define single-user VR as an information technology. However, many researchers [5-7] noted that there is a key difference between VR and other information technologies: VR provides a modifiable and navigable space in which communication takes place.

A communication interface can be considered as the interaction of the physical media, codes and information with the sensorimotor channels of the user [2]. VR can, therefore, be defined as a communication interface in the case of single-user VR [8-10].

The core feature of this single-user VR experience is the perceptual illusion of non-mediation (or the *disappearance of mediation*), a level of experience where both the VR system and the real physical environment disappear from the user's phenomenal awareness. When this happens, the user is not simply an external observer of pictures or one who passively experiences the reality created by a computer, but on the contrary, owing to a condition of complete sensorial immersion, he can actively change the three-dimensional world in which he is acting.

Following this conception, the designer of the interface directs the truth of the user-interface interaction. Particularly, as Laurel [11, 12] outlined, the efficacy of the VE as a representational space where user and designer meet depends on developing convincing "characters" in the "narrative" of the user-interface interaction.

In this way, for instance, a therapist may use VR to advantage the creation of a real experiential world within the walls of the psychotherapeutic setting [13, 14].

11.1.2 VR and patient-therapist communication

A core characteristic of any form of psychological therapy is the relationship between client and therapist. Understanding how to use VR to support this relationship presents a substantial challenge for the designers and users of clinical oriented VEs.

According to Vincelli [13], VR produces a shift in the traditional relationship between client and psychotherapist. The new pattern of this relationship is grounded on the knowledge of being more skilled in the complex operations of the recovery of past experiences, through the memory systems, and of foreseeing future experiences, through the imagination. However, these processes are likely to happen if and only if the "virtual setting" can support the relationship between the therapist and the patient. In fact, as a premise, it was assumed that both of them should have some mental representations about what VR is, how it works, and how they can manage it. It was also assumed that the virtual environment proposed by the therapist should be consistent with the standard expectations and the everyday experiences of the patient [15]. Needless to say that both of these processes – the mental representations and the proposed virtual environment – should converge to support the relationship between patient and therapist. Nevertheless, VR treatment is somewhat critic. As recently pointed out by Baños and Botella [16], VR "can be also seen as a creator of psychopathology" (p. 288) due to its potential of inducing difficulties in judging reality and self-identity. It is also well known that this device can provoke relevant side effects such as cyber sickness and after-effects [17], compelling the psychotherapist to a clear and sequential planning of the approach to reduce the likelihood of inducing harmful consequences for the patients.

As Rodden, Mariani, and Blair [18] pointed out, VEs are designed to serve a purpose, explicitly considering users' tasks and goals. During the VR experience the knowledge relevant to the goal should be distributed, and actions should be coordinated. Particularly, to support collaborative activities VEs should provide task appropriate information representation and communication tools embedded in the environment in which activities happen. In this conception, a VE developer has to face a series of key issues for supporting the negotiation process [19, pp. 5-7]:

- The transition between shared and individual activities: actors should know what is currently happening in the context of the task aims.
- Flexible and multiple viewpoints and representations: tasks often need the application of multiple each related to a different point of view and different subtasks.
- A shared context, composed of symbolic references, which allow actors to orient and coordinate themselves.
- The awareness of others, including a sense of co-presence.
- The support to communication activities. VE should allow a collaborative interaction through a support to negotiation and face-to-face talk. In fact, the possibility of negotiation, both of actions and of their meaning, has a key role in providing a satisfactory *sense of presence*. This is even truer for clinical oriented VEs where empathy and communication are the core features of the experience.

11.1.2.1 Sense of presence

Using the concept of presence it is possible to define VR in terms of human experience [20]. Sense of presence is considered as the *perceptual illusion of nonmediation*. The term "perceptual" indicates that this phenomenon "involves continuous (real time) responses of the human sensory, cognitive, and affective processing systems to objects and entities in a person's environment" [21]. An "illusion of nonmediation" occurs when a person fails to perceive or acknowledge the existence of a medium in his/her communication environment and responds as he/she would if the medium were not there.

The illusion of nonmediation can occur in two distinct ways:

- The medium can appear to be invisible or transparent and function as would a large open window, with the medium user and the medium content (objects and entities) sharing the same physical environment.
- The medium can appear to be transformed into something other than a medium, a social entity.

Beneath the several interrelated but distinct conceptualizations of presence, the present chapter emphasizes the idea of psychological *immersion*. When users feel immersive presence they are involved [7], absorbed, engaged, engrossed. This psychological state typically is best measured via subject self-report (although observation of involved media users might also be a useful indicator). For example, a factor analysis of responses to items used by Heeter [22] in a study of user reactions to consumer virtual reality systems resulted in an "involvement" factor containing the items "intense," "fun," "competitive," "addictive," and "exciting"; scores on this factor were the highest of all factors (8.7 out of 10).

Recently, Mantovani and Riva [23] have proposed a new definition of *presence* that (a) recognizes the mediated character of every possible experience of presence; (b) always conceives experience as immersed in a social context; (c) stresses the component of ambiguity inherent in everyday situations; (d) highlights the function of confirmation which culture (artifacts and principles) plays.

The main consequence of this approach for the design and the development of clinical oriented VR systems is that a patient's presence in an environment exists if and only if that patient can use the VR for cooperating with the therapist and/or other patients, and even for entering into conflict with them. In fact, more than the richness of available images [24, 25], the sensation of presence depends on the level of interaction/interactivity which actors have in both "real" and simulated environments [26]. In this sense, emphasis shifts from quality of image to freedom of movement, from the graphic perfection of the system to the actions of actors in the environment.

This approach shifts the focus of attention on successfully creating psychotherapeutic virtual setting. Reproducing faithfully the physical features of the "real" circumstances is not the only thing to be borne in mind in virtual simulation: the possibility of interaction allowed by virtual environments is important as well. In such a way, the graphic quality of the virtual environment should be combined with freedom of movement, more like a theatre [11, 12]. "Experience of (virtual) space will depend more on the mode of locomotion than on the visual and acoustic images. The reality of a surface will be in its implications for action (e.g., does it impede locomotion) instead of in its appearance (e.g., does it look like a wall). In this approach, the reality of experience is defined relative to functionality, rather than to appearances" [27].

Trying to understand this processes, the psychotherapeutic context was conceptualized as an interaction between two people, in which one person (the patient) meets another person (the therapist) taking with himself/herself a story (psychological sufferance, e.g. anxiety symptoms) to narrate inside a specific request (usually to solve the problem and/or to eliminate the symptoms). This is true independently from the specific theory, model or technique used by the therapist. What changes is naturally the way the story is considered and treated by the therapist.

11.1.3 Using VR in Panic Disorder treatment

In the psychological field it is worthwhile applying the new opportunities offered by VR to treatment of psychic disorders to verify the therapeutic usefulness and efficacy. In fact, the possible impact of VR on health care is even higher than the one offered by other new communication technologies [10].

The analysis of the retrieved papers outlined that the first health care applications of VR started in the early '90s by the need of medical staff to visualize complex medical data, particularly during surgery and for surgery planning [28]. In such a case, the core goal of VR is the presentation of virtual objects to all of the human senses in a way similar to their natural counterpart [29].

However, as it was outlined in a number of studies [30-34], for clinical psychologists the main goal is radically different. Particularly, VR is used in cybertherapy "to provide a new human-computer interaction paradigm in which users are no longer simply external observers of images on a computer screen but are active participants within a computer-generated three-dimensional virtual world" [33]. In such a way, according to Gaggioli *et al.* [35], within the VE the patient has the possibility of learning to manage a critic situation related to his/her disturbance.

Along these lines, VR was used in the current study to support the treatment of Panic Disorder (PD). PD is characterized by "the presence of recurrent, unexpected Panic Attacks (PAs) (...) followed by at least one month of persistent concern about having another PA, worry about the possible implications or consequences of the PAs, or a significant behavioural change related to the attacks" [36]. A PA is a sudden onset period of intense fear or discomfort associated with at least 4 of 13 somatic or cognitive symptoms that include: palpitations, sweating, dizziness or light-headedness, trembling or shaking, sensations of shortness of breath or smothering, feeling of choking, nausea or abdominal distress, derealisation or depersonalization, fear of losing control or "going crazy", fear of dying, chest pain or discomfort, paresthesias, and chills or hot flushes. Therefore, PD is defined by a cluster of physical and cognitive symptoms, which occur unexpectedly and recurrently, such as pervasive apprehension about PAs, persistent worry about future attacks, worry about the perceived physical, social or mental consequences of attacks.

Patients involved in the present study were affected by Panic Disorder with Agoraphobia (PDA), which is characterized by both recurrent unexpected PAs and Agoraphobia. The essential feature of Agoraphobia is "anxiety about being in places or situations from which escape might be difficult (or embarrassing) or in which help may not be available in the event if having a PA (...) or panic-like symptoms" [36]. These patients have been treated following the cognitive-behavioural treatment, which consists of gradual *in vivo* exposition to the feared situations, breathing retraining, applied relaxation, new labeling of somatic sensation, as well as cognitive restructuring.

Cognitive-behavioural treatment (CBT) appears to be the most effective therapy for PD [37, 38]. CBT has been recently enhanced by VR technology, especially for disorders as fear of heights, fear of flying and fear of spiders. It has been regarded as a natural extension of the systematic exposure component of behaviour therapy. The first feasibility studies were conducted at Georgia Tech in Atlanta and used VR to treat the fear of heights [39]. Results suggested that patients did indeed experience a wide range of physical anxiety symptoms consistent with their being present in a threatening situation involving heights. Currently, the use of VR therapy for anxiety disorders such as PDA is rather extensive. To meet the demand, many researchers have developed additional virtual environments for use in CBT. In the present study, VR has been proposed as a new medium for exposure therapy. In particular, it has been assumed that VR technology can offer experiences that reduce the gap between imagination and reality [40], and, thereby, increase the efficacy of therapeutic sessions.

11.2   Objectives and hypotheses

The use of a virtual environment should not be considered only a simple process of attention shifting, but it is useful to regard it as a device to develop the patient-therapist communication in a peculiar way. A study is presented herein to describe patients' communicative style in a treatment supported by VR.

Specifically, we intended to analyze whether there were significant differences in non-verbal communicative style of the patients before and after VR exposure. By means of this analysis it should be possible to discover the cognitive and emotional patterns, in terms of engagement, that influence the communicative patterns adopted by the patients. It was hypothesized that VR influences the level of patient's engagement in some way. To reach this goal, the current study analyzed how patients used a number of non-verbal indexes while interacting with the therapist before and after VR exposure. In particular, we supposed that non-verbal signals of anxiety and tension occurred more frequently before than after VR exposure. For instance, gaze (i.e.: "eye-contact", "looking", "cut off") is used to collect feedback, at strategic points; it is used as a synchronizing signal, and as a signal to accompany or comment on speech [41]; it also plays a major part in turn-taking and in organizing conversational flow. Inability of the communicators to maintain eye contact could reflect a high level of anxiety and a poor engagement [42]. In that case, the act of cutting off gaze is probably performed in order to reduce arousal, or anxiety. Likewise, head movements give a contribution in the flow of discourse and in subjects' speech synchronization [42]. A high emotional involvement, engagement and attention may show a tendency to resort to frequent head movements. Moreover, the general level of arousal is reflected in all parts of the body, in the form of diffuse, and generally meaningless movements. Probably one of the main messages conveyed by hand movements is the level of excitement of a speaker. For instance, tense, strained hands, clutching each other or the arms of a chair may convey anxiety. In general, a great number but a poor variety of bodily gestures is interpreted as a signal of tension.

11.3   Method and materials

11.3.1 Participants

Participants were recruited from people who requested treatment at the Anxiety Units of both the S. Carlo Hospital and the Niguarda Hospital in Milan, Italy. The clinical sessions took place at the Communication Psychology Lab of the Catholic University in Milan. Eighteen female participants were invited. To participate in the study, subjects had to meet DSM-IV research criteria for anxiety disorders for a minimum of 6 months determined by independent clinicians on clinical interviews.

Individuals were excluded in the following cases: if they were among people with psychotic or bipolar disorders, or among those who show high suicidal risks, or those who are medically ill (i.e., cardiac conduction disease, vestibular dysfunction) and, finally, pregnant women. Twelve participants met the inclusion criteria and took part in the study (mean age, 43.83±6.68; range, 35–53 years).

The subjects who satisfied the entry criteria were assigned to the Experiential-Cognitive Therapy (ECT) – a new treatment protocol that integrates the use of VR with the traditional CBT strategy – group and were submitted to an eight-session protocol described in Table 11.1.

People on medication were not allowed to modify the prescribed dosage during the treatment. Before starting the trial, the nature of the treatment was explained to the patients, and their written informed consent was obtained.

11.3.2 The virtual environments

For its use in ECT, Riva designed the Virtual Environments for Panic Disorders (VEPD) virtual reality system. VEPD is a four-zone virtual environment developed using the Superscape VRT 5.6 toolkit.

The four zones reproduce different potentially fearful situations—an elevator, a supermarket, a subway ride, and a large square. In each zone, the therapist, through a set-up menu, defines the characteristics of the anxiety-related experience. Specifically, the therapist can define the length of the virtual experience, its end and the number of virtual subjects (from none to a crowd) to be included in the zone.

- Zone 1: In this zone – an elevator in which the subject has to enter – the subject becomes acquainted with the proper control device, the head mounted display and the recognition of collisions.
- Zone 2: This zone shows a supermarket in which the patient can go for shopping. The subject can pick up objects and pay for them at the cash register.
- Zone 3: This zone reproduces a subway ride. The subject is located in the train that moves between different stations.
- Zone 4: The last zone is a large square in which are located a medieval church, different buildings, and a pub.

The VEPD software can be freely downloaded at the web site www.cyberpsychology.info/try.htm. It can be used on a standard PC with Pentium IV/ Celeron/Athlon 1.2 GHz or better, 64 MB of RAM or better, graphic card with 32 MB of VRam or better, using Windows 95/98/2000/NT/XP.

11.3.3 VR hardware

The VR hardware includes the following:
- The head mounted display: Glasstron PLM-A35 developed by Sony Inc., Japan. The Glasstron uses LCD technology (two 0.7 inch active matrix color LCD's) displaying 180000 pixels (PLM-A35: 800H 2225V) to each eye. Sony has designed its Glasstron so that no optical adjustment at all is needed, aside from tightening two ratchet knobs to adjust for the size of the wearer's head.
- The motion gyroscopic tracker: InterTrax 30 (serial interface; azimuth, ±180 degrees; elevation, ±80 degrees; refresh rate, 256 Hz; latency time, 38 6 2 msec).
- A PC Pentium IV: 2 Ghz processor, 128 MB Ram and a GeForce 4 Ti 200 graphic card.
- A joypad.

11.3.4 Procedure

The Communication Psychology Lab of the Catholic University in Milan was provided with two fixed cameras controlled by an Y/C video mixer placed in an adjacent direction room. Under their agreement, patients were video-recorded during the whole treatment. From the collected material, time samples before VR exposure (3 minutes) and after VR exposure (3 minutes) were randomly extracted from the first, the fourth, and the seventh session of the treatment, in order to examine spontaneous behaviours of the patients. The temporal behavioural sequencing of gesture and face expression was analyzed with the aim of finding out behavioural patterns occurrences. Non-spontaneous, biased behaviours during VR exposure were not taken into account. This kind of analysis was executed with a 'frame by frame analysis' and a successive computational elaboration allowing calculating correlations between single behaviours. Frame by frame analysis is an application of a model developed by Magnusson [43-46] in order to detect real-time behaviour patterns using a system of computer software, called THEME.

Session 1	Description of the etiologic model of PDA according to cognitive-behavioural approach
	Connection between the model and a recent PDA of the patient
	Introduction to Virtual Environments
	Graded exposure to virtual environments and set a hierarchy of the virtual stimulus

Session 2	Homework: diary of panic attacks
Session 3	Homework review Cognitive assessment assisted through graded exposure to virtual environments Introduction and scheduling of in vivo self-exposure Homework: diary of panic attacks, in vivo self-exposure
Session 4	Homework review Cognitive restructuring assisted through graded exposure to virtual environments Homework: diary of panic attacks, in vivo self-exposure
Session 5	Homework review Graded exposure to virtual environments Cognitive restructuring face to face Homework: panic attacks diary, in vivo self-exposure
Session 6	Homework review Interoceptive exposure Interoceptive exposure assisted through graded exposure to virtual environments Homework: in vivo interoceptive exposure, panic attacks diary
Session 7	Homework review Interoceptive exposure assisted through graded exposure to virtual environments Cognitive restructuring face to face Homework: in vivo interoceptive exposure, diary of panic attacks
Session 8	Homework review Interoceptive exposure assisted through graded exposure to virtual environments Cognitive restructuring face to face Homework: in vivo interoceptive exposure, diary of panic attacks
Booster sessions	Homework review Cognitive restructuring and prevention relapse Follow-up session schedule Retest
	Follow-up after 1 month, 3 months, and 6 months Review and reinforcement of patient's tasks Management and prevention of future relapse

Table 11.1 The Experiential-Cognitive Therapy protocol for the treatment of panic disorder with agoraphobia

11.4   Results

11.4.1 Detection of T-patterns

The temporal behavioural sequencing of gestures and face expressions was analyzed in order to find out behavioural patterns occurrences. Table 11.2 presents a grid for the behavioural items considered by this study. The analysis approach highlighted here is based on a process known as T-pattern detection, which allows the detection of the temporal and sequential structure of data sets.

Body part	Items	Source
Face	V1 - Look at the therapist	[47, 48]
	V2 - Take off look	[49, 50]
	V3 - Closed eyes	[49]
	V4 - Open eyes	[48]
	V5 - Tears (to cry)	[49]
	V6 - Open lips	[48, 49]
	V7 - Closed lips	[49]
	V8 - Smile	[47]
Head	T1 - Head up	[47]
	T2 - Head forward	[47]
	T3 - Head back	[47, 48]
	T4 - Head turned sidewise	[50]
	T5 - Tilt head	[47, 48]
	T6 - Shaking left/right	[48, 50]
	T7 - Shaking up/down	[48, 50]
Shoulders	S1 - Shoulders normal	[47]
	S2 - Shoulders forward	[47]
	S3 - Shoulders up	[47]
Trunk	Tr1 - Trunk normal	[47]
	Tr2 - Trunk forward	[47]
	Tr3 - Turn trunk	[47]
	Tr4 - Trunk tilt	[47]
	Tr5 - Dangling trunk	[47]
Hands	M1 - Open hands	[48, 50]
	M2 - Closed hands	[48, 50]
	M3 - Palms up	[48, 50]
	M4 - Palms down	[48, 50]
	M5 - Palms inward	[50]
	M6 - Palms outward	[50]
	M7 - Side palms	[50]
	M8 - Joint hands	[50]
	M9 - Bag	[50]
	M10 - Ring	[50]
	M11 - Moving wrist	[47]
	M12 - Pointing index	[48, 50]
	M13 - To number	[47]
	M14 - Negation	[47]
	M15 - Intertwining fingers	[47]
	M16 - Covering face	[47]
	M17 - Body focused/body	[47]
	M18 - Body focused/head	[47]
	M19 - Handling object	[47]
	M20 - To hit table	[48]
	M21 - Touching hairs	[47]
Arms	Br1 - Stretched arms	[47, 48]
	Br2 - Bent arms	[47]
	Br3 - Arms far from the body	[47, 48]
	Br4 - Arms next to the body	[47]
	Br5 - Crossed arms	[47]
	Br6 - Oscillating arms	[47]
	Br7 - Arms on legs	[48]
	Br8 - Arms on table	[48]
	Br9 - "hanging" arms	[48]
	Br10 - Akimbo	[47, 48]
Turn	Tn1 - Talk	[49]
	Tn2 - Listen	[49]

Table 11.2 Behavioural items.

A T-pattern is essentially a combination of events where events occur in the same order with the consecutive time distances between consecutive pattern components remaining relatively invariant with respect to an expectation, assuming, as a null hypothesis, that each component is independently and randomly distributed over time.

Eight relevant T-patterns are presented here in order to display non-verbal communicative differences between PRE-VR and POST-VR. Four T-patterns were extracted from each interactive format.

Considering PRE-VR format, Figures 11.1, 11.2, and 11.3 show the presence of a low level of complexity with a few number of items per T-pattern. In particular, Figure 11.1 presents a T-pattern observed during session 4. Five behavioural items occurred for three times along the temporal period of observation in a three-level pattern. Gaze direction and head movements co-occurred in the present pattern. Specifically, patient takes off look from the therapist (V2), then he takes the head up (T1) while looking at the therapist (V1). No hands or arms movements were detected along the observed period. Box 2 shows a frequent occurrence of head movements sub-patterns along the overall temporal period.

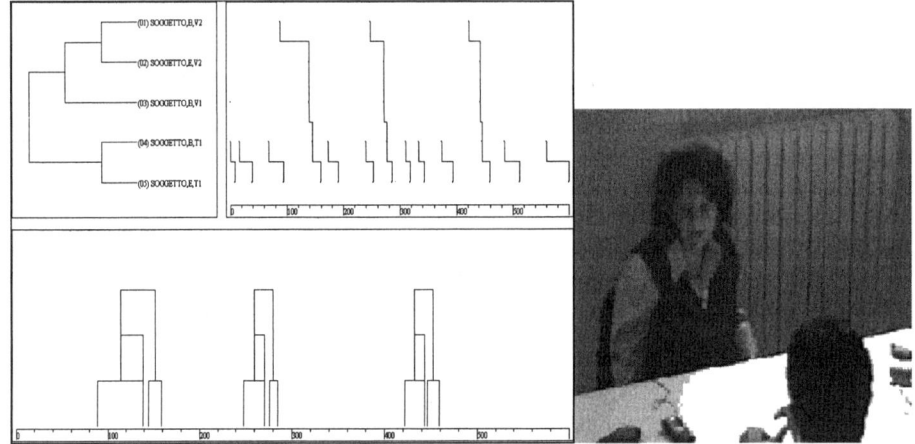

Figure 11.1[1] Subject 5 – Session 4 – "PRE-VR"Min. occ. = 2; $p < .005$. **(1)** SUBJECT, B, *take off look*; **(2)** SUBJECT, E, *take off look;* **(3)** SUBJECT, B, *look at the therapist*; **(4)** SUBJECT, B, *head up*; **(5)** SUBJECT, E, *head up.*

---

[1] Box 1 (top-left) shows the events occurring within the pattern. These events are listed in the order in which they occur within the pattern. The first event in the pattern appears at the top as event number 1 and the last event appears at the bottom. In this case events are coded by using a shortened version of the names of the categories (these abbreviations are explained in the text following each pattern). The pattern connections are shown to the left of the event list. The dots represent event occurrences and the lines between the events represent the pattern connection.

Box 2 (top-right) illustrates the frequency of events within the pattern, each dot means that an event has been coded. The pattern diagram (the lines connecting the dots) shows the connection between events. The number of pattern diagrams illustrates how often the pattern occurs. Subpatterns also occur when some of the events within the pattern occur without the whole of the pattern occurring. For example, if the first two events are connected by a line without being connected to the other events, a subpattern occurs. It is thereby possible to see real-time event distribution, connection between events and how often subpatterns occur, all at the same time. The lines display the connection between events and their time of occurrence.

Box 3 (bottom-left) shows the real-time of the pattern. The lines show the connections between events, when they take place and how much time passes between each event. The timeline is in frames.

A three-level pattern with six items was extracted from session 4 during PRE-VR format (figure 11.2). Patient gaze direction (V1 and V2) is strictly connected to trunk movements (Tr3, "turn trunk") and to body focused movements (M21, "touching hairs"). "Look at the therapist" and "take off look" are repeated twice along a single T-pattern.

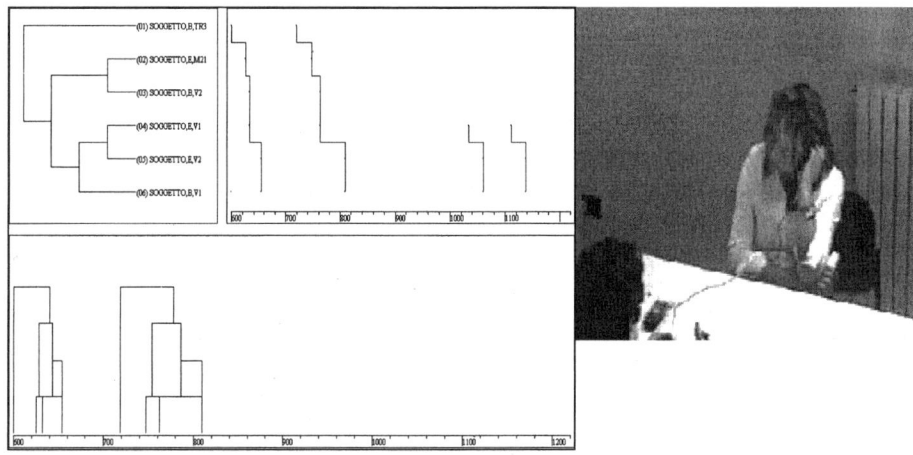

Figure 11.2 Subject 9 – Session 4 – "PRE-VR". Min. occ. = 2; $p < .005$. **(1)** SUBJECT, B, *turn trunk*; **(2)** SUBJECT, E, ***touching hairs***; **(3)** SUBJECT, B, *take off look*; **(4)** SUBJECT, E, *look at the therapist*; **(5)** SUBJECT, E, *take off look*; **(6)** SUBJECT, B, *look at the therapist.*

Figure 11.3 shows a T-pattern at the lower level of complexity. A single level with two behavioural items characterizes it. However, the present T-pattern occurred five times in the same temporal period of observation. As it clearly suggests, patient often took the head forward (T2) during PRE-VR format.

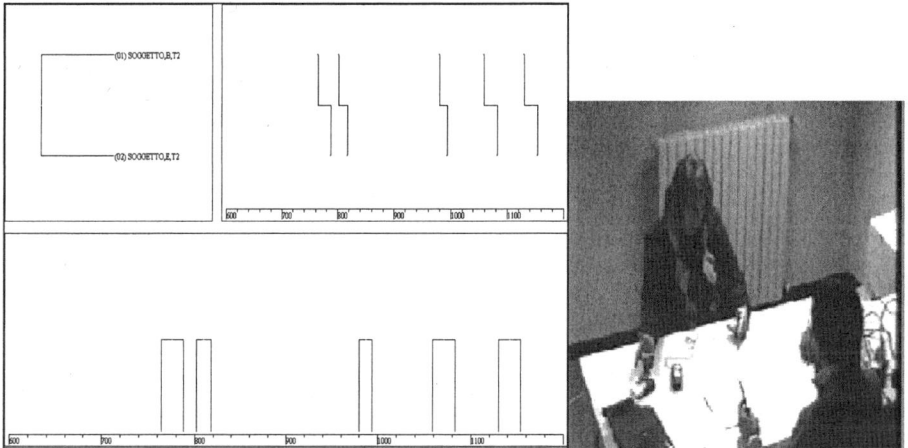

Figure 11.3 Subject 12 – Session 7 – "PRE-VR". Min. occ. = 2; $p < .005$. **(1)** SUBJECT, B, ***head forward***; **(2)** SUBJECT, E, *head forward.*

A T-pattern taken during the PRE-VR condition of session 4 is presented in Figure 11.4. The pattern includes 19 items on seven levels of complexity. Box 3 (bottom) shows how the same pattern recurs combined two times along the communication process during the same period of observation.

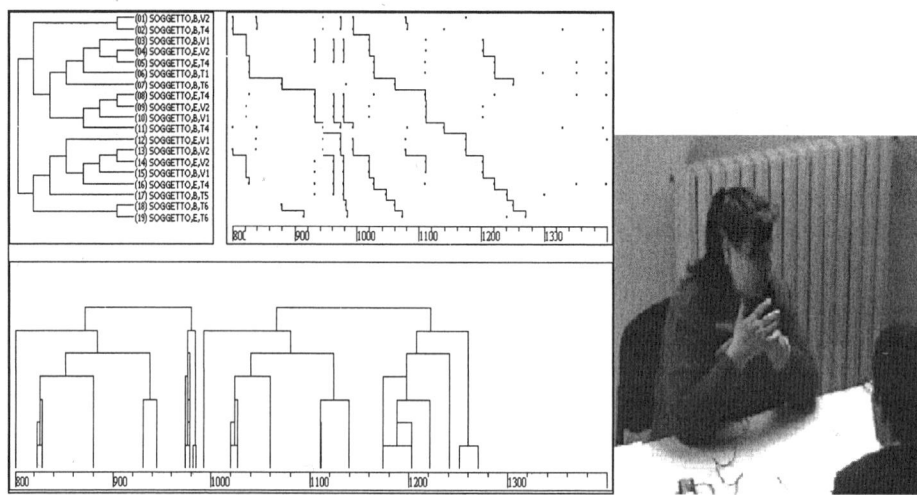

Figure 11.4 Subject 10 – Session 4 – "PRE-VR". Min. occ. = 2; *p* < .005
Keys: (1) SUBJECT, B, *take off look*; **(2)** SUBJECT, B, ***head turned sidewise***; **(3)** SUBJECT, B, *look at the therapist*; **(4)** SUBJECT, E, *take off look*; **(5)** SUBJECT, E, *Head turned sidewise*; **(6)** SUBJECT, B, *head up*; **(7)** SUBJECT, B, *shaking head left/right*; **(8)** SUBJECT, E, *head turned sidewise*; **(9)** SUBJECT, E, *take off look*; **(10)** SUBJECT, B, *look at the therapist*; **(11)** SUBJECT, B, *head turned sidewise*; **(12)** SUBJECT, E, *Look at the therapist*; **(13)** SUBJECT, B, *take off look*; **(14)** SUBJECT, E, *take off look*; **(15)** SUBJECT, B, *look at the therapist*; **(16)** SUBJECT, E, *Head turned sidewise*, **(17)** SUBJECT, B, *tilt head*; **(18)** SUBJECT, B, *shaking head left/right*; **(19)** SUBJECT, E, *shaking head left/right*.

It should be observed here that patient gaze direction (V1 and V2) is strictly connected to head movement's items (T1, T4, T5 and T6). In particular, "look at the therapist" and "take off look" seem to co-occur frequently with "head turned sidewise" and "tilt head". Moreover, it is worth mentioning the frequent presence of a negation behaviour ("shaking head left/right"), which recurs for several times along the same pattern.

Results of the structural analysis of intra-individual real-time behaviour records performed by THEME have shown that observed T-patterns during POST-VR condition generally occurred at a higher level of complexity than T-patterns presented during PRE-VR format. Figure 11.5 shows a representative T-pattern occurred during POST-VR interactive format. It recurs twice along the communicative process, and combines twenty-three items on seven levels of complexity. It could be clearly seen how the patient co-regulates, in particular, arms movements ("arms on the table", "arms far from the body", and "oscillating arms") and head movements ("shaking head up/down").

Two different detected patterns concerning the frequent presence of the smile item for the patient (V8) are presented in Figure 11.6. In particular, top-left box presents a T-pattern that has two items and a level of complexity. A temporal sequence wherein the subject first begins (SUBJECT, B, *smile*) and then stops (SUBJECT, E, *smile*) smiling is clearly outlined. Top-right box illustrates a complex behavioural pattern (fifteen items; eight levels), combining repeated changing of gaze direction ("look at the therapist" and "take off look"), head movements ("head up" and "head forward"), and posture changing ("shoulder forward" and "trunk forward"). Moreover, we observed that the smile T-pattern (top-left box) recurred five times in the same temporal period in which the longer T-pattern (top-right box) repeated twice.

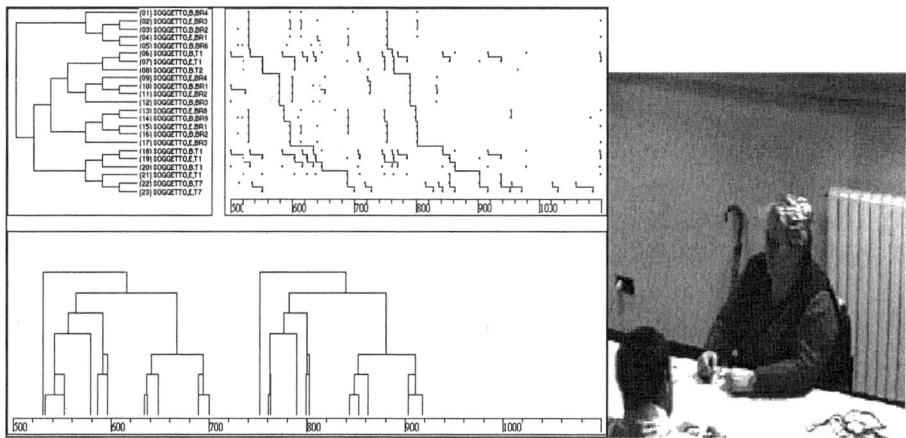

Figure 11.5 Subject 2 – Session 7 – POST-VR. Min. occ. = 2; $p < .005$
Keys: (1) SUBJECT, B, *arms next to the body*; **(2)** SUBJECT, E, *arms far from the body*; **(3)** SUBJECT, B, *bent arms*; **(4)** SUBJECT, E, *stretched arms*; **(5)** SUBJECT, B, *oscillating arms*; **(6)** SUBJECT, B, *head up*; **(7)** SUBJECT, E, *head up*; **(8)** SUBJECT, B, *head forward*; **(9)** SUBJECT, E, *arms next to the body*; **(10)** SUBJECT, B, *stretched arms*; **(11)** SUBJECT, E, *bent arms*; **(12)** SUBJECT, B, *arms far from the body*; **(13)** SUBJECT, B, ***arms on the table***; **(14)** SUBJECT, E, *"hanging" arms*; **(15)** SUBJECT, E, *stretched arms*; **(16)** SUBJECT, B, *bent arms*, **(17)** SUBJECT, E, *arms far from the body*; **(18)** SUBJECT, B, *head up*; **(19)** SUBJECT, E, *head up*; **(20)** SUBJECT, B, *head up*; **(21)** SUBJECT, E, *head up*; **(22)** SUBJECT, B, *shaking head up/down*; **(23)** SUBJECT, E, *shaking head up/down*.

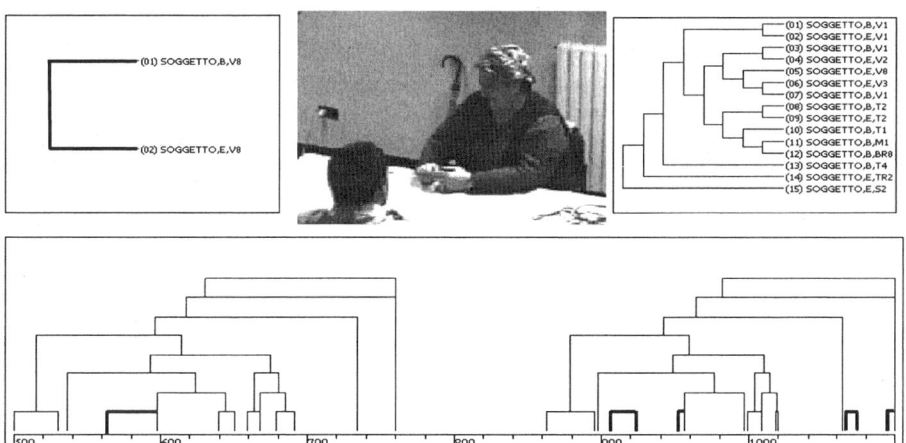

Figure 11.6 Subject 2 – Session 7 – POST-VR. Min. occ. = 2; $p < .005$
Keys: (1) SUBJECT, B, ***smile***; **(2)** SUBJECT, E, *smile*
Keys: (1) SUBJECT, B, *look at the therapist*; **(2)** SUBJECT, E, *look at the therapist*; **(3)** SUBJECT, B, *look at the therapist*; **(4)** SUBJECT, E, *take off look*; **(5)** SUBJECT, E, *smile*; **(6)** SUBJECT, E, *closed eyes*; **(7)** SUBJECT, B, *look at the therapist*; **(8)** SUBJECT, B, *head forward*; **(9)** SUBJECT, E, *head forward*; **(10)** SUBJECT, B, *head up*; **(11)** SUBJECT, B, *open hands*; **(12)** SUBJECT, B, *arms on table*; **(13)** SUBJECT, B, *head turned sidewise*; **(14)** SUBJECT, E, *trunk forward*; **(15)** SUBJECT, E, *shoulder forward*.

A high level of complexity characterizes the T-pattern outlined by Figure 11.7. In fact, fifteen behavioural items along seven levels of complexity describe it.

Hand movements (M1, "open hands"; M11, "moving wrist") are strictly connected to trunk movements (Tr4, "trunk tilt"; Tr5, "dangling trunk") and head movements (T5, "tilt head"; T7, "shaking up/down") which occur repeatedly along the observed temporal period. It is not worth mentioning that patient looks at the therapist all the time. Box 3 reveals that behavioural items are repeated in a long temporal period.

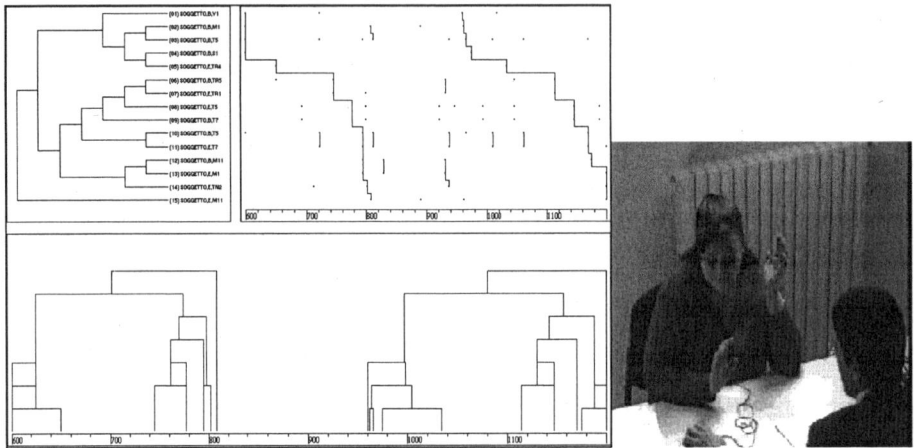

Figure 11.7 Subject 10 – Session 4 –POST-VR. Min. occ. = 2; *p* < .005
(1) SUBJECT, B, *look at the therapist*; **(2)** SUBJECT, B, *open hands*; **(3)** SUBJECT, B, *tilt head*; **(4)** SUBJECT, B, *shoulders normal*; **(5)** SUBJECT, E, *trunk tilt*; **(6)** SUBJECT, B, *dangling trunk*; **(7)** SUBJECT, E, *trunk normal*; **(8)** SUBJECT, E, *tilt head*; **(9)** SUBJECT, B, *shaking up/down*; **(10)** SUBJECT, B, *tilt head*; **(11)** SUBJECT, E, *shaking up/down;* **(12)** SUBJECT, B, *moving wrist*; **(13)** SUBJECT, E, *open hands;* **(14)** SUBJECT, E, *listen;* **(15)** SUBJECT, E, *moving wrist*.

Finally, another complex T-pattern is presented in Figure 11.8 in order to describe patients' communicative behaviour during POST-VR format. It recurs twice along the communicative process, and combines fifteen items on six levels of complexity.

In particular, it could be clearly seen how the patient co-regulates gaze direction, hand movements and head movements. Patient looks at the therapist during the whole behavioural sequence (V1), shaking the head up and down (T7), oscillating his arms (Br6) and, at the same time, moving wrist (M11) repeatedly.

11.4.2 Analysis of T-patterns' complexity

THEME was also used to analyze the complexity of non-verbal communication for each interactive format. Complexity is the result of two different variables: Pattern Length and Maximal Level Frequency. Seventy-two different temporal periods (twelve patients; three sessions: 1, 4, 7; two conditions: PRE-VR, POST-VR) were analyzed. The overall number of T-patterns, their length and level were treated as dependent variables. As independent variable, two-level Format (PRE-VR and POST-VR) was used. The GLM Repeated Measures procedure was considered in order to carry out the statistical analysis. Because of the nature of the current analysis, carryover effects were not significant. In fact, the hypothesized differences between PRE-VR and POST-VR would not be due to fatigue or to practicing effects.

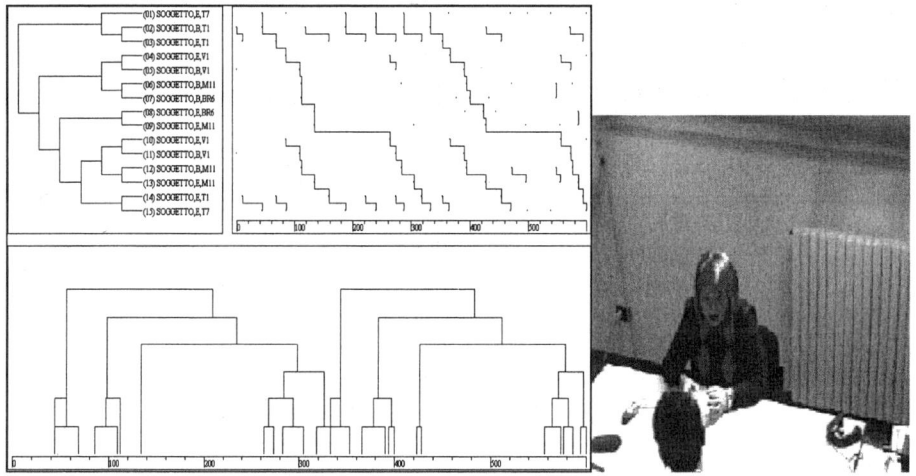

Figure 11.8 Subject 12 – Session 7 – POST-VR. Min. occ. = 2; $p < .005$
(1) SUBJECT, E, *shaking head up/down*; **(2)** SUBJECT, B, *head up;* **(3)** SUBJECT, E, *head up*; **(4)** SUBJECT, E, *look at the therapist*; **(5)** SUBJECT, B, *look at the therapist;* **(6)** SUBJECT, B, ***moving wrist***; **(7)** SUBJECT, B, *oscillating arms*; **(8)** SUBJECT, E, *oscillating arms*; **(9)** SUBJECT, E, *moving wrist*; **(10)** SUBJECT, E, *look at the therapist*; **(11)** SUBJECT, B, *look at the therapist;* **(12)** SUBJECT, B, *moving wrist*; **(13)** SUBJECT, E, *moving wrist;* **(14)** SUBJECT, E, *head up*; **(15)** SUBJECT, E, *shaking head up/down*.

From the collected data, subject 3 was treated as an outlier and not submitted to GLM Repeated Measures test. Data analysis outlined the presence of significant differences between the two-level format variable in both the complexity variables. Both variables reported a general improvement from PRE-VR to POST-VR. Mean values and standard deviations are reported in Table 11.3. In particular, mean values of Pattern Length ($F_{1, 10} = 40.44$; $p < .01$) were significantly different between PRE-VR and POST-VR. Moreover, as it concerns the Maximal Level Frequency of T-patterns' occurrence, GLM Repeated Measures test outlined significant differences ($F_{1, 10} = 8.52$; $p < .05$) between the considered communicative formats. No differences were detected in the overall Number of T-patterns between PRE-VR and POST-VR.

Format	T-pattern Complexity					
	Number of T-pattern		*Pattern Length* **		*Maximal Level Frequency* *	
	M	SD	M	SD	M	SD
PRE-VR	58.03	27.68	10.68	3.22	6.42	1.38
POST-VR	114.88	116.22	13.21	3.51	7.82	1.6

* Mean scores were significantly different between the two formats ($p < .05$ – GLM Repeated Measures Test).
** Mean scores were significantly different between the two formats ($p < .01$ – GLM Repeated Measures Test).

Table 11.3 Means and Standard Deviations for T-pattern Complexity

11.5 Discussion and conclusions

In order to describe patients' communicative style in a treatment supported by VR, this research proposed two different analyses. Firstly, a descriptive analysis of the temporal behavioural sequencing of gestures and facial expressions was carried out. In particular, the structural analysis of intra-individual real-time behaviour records performed by THEME could enable us to verify whether the level of engagement and emotional involvement should increase from PRE-VR to POST-VR interactive condition.

Before discussing the results of data analysis, it is not worth considering two caveats that limited the present study. First, non-verbal analysis could not take into account the patient-therapist communicative interaction, since only the patient sequences of gestures and facial expressions were videotaped. Second, the analysis was limited to PRE-VR and POST-VR formats. A comparable descriptive observation for VR condition was not feasible, since part of the senses of the subjects was immersed in the virtual world: the eyes were covered by a head-mounted display, and the hands constantly manipulated a joypad.

Otherwise, the effect of VR on non-verbal communication could be verified comparing PRE-VR and POST-VR conditions. First of all, the T-patterns taken during the PRE-VR format have some interesting traits in common. In particular, we observed that patients gaze direction is strictly connected to head movements' items. For example, the items "look at the therapist" and "take off look" co-occurred frequently with "head turned sidewise" and "tilt head" items. These data suggest that a high level of anxiety, with a continuous shift of gaze direction characterizes non-verbal communication of patients during PRE-VR [43]. This process is reduplicated by a frequent presence of a "negation" behaviour ("shaking head left/right"). Likewise, the high level of emotional arousal seems to be strengthened by a continuous repetition of hand movements (i.e., "touching hairs") and trunk movements ("turn trunk") along many observed periods [43].

On the contrary, observed T-patterns during POST-VR condition show an increase of level complexity and of the ability of co-regulating different behavioural items. On one side, the present results indicate a reduced level of emotional arousal in POST-VR. On the other, the presence of different items expressing posture changing ("shoulder forward" and "trunk forward") and the frequent temporal sequences regarding smile items seem to outline an increase of the level of engagement of the subjects. Similar considerations can be made for the presence of many arms movements ("arms on the table" and "arms far from the body") and of "affirmation" behaviour ("shaking head up/down"), which give the subject an increased self-control and express a reduced emotional distance during the communicative interaction [42]. This consideration is reduplicated by an increased ability of the patient to maintain eye contact, which plays a major part in turn-taking and in organizing conversational flow. Moreover, a quantitative analysis of non-verbal communication complexity was carried out for each interactive format. Results reduplicated the findings of the descriptive analysis of the temporal behavioural sequencing of gestures and facial expressions. In fact, an increasing in mean values of Pattern Length and in Maximal Level Frequency was showed in POST-VR. It suggests the presence of a higher variety of bodily gestures that could be interpreted as a signal of self-control and of an increased ability in organizing conversational flow by the patients.

To summarize, the current study analyzed how patients used a number of non-verbal indexes while interacting with the therapist before and after VR exposure. To achieve this goal, the ECT was presented here, a new treatment protocol that integrates the use of VR with the traditional multi-component cognitive-behavioural treatment strategy [51, 52]. Results of the current study offered some interesting points about the influence of VR on patients' communication. As for the theoretical perspective, this research can shed some light on the possible contribution of non-verbal analysis to the study of VR effects on patient-therapist interaction. The development of this theoretical perspective presents a challenge to be met with further research.

Taken together, both descriptive and statistical analysis of non-verbal communication should suggest that VR – added to traditional cognitive-behavioural treatment – offers a new and promising approach for the treatment of PD. In fact, the feeling of actual presence offered by the realistic reproduction of cybernetic environments and by the involvement of all the sensorimotor channels, enables the subject undergoing treatment to live the virtual experience in a more vivid and realistic manner than he could through his own imagination [40]. Moreover, VR constitutes a highly flexible tool, which makes it possible to program an enormous variety of procedures of intervention on psychological distress. The possibility of structuring a large amount of controlled stimuli and, simultaneously, of monitoring the possible responses generated by the user of the program offers a considerable increase in the likelihood of therapeutic effectiveness, as compared to traditional procedures. Further research should verify the possibility of extending these considerations also to other phobias and anxiety disorders.

11.6   References

[1]   F. Biocca, Communication within virtual reality: Creating a space for research, *Journal of Communication* **42** (1992) 5-22.

[2]   F. Biocca and B. Delaney, Immersive virtual reality technology, in *Communication in the age of virtual reality*, F. Biocca and M. R. Levy, Eds. Hillsdale: Lawrence Erlbaum, 1995, pp. 57-124.

[3]   W. Bricken, Virtual reality: Directions of growth, University of Washington, Seattle, WA HITL Technical Report R-90-1, 1990.

[4]   S. R. Ellis, Nature and origins of virtual environments: a bibliographical essay, *Computing Systems in Engineering* **2** (1991) 321-347.

[5]   F. Biocca and M. R. Levy, Virtual reality as a communication system, in *Communication in the age of virtual reality*, F. Biocca and M. R. Levy, Eds. Hillsdale: Lawrence Erlbaum, 1995, pp. 15-31.

[6]   R. Schroeder, *Possible worlds: The social dynamic of virtual reality technology*. Boulder: Westview Press, 1996.

[7]   M. T. Palmer, Interpersonal communication and virtual reality: Mediating interpersonal relationships, in *Communication in the age of virtual reality*, F. Biocca and M. R. Levy, Eds. Hillsdale: Lawrence Erlbaum Associates, 1995, pp. 277-299.

[8]   G. Riva, From technology to communication: Psycho-social issues in developing virtual environments, *Journal of Visual Languages and Computing* **10** (1999a) 87-97.

[9]   G. Riva, Virtual Reality as a communication tool: a socio-cognitive analysis, *Presence, Teleoperators, and Virtual Environments* **8** (1999b) 460-466.

[10]   G. Riva, Design of clinically oriented virtual environments: A communicative approach, *CyberPsychology & Behaviour* **2** (2000)351-358.

[11]   B. Laurel, Interface agents: Metaphors with character, in *The art of human computer interface design*, B. Laurel, Ed. Reading: Addison-Wesley, 1990, pp. 355-365.

[12]   B. Laurel, *Computers as theatre*. Reading: Addison-Wesley, 1996.

[13]   F. Vincelli, From imagination to virtual reality: the future of clinical psychology, *Cyberpsychology & Behaviour* **2** (1999) 241-8.

[14]   F. Vincelli and E. Molinari, Virtual reality and imaginative techniques in clinical psychology, in *Virtual environments in clinical psychology and neuroscience: Methods and techniques in advanced patient-therapist interaction*, G. Riva, B. Wiederhold, and E. Molinari, Eds. Amsterdam: IOS Press, 1998, pp. 67-72.

[15]   T. Bardini, Bridging the Gulfs: From Hypertext to Cyberspace, *Journal of Computer Mediated-Communication* (On-line) **3** (1997)

[16]   R. M. Baños and C. Botella, Virtual Reality and Psychopathology, *CyberPsychology & Behaviour* **2** (1999) 283-292.

[17]   A. Rizzo, M. Wiederhold, and J. G. Buckwalter, Basic issues in the use of virtual environments for mental health applications, in *Virtual environments in clinical psychology and neuroscience: Methods and techniques in advanced patient-therapist interaction*, G. Riva, B. Wiederhold, and E. Molinari, Eds. Amsterdam: IOS Press, 1998, pp. 21-42.

[18]   T. Rodden, J. Mariani, and G. Blair, Supporting cooperative applications, *International Journal of Computer Supported Cooperative Work* **1** (1992) 1-2.

[19]   E. F. Churchill and D. Snowdon, Collaborative virtual environments: an introductory review of issues and systems, *Virtual Reality* **3** (1998) 3-15.

[20]   J. S. Steuer, Defining virtual reality: Dimensions determining telepresence, *Journal of Communication* **42** (1992) 73-93.

[21]   M. Lombard and T. Ditton, At the heart of it all: The concept of presence, *Journal of Computer Mediated Communication* (On-line) **3** (1997)

[22]   C. Heeter, Communication research on consumer VR, in *Communication in the age of virtual reality*, F. Biocca and M.R. Levy, Eds. Hillsdale: Lawrence Erlbaum Associates, 1995, pp. 191-218.

[23]   G. Mantovani and G. Riva, "Real" presence: How different ontologies generate different criteria for presence, telepresence, and virtual presence, *Presence, Teleoperators, and Virtual Environments* **8** (1999) 538-548.

[24]   T. B. Sheridan, Musing on telepresence and virtual presence, *Presence, Teleoperators, and Virtual Environments* **1** (1992) 120-125.

[25]   T. B. Sheridan, Further musing on the psychophysics of presence, *Presence, Teleoperators, and Virtual Environments* **5** (1996) 241-6.

[26]   C. van der Mast, K. J. Overbeeke, G. J. F. Smets and P. J. Stappers, Designing in virtual reality: Perception-action coupling and affordances, in *Simulated and virtual realities*, K. Carr and R. England, Eds. London: Taylor & Francis, 1994, pp. 189-208.

[27]   J. M. Flach and J. G. Holden, The reality of experience, *Presence, Teleoperators, and Virtual Environments* **7** (1998) 90-95.

[28]   C. Chinnock, Virtual reality in surgery and medicine, *Hospital Technology Series* **13** (1994) 1-48.

[29]   G. Székely and R.M. Satava, Virtual reality in medicine, *British Medical Journal* **319** (1999) 1305-1318.

[30]   G. Riva, A. Rizzo, D. Alpini, E. A. Attree, E. Barbieri, L. Bertella, J. G. Buckwalter, R. C. Davies, L. Gamberini, L. Johansson, N. Katz, S. Marchi, L. Mendozzi, E. Molinari, L. Pugnetti, F. D. Rose, and P. L. Weiss, Virtual environments in the diagnosis, prevention, and intervention of age-related diseases: A review of VR scenarios proposed in the EC VETERAN project, *CyberPsychology and Behaviour* **2** (1999) 577-591.

[31]   A. A. Rizzo, B. Wiederhold, G. Riva, and C. Van Der Zaag, A bibliography of articles relevant to the application of virtual reality in the mental health field, *Cyberpsychology & Behaviour* **1** (1998) 411-425.

[32]   F. Morganti, A. Gaggioli, G. Castelnuovo, D. Bulla, M. Vettorello, and G. Riva, The use of technology-supported mental imagery in neurological rehabilitation: a research protocol, *Cyberpsychology & Behaviour* **6** (2003) 421-427.

[33]   G. Riva, C. Botella, G. Castelnuovo, M. S. Giaggioli, F. Mantovani, and F. Molinari, (2004), Cybertherapy in practice: The VEPSY Updated project, in *Cybertherapy: Internet and Virtual Reality as assessment and rehabilitation tools for clinical psychology and neuroscience*, G. Riva, C. Rotella, P. Lègeron, and G. Optale, Eds. Amsterdam: IOS Press, 2004, pp. 3-14.

[34]   F. Vincelli, L. Anolli, S. Bouchard, B. K. Wiederhold, M. B. A. Bcia, V. Zurloni, and G. Riva, Experiential cognitive therapy in the treatment of panic disorders with agoraphobia: A controlled study, *Cyberpsychology & Behaviour* **6** (2003) 321-328.

[35]   A. Gaggioli, F. Mantovani, G. Castelnuovo, B. Wiederhold, and G. Riva, Avatars in clinical psychology: a framework for the clinical use of virtual humans, *Cyberpsychology & Behaviour* **6** (2003) 117-125.

[36]   American Psychological Association, *Diagnostic and statistical manual of mental disorders*, (4th edition) (DSM-IV). Washington, DC: American Psychiatric Press, 1994.

[37]   D. Clark, P. Salkovskis, and A. Chalkley, Respiratory control as a treatment for panic attacks, *Journal of Behaviour Therapy and Experimental Psychiatry* **16** (1985) 23-30.

[38]   M. K. Shear, G. Ball, M. Fitzpatrick, S. Josephson, J. Klosko, and A. Francis, Cognitive-behavioural therapy for panic: An open study, *Journal of Nervous and Mental Desease* **179** (1991) 467-471.

[39]   B. O. Rothbaum, L. Hodges, R. Kooper, D. Opdyke, J. Williford, and M. M. North, Effectiveness of virtual graded exposure in the treatment of acrophobia, *American Journal of Psychiatry* **152** (1995) 626-628.

[40]   M. M. North, S. M. North, and J. R. Coble, Virtual reality therapy for fear of flying, *American Journal of Psychiatry* **154** (1997) 130-149.

[41]   M. Argyle, *Bodily communication*. London: Metheun, 1996.

[42]   L. Anolli and L. Lambiase, "Giochi di sguardo" nella conversazione, *Giornale Italiano di Psicologia* **17** (1990) 27-58.

[43]   M. S. Magnusson, *THEME and Syndrome: Two programs for behaviour research*, Symposium in Applied Statistics, H.C. Hoersted Institut, University of Copenhagen, 1983.

[44]   M. S. Magnusson, Le temps et les patterns syntaxiques du comportement humain: modele, methode et le progremme THEME. *Revue des Conditions de Travail. Les actes du Premier Colloque Natural d'Ergonomie Scolaire, Université de Lille*, Marseille: Octares, 1988, p. 284-314.

[45]   M. S. Magnusson, Hidden real-time patterns in intra- and inter-individual behaviour: Description and detection, *European Journal of Psychological Assessment* 12 (1996) 112-123.

[46]   M. S. Magnusson, Discovering hidden time patterns in behaviour: T-patterns and their detection, *Behaviour Research Methods, Instruments & Computers* 32 (2000) 93-110.

[47]   K. Grammer and M. S. Magnusson, The courtship dance: Patterns of nonverbal synchronization in opposite-sex encounters, *Journal of Nonverbal Behaviour* 22 (1998) 3-29.

[48]   D. Givens, *The nonverbal dictionary of gestures, signs and body language cues*. Spokane: Center for Nonverbal Studies Press, 2001.

[49]   P. Ekman and W. V. Friesen, Hand movement, *Journal of Communication* 22 (1972) 353-374.

[50]   D. Morris, *Bodytalk: A world guide to gestures*. London: Vintage/Ebury, 1994.

[51]   F. Vincelli, Y. H. Choi, E. Molinari, B. K. Wiederhold, and G. Riva, Experiential cognitive therapy for the treatment of panic disorder with agoraphobia: Definition of a clinical protocol, *CyberPsychology and Behaviour* 3 (2000) 375-85.

[52]   F. Vincelli, Y. H. Choi, E. Molinari, B. K. Wiederhold, and G. Riva, A VR-based multicomponent treatment for panic disorders with agoraphobia, *Studies in Health Technology and Informatics* 81 (2001) 544-50.

SECTION V

HIDDEN PATTERNS IN NON-VERBAL COMMUNICATION WITH ATYPICAL CHILDREN

The question of what T-pattern mean has often been asked, and there is no single answer. It might be somewhat like asking, generally, What do phrases mean?
Obviously, the answer would, at least, depend on the content of the phrase, how it is performed, and the general context.

Magnusson, 2000

The ability to interpret nonverbal communication is acquired at a very young age. Recent studies showed a two-year-old child is able to identify the direction of the eye gaze and to what specific object or person the gaze is referring. Other nonverbal cues like pointing and dyadic eye gaze, are used by children from an even earlier age. What does it happen when this ability is limited by some impairments or an atypical development? This section tries to answer to this question through the analysis of non verbal communication an social interaction's structure in children with cognitive impairments and atypical development.

Chapter 12, written by PLUMET and TARDIF, was focused on interactions involving autistic children and their relatives. Autistic children have severe difficulties in social interactions and communication. The majority of studies conducted so far with these children are designed to identify what is missing in their behaviour or in their cognitive abilities that could explain their social impairment. However, relatively little research has been done analysing the actual interpersonal functioning existing with familiar partners in everyday life using methods adjusted to catch the idiosyncratic repertoires and temporal structures of specific dyads in specific contexts.

The authors used the THEME software to identify idiosyncratic repertoires and temporal structures of behaviour in specific contexts, paying attention, not only to the intraindividual level, but above all to the dyad's interactive interindividual dynamics.

The results support the possible use of the software as a very useful complementary tool for the understanding of social-communicative dysfunctions and functioning in autistic children. Findings were encouraging because they suggest that despite social impairments, children with autism do develop relationships with others that cannot be reduced to dysfunctions or lack of social-cognitive skills. In fact, autistic children are not only very different from one another, but often fail to display, in the appropriate circumstances, social skills they may have already developed. Taking into account the high inter-individual and intra-individual heterogeneity of autistic children's social functioning and social understanding is a key in testing theoretical models linking their communication problems with circumscribed cognitive deficits.

In the second chapter of this section, 13, SASTRE-RIBA discussed a study about non-verbal communication in educational interactions and tutoring. According to the neuroconstructivist approach, tutoring is considered a complex form of human interaction that affects in different ways the cognitive development of children. For this reason, Sastre-Riba compared tutoring interactions with normal and pathological children (Down-Syndrome), aiming at identifying links between different tutoring types and cognitive gains. Research was focused on infants' capacity to learn and benefit from the logical activity in relation to objects and information provided by an adult. The application of THEME was useful to identify hidden patterns of behaviours of tutoring interactions from ecologically valid situations. Different types of tutoring, ordered from the adult management of activity to the infant's management of activity, were detected: Directive, Maintenance, Integrative and Laissez-faire tutoring.

Results show that infants' gains are related to their capacity to generate action project, flexibility (executive functions), type of tutoring, and the adjustment of adults' proposals based on feedback from the situation. However, the infants' group with more structural and functional difficulties received a more non-adjusted type of tutoring that involves less resistance to interference.

The conclusions of the authors suggest that early educative intervention should not only be centred on formal consistency, but also has to be particularly sensitive to (1) infants' initiation of logical organization of the content and executive control of their actions, and (2) adult adjustment to infant competencies. Not to redefine such intervention may contribute to a continuing deficiency in the tutorial process.

12. Understanding the Functioning of Social Interaction with Autistic Children

Marie-Hélène PLUMET, Carole TARDIF

Abstract. Autistic children have severe difficulties in social interactions and communication. The majority of studies conducted so far with these children are designed to identify what is missing in their behaviour or in their cognitive abilities that could explain their social impairment. However, relatively little research has been made analysing the actual interpersonal functioning existing with familiar partners in everyday life using methods adjusted to catch the idiosyncratic repertoires and temporal structures of specific dyads in specific contexts. Autistic children are not only very different from one another, but often fail to display, in the appropriate circumstances, social skills they may have already developed. Taking into account the high inter-individual and intra-individual heterogeneity of autistic children's social functioning and social understanding is a key in testing theoretical models linking their communication problems with circumscribed cognitive deficits.

In this chapter we first consider some limits of the existing methods used to study social functioning and understanding in autistic children, and we offer work we are conducting in our research team at Paris 5 University. We will illustrate the contribution of THEME analysis to our comparative studies on the development of communication and theory of mind in normal and autistic children. We conclude by showing the interest of the data obtained with this method for the interpretation of cognitive and social processes involved in the particular modes of interaction occurring between autistic children and their social partners.

Keywords: Autistic children; non verbal idiosyncratic repertoires; interpersonal functioning; social impairment.

Contents

12.1   Introduction

Autism, first described by Kanner [1], is a developmental disorder characterized by severe dysfunctions of social interaction and communication. It is not solely a quantitative impairment (fewer interactions and language), but a qualitative deviance (severe problems with the use of verbal as well as non verbal behaviours for communicative purposes) [2]. Even when language develops, semantic and pragmatic dimensions are usually much more affected than phonetics, vocabulary or syntax [3]. The understanding of the underlying cognitive deficits thus depends on facing the complexity of communication processes.

12.1.1   Social-communicative dysfunctions and underlying cognitive deficits

In a social-pragmatic approach, communication is considered as the use of appropriate communicative means to achieve social goals, adjusted to specific contexts. This activity involves different types of abilities. One of them, which has retained the attention of a very large number of recent studies on autism, is the development of *social knowledge*, and particularly the ability to represent interpersonal mental attitudes (*Theory of Mind*) [4, 5]. Taking into account another person's intentions, feelings, desires or knowledge is a condition for the establishment of communicative exchanges that serves more than simply instrumental purposes. Another important component of communication is the involvement of *temporal inter- and intra-regulation* of behaviours. This relies on *control and executive processes* during the course of social interactions in order to adjust the selection of context-relevant communicative means to the expression and understanding of intentions. The relationships between forms and functions of communicative acts have to be monitored, on line, in a temporal flow of constant changes [6]. Each partner of the social interaction contributes, with varying degrees, to these control processes through dynamic co-regulation processes.

Up to now, there has been a lot of theoretical work on how cognitive deficits, in either of these components (theory of mind/executive functions) could be responsible for autistic social-communicative dysfunctions [7-9]. However, very few studies investigate these relationships directly, testing precise operational predictions derived from such models. According to mind-reading deficit hypothesis, as far as theory of mind develops in autistic children (by therapeutic intervention, or by compensation processes through experience), their communicative functioning should improve. If executive dysfunctions impair more widely the activation/guiding of appropriate social behaviours and knowledge in various interpersonal contexts, then the former prediction should be at least partially disproved. Even if autistic children do acquire some pertinent social behaviours or understanding capacities, difficulties should persist in using them within various communicative exchanges. Moreover, problems may be more salient when theory of mind is involved, but may also extend to instrumental interpersonal relationships.

Consequently, testing the links between theory of mind and social functioning in autism requires making several important distinctions: a) the evaluation of *competences vs.* the evaluation of *performances*; b) the coding of *forms* (behavioural components, intra-personal and interpersonal temporal structure...) *vs.* the coding of *functions* of communicative behaviours (social goals they intend to serve). Such a pragmatic approach has been relatively rarely adopted.

In earlier studies, the attempts to answer these questions have been hindered by several methodological problems which we consider in the next section.

12.1.2 Evaluating social functioning and theory of mind in autistic children: methodological problems

12.1.2.1 Social interactions
A first limitation in current research on autistic children's social interactions is the relative scarcity of studies that directly observe and investigate children's functioning in naturally-occurring, everyday interactional settings [10-12]. A majority of studies provide information on indirect observations obtained through the use of clinical inventories/checklists with parents or teachers [13, 14]. Although theses procedures are not very time consuming and are helpful in the establishment of diagnostic, they tend to overemphasize what is lacking and dysfunctioning, while little is revealed about what does function more or less adequately, whether it comes from typical or vicarious processes of development. When direct observation tools are used [e.g.15, 16], most of them focus solely on measuring the child's social behaviours, and rarely take into account the interactive dynamics between the child and her/his partner(s).

A few studies do integrate measures of interactivity, but they come up against two types of difficulties in their application to autistic children. Some authors use *predefined categories,* generally based on normal development framework, thus searching for typically coordinated structures of interaction that are characteristic of different developmental stages (e.g. "joint attention", "social referencing" [17, 18]). This method may not only prove hard to apply (such structures are often only partially present), but possibly omits idiosyncratic or hidden structures that might exist when interacting with an autistic child. For this reason, other studies choose to *detect empirically* the occurring behavioural combinations through correlational or sequential analysis [16, 19] but still may fail to catch the underlying structures of interactivity: correlational approaches miss real-time organization, and sequential analysis need to define time windows between related behaviours, thus neglecting idiosyncratic response intervals (delayed, or differed after other unrelated behaviours). Another type of problem concerns the application of standard quantitative data analysis to subjects with developmental disorders. Comparisons are usually made between groups (autistic *vs.* controls with typical development of other handicaps), with the resultant difficulty of choosing the relevant matching variable (chronological age? verbal or non-verbal mental age? developmental level in a more circumscribed domain?), and of interpreting comparisons based on means statistics. Mean level of social functioning has indeed very little sense with autistic children, standard deviations being often higher than mean values. They reflect extreme inter-individual variations, which may be greater within group than between groups, and high intra-individual sensibility to contexts variables (e.g. structured/unstructured situations [20]). The characterization of autistic children's social functioning thus requires alternative methods of data analysis, better adjusted to the identification of internal regularities in their interactional repertoires implemented within specific contexts.

12.1.2.2 Theory of Mind (ToM)
While there is a certain theoretical agreement on the idea that autistic children's disabilities in attributing mental states underlie their peculiar socio-pragmatic functioning [4, 5], theory of mind (ToM) is usually not tested in real and familiar interactional situations. Most studies use experimental tasks, measuring metacognitive knowledge through commentaries (predictions or justifications) about the behaviour of figures in fictitious stories. This has two main drawbacks. First, such tasks cannot be easily applied to young or low-functioning autistic children. Secondly, they evaluate capacities of social understanding/reasoning potential, not their actual usage in ecologically meaningful interactive situations. A series of recent studies showed, however, that autistic children who pass ToM tasks still have

important difficulties in interpreting mental states in everyday communicative situations [21, 22]. Thus, complementary methods of assessment are needed in order to investigate the reasons for this apparently paradoxical finding: autistic children seem to show poorer ToM capacities in social situations involving real interpersonal motives and familiar partners than in experimental contexts. Differences in the requirements of regulation processes could play an important role. Developing methods adjusted to the analysis of ToM application *in vivo* is an important issue, and a first step would be to identify, through the flow of naturally occurring social interactions, when and how ToM is more likely to be activated. The selection of relevant episodes in observational *corpora*, as well as the behavioural coding systems used, should thus be guided by an attempt to index functional markers allowing to distinguish interactional sequences that are more likely to request mentalistic capacities, from more elementary exchanges in which behaviour manipulation is sufficient. In our research team, this approach has been adopted in two complementary directions: a) the elaboration of social interaction behavioural grids, applicable to various contexts, in which some behaviours are indexed as potential ToM markers (e.g. clarification request, joint attention attempt, non literal use of a behaviour or statement such as teasing, irony, etc.); b) a focus on more specific interactive contexts that may particularly solicit the participants to draw from their ToM resources (such as oppositional episodes), and an extensive structural and functional analysis of interpersonal strategies followed by the social partners involved. Given these conceptual and methodological considerations, the questions about the links between ToM and social functioning can now be reformulated more precisely for empirical testing:

a) *Is ToM level measured in experimental tasks predictive of social functioning quality in real life?* Is it related to the functional quality (mentalist vs. instrumental) and/or to the structural quality (behavioural coordination and temporal regulation) of social interactions?

b) *Where and how is ToM likely to be activated during real life interactions?* Are there specific structures that organize mentalistic exchanges? Are they specifically disorganized in autistic children?

12.1.3 Interest of THEME program for the study of interactions involving an autistic child

The use of a computerized program such as THEME [23, 24] seems to be an interesting opportunity to explore some of the methodological difficulties reviewed above. First, this method is open to detection of unexpected or non conventional structures of interaction, in terms of *content* (behavioural elements and combinations) and of *time* duration and intervals. Second, the algorithm of patterns detection is independent of the coding system, and is not constrained by presupposed links between forms and functions of behaviours, whether in terms of time intervals, succession or co-occurrence of elementary events. Third, it is based on the detection of statistical regularities that are intrinsic to the segment analysed, allowing the identification of individualized rather than "mean" interactive repertoires, more suitable for taking into account the high heterogeneity within and between subjects . Finally, such a program could be a useful tool for investigating the place and role of ToM requirements in the flow of naturalistic interactive moves. In particular, it could help to analyse whether there exist some specific structural characteristics in patterns which regulate social exchanges that are more demanding in mentalistic competences.

12.2   Research illustration

Data presented here are part of a larger project. The first part has been published elsewhere [25] and will be only summarized here, in order to present the next step, in which THEME program was used. The central purpose of this project was to determine whether the level of success of children in experimental ToM tasks would predict the quality of their social functioning in naturalistic interactive contexts, as measured by communicative functions (part 1) and interactional structures (part 2). A developmental and comparative approach (autistic *vs.* normal) was adopted.

12.2.1 Part 1: Summary of method and findings

12.2.1.1 Subjects
Participants were 14 autistic children aged 5 to 12 years, and 14 normal children matched on verbal mental age (Vocabulary test [26]), aged 3 to 6 years. This range of developmental ages was chosen because it covers a period of critical progress in ToM in typical development. Autistic children were all diagnosed by experienced clinicians on the basis of international criteria (DSM-IV and ADI-R, [27, 28]). They were recruited through the Psychopathology Unit for Children and Adolescents at the Robert Debré Hospital in Paris and through an organization called the SESSAD (Service d'Education Spécialisée et de Soins à Domicile), specialized in the evaluation and guidance of autistic children. None of the autistic children was reported to have associated organic pathologies. Normal children were recruited in Paris schools. All children had at least one sibling.

12.2.1.2 Method
All children were observed in two types of situations:

a) A *developmental battery* of *Theory of mind* experimental tasks derived from classical tasks of the literature [29]. Sub-tests investigated the understanding of different mental states (perceptions, emotions, and cognitions), from implicit to explicit knowledge, corresponding to developmental levels from 1 to 8 years. Children were individually tested at the hospital (autistic) or at school (typical children).

b) *Videotaped samples of spontaneous familial interactions*, filmed at home, in familiar contexts with the usual partners (meals and play, with parents and siblings). Results presented here are based on systematic coding of meal episodes (25 first minutes *per* child).

Films were first submitted to a functional analysis, recording the frequency of children's communicative acts classified in four pragmatic categories: 1) *instrumental* (attempts to manipulate the other's behaviour- e.g. request action, object, permission; positive response; negative response...); 2) *mentalistic* (attempts to share or manipulate another person's mental states - e.g. direct attention, request/provide information, clarification, argument; comments; deny; lie...); 3) *evaluations* (e.g. positive/negative evaluations of objects, actions, events...); 4) *other* (e.g. echoes a statement; undetermined function). Codings also rated the presence or absence of gaze towards partners, and whether the communicative act was initiated by the child or produced in response to the partner's solicitation.

12.2.1.3 Main findings
In concordance with previous research [21, 22], autistic children were found to be impaired in both experimental ToM and mentalistic communicative measures when compared with normal children matched on verbal mental age. However, the profiles of the more advanced autistic children (verbal mental age - VMA: 5 to 8 years) present remarkable similarities with those of younger normal children (VMA: 3 to 4 yrs). This probably does not reflect a simple delay in the emergence of at least some mentalistic capacities, because qualitative abnormalities persist in autistic children's ToM usage (e.g. use of eye contact). But despite deviant processes of acquisition, the progression could follow more general developmental constraints, a fact that is often masked by comparative group studies. Results moreover confirmed that experimental ToM level is less systematically linked to effective

communicative functioning in autistic than in normal children. Autistic children with the highest ToM scores still use a majority of instrumental communicative functions in everyday social interactions.

12.2.2 Part 2: Contribution of THEME to structural analyses

12.2.2.1 Subjects

Since we found that verbally advanced autistic children more resembled younger normal children than they resembled children matched on VMA, we chose to present results of structural analyses on 2 subjects (one autistic/one normal), showing the most similar profiles on both ToM measures and distribution of communicative functions.

This contrast places the autistic child in an apparently more advantageous position than the normal child regarding development of formal language (vocabulary: 6 yrs vs. 3; 6 yrs) and experience (chronological age: around 8 yrs vs. 4 yrs). However, at functional level, they're more closely matched than in the majority of studies of this type. It can be noted that the autistic child still presents inferior rates of spontaneous mentalistic communications than the normal child. Table 12.1 presents the characteristics of these subjects.

Subject	Chrono -logical age	Verbal mental age	Scores on experimental ToM Tasks				Distribution of Communicative functions in natural contexts			
			Total (max=24)	Perceptions (max=8)	Emotions (max=8)	Cognitions (max=8)	Instrumental	Mentalistic	Evaluations	Other
John *autistic*	7;11	6; 0	12	6	5	1	68,5 %	20,4 %	9,3 %	1,8 %
David *normal*	3;11	3;6	15	7	5	3	46,3 %	41,5 %	7,3 %	4,9%

Table 12.1 Subjects characteristics

12.2.2.2 Method

We used the same films as above, and submitted them to a second type of coding adjusted for the purposes of a dynamic structural analysis: behaviours were coded in all interactants (child and partners), and more fine-grained categories were employed, both for form and function. The behavioural grid (Table 12.2) was derived from our earlier work [30, 31]. For the specific purpose of this study, more functional codings in relation to theory of mind were introduced. A specific category was added for pragmatic functions (instrumental vs. mentalistic), coded independently from the category of behavioural forms.

Moreover, additional potential «ToM markers» were rated: whether an explicit term designing a mental state had been used; cases when behaviours are produced «non literally», with an intention clearly different from the apparent overt behaviour (teasing, pretending, irony, prosody, etc.); cases when the topic of co-reference is not present (past or future event, object, etc.) and must be represented.

We also quoted each time a verbal production was not clearly understandable, because it was frequent in autistic children, and could elicit explicit demands for clarification of intention from the social partners.

Actor	Target child; Mother; Father; Brother1; Brother2; Sister1; Sister2; Other
B_E	Begin; End
Canal	Non Verbal; Vocal; Verbal
Behaviour	Look; Manipulate; Take; Give; Touch; Point to; Emotion+; Emotion-; Approach; Go Away; Stereotypy; Hit/slap
Focus	Object; Other Object; Action; Event; Face
Addressee	Target Child; Mother; Father; Brother1; Brother2; Sister1; Sister2; Other
Function	Asking (*Types*: Object; Action; Permission; Information*; Clarification*); Direct attention*; Provide information*; Comment*; Deny a statement*; Lie*; Threaten*; Explain/Justify*; Response+ (agree, accept); Response- (refuse, protest); Prevent action; Evaluate+; Evaluate-; Echo reproduction; Self-regulative statement; No response (when expected)
ToM markers*	Psychological term (*Types*: Emotion*; Desire*; Cognition*; Perception*); Non literal behaviour (*Modality*: Behavioural, e.g. tease/pretend*;Verbal, e.g. irony*; Vocal, 2nd degree prosodic mark*); Not present (evocation of past/future)*; Not understandable

Table 12.2 Behavioural grid used for structural analysis. (*ToM specially required)

Principles of the analysis with THEME program [23, 24] will not be detailed here since they are presented in the first chapter of this volume.

12.2.2.3 Results

Patterns quantitative characteristics: Figures 12.1, 12.2 and 12.3 present the distribution of T-patterns detected in interactions with the autistic and with the normal child by length, level and degree of interactivity. Longer and higher levels of T-patterns were found in behavioural episodes involving the autistic child than the normal child. This apparently surprising finding is illuminated by the third figure. For the autistic child, patterns are mostly of low interactivity (single child patterns). Keeping in mind that the behavioural grid includes very elementary aspects of behaviours (such as «touch», «look», «approach», etc.), and that they compose many of the T-patterns, the increase in T-patterns' length and level may reflect mainly the existence of more repetitive intra-individual structures of behavioural combinations in the autistic child.

Patterns qualitative content: Figure 12.4 presents T-patterns that have been detected for the *normal child* and account for the majority of the interactive course, with the following parameters: minimum of occurrences = 3, $p < .005$.

The total number of T-patterns detected, after redundancy reduction, was 12. These are mostly T-patterns of alternative looks between the child and the partners (father and sister), during instrumental interactions, the father trying to control children's behaviour during meal.

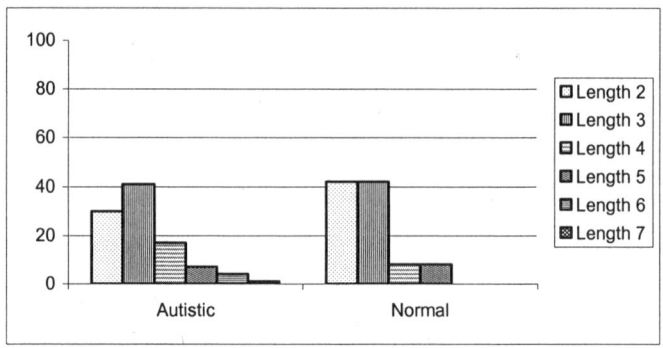

Figure 12.1 Percentage of patterns by length and type of subject

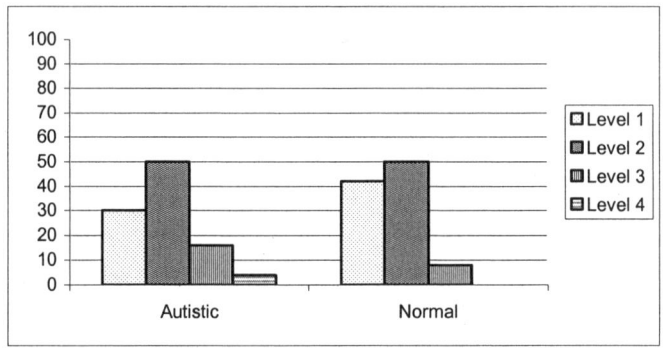

Figure 12.2 Percentage of patterns by level and type of subject

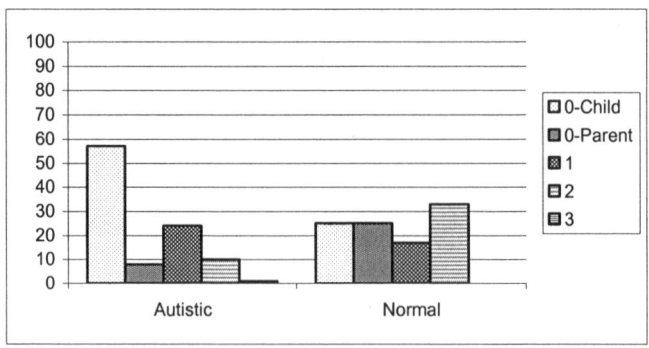

Figure 12.3 Percentage of patterns by degree of interactivity and type of subject

Figure 12.5 shows the T-patterns that have been detected for the *autistic child* and account for the majority of the interactive course, with the same detection parameters (minimum of occurrences = 3, $p < .005$). The total number of T-patterns detected, after redundancy reduction was 179.

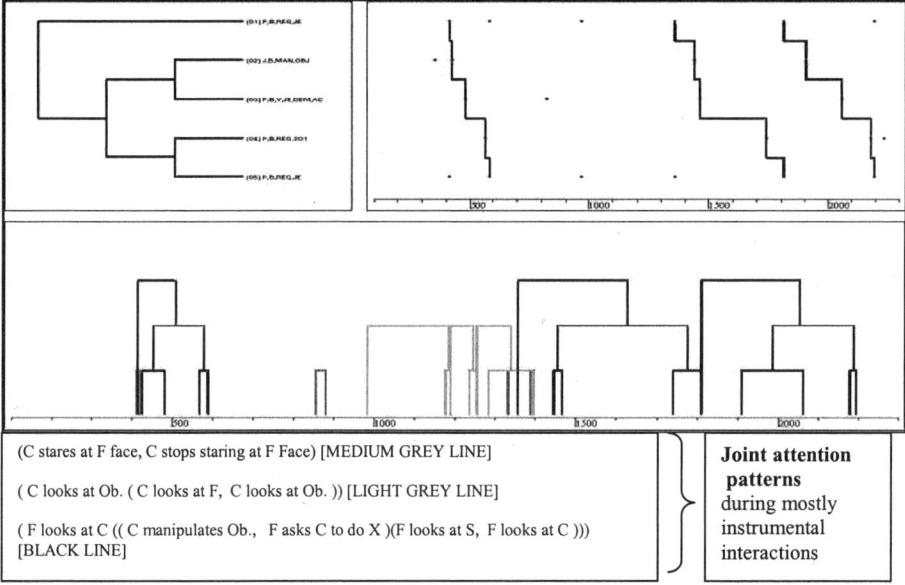

(C stares at F face, C stops staring at F Face) [MEDIUM GREY LINE]

(C looks at Ob. (C looks at F, C looks at Ob.)) [LIGHT GREY LINE]

(F looks at C ((C manipulates Ob., F asks C to do X)(F looks at S, F looks at C))) [BLACK LINE]

Joint attention patterns during mostly instrumental interactions

Figure 12.4 Detection of T-patterns in a normal child (aged 3; 11) (min occ. = 3, $p < .005$). (Total Nb. = 12, max. length = 5, ma12. level = 3). C= Child; F= Father; Ob= Object;

From the analysis of the content and meaning of the T-patterns detected emerge the following findings:
- A very large part of the T-patterns (65%) were composed of behaviours from a single actor (57% child, 8% mother)
- The most complex or long interactive patterns reveal unadapted exchanges (example A). Despite an explicit request from the mother that the child clarifies his intention (solicitation of mentalistic capacities), the child is unable to do it clearly, although he is able to speak with perfectly intelligible words or whole sentences.
- Some T-patterns reveal typically autistic structures (example B): poorly coordinated behaviours (gaze/verbal-vocal), self-centred behaviours, alternance of approach/ withdrawal. Some of these child patterns could be communication attempts that fail.
- mother T-pattern (example C): the longest patterns including only the mother are often attempts to understand, supervise and control the children, while she is serving the dinner.
- Although behaviours indexed as ToM markers had been coded in the autistic child, they almost never appeared in T-patterns detected. Only ToM markers associated to partners' behaviours appeared in T-patterns.

Because autistic children are known to have more difficulty engaging in conventional interactions, we wondered if the parameter of a minimum of 3 occurrences for the detection of T-patterns was not too high for them, at least for the detection of T-patterns with higher levels of interactivity. Figure 12.6 thus presents the results of THEME analysis for the autistic child, with a lower minimum of occurrences (2), but a more stringent threshold ($p < .001$). We found an important increase of the number of T-patterns detected (n= 1179 after redundancy reduction), of their maximal length (20) and level (11).The content analysis of the more complex T-patterns shows that there is an entanglement of adapted interactions (Fig. 12.6, example 6.a) and unadapted exchanges (Fig. 12.6, example 12.6.b).

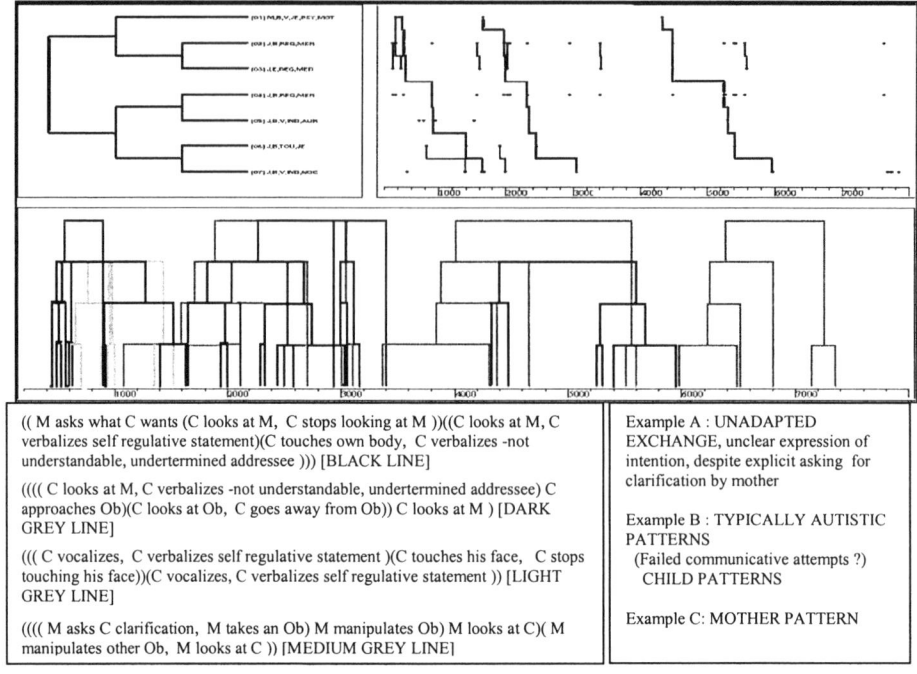

((M asks what C wants (C looks at M, C stops looking at M))((C looks at M, C verbalizes self regulative statement)(C touches own body, C verbalizes -not understandable, undertermined addressee))) [BLACK LINE]	Example A : UNADAPTED EXCHANGE, unclear expression of intention, despite explicit asking for clarification by mother
(((((C looks at M, C verbalizes -not understandable, undertermined addressee) C approaches Ob)(C looks at Ob, C goes away from Ob)) C looks at M) [DARK GREY LINE]	Example B : TYPICALLY AUTISTIC PATTERNS (Failed communicative attempts ?) CHILD PATTERNS
(((C vocalizes, C verbalizes self regulative statement)(C touches his face, C stops touching his face))(C vocalizes, C verbalizes self regulative statement)) [LIGHT GREY LINE]	
(((((M asks C clarification, M takes an Ob) M manipulates Ob) M looks at C)(M manipulates other Ob, M looks at C)) [MEDIUM GREY LINE]	Example C: MOTHER PATTERN

Figure 12.5 Detection of T-patterns in an autistic child (aged 7;11, VMA= 6;0) C= Child; M= Mother; Ob= Object.

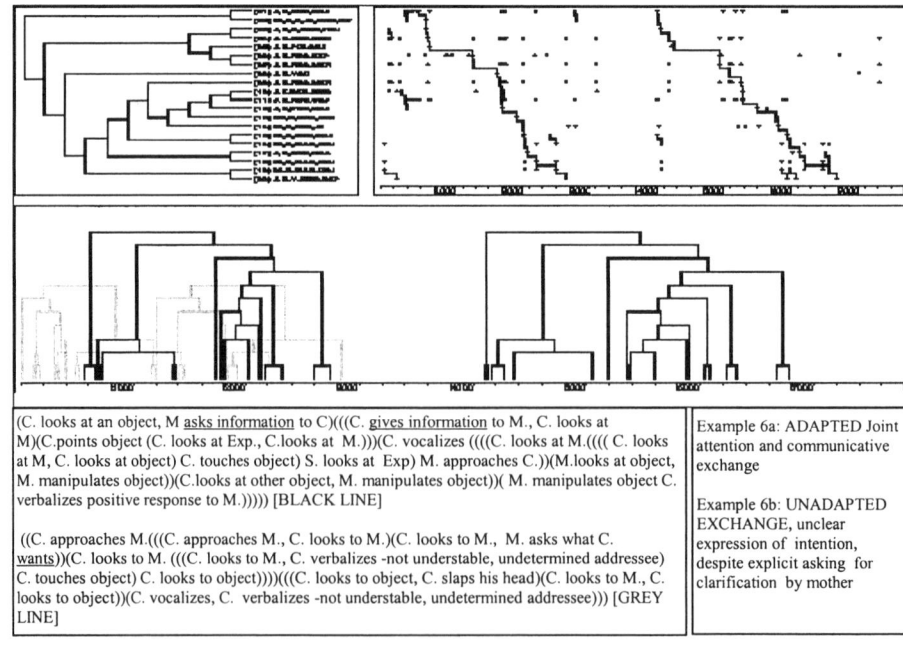

(C. looks at an object, M asks information to C)(((C. gives information to M., C. looks at M)(C.points object (C. looks at Exp., C.looks at M.)))(C. vocalizes ((((C. looks at M.(((((C. looks at M, C. looks at object) C. touches object) S. looks at Exp) M. approaches C.))(M.looks at object, M. manipulates object))(C.looks at other object, M. manipulates object))(M. manipulates object C. verbalizes positive response to M.))))) [BLACK LINE]	Example 6a: ADAPTED Joint attention and communicative exchange
((C. approaches M.((((C. approaches M., C. looks to M.)(C. looks to M., M. asks what C. wants))(C. looks to M. (((C. looks to M., C. verbalizes -not understable, undetermined addressee) C. touches object) C. looks to object))))(((C. looks to object, C. slaps his head)(C. looks to M., C. looks to object))(C. vocalizes, C. verbalizes -not understable, undetermined addressee))) [GREY LINE]	Example 6b: UNADAPTED EXCHANGE, unclear expression of intention, despite explicit asking for clarification by mother

Figure 12.6 T-Patterns detection with a minimal occurrence (autistic child) (min Occ. = 2, *p* < .001) (Total Nb. = 1179, max. length = 20, max. level = 11) C= Child; M= Mother; Exp= Experimenter; S= Sister.

At the beginning of the sequence, there is a quick repetition of a T-pattern containing 16 behavioural events, in which the autistic child has problems in communicating his intentions despite the mother's efforts to make it clearer (same as in the previous analysis). But another pattern containing 20 events emerges, on a larger time scale, revealing an appropriate succession of communicative behaviours (asking/giving information, joint attention involving adapted coordination of gaze alternance, manipulations, and explicit verbal positive comments).

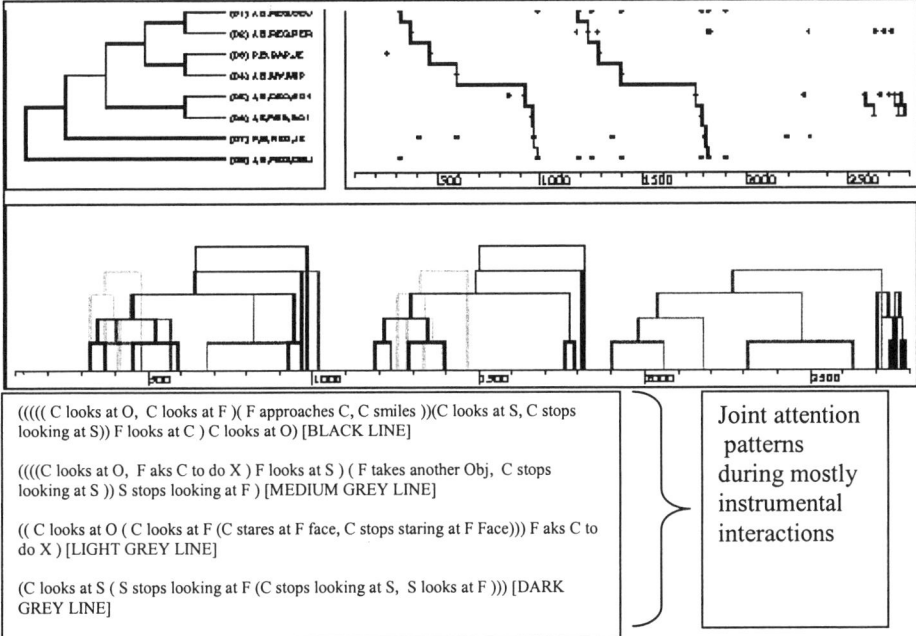

(((((C looks at O, C looks at F)(F approaches C, C smiles))(C looks at S, C stops looking at S)) F looks at C) C looks at O) [BLACK LINE]

(((((C looks at O, F aks C to do X) F looks at S) (F takes another Obj, C stops looking at F)) S stops looking at F) [MEDIUM GREY LINE]

((C looks at O (C looks at F (C stares at F face, C stops staring at F Face))) F aks C to do X) [LIGHT GREY LINE]

(C looks at S (S stops looking at F (C stops looking at S, S looks at F))) [DARK GREY LINE]

Joint attention patterns during mostly instrumental interactions

Figure 12.7 T-patterns detection with a minimal occurrence (normal child) (min Occ = 2, $p < .001$) (Total Nb. = 52, max. length = 8, max. level = 5). C= Child; F= Father; S= Sister; O= Object.

In comparison, the same analysis conducted with the *normal child* (minimum of 2 occurrences) also increases the length and levels of patterns detected, but to a much lower extent (maximal length = 8, maximal level = 5) than for the autistic child. Moreover, the qualitative content was very similar to the previous analysis (joint attention during instrumental patterns).

12.2.2.4 Discussion
Structural analyses conducted with THEME program provided several important findings. While a high number of T-patterns were detected in episodes involving the autistic child, it seemed to be linked more to intra-individual repetitive tendencies, than to high degrees of reciprocal interactive combinations of behaviours. The analysis confirmed the existence of forms/functions dissociations in the structures detected, and of difficulties in the regulation of communicative intentions (e.g. initiating, planning, maintaining, and modifying in order to be better understood). Moreover, data showed the variability of coordination and adjustment (sometimes very poor, sometimes better) in the dynamic of social interactions between autistic children and their social partners. As regards theory of mind, inappropriate selection of context-relevant communicative means for the expression and the understanding of intentions was found even within simple instrumental communicative

functions, such as asking for an object. Disregulation of control and executive processes appear to play a more general role in the autistic child's interactive peculiarities. Few T-patterns contained "ToM markers", although they occurred in events coded. When ToM markers occurred in patterns, they usually qualify the parents' behaviours (e.g. "asks for clarification"). Several interpretations could be proposed for that finding. It might be a property of "ToM markers", intrinsically linked to potentially "trap-social situations" (non literal messages, jokes, etc) and, as such, require innovative and flexible strategies. They would consequently appear in less regular communicative structures than more elementary and automaticized communicative regulation behaviours. It may also be that children from this study are not sufficiently advanced in ToM to show integrated communicative patterns including those markers. Moreover, it might be due to specific limitations of the observational context. Meal episodes may elicit more instrumental exchanges than mentalistic communications with children of this age. The extension of this kind of analyses to other contexts (especially play with adults or siblings, with a focus on oppositional episodes, [32]) will offer important information in this regard.

12.3   Conclusion and perspectives

Data presented here are only first results of a work in progress. Although there is still a lot to explore, such as peculiarities in timing structures, the exact location of critical behaviours (eye contacts, smiles, etc.) inside or outside patterns, THEME program seemed a very useful complementary tool for the understanding of social-communicative dysfunctions and functioning in autistic children. Findings were encouraging because they suggest that despite social impairments, children with autism develop relationships with others that cannot be reduced to dysfunctions or lack of social-cognitive skills. This type of analysis offers stimulating opportunities to investigate how theory of mind is implemented *in vivo*, as a function of contexts varying in executive processes demands. More generally, because it enables an individualized identification of communicative repertoires activated in specific contexts (as defined by partners and social goals), this method may contribute to both theoretical and clinical research, by offering possibilities of more precise adjustments in educational interventions to the individuals.

12.4   Acknowledgements

This research has been supported by Fondation de France and by France Telecom foundation. The authors are grateful to Thomas Calder for his skilful help, and to the families for their kind cooperation.

12.5   References

[1]   L. Kanner, Autistic disturbances of affective contact, *Nervous Child* **2** (1943) 217-250.
[2]   H. Tager-Flusberg, Current theory and research on language and communication in autism, *Journal of Autism and Developmental Disorders* **26** (1996) 169-172.
[3]   I. Rapin and M. Dunn, Update on the language disorders of individuals on the autistic spectrum, *Brain and Development* **25** (2003) 166-172.
[4]   S. Baron-Cohen, H. Tager-Flusberg, and D. Cohen, *Understanding other minds: Perspectives from developmental cognitive neuroscience, 2nd Edition.* Oxford: Oxford University Press, 2000.
[5]   U. Frith, A new look at language and communication in autism, *British Journal of Disorders of Communication* **24** (1989) 123-150.
[6]   J. Beaudichon, *La communication: processus, formes et applications.* Paris: Armand Colin, 1999.

[7]   J. Russell, *Autism as an executive disorder*. Oxford: Oxford University Press, 1998.
[8]   M. H. Plumet, C. Hughes, C. Tardif., and M. C. Mouren-Siméoni, L'hypothèse d'un déficit des fonctions exécutives dans l'autisme, *Psychologie Française* **43** (1998) 157-167.
[9]   I. Martin and S. McDonald, Weak coherence, no theory of mind, or executive dysfunction? Solving the puzzle of pragmatic language disorders, *Brain and Language* **85** (2003) 451-466.
[10]   V. Bernard-Orpitz, Pragmatic analysis of the communicative behaviour of an autistic child, *Journal of Speech and Hearing Research* **47** (1982) 99-109.
[11]   K. A. Loveland, S. H. Landry, S. O. Hughes, S. K. Hall, and R. E. McEvoy, Speech acts and the pragmatic deficits of autism, *Journal of Speech and Hearing Research* **31** (1988) 593-604.
[12]   A. M. Wetherby and C. A. Prutting, Profiles of communicative and cognitive-social abilities in autistic children, *Journal of Speech and Hearing Research* **27** (1984) 364-377.
[13]   D. V. Bishop, Development of the Children's Communication Checklist (CCC): A method for assessing qualitative aspects of communicative impairment in children, *Journal of Child Psychology and Psychiatry* **39**(6), (1998) 879-91.
[14]   S. Sparrow, D. R. Balla, and D. Cicchetti, *Vineland adaptive behaviour scales: Interview edition*. Circle Pines: American Guidance Service, 1984.
[15]   J. L. Adrien, C. Barthelemy, A. Perrot, S. Roux, L. Hameury, and D. Sauvage, Validity and reliability of the infant behavioral summarized evaluation (IBSE): a rating scale for the assessment of young children with autism and developmental disorders, *Journal of Autism and Developmental Disorders* **22** (1992) 375-394.
[16]   H. Van Engeland, F. A. Bodnar, and G. Bolhuis, Some qualitative aspects of the social behaviour of autistic children: an ethological approach, *Journal of Child Psychology and Psychiatry* **26** (1985) 879-893.
[17]   P. Mundy, M. Sigman, J. Ungerer, and T. Sherman, Defining the social deficits of autism: The contribution of non-verbal communication measures, *Journal of Child Psychology and Psychiatry* **27** (1986) 657-669.
[18]   F. Knott, C. Lewis, and T. Williams, Sibling interaction of children with learning disabilities: a comparison of autism and Down's syndrome, *Journal of Child Psychology and Psychiatry* **36** (1995) 965-976.
[19]   J. H. Buitelaar, H. Van Engeland, C. H. De Kogel, H. De Vries, and J. A. Van Hooff, Differences in the structure of social behaviour of autistic and non autistic retarded controls, *Journal of Child Psychology and Psychiatry* **26** (1991) 879-893.
[20]   S. H. N. Willemsen-Swinkels, J. H. Buitelaar, and H. Van Engeland, Children with a pervasive developmental disorder, children with a language disorder and normally developing children in situations with high- and low- involvement of the caregiver, *Journal of Child Psychology and Psychiatry* **32** (1997) 995-1015.
[21]   U. Frith, F. Happé, and F. Siddons, Autism and theory of mind in everyday life, *Social Development* **3** (1994) 108-124.
[22]   E. Fombonne, F. Siddons, S. Achard, U. Frith, and F. Happé, Adaptive behaviour and theory of mind in autism, *European Child and Adolescent Psychiatry* **3** (1994) 176-186.
[23]   M. S. Magnusson. *THEME user's manual: with notes on theory, model and pattern detection method*. Reykjavik: Human Laboratory, University of Iceland, 1993.
[24]   M. S. Magnusson, Discovering hidden time patterns in behaviour: T-patterns and their detection, *Behaviour Research Methods, Instruments, & Computers* **32** (2000) 93-110.
[25]   M. H. Plumet and C. Tardif, Théorie de l'esprit et communication chez l'enfant autiste: une approche fonctionnelle développementale, *Cahiers d'Acquisition et de Pathologie du Langage* **23** (2003) 121-141.
[26]   J. J. Deltour and D. Hupkens, *Test de Vocabulaire Actif et Passif, TVAP*. Paris: Editions EAP, 1980.
[27]   American Psychiatric Association. *Diagnostic and statistical manual of mental disorders (DSM-IV)*, 3rd ed. Washington: American Psychiatric Association, 1994.
[28]   C. Lord, M. Rutter, and A. LeCouteur, Autism Diagnostic Interview-Revised: A revised version of a diagnostic interview for caregivers of individuals with possible pervasive developmental disorders, *Journal of Autism and Developmental Disorders* **24**(5), (1994) 659-85.
[29]   P. Mitchell, *Introduction to theory of mind: children, autism and apes*. London: Arnold, 1997.
[30]   C. Tardif, M. H. Plumet, J. Beaudichon, D. Waller-Perrotte, M. Bouvard, and M. Leboyer, Micro-analysis of social interactions in autistic child-adult dyads in semi-structured play situations, *International Journal of Behavioural Development* **18** (1995) 727-747.
[31]   C. Tardif, Apport d'une nouvelle méthode pour l'étude des interactions observées dans des dyades composées d'un enfant autiste, *Approche Neuropsychologique des Apprentissages chez l'Enfant* **36** (1996) 11-16.

[32]   E. Veneziano, M. H. Plumet, S. Cupello, and C. Tardif, Pragmatic functioning in natural setting and the emergence of "theory-of-mind" in autistic and control children: A comparative study, *Psychology of Language and Communication,* in press.

The Hidden Structure of Interaction
L. Anolli et al. (Eds.)
IOS Press, 2005
© 2005 *The authors. All rights reserved.*

13. Tutoring Adjustment and Infants' Cognitive Gain

Sylvia SASTRE-RIBA

Abstract. Within the neuroconstructivist approach to cognitive development, tutoring is considered as a complex and essential form of human interaction in an educational context. Types, dynamics, and effects of tutoring (infant–infant and adult–infant) are heterogeneous and potentially have various effects on cognitive development. The identification of such interactive patterns among the participants and their successive regulations is essential to understand tutoring phenomenon. Investigating these tutoring types, dynamics and effects requires the observation of otherwise hidden patterns of tutoring in real time from ecologically valid situations involving a range of participants. The application of THEME program for the study of tutoring yielded these most relevant results: (1) the identification of various types of tutoring; (2) the importance of a tutor's adjustment to the tutored activity and the infant's competence; and (3) the possible effects of interference, and the determination of a tutor's optimal response to it.

Keywords: Tutoring; cognitive development; interaction; adjustment; executive functions.

Contents

13.1   Introduction

13.1.1 Cognitive development understanding

Cognitive development understanding requires an interdisciplinary and neuropsychological investigation of the continuous interaction among genes, neuropsychological substructure, and social context [1, 2]. From this perspective, cognitive development is interpreted as a continuous and differential transformation of cognitive competencies during which a human mind emerges from a developing brain as Quartz and Sejnowski reported [3]. Individual action and interpersonal interaction are essential components of this transformational process because they favour the progressive action organization as well as their cognitive consequences, demonstrate the emergent mechanisms and facilitate inferencing the intellectual structure. In sum, cognitive development would be a continuous redescription [4] of structures and cognitive functions during human life span, in which the subject has an active role. In this process, cognitive capacities are constructed and reconstructed step-by-step. Our interest focuses not only on the human intellectual capacity but also on its functioning, control and different manifestations.

Cognitive functioning is facilitated to a large extent by executive functions that coordinate various processes to achieve goals, flexibility [5] and the regulation of cognition [6], what is referred to as "executive control". Executive functions enable problem solving, creativity, and information processing. Concretely, such functions favour: 1) action as result of decision-making (intentionality), and 2) the selection and maintenance of information in the mind (representation), and 3) logical organization, decision-making, and planning [7]. Executive functions change with age, have differential expressions depending on types of development, may explain important aspects of typical and atypical development, and are crucial for successful social and academic performance.

Actual research on differential cognitive development focuses on the analysis of the microgenetic functioning of executive functions [8], in particular, inhibition, activation, planning, and shifting mechanisms. Cognitive development is no longer conceived as the activation of structural units - as Piaget postulated [9] - but is viewed as dependent on the inhibition of one structure or non-pertinent competence, the resistance to interference and the efficiency of activation.

The first years of life are essential in this redescriptional change because of their important role in the developmental process; in particular, occur concrete changes in the structure and functioning of the frontal lobe, changes in the prefrontal cortex related to myelinizaton, dendritic and cellular growth, new synaptical connections, and the activation of neurochemical systems [11-13]. These structural and functional brain's changes are associated with relevant gains in infant's first cognitive competencies and executive functions [7, 13 and 14], and in the organization of logical action and knowledge [15-17].

It is not only *nature* that produces developing minds; also social interaction pass beyond and modulate the neurobiological functioning, cognitive development is not only individual neither social, but both in a closed interrelation [18]. We postulate a tripolar subject–object–subject framework in which interpersonal interaction occurs in relation to a common object [18-20]. The flow of information in such interactions is not unidirectional, i.e., from the more competent (adult) participant to the less competent (child) as Vygotskian perspectives postulated, but bidirectional and dynamic, with continuous feedback among participants (e.g., child–child, child–adult). The patterns of information flow determine the modality of such processes, while the characteristics of the participants (e.g., their age and cognitive competence) and the form of their exchanges produce various modalities of interaction, as imitation or co-construction [18].

Tutoring is a modality that has particular relevance to the early years of human life [20]. Tutoring implies the existence of different competencies among participants (e.g., expert versus non-expert) and different roles [18] during interaction. Furthermore, as previous research has shown [21-23], tutoring varies according to: 1) the "action project" management (an infant's or an adult's action management), 2) an adult's adjustment to child competency and activity, 3) the focalization of an adult's proposal on the action results or process, and, 4) the proactive (during) or retroactive (after a result) maintenance by an adult of an infant's activity.

These types of tutoring, ordered from the adult management of activity (more adult guidance) to the infant's management of activity (lower adult's management), and from the more to less adult's adjustment are identified and defined through pattern extraction using the THEME program [24] as the following types: directive, integrative, maintenance, and laissez-faire (more information in [20, 21]). Because all of these tutoring types could be differentially related to cognitive gain and close cognitive progress [21, 22], the knowledge of an infant's action logical organization related to the impact of the tutoring types is important, as well as the role of inhibition (as an infant's "interference resistance") in front of some discordant information obtained (intrapersonal) or non-pertinent schemes of action, or in front of a non-adjusted adult proposal (interpersonal).

The manifestation of an infant's differential inhibition to an adult's proposals—adjusted or non-adjusted—would allow us to infer the infant's capacity to resist the interference as a result of the differentiated, selective, and effective inhibition. The manifestation of undifferentiated inhibition demonstrates the existence of "non-resistance to interference"; all of these factors demonstrate the efficacy or lack of efficacy in the infant's early executive functioning. There is little scientific evidence of what happens regarding alternative developmental courses. Some courses could be determined by functional brain differences, e.g., intra-uterine metabolopaties or nutritional problems, or by other functional and structural differences, e.g., resulting from Down Syndrome [25, 26]. In all cases, data related with these functional or structural matters improve our knowledge.

Our research is thus focused on infants' capacity to capture and benefit from the information obtained through their logical activity in relation to objects, and the information proposed by an adult. The comprehension of this question centers on understanding "how does the infant do" and "what does the infant do" in an interactive context during the first years of life. The research focuses on the action logical organization, the action content and on the own executive functions of the individual and the interference or facilitation provided by the adult's proposals (between individuals). Research must be applied to alternative developmental courses during the first three years of life, to identify differences in action logical organization [27, 28], executive functioning, and the effects of types of tutoring on those factors [22]. Our hypothesis was that different courses of development are associated with brain structural differences and differential models of efficacy in the previous-mentioned functions. A methodology adjusted to research objectives and data characteristics was necessary.

13.1.2 What a differential study of cognitive development can investigate

The subject of "knowing" is complex and multifaceted. It is commonly assumed to encompass hidden structures in individual and interpersonal functioning during early childhood cognitive development. From our point of view, it involves the following matters:

1. *An infant's activity on objects.* According to Langer [29], to act is to know, but acting is not sufficient for knowing, because acting must be intentional and logically

organized to obtain cognitive products. Furthermore, simple actions are embedded in more complex actions, in which goal achivement requires other steps that depend on higher-order factors [30]. We must know, step-by-step, the content of the infant's intentional activity, its action project and the flow of actions, results and their consequences on the activity redescription, as well as the role of executive functions in achieving such results (concretely: inhibition and activation regarding their correlates on control and planning, flexibility or perseveration). As Langer [29, 31] and Pastor & Sastre [27] reported, the logical classification of operations and functions will be used to operationalize the content of action.

2.   *Executive functions.* Action planning and control are determined by the differential application of executive functions. The most relevant functions with respect to cognitive control, planning, and flexibility are inhibition and efficient activation (or shifting). Inhibition is related to control and planning that: (a) stops the execution of a dominant action or the processing of irrelevant information, (b) selects representations and pertinent actions in an action procedure, and (c) favours consequent shifting or efficient activation after a stop-signal. In summary, inhibition allows the emergence of a new or modulative (shifting) scheme and resistance to interference, and is thus associated with mental flexibility. Shifting is the result of efficient inhibition and activation. It appears after the stopping of one potential interference of irrelevant information (or action), and is accompanied by a pertinent activation. The unsuitable manifestation of shifting is associated with perseveration. Perseveration appears when efficient inhibition is lacking but the activation of a dominant action is continued repetitively and without modification [32]. Then, it is also associated with non-appropriate cognitive functioning. All of these executive functions must be studied with reference to an infant's ability to resist interference (non-pertinent information) and goal maintenance (action project).

3.   *Interaction.* Because infants do not act alone, it is necessary to investigate the interactive context during the flow of task activity. According to Haan & Johnson [1], genetic factors and *interactions* with external factors contribute to the developmental process, even when an infant is still in the protective environment of the womb. Table 13.1 shows the components of an interactive situation that we studied from a tripolar perspective, in which we postulated the bi-directionality of interaction, the active and regulating role of the infant, and the importance of object determinants.

Consequently, we studied the following issues. First, we aimed at determining which types of tutoring are optimal in cognitive management, what do an infant and adult do during interactive activity, and which are the possible modulating parameters of tutoring. We had studied these parameters in previous research that identified tutoring types [21, 33] through the patterns detected by the THEME program [34]. The present study aimed at corroborating these findings in relation to executive functions and different participants. Tutoring types were identified using relevant parameters extracted from previously studied categories [20] related to:

- *Action project*: This was defined as the action goal maintenance that generates, organizes, and maintains activity, and attributes its meaning. This tutoring type can emerge from an infant, an adult, or both. The subcategories were the type, content, signification, and attention characteristics of an infant's activity.
- *Activity management*: This concerned the determination of which participant is the agent of activity (infant or adult) to understand the beginning and management of projects and actions realized.

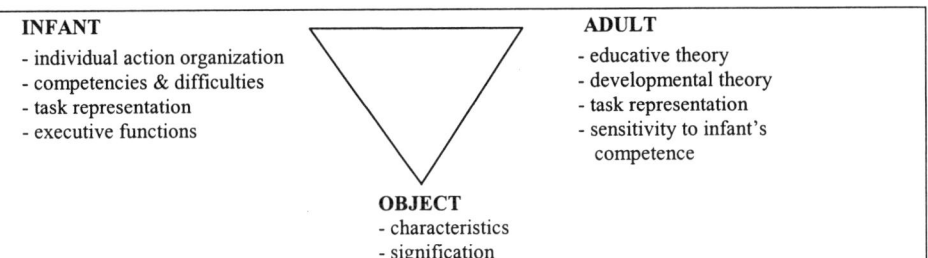

INFANT		ADULT
- individual action organization		- educative theory
- competencies & difficulties		- developmental theory
- task representation		- task representation
- executive functions		- sensitivity to infant's competence
	OBJECT	
	- characteristics	
	- signification	

Table 13.1 Components of the interactive activity

- *The adult's focus*: It consisted of determining whether an adult focused on the result of an infant's activity or on the process of obtaining it.
- *Maintenance*: This concerned whether an adult's proposals accompanied the process or the result of an infant's action. The subcategories were proactive (during activity) and retroactive (ending activity).
- *Adjustment*: This involved the proximity between an adult proposal and an infant's action project and/or his/her competence. Intersubjectivity and common representation of task was needed. The subcategory was adult information.

Second, the discovering of immediate infant gains during the interactive relationship related on the tutoring modalities is detected. These gains are referred to the micro-categories of "knowing result". Third, the understanding of infant's ability to resist the interference produced by lack of adjustment of the adult proposals, related to the types of tutoring. It is contained on the "type of activity" and "inhibition/activation" components [35].

All of these components and conditionings were necessary to the research goal; they were collected by the components of the mixed system analysis of field formats, as explained in the procedure paragraph. The understanding of the behavioural mechanisms of human activity; their content and effects, are not always evident and easily perceived. Furthermore, interaction relationships are subject to problem analyses concerning temporal organization (verbal or nonverbal, intra- or inter-individual). In this respect, time is central to the behavioural organization determining the methodology to apply.

13.1.3 Methodology decision

According to the previous concepts, methodology must allow to capture reality through the continuum in which is produced and its meaning. Methodology must allow to structure reality according to their behavioural units and it must allow the reality's simplification in order to interpret it. The methodology was designed to measure the elements set out in Table 13.2.

Consequently, the methodology consisted of the following points:

1) To infer intra- and inter-individual processes conferring psychological meaning: (a) the systematic observational methodology [36] for the reliable capture of reality in their continuum, extracting and codifying behavioural units and their sequential components; (b) the micro-genetic analysis of the reality content. This analysis was: (i) functional, extracting content and showing its emergence and sequential organization; (ii) intensive, i.e., based on a large number of reality observations; and (iii) sequentially realized.

2) To objectify the micro-genetic inferences, respecting the flow of real activity and its organization, the THEME program analysis [24, 34] permits the discovering of hidden structures and intra- and inter-individual patterns of functioning and their components. It also permits to identify the transition between events and patterns.

-The flow of action and its organization	-The adult proposals' adjustment
-Number of participants	-The nature of exchanges
-The characteristics of each participant	-The cognitive prerequisites
-The role of each participant	-Motivational aspects
-The types of tutoring used	-The dynamics of interaction
-The differential effects of tutoring	

Table 13.2 Reality elements to capture

13.2   The application of THEME program analysis to the study of tutoring and cognitive development

13.2.1 Participants

We studied 24 infants with alternative courses of development: 15 typical infants and 9 Down Syndrome infants, at the age of 1–3 years old (typical) or a developmental level equivalent to 1–3 years old (Down Syndrome). All infants were drawn from the Neonatology Service of the Saint Millan's Hospital at Logroño. Their initial cognitive developmental level was tested and found to be equivalent to 1–3-years-old [37].

13.2.2 Material

The material presented to the infants is designed to study the variation-selection mechanisms (activation–inhibition–shifting). It consisted of a task oriented to nonverbal behaviour to allow infants to execute proto-substitution and proto-addition logical operations (Figure 13.1).

Figure 13.1 Material

13.2.3 Procedure

Infants' spontaneous activity was videotaped longitudinally for a 10-minute period. The infant sat in front of the material and beside a familiar adult who acted according to the instruction: "act only if the infant's action stops, in which case offer a motivating proposal". Data analysis was designed to detect the content and logical organization of the infants' actions, and the associated executive functions and interactive dynamics. Three levels of analysis are proposed, from the less to the more reality-abstracted, ending with statistical analysis on the third level.

1) First-level analysis: Reality description. It included: (a) The reality depiction, step by step, exhaustively and consistently [38] recorded on specific sheets, elaborated ad-hoc for the extraction of successive behavioural units and their content; (b) The mixed analysis system (field formats) for reality coding. This system was essential for the analysis, and included the relevant content-components extracted from the theoretical background and experimentally applied to reality: the infant's activity, logical content, executive functions, and adult proposals and their adjustment. Table 13.3 shows the major components; (c) The inter- and intra-observer data quality control [38]. If the inter- and intra-observer concordance indices were satisfactory, we proceeded to the depiction and coding of all empirical data from the participants.

The product of this level of analysis was the generation of reality-depiction sheets, including the record of the acting content and the succession of actions.

	Macro-components	Micro-components	Codes
	activity management	infant	ch
		adult	ad
		both	com
	type of activity	repetitive	re
		modified	mopa
Infant	inhibition/activation	shifting	sh
		....	...
activity	action content	continent/content function	fcc
		...	
	knowing result	result	re
		...	...
	communicative demand	show result	mr
		...	...
	proposal	object	porel
Adult		....	
	adult information	related	infvarel
intervention	(adjustment)	non-related	infvanrel
		...	...
	focus on	process	ca
		result	

Table 13.3 Some components of the mixed system analysis (adapted from [39])

2) Second-level analysis: Reality codification and first inferences. This level consisted of the extraction and codification of behavioural units (Type III data—sequential and time-based). Reliability was calculated by intra- and inter-observer concordance [37]. In this way, we proceeded to the micro-genetic extraction of action projects: their start and end, chaining and meaning organization, logical content, and adult proposals. Activity sequences were established according to the stability of the action projects that were developed (by infant or by adult). The product consisted of detailed tables showing the organization of intra- and inter-group activity and participants' management of such activity [38]. This was an important approach to the psychological meaning of activity, which must be objectified and integrated.

3) Third-level analysis: Hidden pattern extraction (THEME program) and corroboration of micro-genetical interpretation. Digitalised image of reality is coded in real time applying the mixed analysis system constructed on the first level analysis and now introduced into the *.vvt folder* (THEME coder) . Then, we proceed to pattern extraction ($\alpha = .01$). Figure 13.2 shows one frame of the THEME coder.

After pattern extraction, we statistically analysed the components according to the research objectives, particularly oriented towards identifying whether there were significant differences between the groups (i.e., typical versus Down Syndrome infants).

The results consisted of hidden structures of functioning, including patterns of the tutoring types, adjustment, and infants' interference resistance to adult proposals.

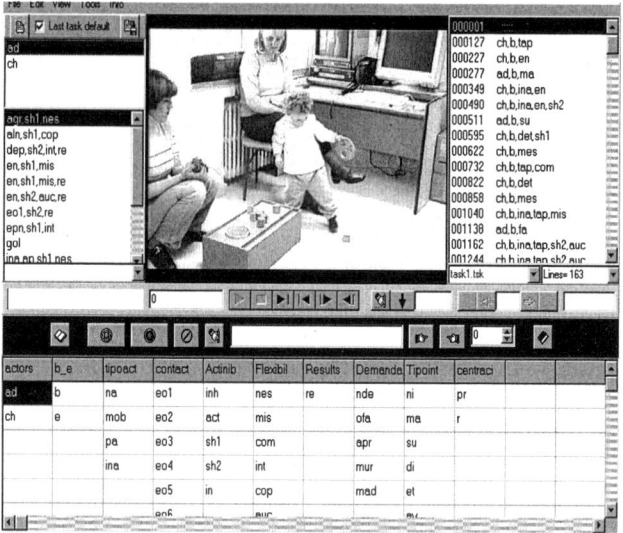

Figure 13.2 THEME coding frame

13.2.4 Results

Only the results of the third level analysis derived from the THEME program are presented; the results are grouped into the three issues studied: (a) tutoring types, (b) logical content, and (c) resistance to interference [38]. This extraction was started by the generation of a coefficient of concordance, with $\alpha= 80\%$ as the acceptable threshold.

13.2.4.1 Tutoring types

Previously established tutoring types [21] were supported. Patterns obtained were constituted by the same categorical elements, with a frequency of regularity of almost the 85%. Table 13.4 shows the types of tutoring extracted according to the parameters described. Figure 13.3 shows one of the representative patterns obtained.

A brief description of each tutoring type is now given, from less to more adult-oriented management of activity.

i. *Directive tutoring* was defined because the adult's managed activity. Infants followed adult proposals, incorporating these proposals into their own activity. Adult proposals were not adjusted to infants' actions, but to their own activity.

ii. *Integrative tutoring* was evidenced when adults managed an activity facilitating the infants participation in the adult' action project. Adult proposals were adjusted to the infants' level of competence, but did not favour infants' initiatives.

iii. *Maintenance tutoring* was evidenced by patterns composed of behaviors concerning infants' management activity, with adults' proposals adjusted to infants' action projects and competence. Adults offer new information that helps infants to excel their own initiative.

iv. *Laissez-faire tutoring*. This assumed that there was no adult intervention while infants were acting on objects; therefore there were no proposals or expressions of maintenance. Activity management was thus entirely infants' responsibility.

Action project	Focus on	Maintenance	Adjustment	Tutoring type
adult	result process	proactive retroactive	no	directive
adult to child	result process	proactive retroactive	yes	integrative
child	result	proactive retroactive	yes	maintenance
child	no result no process	no proactive no retroactive	no	laissez-faire

Table 13.4 Types of tutoring

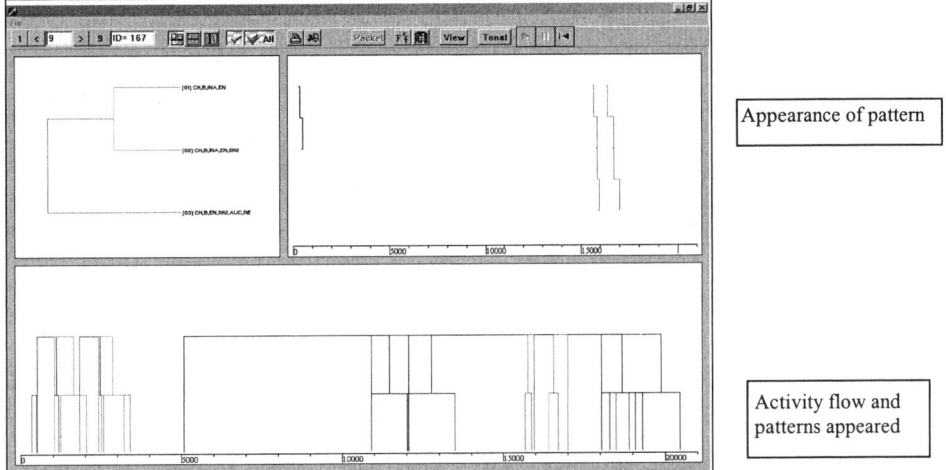

Figure 13.3 Example of a THEME pattern and their participation on the flow of activity

Among the Down Syndrome babies, the more frequently occurring tutorial type was directive tutoring; among the typical babies, the more frequent type was maintenance tutoring. This suggests that infants' development may depend in part on the extent to which adult proposals assist them.

13.2.4.2 Immediate gain in action
To determine the relationship between tutoring type and infant development, we have summed all the codes referred to as "gain", constituting the patterns obtained and corresponding to each kind of tutoring. The results are set out in Table 13.5.

Tutoring type	Cognitive gain
Maintenance	n= 28
Integrative	n= 16
Directive	n= 2
Laissez-faire	n= 0

Table 13.5 Gain and non-gain frequencies

The ground with higher gain was produced with "maintenance tutoring", i.e., adult proposals are related to the infant and accompanied by proactive and retroactive adult's maintenance during infant activity. On the other hand, directive tutoring showed some gains as the result of the copy of non-adjusted adult proposals, but not as the product of infants' initiative and elaboration.

We also represent, the emergence of executive functions on infants' activity to determine their effect on cognitive control and flexibility. As Table 13.6 shows, there are significant differences between the groups with respect to the levels of shifting, i.e., efficient inhibition and activation on typical babies, and perseveration, i.e., inefficient inhibition among the Down Syndrome infants. This result suggests that adults' adjusted proposals play a significant role in the favouring of cognitive development and in stimulating flexibility rather than perseveration.

Efficient inhibition/activation	Typical/Down Syndrome infants
Shifting	$p = .032$
Perseveration	$p = .050$

Table 13.6. Inter-group differences in efficient inhibition/activation ($\alpha = .05$).

13.2.4.3 Infants' resistance to interference

Resistance to the interference produced by adult's non-adjusted information was extracted from the data; the resulting significant differences are set out in Table 13.7. The data show more adult's non-adjusted proposals and less resistance to interference among Down Syndrome babies. This is an important finding for educators who wish to minimize the effects of their non-adjusted proposals, they have to be particularly sensitive to alternative courses of development because they may increase the potential for adult intervention, if not adjusted, to add to the structural and functional difficulties of Down Syndrome infants from the early stages of their development.

	Tutoring types			
Infants	Adjustment	Non adjustment	Interf. resistance	Goal maintenance
Typical infants	$p = .001$	---	$p = .003$	Yes
Down Syndrome infants	---	$p = .002$	---	No

Table 13.7. Significant inter-group differences in adjustment and resistance to interference ($\alpha = 0.5$)

13.3   Conclusions

The THEME program has produced significant evidence of the types and dynamics of tutoring, and of the organization, content, and associated executive functions of action sequences. It has shown the importance of the adjustment of adult proposals to infants' action project and competencies in the task of optimising their cognitive development.

We have identified various types of tutoring associated with both adult and infant management of activity. Infant management appears to be enhanced with maintenance tutoring, which is in correspondence with a greater level of cognitive improvement. A reduced level of infant's gains accompanies adult management activity - directive tutoring.

These types of tutoring are also characterized by the level of adult proposal adjustment to an infant; the more adjusted proposals are likely to be associated with maintenance tutoring and the less adjusted proposals with the directive or laissez-faire tutoring. In this respect, adult adjustment depends on the type of tutoring and the existence of an infant's project of action (goal maintenance). On the other hand, infants' gains are related to infants capacity to generate action project, flexibility (executive functions), type of tutoring, and the adjustment of adults' proposals based on feedback from the situation.

There are significant inter-group differences in efficient inhibition/activation mechanisms: the main one is not centred on a stop-signal but on perseveration, which is more frequent among Down Syndrome infants and which is associated with less combination and redefinition of efficient inhibition/activation function (shifting). Such infants also show a lower capacity to generate or modulate new action schemes, where flexibility on action organization is lower.

Deriving educational implications from these findings is necessary to help infants in their cognitive development. This is particularly important with respect to alternative courses of development because, adding to the individual structural differences on the competence to organize and control cognitive acting, it appears the influence of non-adjusted adult's intervention.

Results show that the infants' group with more structural and functional difficulties receives a more non-adjusted type of tutoring that involves less resistance to interference. It suggests that their developmental process could be impaired.

In sum, early educative intervention must be redefined: it should not only be centred on formal consistency, but also should be particularly sensitive to (1) infants' initiation of logical organization of the content and executive control of their actions, and (2) adult adjustment to infant competencies. Not to redefine such intervention may contribute to a continuing deficiency in the tutorial process.

13.4 Acknowledgements

This work was made possible by grants from the Health Ministry of the La Rioja Autonomous Government and the Spanish Ministry of Education, PB98 C-0207.

13.5 References

[1] M. Haan and M. Johnson, Eds. *The cognitive neuroscience of development.* London: Sage, 2003.

[2] S. A. Petrill, R. Plomin, J. C. DeFries, and J. K. Hewitt, Conclusions, in *Nature, nurture, and the transition to early adolescence*, S. A. Petrill, R. Plomin, J. C. DeFries, and J. K. Hewitt, Eds. New York: Oxford University Press, 2003, pp. 310-316.

[3] S. R. Quartz and T. J. Sejnowski, The neural basis of cognitive development: A constructivist manifesto, *Behavioral and Brain Sciences* **20** (1997) 537–596.

[4] A. Karmiloff-Smith, Promissory notes, genetic clocks, and epigenetic outcomes, *Behavioral and Brain Sciences* **20** (2), (1997) 355–360.

[5] S. Funahashi, Neuronal mechanisms of executive control by the prefrontal cortex, *Neuroscience Research* **39** (2001) 147-165.

[6] A. Miyake, N. Friedman, M. Emerson, A. Witzki, and A. Hoerter, The unity and diversity of executive functions and their contributions to complex «frontal lobe» tasks: a latent variable analysis, *Cognitive Psychology* **41** (2000) 49–100.

[7] A. Diamond, Normal development of prefrontal cortex from birth to young adulthood: Cognitive functions, anatomy and biochemistry, in *Principles of Frontal Lobe Function,* D. T. Stuss and R. T. Knight, Eds. London: Oxford University Press, 2002, pp. 466–503.

[8] A. D. Baddeley, Working Memory, *Science* **255** (1992) 566-569.

[9] J. Piaget, *The construction of reality in the child.* New York: Basic Books, 1954.

[10] F. M. Benes, J. B. Taylor, and M. Cunningham, Convergence and plasticity of monoaminergic systems in the medial prefrontal cortex during postnatal period: Implications for the development of psychopathology, *Cerebral Cortex* **10** (2000) 1014–1027.

[11]   K. Christoff and J. Gabrieli, The frontopolar cortex and human cognition: evidence for a rostrocaudal hierarchical organization within the human prefrontal cortex, *Psychobiology* **28** (2000) 168–186.
[12]   D. T. Stuss and R. T. Knight, Introduction, in *Principles of Frontal Lobe Function*, D. T. Stuss and R. T. Knight, Eds. New York: Oxford University Press, 2002, pp. 1–7.
[13]   A. Diamond, Neuropsychological insights into the meaning of object concept development, in *Brain Development and Cognition*, M. H. Johnson, Ed. Cambridge: Blackwell, 1996, pp. 208-247.
[14]   A. Diamond, Prefrontal cortex development and development of cognitive functions, in *The International Encyclopedia of the Social and Behavioral Sciences*, Vol. 4.3 Article: 198, N.J.Smelser and P. B. Baltes, Eds. London: Elsevier Press, 2001.
[15]   J. Langer, The heterochronic evolution of primates. Cognitive development, in *Biology, Brains and Behavior*, S. T. Parker, J. Langer, and L. McKinney, Eds. Oxford: James Currey, 2001, pp. 215–236.
[16]   O. Houdé, Inhibition and cognitive development: object, number, categorisation and reasoning, *Cognitive Development* **15** (2000) 63–67.
[17]   F. M. Crinella and J. Yu, Brain mechanisms and intelligence. Psychometric g and executive function, *Intelligence* **27** (4), (2000) 299–327.
[18]   M. Verba, The beginnings of collaboration in peer interaction, *Human Development* **37** (1994) 125–139.
[19]   J. Beaudichon, S. Legros, and M. Magnuson, Organisation des régulations inter e intrapersonnelles dans la transmission d'informations complexes organisées, *Bulletin de psychologie* **399** (1991) 44–60.
[20]   M. Verba, Tutoring interactions between young children: how symmetry can modify asymmetrical interactions, *International Journal of Behavioral Development* **22** (1), (1998) 195–216.
[21]   S. Sastre and E. Pastor, Modalidades de tutela de gestión cognitiva en bebés trisómicos, *Infancia y aprendizaje* **93** (2001) 35–52.
[22]   S. Sastre and M. Verba, Les interactions de tutelle avec les bébes normaux et les enfants trisomiques: l'apport de l'enfant dans l'ajustament de l'adulte, *Enfance* **2** (2001) 197–214.
[23]   L. Villares, S. Sastre, and J. D. Vargas, Modalidades de tutela paterna y efectos en el desarrollo cognitivo del hijo (1;0–2;0 a.), *Iberpsicología* **8.**1.3 (2003).
[24]   M. Magnusson, *THEME 4.0*. Amsterdam: PatternVision Ltd. and Noldus Information, 2003.
[25]   J. Flórez, Bases neurológicas del aprendizaje, *Siglo Cero* **30** (3), (1999) 9–27.
[26]   J. Flórez, V. Troncoso, and M. Diersen, *Síndrome de Down: biología, desarrollo y educación*. Barcelona: Masson, 1996.
[27]   E. Pastor and S. Sastre, Desarrollo de la inteligencia, in *Desarrollo cognitivo*, V. Bermejo, Ed. Madrid: Sintesis, 1994, pp. 191–213.
[28]   S. Sastre, Estudios del desarrollo cognitivo precoz: alcance, aplicaciones y límites en el proceso de deficienciación, *Universitas Tarraconensis (Revista de Psicología)* **XVIII** (2), (1996) 77–107.
[29]   J. Langer, Early cognitive development: Basic functions, in *Developmental Psychology: Cognitive, perceptuo-motor and neuropsychological perspectives*, C. A. Hauert, Ed. Amsterdam: North Holland, 1990, pp.19–42.
[30]   J. Jeannerod, *The Cognitive Neuroscience of Action*. Cambridge: Blackwell Publishers, 1997.
[31]   J. Langer, *The origins of logic: six to twelve months*. New York: Academic Press, 1980.
[32]   F. N. Dempster and C. J. Brainerd, *Interference and inhibition in cognition*. New York: Academic Press, 1995.
[33]   E. Pastor and S. Sastre, Patrones de interacción adulto–niño en la construcción del significado: Aplicación del progama THEME, in *Observación de conducta interactiva en contextos naturales: aplicaciones*, M. T. Anguera, Ed. Barcelona: E.U.B., 1999, pp. 125–150.
[34]   M. Magnusson, Hidden real-time patterns in intra and interindividual behavior: description and detection, *European Journal of Psychological Assessment* **12** (2), (1996) 112–123.
[35]   S. Sastre and N. Merino, Tipos de tutela e interferencia, *Contextos educativos,* in press.
[36]   M. T. Anguera, Metodología observacional, in *Metodología de la investigación en ciencias del comportamiento*, J. Arnau, M. T. Anguera, and J. Gómez, Eds. Murcia: Secretariado de Publicaciones de la Universidad de Murcia, 1999, pp. 125–236.
[37]   A. Cambrodí and S. Sastre, *Escales d'Observació Sistemàtica 0–3 anys*. Barcelona: P.P.U. 1993.
[38]   K. L. Krippendorf, *Content analysis. An introduction to its methodology (V)*. London: Sage publications, 1983.
[39]   S. Sastre, P. Bretón, J. Escorza, E. Escolano, N. Merino, M. Poch, M. Pascual, and Y. Soares, *Desarrollo cognitivo e inhibición, prevención e intervenció*. Logroño: Consejería de Salud de la Comunidad Autónoma de La Rioja, 2000.

SECTION VI

HIDDEN PATTERNS IN SOCIAL AND CULTURAL CONTEXTS

> *No single theory seems to predict or explain the emergence of T-patterns in behavior and interactions. Suggestions may, however, be found within the area of dynamic patterns and complexity studies since key terms describing complex dynamic and self organizing systems - that is, mechanism, agents, interaction, recurring patterns, and hierarchical organization - also surround the definition and detection of T-patterns.*
>
> *Magnusson, 2000*

Even though unaided observers often perceive human behavior in social interactions as somewhat structured and repetitive, they find it difficult or impossible to specify what kinds of patterns are being repeated or when. This is particularly true when the observers consider interactions occurring in daily life, usually strongly shaped by the social and cultural context in which they happen.

This section tries to provide a general method for analyzing hidden patterns in social and cultural non-pathological contexts based on the use of the THEME software. To provide a wide reference framework, the interactions discussed were taken from very different daily situations: starting from the analysis of the structure of a familiar conflict, this section ends with the analysis of the interaction in a work context. Also analyzed were the cultural behavioural differences displayed during friendly conversations, the hidden movements of soccer players and the facial expression of people looking at the TV news.

In the first study, chapter 14, HARDAWAY and DUNCAN JR. report an intensive, exploratory study of a single, protracted conflictual interaction involving three of the four family members: the father and two daughters. The two children were 14–months and 5.5–years old. Speech and body motion were transcribed to the accuracy of a single video frame. THEME analyses were used to detect sequential patterns in the transcribed data.

The Authors suggested that the behaviour has to be considered within the streams of actions and re-actions displayed. Structure is a key notion of this study, considered as an assumption about the nature of relationship that ties successive actions. In particular the chapter discussed the notion of *attack series*: sequences of conflictual actions, beginning with the child's non-reactive attack and subsequent actions by the father and sister directly responsive to the child's attack. The analysis of these parent–child interactions having "real emotional significance" seems also particularly useful to enhancing comprehension of the child's social and cognitive development.

Maintaining the focus on the structure of interaction, in chapter 15, AGLIATI, VESCOVO and ANOLLI compared conversational T-patterns in two different cultures, specifically Italian and Icelandic ones. THEME was used to investigate non verbal behaviors that participants displayed during the conversation flow: gestures, turn-taking and body movements. Data highlighted the country effect on conversation rhythm: number and frequency of time patterns were deeply different between Icelandic and Italian couples, as the former turned out to manage the temporal organization in a more synchronous and regular way than the latter. Furthermore, peculiar gestures were recognized for Icelandic and Italian couples, underlining systematic differences in the cultural framework. The research also sketched out that conversation may be considered a domain –specific activity, at least as it concerns gestures and time allocation.

In chapter 16, BLOOMFIELD, JONSSON, POLMAN, HOULAHAN, and O'DONOGHUE faced with the issue of physical conditioning and coaching techniques, practices that aim at improving sports performance. Many sporting skills require a very precise moment and direction of force application and the neural pattern for the precise force application is acquired only by repetition of the desired skill. Thus, precise movement patterns of specific motor skills are needed to effectively entrain appropriate motor programs for efficient co-ordination of muscular contraction. Following this line, the chapter first reviewed and critiqued the current research into the physical demands of soccer. Then it offered an alternative method of detailing the movements performed by the players, and finally provides a methodology for the identification of hidden patterns within the movements through use of T-pattern detection. The final aim is the reproduction of specific patterns of movement, which can be used to enhance physical conditioning and coaching practices.

Chapter 17 details a study carried out by UNZ and SCHWAB, regarding media reception and emotional processes following the watching of TV-news. The investigation of media reception was done by combining both timeline data of TV-news (describing formats and content of TV-news by using a computer assisted media analysis) and data about facial expressions as indicators of emotional appraisal processes (EmFACS). The results show a large number of temporal patterns in facial expressions data. A remarkably high proportion of these patterns can be interpreted as cognitive appraisal-processes according the assumptions of Scherer and colleagues. Furthermore, the authors found patterns between the formal aspects of TV-news and the facial expressions of the viewers, suggesting a connection between the presentation of TV news events and the emotional processes of the viewer. These results also showed how the study of facial expressions and behavioural manifestation of emotion could contribute to a deeper comprehension of the emotional processing.

Last chapter, 18, written by KOCH, MÜLLER, SCHROEER, THIMM, KRUSE and ZUMBACH, reported a study dealing with gender-related communicative patterns in two token work teams: they considered how gender-token status may affect verbal and nonverbal communication. The authors considered two teams with one gender-token each: a female token in an industrial team of eleven persons and a male token in a kindergarten team of eight persons. Patterns of talking times, back channelling, gaze behaviour, affect display, and movement qualities were assessed. As highlighted by data, the female token showed more nonverbal behaviour patterns than the male token. In a sequence with some underlying conflict potential, women used more nonverbal communication, regarding dominance, support and defensive behaviour. On the other hand, considering that defensive behaviour appears when self image is threatened, it seemed worth to acknowledge that this behaviour is displayed both by female gender-token and, with some degree, by female leader when interacting with male gender-token. This occurrence supported previous research findings according to which gender-token status has frequently negative consequences only for women.

The Hidden Structure of Interaction
L. Anolli et al. (Eds.)
IOS Press, 2005

14. "Me First!" Structure and Dynamics of a Four-Way Family Conflict

Christina HARDWAY, Starkey DUNCAN Jr

Abstract. This study reports an intensive, exploratory study of a single, protracted conflictual interaction involving all four members of a family. Within the larger interaction, there were four subinteractions. Because of space limitations, only the central conflictual subinteraction will be described. This interaction involved three of the four family members: the father and two daughters. The two children were 14–months and 5.5–years old. Speech and body motion were transcribed to the accuracy of a single video frame. THEME analyses were used to detect sequential patterns in the transcribed data. These patterns were used, in turn, to generate hypotheses concerning the rule–governed structure of the interaction. Results are discussed in terms of the structure of conflictual interactions, the implications of the hypothesized structures for the conflict process in the interaction studied, and the description of multiway influence in interaction.

Keywords: Conflict; family; conflictual interaction structure; convention-based interaction; speech; body motion.

Contents

14.1   Introduction

This study proceeds from several presuppositions involving interaction in general and early parent-child interaction in particular. (a) Interaction is defined in terms of participants' mutually contingent action sequences. (b) These sequences involve bidirectional influence between participants. That is, each participant is, to some empirically definable extent, influencing the actions of the partner. (c) Much of adult interaction is convention based or rule governed. There are rules for conducting various types of interactions, just as there are rules governing participants' actions in games such as chess or basketball. However, the rules for games are explicit while the rules for interaction (as well as for language) are largely unknown by participants and must be hypothesized based on empirical, exploratory research. In this discussion, a *structure* is an empirically based hypothesis concerning the rules operating in a set of observed interactions. (d) The extent to which a child is capable of convention-based interaction is similarly an empirical issue, as are the nature and extent of these convention-based interactions when they eventually emerge as a component of socialization. A special form of interaction, probably inevitable in any extended relationship, is conflict. There appears to be broad agreement that, while conflict may often be a strong experience for participants, its developmental implications may be either positive or negative [1, 2]. There is cumulating evidence that the way in which conflict contributes to socialization is deeply affected by factors such as the nature of the interaction process through which conflict is pursued, the actions involved, the duration of the conflict, and the way it is concluded [2, 3]. While the child's early conflicts may be important socialization experiences, they need not be prolonged. Two reviewers of conflict between peers [2, 3], using partially overlapping evidence, reported that, depending on the methods used, the duration of these interactions was typically brief, averaging 12 to 31 s. The brevity of many early peer conflicts is strongly supported by our observations of videotapes made in the homes of families (described in the Method section). Conflicts observed on these tapes, though relatively frequent, were typically quite brief.

14.2   The conflict

The conflict reported in this paper was chosen because of its several distinctive properties. (a) The conflict interaction as a whole was by far the longest one that we have found on our tapes of early parent–child interaction in the home, spanning a period of 14 min 37 s. The interaction included four subinteractions, one of which is described in this paper. This permitted our studying the dynamics of a single protracted conflict, as opposed to aggregating a number of briefer conflicts possibly exhibiting different interaction characteristics. (b) The duration of the interaction permitted a more detailed scrutiny of the mechanisms and characteristics of bidirectional or multidirectional processes operating within it. (c) Although the larger interaction included all four members of the family, the conflict described here involved three: the father, child, and big sister. Thus, it was possible to examine the characteristics of triadic interactions. (e) The main antagonist and clear winner was a 14 months–old child who succeeded in fully exploiting her relative immaturity, lack of productive language, and the fact that other family members appeared to underestimate her receptive ability and grasp of the situation. Thus, the conflict provided the opportunity to consider issues of analysis and interpretation of longer, more complex, multiparty interactions in which a relatively young child was involved.

The interaction as a whole may be described as comprised of four main phases. After the father returns home from work, he sits on the couch with the mother and two girls. Each girl promptly perches herself on one of father's legs. The conflict to be described begins at this point. The child immediately hits the big sister, beginning a number of physical attacks involving hitting, pushing, shoving, and kicking, accompanied by continual fussing, crying, and screaming. These attacks and the father's and big sister's responses to them form the most salient aspects of the conflict. The child clearly wants to be with the father without the big sister's co–presence. In contrast, the big sister appears willing (or obliged) to settle for peaceful coexistence. The attacks and general fussing continue throughout this subinteraction with the exception of a relatively brief interlude during which the child, big sister, and father have several episodes of playing. However, in each case the child abruptly terminates the play and renews the attacks. This subinteraction lasts 6 min 45 s.

There is a second conflictual subinteraction in which the big sister returns to the father's side, and the child resumes her attacks and fussing. The phase ends when the father requests the big sister to get a carrot from the kitchen for the child. The big sister's departure ends the conflict and the broader interaction. This final phase lasts 1 min 7 s. Taken as a whole, and considering the parents' definition of the problem, the child's strategy of remaining implacable and continually attacking the big sister when both are on the father's lap is both effective and ultimately successful. At the end, the big sister capitulated by joining the mother in the kitchen. This left the child alone with the father and showing every sign of being entirely satisfied with this new arrangement.

14.3   Convention-based interaction

The notion of convention-based interaction is widely discussed in the literature [4-12]. The use of conventions by participants introduces strong regularities of a specifiable sort in the sequences of actions comprising the interaction. Exploratory analyses aimed at detecting these sequential regularities may lead to the hypothesis of conventions underlying them. As mentioned earlier, a hypothesis concerning one or more conventions used in an observed interaction will be termed a *structure*.

14.3.1 Describing interaction structure

Describing interaction structure is considered at length in [7, 8]. Interaction structure is described in terms of two main components: elements and rules connecting them. Each *element* is composed of one or more actions by one or more participants. In most structures, when two or more actions comprise an element, the element is considered to occur when any one or more of its constituent actions occur. That is, the actions are considered to be *interchangeable* [6] within the element. Grouping different actions within a single structural element is an empirical issue, based on evidence that the actions have the same effect on the course of the interaction. Thus, the groupings were based on sequential analysis, as opposed to intuition or theory. *Rules* define appropriate sequences of elements within the structure. A distinction is made between obligatory rules and optional rules. An *obligatory rule* states that, at a specified point in the stream of interaction, an element must or must not occur. An *optional rule* states that, at a specified point in the stream of interaction, the partner may legitimately choose from a set of two or more alternative actions. In some cases these alternative actions will involve contrasts, such as saying "yes" or saying "no". In other cases, the alternatives will involve a participant's performing or not performing an action, such as hitting or not hitting the big sister. In any event, each available option must have a different effect on the ensuing interaction. That is, the interaction must take a different course, depending on how the option is exercised.

14.3.2 Flowcharts

Hypothesized structures are represented as flowcharts. Four flowchart shapes are used in this paper. The beginning of a structure is indicated by a large arrow shape, and the ending by an oblong shape. Obligatory elements are represented by rectangular shapes. Optional elements are represented by diamond shapes. Indicated within these shapes are one or more actions and the participant(s) responsible for them. The lines leading out of diamonds indicate the course the interaction takes as a result of the way the option was exercised.

14.3.3 Development of hypothesized structures

Analysis of action sequences in the transcribed data permits the development of empirically based hypotheses concerning interaction structures. For example, patterns involving the child's hits, pulls, pushes, and shoves were carefully scrutinized in order to develop a hypothesized structure involving actions by the child, big sister, and father that systematically preceded or followed these actions. Potential structures were then evaluated in terms of their effectiveness in fitting the transcribed data.

14.4   Conflict

When structures are hypothesized for interactions, it becomes possible to identify each participant's actions within the structure as ratifying, not ratifying, or neither with regard to the partner's preceding action [4, 5]. *Ratification* is used in its usual sense of a participant's explicitly or implicitly agreeing to, permitting, or going along with, something. In the context of this discussion the "something" is the partner's preceding action within the structure. In interaction structures, ratifying or non-ratifying actions can be identified on the basis of low–level judgments concerning whether or not each participant is acting in concert with the preceding actions of the partner. Ratification in face–to–face interaction was considered by [10]. It was further elaborated in a conceptual framework for rule–governed interaction [7, 8]. Ratification was a key element in treatments of convention–based conflict [4, 5].

Two types of conflict were identified: conflict concerning convention, and conflict within convention. In *conflict concerning convention*, participants do not agree on the use of a particular convention in an interaction, a change in a currently active convention, or the ending of a currently active convention. This study focuses on conflict within convention. In this form of conflict participants agree on a convention to be used in an interaction, and conform to the rules of the convention, but disagree on the course the interaction should take within the convention. Such disagreement becomes possible when the convention permits participants to perform the convention in more than one way—that is, when the interaction structure provides one or more options. When a participant exercises an option, the partner may not agree with that choice. Thus, conflict or the possibility of conflict is part of the convention itself. A simple example would be competitive games, such as chess or football, in which participants agree to engage in conflict within the bounds of explicit rules that include both cooperation and conflict.

In [5] *conflict within convention* was defined as being created when there are two successive failures to ratify, one by each participant. Conflict within convention is concluded when either participant ratifies the partner's action. Definitions of conflict concerning and within convention require (a) a hypothesized structure for the interaction, and (b) the evaluation of elements in the structure as ratifying, non-ratifying, or neither.

14.5   Method

14.5.1   Subjects

The subjects of this study were members of a family of four: a 14 months–old child (the focus of our taping), her 5.5 years–old big sister, and their father and mother. Videotaping of this family began when the child was 6 months old and ended when she was 18 months old. The family was taped all day, two consecutive days each month. Taping focused on the child's interactions with other family members.

14.5.2   Transcription

14.5.2.1   Interaction transcribed and analyzed
All of the interaction (14 min 37 s) was transcribed and analyzed. The interaction included four distinct phases, of which two were conflictual. However, space constraints permit description of the analysis of only the first conflictual phase. More extended description of the entire interaction is available from the second author.

14.5.2.2   Actions
Because this was an exploratory study designed to generate hypotheses concerning rules within the interaction, a number of actions were transcribed for each of the four participants: 17 for the child, 17 for the big sister, 19 for the father and 5 for the mother. Transcription included the beginning and ending times for each action to the accuracy of a single video frame. Each type of action was defined as concretely as possible. From the larger set of transcribed actions, the following appear in the results: (a) child: hit, pull, push, and shove big sister; (b) big sister: shield self from the child's attacks, reposition herself on the father's knee; (c) father: physically intervene in child's action.

14.5.2.3   Speech
Transcribing speech and locating syllables with respect to actions was facilitated by the Sequel - Analysis Module (SAM-259) [13]. SAM-259 produces a distinctive visual representation of phonemes. This representation can be written to videotape so that the transcription of speech can be carried out at any tape speed, including stop frame.

14.5.2.4   Reliability
Interjudge reliability was evaluated for the beginning and ending of each action appearing in the hypothesized structures reported in the Results section. The reliability judge had no prior experience with this sort of research and was not acquainted with the hypotheses described in the Results section. Reliability was assessed for 12.7% of the transcribed actions using *kappa* [14]. Overall agreement was 91%, yielding a *kappa* of .90.

14.5.3   Data analysis

Exploratory analyses of interaction sequences based on THEME [15, 16] were designed to develop hypotheses of interaction structure. As reported in the results section, evaluation and revision of emerging hypotheses were based entirely on the extent to which they fit the transcribed data.

In the pattern search the following parameters were set for THEME: (a) the minimum significance level for pairs of pattern constituents was $p < .005$, and (b) the minimum number of action sequences required to form a pattern was four.

For this study THEME was used for two crucial purposes: hypothesizing the structure of this interaction, and identifying bouts of attacks by the child. THEME patterns were used to develop hypotheses concerning the organization of the interaction. This required examining and combining a number of THEME patterns in order to hypothesize both the constituents of each element, and the optional or obligatory rules connecting these elements. Thus, the patterns detected by THEME were not, in themselves, the final results, but they made possible the development of the structure. However, there was one particular in which information from THEME patterns was directly incorporated in the results. As described in the Results section, hypotheses regarding the structure of the child's attacking the big sister include the notion of an *attack series*: sequences of conflictual actions, beginning with the child's attacking, in which the child's initial attack is not regarded as being directly responsive to a preceding action, and subsequent actions by the father and big sister are regarded as directly responsive to the child's attack. Definition of these sequences of related actions was based on THEME patterns indicating that the actions occurred within a temporal interval (the critical interval) more frequently than expected at the specified level of significance. Action sequences falling outside such an interval were not regarded as elements of an attack series though they were part of the larger conflictual interaction.

Thus, while the actions actually comprising an attack series were based on a more general exploratory analysis, temporal intervals within THEME patterns were used to define those actions that were linked in a series and those that were not. Critical intervals for relevant actions and associated levels of significance are presented in Table 14.2.

14.6   Results

The most salient action of the conflict is the child's repeated hitting, pushing, pulling, and shoving the big sister. On average there was one of these actions about every 17 s. Although this seems a high rate of Attack, we regard 17 s as a fairly extended period of time because of the considerable rapidity of some aspects of the interaction. All these actions were brief. The longest was 9.25 s long. The mean was 1.8 s; the standard deviation was 1.8 s. Because sequential analyses indicated that the child's actions had essentially the same effect on the course of the interaction, they were grouped as interchangeable actions [6] into a single structural element: *Attack*. Results indicated these actions were not evenly distributed across the interaction. Three actions were systematically related to these Attacks: one action by the father: *Physically Intervening* in the child's Attacks, and two actions by the big sister: *Shielding* herself from the Attack, and *Repositioning* herself on the father's leg. Because these actions, singly or in combination, had the same effect on the interaction, they also were treated as interchangeable within a single structural element: *Respond*.

Figure 14.1 presents the structure hypothesized for the interaction related to Attacks. The structure represents an Attack series, defined as one transit of the structure from beginning to end. An Attack series involves at least one Attack by the child, and may include one or more Responses by the father and big sister. Given the nature of the structure, the interaction may, but need not, loop within the structure one or more times before reaching the end. After the end of an Attack series, the next series is initiated by the child's next Attack. An Attack series may include a single Attack that is not Responded to by the father or big sister, or a string of tightly spaced Attacks and Responses. The length of an Attack series is determined by the rules of the structure and by the choices made by participants at the option points in the structure. The structure applies to all Attacks by the child and to all Responses occurring during an Attack series. To aid discussion, each element in Figure 14.1 is labelled with (a) a letter (A, B, C, D), (b) the participant(s) involved (the child (Ch) and the father or big sister (FS)), and (c) a brief indication of the action constituting the element (Attack or Respond). In addition, each line is labelled with respect to ratification (+ or −), indicating whether or not the preceding element was considered to be ratifying.

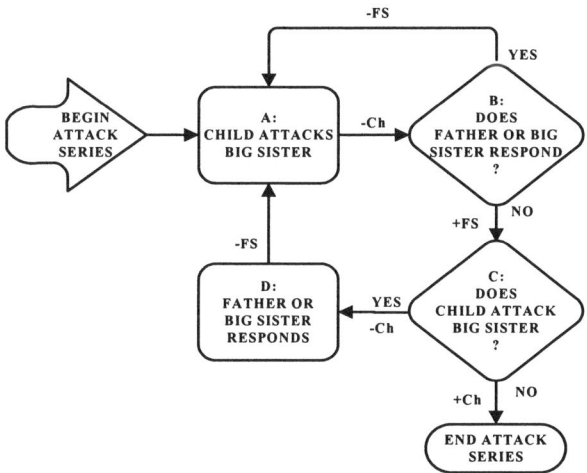

Figure 14.1 Hypothesized structure of attack interaction

14.6.1 Composition of elements

The following definitions, rules, and dynamics characterize the structure. (a) There are only two elements in this structure: Attack by the child (elements A and C), and Response by big sister or father (elements B and D). However, each element appears twice in the structure, once as obligatory (elements A and D), and once as optional (elements B and C). (b) The four actions constituting an Attack by the child (hit, push, shove, pull) are interchangeable [6]. That is, the occurrence of any one or more of these actions constitutes an Attack, and all, singly or in combination, are equivalent in their effect. That is, the conjoint occurrence of two, three, or four Attack actions has no effect on the structure beyond that of a single Attack. (c) The three actions by the father or big sister, defined as a Response (big sister's shielding or repositioning, and father's physical intervention), are similarly interchangeable. The conjoint occurrence of two or three Response actions has no effect on the structure beyond that of a single action.

14.6.2 Rules

(1) The father and big sister have the option of Responding or not to any single Attack (B: ±FS). (2) However, if the child makes two consecutive Attacks without an intervening Response (A: −Ch → B: +FS → C: −Ch), a Response is obligatory after the second Attack (D: −FS). (3) If there is a Response (B: −FS or D: −FS), a subsequent Attack by the child is obligatory (A: −Ch). (4) If there is no Response to an Attack (B: +FS), the child has the option of making or not making a second Attack (C: ±Ch). These rules apply to the first Attack and all subsequent Attacks in a series.

14.6.3 Attack results

Table 14.1 presents action sequences observed during the conflict. The eight Attack series are shown as rows separated by lines.

Attack Series	Preceding action(s) Father's Physical Intervention	Big Sister's Reposition	Big Sister's Shield	Child's Attack		Following action(s) Father's Physical Intervention	Big Sister's Reposition	Big Sister's Shield
1				1	Attack			
2				2	ATTACK			
				3	ATTACK			Shield
			Shield	4	Attack			
3				5	Attack	Physical	Reposition	
	Physical	Reposition		6	ATTACK	Physical		
		Reposition		7	ATTACK			
		Reposition		8	ATTACK			Shield
			Shield	9	Attack			
4				10	Attack			
5				11	Attack			Shield
			Shield	12	Attack			
6				13	ATTACK			
				14	ATTACK	Physical		
	Physical			15	ATTACK	Physical		
	Physical			16	Attack	Physical	Reposition	
		Reposition		17	Attack			
7				18	ATTACK			
		Reposition		19	ATTACK	Physical	Reposition	
	Physical	Reposition		20	Attack	Physical		Shield
	Physical		Shield	21	Attack	Physical	Reposition	Shield
	Physical	Reposition	Shield	22	ATTACK			
		Reposition		23	ATTACK		Reposition	
		Reposition		24	Attack	Physical		
	Physical	Reposition		25	ATTACK	Physical	Reposition	
	Physical	Reposition		26	ATTACK	Physical		
				27	Attack*	Physical	Reposition	
8				28	Attack	Physical		
	Physical			29	Attack			

Table 14.1 Child's attacks and responses by father and big sister

The structure includes all 29 Attacks, all five Shields, and all 13 Physical Interventions. There are occurrences of the big sister's Repositioning outside the context of an Attack series, for example, during other interaction phases. These are not included in the Attack structure. The structure fits 28 of the 29 Attacks (96.5%). The one failure occurs in connection with the starred Reposition at the bottom of series 7. This Attack fits the structure, but the structure requires a further obligatory Attack following the Response (Repositioning and Physical Intervention). This second Attack does not occur. There are eight Attack series in the interaction studied, and thus eight series–initial Attacks and seven series–ending Attacks (due to the faulty ending of series 7). The Attack series include (a) two isolated Attacks (1 & 4); (b) two series containing two Attacks (5 & 8); (c) one series containing three Attacks (2); (d) two series containing five Attacks (3 & 6); and (e) one series containing 10 Attacks (7). Table 14.2 presents results from THEME patterns relevant to the structure. These data are presented to provide information on the time scale of the action sequences in the hypothesized structures. The table shows for two–action patterns (a) the outside limit of the critical interval for selected patterned actions, that is, the maximum time (in seconds) separating actions considered to be patterned, and (b) the significance of the relationship between the actions. In general, the maximum interval between paired actions in patterns was less than 3s. The significance levels were well beyond the $p < .005$ criterion specified in the analysis.

Action Pair	Maximum Interval (s)	*p*
End Child's Attack - Begin Attack	2.5	.0028
Begin Child's Attack - Begin Father's Physical Intervention	2.3	.0021
Begin Child's Attack - Begin Big Sister's Shield	0.5	0
End Big Sister's Reposition - Begin Child's Attack	1.7	.0009
End Big Sister's Shield - Begin Child's Attack	7.5	.0006

Table 14.2 Maximum critical intervals and significance of action pairs

14.7   Discussion

We agree with [17] that "it is both crucially important and practically possible to study young children, with their families, in situations of real emotional significance to them." [18, p. 217] adds that "we gain immeasurably by studying children in their own world; indeed, if we do not do so we run a grave risk of misrepresenting the nature of their social intelligence, and stand little chance of clarifying what may be important in the development of that understanding" (p. 321). Thus, careful examination of these parent–child interactions having "real emotional significance" may be particularly fruitful in contributing to our understanding of the child's social and cognitive development.

We chose to study this particular conflict because (a) it was the most extended conflict we have found on our videotapes of family interaction, and (b) it included triadic interactions, permitting a move beyond analysis of dyads. For these reasons, it presented an interesting interaction to analyze and model.

14.7.1 Interaction structure

We approached the description of the conflict from the perspective of convention-based or rule-governed interaction. In attempting to move inside this conflict as much as possible, our primary goals were (a) to examine the characteristics of the structures hypothesized for this interaction, (b) to consider the implications of a structural approach to interaction in general and conflict in particular, and (c) to consider the relation between the dynamics of interaction structures and the processes of bidirectional or multidirectional influence in interactions. Taken as a whole, we regard several characteristics of this complex, extended conflict as especially notable.

The interaction sequences described in the Results section involve a remarkable degree of consistency and coordination in the interaction of family members. We have interpreted these regularities as reflecting in part the operation of convention within the conflict [5, 8], just as these conventions operate in other familiar family interactions, such as games, meals, or discipline [6, 9, 18, and 20]. We regard the issue of whether or not a particular family interaction is structured as strictly empirical. In this case, the strength of the sequential regularities in the interaction reported appears to justify the hypothesized structure. Although our data do not provide information on the extent to which this conflict reflects the properties of other, preceding conflicts in this family, these hypothesized structures appeared firmly in place from the beginning of the respective interactions. The results do not suggest, nor did we detect, an initial period during which the structures were forming. The structure facilitates the coordination of action by participants, even within conflicts, through common expectations of appropriate action within the structure [12, 23]. The importance of such shared expectations in interaction has been frequently noted [4, 7 and 21-23]. Continuing study of interaction structures has the potential for extending our understanding of the child's capacity for developing expectations of their own and others' actions in natural situations, and thus of the child's developing social capabilities and social cognition. Structures containing optional rules have been termed *variable–sequence* structures [6]. Although only certain actions and action sequences are appropriate within a structure, an interaction may take different courses, based on the participants' respective, sequential choices of available options. Each instance of the rule-governed interaction – in this case, an attack series - is jointly constructed by the participants based on the choices each participant makes at each choice point.

Table 14.1 suggests, but does not exhaust, the variety of interaction sequences that can be generated from the variable–sequence structures shown in Figure 14.1. The structure clearly illustrates the way in which each participant's action defines the subsequent action(s) available to the partner, including whether that subsequent action is obligatory or involves options. Responding appropriately to the partner, including choosing between available options, is an important component of the child's social competence. Interaction structures define appropriate responses in specific types of interactions. By the same token, the structure makes strategies interpretable to partners (and to investigators). That is, choosing a particular action when options are available (as in elements B and C in Figure 14.1) becomes interpretable because both the alternative actions and the partner's appropriate response to each of these alternatives are known. Thus, each participant knows not only what actions are appropriate at each point in the interaction, but also the possible consequences of those actions [23].

14.7.2 Hypothesized attack structure

The hypothesized structure for the child's Attacks (Figure 14.1) has a number of contrasts and symmetries that are quite striking when compared to structures we have developed for other parent–child interactions [6, 8]. There are only two elements in the structure: the child's Attacks, and Responses by father or big sister. Each of these two elements appears twice in the structure, once as obligatory and once as optional. This characteristic of the structure is unique in our experience. Whether an element is obligatory or optional thus depends upon its placement in the stream of interaction.

In the Attack structure, all occurrences of Attacks and Responses play a role in the structure, but the nature of that role depends on the interactional context of the element. The notion of obligatory/optional alternation for an element complicates the notion of interpersonal influence in interaction. It is not only that the participants are influencing each other bidirectionally through the medium of the structure, but also that the effect of a participant's action may vary, depending on where in the stream of interaction the action occurs. This fits with intuition; it seems reasonable to expect that the effect of an action may not be entirely constant but may vary according to the immediate context of its occurrence. Both this context and the specific effect of actions within the context are clearly defined by the structure.

14.7.3 Dynamics within the structure: Beginning, continuing, and ending an Attack series

Figure 14.1 can be described as a single conflictual loop. The circular shape of the structure suggests that the structure facilitates continuing an Attack series once it begins. It is clearly easier to begin an Attack series than to end one. This impression can be verified by tracing the various possible paths within the structure.

Beginning an Attack series requires a single action: the child Attacks the big sister (A: – Ch). The big sister initiates no Attacks. While the father often physically intervenes in an Attack, he never takes an action that effectively prevents the child from repeating an Attack. In this he appears to be guided in part by his stated notion that the big sister should be instrumental in concluding the conflict. Notice that both obligatory elements have the same effect: propelling the conflict forward, and locking all participants into continued conflict. Although the structure favours continuing an Attack series once it begins, the structure does provide a definite, though somewhat complex, way to end a series, based on sequences of optional actions. The structure provides that an Attack series can be ended only by the conjoint action of all three participants: all must have the option to desist and choose to do so. As described in the Results section, once begun, an Attack series can be ended only by a single path within the structure: (A: –Ch → B: +FS → C: +Ch). That is, the child attacks, the father and big sister refrain from responding, and the child chooses not to attack again. This ending process obtains regardless of which one of the three possible ways element (A) is reached. Thus, while an Attack series is always begun unilaterally by the child, it can only be ended through the coordinated, abstemious self–regulation of all three participants across a stretch of interaction. Notice that, paradoxically, the structure requires that the conflict be ended only by the father's and big sister's implicitly ratifying the child's immediately preceding attack by failing to respond to it. The structure provides for an Attack series being ended after a single Attack. After the initial attack the father and big sister ratify the Attack, and the child chooses not to attack again (B: +FS → C: +Ch). This occurs in series 1 and 4. In this case, there is an attack but no conflict. This possibility of aggression without conflict is noted by [2].

When the interaction reaches element (C), if the child chooses to attack (C: –Ch), the father or big sister is obliged to respond (D: –FS), and the child is obliged to attack again (A: –Ch). This perpetuates the Attack series but also sets once again up at least the possibility of ending the attack series. Characteristics of the Attack structure exemplify the observation by [2] that "examining conflict as a temporally extended phenomenon permits a more complete account of its determinants, since those factors that regulate the beginning of a conflict may or may not affect the way in which it ends" [2]. When there is a structure hypothesized for a conflict or other interaction, the way the interaction begins, continues, and ends can be described in a highly differentiated manner. The contrast between the ease of starting an Attack series and the complexity of ending it may be an important property of a certain class of conflicts. However, conflict structures may be exited in much simpler ways [9].

14.7.4 Multiparticipant Interaction Structures

The Attack structure involves a three–person interaction. This structure, although nested within a broader interaction, provides an empirical example of the multidirectional family interaction emphasized by [22].

14.7.5   Conflict strategy

Figure 14.1 and Table 14.1 illustrate the manner in which interaction may be examined in a way that extends beyond "isolated acts of aggression," in this case, a set of Attack series involving patterned sequential regularities. These Attacks occur within the context of an interaction structure in which three participants' actions are systematically interrelated. The behavioural regularities underlying the hypothesis of the Attack structure indicate the degree to which "one child's acts were contingent on the other's, and different types of actions were used at different points within the conflicts" [2, p. 16]. The structure represents a hypothesis regarding the nature of the relationship between successive actions, and the way this relationship depends upon where an action is located in the stream of interaction.

Because of the deep interconnectedness of participants' actions in interaction, it may be counterproductive to attempt describing one participant's strategy independently of those of other participants [8]. What one participant does is appropriately influenced by the partner's preceding actions, the availability of options, and the partner's anticipated responses to the participant's action. Thus, all participants are bidirectionally influencing each other. For this reason, it becomes necessary to describe each participant's action in the context of the respective actions of all other participants. This is accomplished in the structure (Figure 14.1). Bidirectionality is not a particularly easy phenomenon to model. Once a structure is hypothesized, it becomes possible to examine the extent to which preceding actions by both participant and partner influence a participant's choice of alternative actions at each option point [9]. This line of inquiry is beyond the scope of this discussion.

14.8   Conclusion

The results may be interpreted as lending cumulative support to the following conclusions, presented roughly in order of increasing generality. (a) Substantial sequential regularities suggest the operation of convention in face–to–face interaction. (b) This and other studies [6] provide evidence that children at least 14-months old are capable of participating fully in at least some interaction structures. (c) Conflictual interactions may exhibit structure in the same manner as nonconflictual ones. (d) Some structures may be concerned exclusively with conflict (Figure 14.1) or make no provision for conflict. (e) Other structures provide for both conflictual and nonconflictual interactions [9]. In this case whether or not an interaction based on such a structure becomes conflictual depends on the respective choices of action by the participants. (f) It becomes apparent that, within the context of interaction structure, there are several ways in which interactions can be compared and contrasted, including the interaction structure itself, the specific actions comprising the elements in the structure, the participants in the structure, and the way in which options may be exercised within the structure. This provides the possibility of a highly differentiated description of interaction process. (g) Descriptions of these phenomena in observed interactions permit detailed scrutiny of the child's interactions with others. (h) Continued investigation of these phenomena has the potential for yielding useful information both on the child's social and cognitive development, including social cognition, and on the contribution of the child's interaction with others to the child's socialization. (i) Interactions both within and between families, including the identification of subtle differences between apparently comparable interactions, may be examined. (j) Interaction structures not only exemplify the notion of bidirectional influence in parent–child interaction, but also permit detailed specification of the nature of that influence in observed interactions. (k) If face–to–face interaction is a rule–governed or structured process, then research designed to discover structure, strategy, and related phenomena becomes the approach of choice in studying family interaction.

Longitudinal studies are currently underway on the early development and evolution of structures for a wide variety of conflictual and nonconflictual parent–child interactions.

14.9   Acknowledgements

This research was done by the first author in partial fulfilment of the requirements for special honours in the college. Preparation of this paper was supported in part by National Institute of Mental Health grant MH–38344 to Starkey Duncan. We are indebted to Anne Farley for making the videotapes, to Rich Sayre for invaluable aid in working with C–QUAL, to Magnus Magnusson for developing THEME and aiding in its use, and to Ann Jankowski for helping with data analysis. Amanda Woodward, Michael Silverstein, and David McNeill provided useful comments on research issues and earlier drafts. We are deeply grateful to members of the family for their hospitality and patience during the videotaping process.

14.10   References

[1]   J. F. Cohn and E. Z. Tronick, Communicative rules and the sequential structure of infant behavior during normal and depressed interaction, in *Social interchange in infancy: Affect, cognition, and communication*, E. Z. Tronick, Ed. Baltimore: University Park Press, 1982, pp. 59–77.

[2]   D. F. Hay, Social conflict in early childhood, in *Annals of child development. Vol. 1*, G. Whitehurst, Ed. Greenwich: JAI, 1984, pp. 1–44.

[3]   C. U. Shantz, Conflicts between children, *Child Development* **58** (1987) 283–305.

[4]   S. D. Duncan Jr., Convention and conflict in the child's interaction with others, *DevelopmentalReview* **11** (1991) 337-367.

[5]   S. D. Duncan Jr., Convention, conflict, and compliance in parent-child interaction, in *Festschrift for David McNeill*, S. Duncan, Ed. Washington: American Psychological Association, in press.

[6]   S. D. Duncan Jr. and A. M. Farley, Achieving parent–child coordination through convention: Fixed– and variable–sequence conventions, *Child Development* **61** (1990) 742–753.

[7]   S. D. Duncan Jr. and D. W. Fiske, *Face-to-face interaction: Research methods, and theory*. Hillsdale: Erlbaum.

[8]   S. D. Duncan Jr., D. W. Fiske, R. Denny, B. G. Kanki, and H. B. Mokros, *Interaction structure and strategy*. New York: Cambridge University Press, 1985.

[9]   F. Friedman, S. D. Duncan, Jr., K. Rasinski, and L.V. Hedges, *Infant-Caregiver bidirectional in interaction structure and strategy*. Submitted for publication.

[10]   E. Goffman, *Relations in public*. New York: Basic Books, 1971.

[11]   A. Kendon, *Conducting interaction: Patterns of behavior in focused encounters*. Cambridge: Cambridge University Press, 1990.

[12]   D. K. Lewis, *Convention*. Cambridge: Harvard University Press, 1969.

[13]   S. Frey, H. P. Hirsbrunner, A. Florin, W. Daw, and R. Crawford, A unified approach to the investigation of nonverbal and verbal behavior in communication research, in *Current issues in European social psychology*, W. Doise and S. Moscovici, Eds. Cambridge: Cambridge University Press, 1983, pp. 143–199.

[14]   J. Cohen, A   coefficient of agreement for nominal scales, *Educational and Psychological Measurement* **20** (1960) 37–46.

[15]   M. S. Magnusson, Structures syntaxiques et rythmes comportementaux: Sur la détection de rythmes cachés, *Science et Techniques de l'Animal du LA Boratoire* **14** (1989) 143–147.

[16]   M. S. Magnusson, Discovering Hidden Time Patterns in Behavior: T-Patterns and their Detection, *Behavior Research Methods, Instruments and Computers* **32** (2000) 93-110.

[17]   J. Dunn and C. Kendrick, *Siblings: Love, envy, & understanding*. Cambridge: Harvard University Press, 1982.

[18]   J. Dunn, *The beginnings of social understanding*. Cambridge: Harvard University Press, 1988.

[19]   E. J. Doolittle, *Mother–daughter interaction in lower–socioeconomic African American families and its implications for academic achievement*. Unpublished doctoral dissertation, University of Chicago, 1995.

[20]   J. K. J. Enders, *Meal time interactions from infancy to toddlerhood: The case of one mother–son dyad*. Unpublished doctoral dissertation, University of Chicago, 1997.

[21]   C. B. Kopp, Antecedents of self–regulation: A developmental perspective *Developmental Psychology* **18** (1982) 199–214.

[22]   R. D. Parke, Families in life–span perspective: A multilevel developmental approach, in *Child development in life–span perspective*, E. M. Hetherington, R. M. Lerner, and M. Perlmutter, Eds. Hillsdale: Erlbaum, 1988, pp. 159–190.

[23]   T. C. Schelling, *The strategy of conflict*. New York: Oxford University Press, 1960.

The Hidden Structure of Interaction
L. Anolli et al. (Eds.)
IOS Press, 2005

15. Conversation Patterns in Icelandic and Italian People: Similarities and Differences in Rhythm and Accommodation

Alessia AGLIATI, Antonietta VESCOVO, Luigi ANOLLI

Abstract. Conversation may be considered as a *universal communication system* which performs social and interactive cue of communication. Although it could appear casual, even chaotic and confused, due to its spontaneous nature, a deep and intrinsic organization, grounded on a shared social order, is involved in conversational stream which follows given cultural standards. In the present study a *sequence structural analysis* of conversation was carried out. In particular, rhythm and accommodation in conversation patterns in Icelandic and Italian people were focused to detect specific kinetic T-patterns by using the software THEME 2001.
Forty conversations between Icelandic and Italian couples of known and unknown individuals have been videotaped and analysed zooming on gestures, turn-taking and body movements displayed during the conversation flow. Data highlighted the country effect on conversation rhythm: number and frequency of time patterns were deeply different between Icelandic and Italian couples, as the former turned out to manage the temporal organization in a more synchronous and regular way than the latter. Furthermore, peculiar gestures were recognized for Icelandic and Italian couples, underlining systematic differences in the cultural framework.

Keywords: Conversation; rhythm; gestures; accommodation; cultural differences.

Contents

15.1   Introduction

15.1.1 Variability and regularity in conversation patterns

Conversation is among the most pervasive form of human interaction [1]. Cherry [2] argued that "it [...] is the fundamental unit of human communication", drawing attention to the practices through which conversation is organized, as such analysis enables to understand how human beings communicate each other in a given cultural framework. Generally speaking, conversation may be considered as a sequence of communicative turnovers, variable from few quips to hours lasting, involving two or more participants, who are speaking in a more or less formal way, referring to any kind of topic in nature. Due to this wide variability and flexibility, conversation comes to be a basic communicative activity suitable to a wide range of conditions in different contexts [3].

Although conversation might appear casual, even chaotic and confused, due to its spontaneous nature, a deep and intrinsic organization, grounded on a shared social order, is involved in conversation stream which follows defined cultural standards. As a rule, three main portions may be recognized in a standard conversation: a) the beginning (opening) in which identification and acknowledgment of participants occur; b) the topic's development; c) the end (closing) which points out the leave taking. Starting from this partition, conversation analysis enables to find out a comprehensive format in which regularities, routines and patterns are detectable and recognizable, so that it becomes a graspable and interpretable human activity [3]. Apparently disorganized and sometimes purposeless, conversation is actually organized and ruled out by cultural standards and norms that produce and reproduce social organization in a reflexive manner. In such a way patterns of repetitive action units may be taken in evidence and analysed.

The present study follows the *social pragmatic perspective* on conversation, according to which conversation is a sequence of exchanges based on defined rules. The pragmatics is the study of how people use language to communicate and accomplish their goals in interaction, in other words it is a speech act model. This perspective differs from others approaches to the study of language in that it focuses on how speakers design their talk to convey particular social actions and how participants organize their talk [4, 5]. The words used in conversation do not primarily and strictly reproduce internal concepts and mental representations; rather, participants, talking together, make conversation by uttering and answering to words; in such a way they co-construct their interaction by using words. In a similar manner, they co-construct images and representations of themselves, the interlocutor, their relationship, and their culture. As an outcome, participants in conversation co-construct their personal, social and cultural worlds [6].

15.1.2 Rhythm, accommodation and behaviour richness in conversation

Herein two main principles of the social pragmatic perspective on conversation will be briefly taken in consideration. First, conversation is ruled out by a given *rhythm of turnover* and *accommodation*. People need to coordinate their talk, *taking floor* (becoming speaker in interaction) in a well-timed way, so that actions of a participant dovetail with those of the other. By turns and in a sequence of turns, participants make their participation synchronous and accomplish action together. The synchronous rhythm of communication may be deemed as a basic feature of conversation, as it makes fluent and smooth turnover possible.

In this domain Accommodation Theory, sketched out by Giles [7], provides a useful device to analyse and understand the processes by which participants adjust their communicative action within the conversation stream, and by which they accommodate each other via a gradual, continuous and mutual approaching. Such a theory foresees that, in case participants want to show agreement, harmony, and linking, or enhance the communication effectiveness, or else obtain social approval, they should accommodate each other. In the same vein, to produce, share and understand the meaning of utterances' flow, they should act together taking into consideration what the interlocutor communicates in verbal or nonverbal way, and participating to the development of a given meaning path.

Second, according to the social pragmatic perspective, conversation is distinguished by *behaviour richness*, as it consists of more than spoken language. Conversation is a basic social activity involving two or more participants ("having a conversation") who weave the sequence of their communicative exchanges ("speaking or conversing") in that, at the same time, they are made up. As social activity, conversation faces the issue of coordination and co-regulation. In this field, gesture, gaze, body posture, facial mimics, and other nonverbal expression are important and useful devices to promote and further the conversation coordination between participants. As an outcome, participants communicate much more than they say, as in an aware or unaware way they leave each other many cues about their communicational intention. So, in the conversation stream there is much room for inferential process in the ascription of given mental representations and intentions to speech of interlocutors [3].

To sum up, conversation may be regarded as a universal communication system which in a polyphonic way performs social interaction between participants through a wide range of situations, from very formal ones (like a trial in a court) to very informal (like an occasional talk with an unknown) [3].

15.1.3 Culture and conversation

As a relevant issue, the social pragmatics principles should be deepened to analyse whether they display (or not) some variability among different cultures. On the one hand, pragmatics [8, 9] seems to provide arguments in favour of a universal position, according to which there are many invariables features that define what is for behaviour to constitute interaction. For example, some scholars like Grice [9], Turnbull [6], Boden and Zimmerman [10] argue that everywhere each participant has to coordinate his/her action with the interlocutor's action. In every culture the conversation format shows more or less the same design and sequence of patterns, as greetings, turn-taking, leave-taking, and the like. On the other hand, it is presupposed that in conversation participants co-construct their personal, social, and cultural worlds, and, as a consequence, their mental disposition towards those co-constructed worlds thoroughly influences the global organization of conversation [11, 12]. According to other scholars like Ochs, Duranti, Goodwin, and Levinson, cultural format severely shapes the communicative process in nature, conversation included. As Grader [13] pointed out, a comparative conversation analysis among different cultures highlights how people manage the time use in a very different way during the conversation stream.

Within this domain, it is worthwhile to deepen time and word, as they are two key facets of conversation.

First, as regards *time*, within talk-in-interaction, a given culture provides people with standards and resources that may be employed both to manage time in the world being represented through talk, and to extrapolate future events in the current and future interactions. Such time management in the conversation stream is framed, among other cues, also by participants' movements. Through their gestures and body postures which are interactively arranged, they display crucial information about the temporal and sequential organization of their joint participation in the current interaction [14].

So-called *chronemics* analyses the way people manage and design their use of time in conversation setting. According to Hall [15, 16], only within certain societies time is a matter of great importance and significance. Some cultures, defined "slow cultures", relate to time as a circular phenomenon, in which there is no pressure or anxiety about the future. In these societies, such as Asian, or African, or else South American ones, polychronic time use, in which many things occur simultaneously, is prevailing. As a consequence, for these societies there is no imperative need to achieve or create newness, or to produce more than absolutely necessary to survive. In these cultures, people slowly talk, slowly eat, and slowly walk. According to Hall, such societies have successfully integrated the past and future into a peaceful sense of present. Conversely, the so-called "fast cultures", like Western societies, devise a linear perspective of time, ruled by the principle "one-thing-at-a-time". In these societies, people are expected to lean more toward strict planning, time allocation, and prioritizing in attempting to meet their obligations. They have a monochronic time use, and, as a rule, they anxiously run towards the future and the progress. Usually, they fast talk, fast walk, fast eat, and so on.

Second, as for *word*, cultures display great differences referring to turn-taking, silence, and word use. In many countries in Africa, South America, Mediterranean area people are talkative and chattering, as they are prone to speak and gossip. Remarkably, in these so-called "word cultures", a quick rhythm in uttering with short (full and empty) pauses occur in standard conversation. Likewise, speedy turn-taking and short transitional times take place. In opposite way, silence is deemed to be a kind of thread, as it becomes charged with negative meanings of indifference, resistance, mistrust, even hostility in some circumstances.

Conversely, there are cultures that do not like to talk and are much less loquacious. In these so-called "silence cultures" like Japanese, Apache, Navajos, and Paliyan, participants have long silence pauses in turnover, as a signal of cogitation and circumspection. For instance, in the conversation among Lapp some minutes of silence may occur between a plain request and the consequent reply. As a consequence, the conversation rhythm is rather slow, and silence is conceived as an evidence of trust, confidence, agreement, and harmony.

15.2 Objectives and hypotheses

Assuming culture as a general framework, the current research took into consideration how rhythm, sequential order of turns, word use, gestures and other nonverbal behaviours may be affected by culture during conversation in Icelandic and Italian people. The general aim was focused on analysing and describing the Icelandic and Italian style of interaction in a cooperative situation. In particular, we aimed at investigating how both the temporal management of conversation and non verbal behaviour as displayed by gestures and posture varied in conformity with cultural standards.

In this field three research hypotheses were outlined. First, in agreement with Moraro [17] study, it was hypothesized that nonverbal patterns were differently organized and managed by Icelandic and Italian people. Distinctly, according to the extant literature it was supposed that North European people would have coordinated their conversation following most regular shaped sequences of repetitive actions than Mediterranean one. In particular, it was expected that higher number of action patterns would be detected in Icelandic interaction than in Italian one. Second, according to the previous researches of Graham and Argyle [18], and in conformity with the cultural stereotypes, it was hypothesized that Icelandic and Italian people would have shown a great difference in gesture during conversation. Particularly, it was expected that Italian people would have displayed a higher number of gestures than Icelandic ones. Third, in agreement with the studies of

Goodwin [14], it was supposed that Icelandic and Italian people would have used different types of gestures. In particular, it was hypothesized that Icelandic people in conversation would have displayed gestures not available in Italian ones, and vice versa.

15.3 Method and instruments

15.3.1 Participants

Twenty Icelandic and twenty Italian couples of participants took part in this experiment. Icelandic subjects were recruited in University of Iceland in Reykjavik and Italian ones in Catholic University in Milan. All participants belonged to the middle socio-economic class. Half of couples were formed by individuals who knew each other, and half of them were composed by individuals who were unknown. Subjects' gender was balanced in the experiment, so that half of individuals were males and half of them females. All participants were between 20 and 30 years. Italian subjects' age was 23.75 years on average. In particular, the age mean for couples of individuals who knew each other was 23.35 years, while for individuals who were unknown was 24.15; males were 24 years old on average, while females were 23.5. The age mean for Icelandic subjects was 22.8 years. For couples of friends the age mean was 22.65, while in couples of unknown was 22.95; males were 23.10 years old on average, while females were 22.5. Videotaping each participant and the subsequent use of data for research purposes were approved and authorized by each of subjects.

15.3.2 Procedure

The present research was partly carried out in the Communication Psychology lab at Catholic University, and partly in the Human Behavior Laboratory of Reykjavik, both equipped with two cameras (split-screen technique). Each couple of participants was invited to enter the room accompanied by the experimenter. Before beginning the experiment, subjects who formed couples of friends were invited to compile individually a questionnaire about the characteristics of their friendship [19]. The experimental task was then introduced: the experimenter suggested a cooperative creative task to each couple. In particular, participants were asked to think up and to talk about an advertising of a bubble bath, as if they were creative and advertising experts, inventing the mood, the story, the leading character, the music, and the like for television advertising. Each interaction lasted 15 minutes and was video recorded. However, only a segment was taken into consideration for subsequent analysis: from second to seventh minute.

15.3.3 The nonverbal behaviour grid

To code the participants' behaviour a nonverbal grid, named *Variable Value Table* (VVT), was ad hoc developed. Forty-eight behaviour units (minimal coded action units), portioned in nine categories, were mapped into the grid: hands, arms, head, fingers, trunk, shoulders, gaze direction, face, turn-taking, as shown in table 15.1. The mostly behaviour units were taken from grids used in previous studies on nonverbal behaviour [20, 21].

Items	Description	Items	Description	Items	Description
1. Hands		*2. Fingers*		*5. Trunk*	
M1	Rotation	D1	Pointing	BU1	Trunk forward
M2	Hand contact	D2	Counting	BU2	Tilt trunk left or right
M3	Crossed hands	D3	Negation by fingers	BU3	Trunk back
M4	Hand on face	D4	Pianist	BU4	Swinging
M5	Hand on body				
M6	Hand on chair	*3. Arms*		*6. Face*	
M7	Hand on hair	BR1	Arms upward	SO1	Smile (AU6+12)
M8	Palm inward	BR2	Crossed arms	SO2	Laugh (AU6+12+25and/or26)
M9	Palm forward	BR3	Arms forward		
M10	Palm down	BR4	Open arms	*7. Gaze*	
M11	Palm upward	BR5	Dangling arms	S1	Avert gaze
M12	Palm back	BR6	Arms back		
M13	Palm outside	BR7	Bend arms	*8. Shoulders*	
M14	Fist			SP1	Shoulders shrug
M15	Bag-hand	*4. Head*			
M16	Mirror-hands	T1	Head forward	*9. Turn*	
M17	Rubbing hands	T2	Head down	TU	Speak
M18	Ax-hand	T3	Head back		
M19	Hitchhiking	T4	Tilt head l/r		
M20	Ring	T5	Tilt head up/down		
M21	Hands away	T6	Negation by head		
M22	Ball-hands				

Table 15.1 List of behaviour units included in the grid

The categories were then coded frame by frame using THEME Coder. The coding was done separately for each behaviour unit, that is, first of all occurrences of behaviour A were recorded, then all of behaviour B and so on. This procedure yielded a highly reliable scoring. Ten sequences were recorded by a second observer. Reliability was calculated according to McGrew formula [22] as an index of concordance: a reliability of 85% was found between the coders. The behaviour units were then analyzed with THEME [23, 24], by which T-patterns were detected. Each T-pattern is made of *events* that include the actor involved and the beginning or ending behaviour unit.

15.4   Analysis and results

15.4.1 Analysis of conversation rhythm

A univariate analysis of variance was conducted on the number and the length of T-patterns as dependent variable, in order to examine the temporal management of conversation in Icelandic and Italian couples. Significant differences were found both for number and length of T-patterns. Icelandic participants coordinated their actions and gestures through longer and more frequent T-patterns than Italian ones. In particular, on average in the Icelandic couples 412 types of T-patterns were detected, while in Italian ones 318 types of T-patterns were observed on average.

Moreover, the length mean of T-patterns in Icelandic couples was 14.80 events long (i.e. it included 14.80 behaviour units on average), while mean length for Italian ones was 11.70. Two occurrences of these T-patterns are described in figure 15.1. On the left of the figure 1, a T-pattern was detected in an Italian known couple during their conversation. Such a T-pattern included five events and, in particular, highlighted how often these two Italian fellows overlapped in their conversation. The first two events were related to turn-taking – actorA, b, talking; actorB, b, talking – and showed that the two Italian participants simultaneously began to take floor ten times. The whole T-pattern recurred three times in the same critical interval of time and embodied a third event, the *bag-hand*, a typical Italian gesture, as shown in the picture. On the right of the figure 1, another T-pattern was detected in Icelandic known couples during their conversation. Such a T-pattern, longer than Italian one, encompassed twelve events and displayed how often each one of the two Icelandic known participants took turn only after his/her partner has stopped. The first two events in this T-pattern concerned turn-taking – actorA, e, talking; actorB, b, talking – and they repeated, in the same order, twenty-one times into the same critical period of time.

Three other events (the sixth, the seventh, and the ninth) comprised in this T-pattern regarded gaze direction: actorA, b, avert gaze from his interlocutor; actorB, b, avert gaze from her interlocutor. The last two events included in this T-pattern concerned the *pianist*, a typical Icelandic gesture, displayed in the picture by both the participants simultaneously.

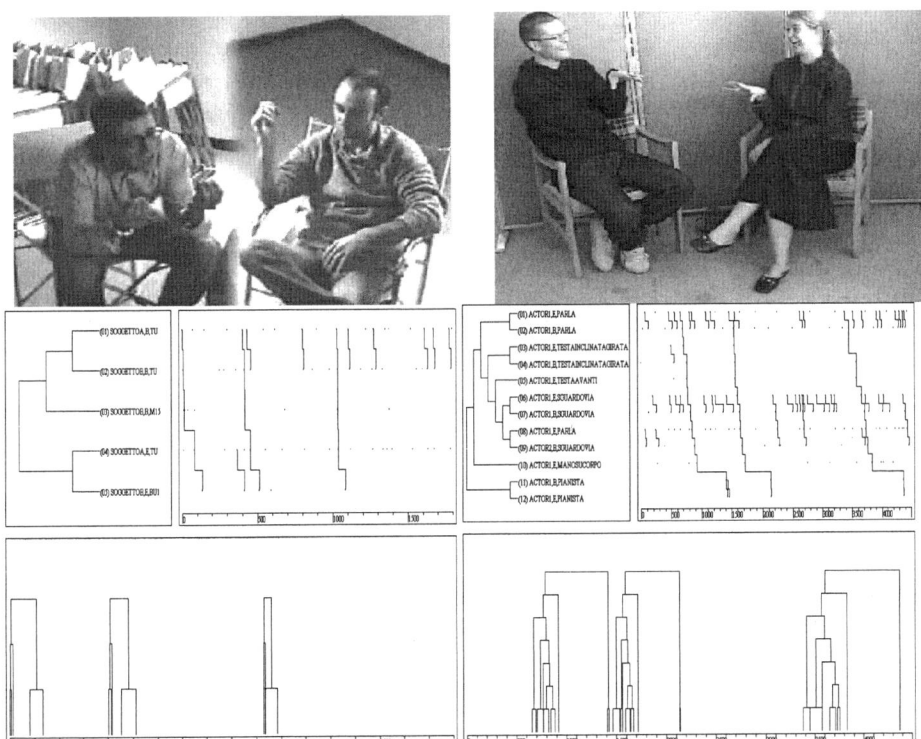

Figure 15.1 *This* figure includes a picture and a T-pattern both for Italians interaction and for Icelandic one. The picture on the left shows the "bag-hand", the typical Italian gesture; the picture on the right presents the "pianist" displayed only by Icelandic subjects. The T-patterns show the different use of turnover displayed by Italians and Icelanders. The T-pattern on the left refers to an Italian interaction between friends, it includes five events ((1) *subjectA, b, turn*; (2) *subjectB, b, turn*; (3) subjectB, b, bag-hand; (4) subjectA, e, turn; (5) subjectB, b, trunk forward) and recurs three times in the same observation period. The T-pattern on the right refers to an Icelandic interaction between friends, it includes twelve events ((1) *subjectB, e, turn*; (2) *subjectA, b, turn*; (3) subjectA, b, tilt head; (4) subjectA, e, tilt head; (5) subjectA, b, head forward; (6) subjectA, e, look away; (7) subjectB, b, look away; (8) subjectA, e, turn; (9) subjectB, b, look away; (10) subjectA, e, hand on body; (11) subjectA, b, pianist; (12) subjectA, e, pianist), and it recurs three times in the same observation period.

15.4.2 Analysis of non-verbal behaviour in Icelandic and Italian conversation

To examine which kind of nonverbal cues Icelandic and Italian participants displayed in a cooperative interaction, a second analysis of variance was carried out on behaviour units frequency as dependent variable (48 items of the grid). Means and standard deviations are shown in table 15.2 and a comparison between Italian and Icelandic behaviour units is visible in figure 15.2.

Items	Icelanders M	SD	Italians M	SD	F	η^2	$p^{(a)}$
Hand contact	1.55	1.83	2.85	2.43	7.391	.093	**
Crossed hands	.86	1.11	.64	.79	1.182	.016	
Hand on face	1.87	1.37	2.89	1.78	8.843	.109	**
Hand on hair	.22	.38	.82	1.21	8.493	.106	**
Palm inward	.31	.50	.68	.71	7.318	.092	**
Palm upward	.25	.52	.65	.81	7.222	.091	**
Palm back	.00	.00	.20	.44	8.592	.107	**
Bag-hand	.06	.18	.94	1.03	27.647	.277	**
Mirror-hands	.16	.36	.44	.69	5.314	.069	*
Ring	.01	.07	.10	.26	4.657	.061	*
Ball-hands	1.65	1.53	.03	.11	45.816	.389	**
Negation by finger	.04	.12	.00	.00	4.866	.063	*
Pianist	.43	.66	.03	.13	14.175	.164	**
Crossed arms	.09	.24	.07	.27	.231	.003	
Open arms	.06	.21	.18	.33	3.948	.052	*
Dangling arms	.05	.18	.05	.19	.019	.000	
Arms back	.11	.26	.00	.00	6.864	.087	*
Bend arms	.58	.63	.77	.65	1.875	.025	
Head forward	3.21	2.11	5.10	2.53	12.753	.150	**
Head back	.11	.24	.12	.33	.021	.000	
Tilt head left or right	1.68	1.47	.70	.61	15.903	.181	**
Trunk forward	.40	.71	.85	.95	6.988	.088	**
Swinging	.07	.25	.54	1.36	4.826	.063	*
Laugh	.90	1.11	2.17	1.52	17.987	.200	**
Avert gaze	7.78	3.29	6.27	2.26	5.792	.074	*
Speak	12.52	3.68	7.69	2.41	47.539	.398	**

Table 15.2 Means and standard deviations of behaviour units in Italian and Icelandic interactions

In the IR analysis, a significant main effect was found for Culture variable ($F_{1,29} = 14.01$, $p < .0001$). In the experimental cooperative interaction, Italian participants turned out to produce a higher number of gestures than Icelandic ones. In particular, Italian participants displayed self-contact gestures like *hand contact, hands on hair* and *hands on face* more frequently than Icelandic ones. Moreover, they also moved their *palms inward, upward* and *back* more frequently than North European individuals.

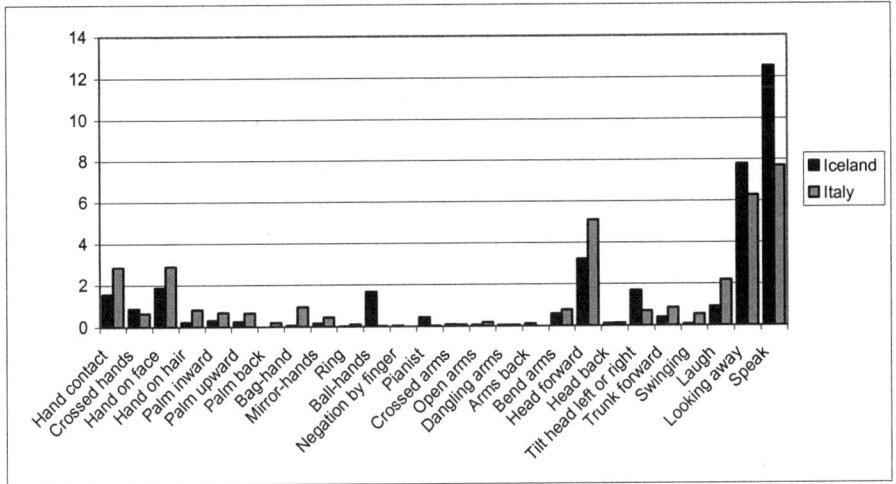

Figure 15.2 Comparison of Italian and Icelandic behaviour units.

Likewise, Italian and Icelandic participants resorted to different kinds of gestures, as only the former displayed the *ring*, the *mirror-hands* and the *bag-hand* gestures that were never used by the latter. Figure 15.3 illustrates these gestures. Conversely, Icelandic people displayed *ball-hands* and *pianist* gestures that were never present in Italian participants (see figure 15.3). Furthermore, Italian gestures turned out to be waver and opener than Icelandic ones, as *open arms* were displayed more frequently by Italian people, while Icelandic participants used more *arms back*. In a similar way Italian subjects often moved themselves on the chair and changed posture: they *moved trunk forward*, *swinging* and *tilt head forward* more than Icelandic ones. Eventually, Italian participants more frequently *laughed* than Icelandic ones. Significant differences were found also for *turn-taking* and *avert gaze*: Icelandic subjects seem to *avert gaze* and to *take-turn* more frequently than Italian ones.

15.5 Discussion

15.5.1 Icelandic and Italian conversation management: "gesture" vs. "word" style

The current research gives support to the social pragmatic perspective, as conversation appears to be a social activity ruled out by specific standards and expectations that are culturally defined. Although conversation as human activity holds general and universal features in its organization as a necessary interaction among two or more interlocutors, a temporal and formal partition in different phases (like opening, topic's development, and closing), the data herein observed point out that conversation is culturally shaped in nature. Under the superficial appearance of a universal format, conversation displays different styles in conformity to the culture of reference. In the present study between North European and Mediterranean people, it was observed that Icelandic participants deeply diverged from Italian ones by producing longer and more regular sequences of turns.

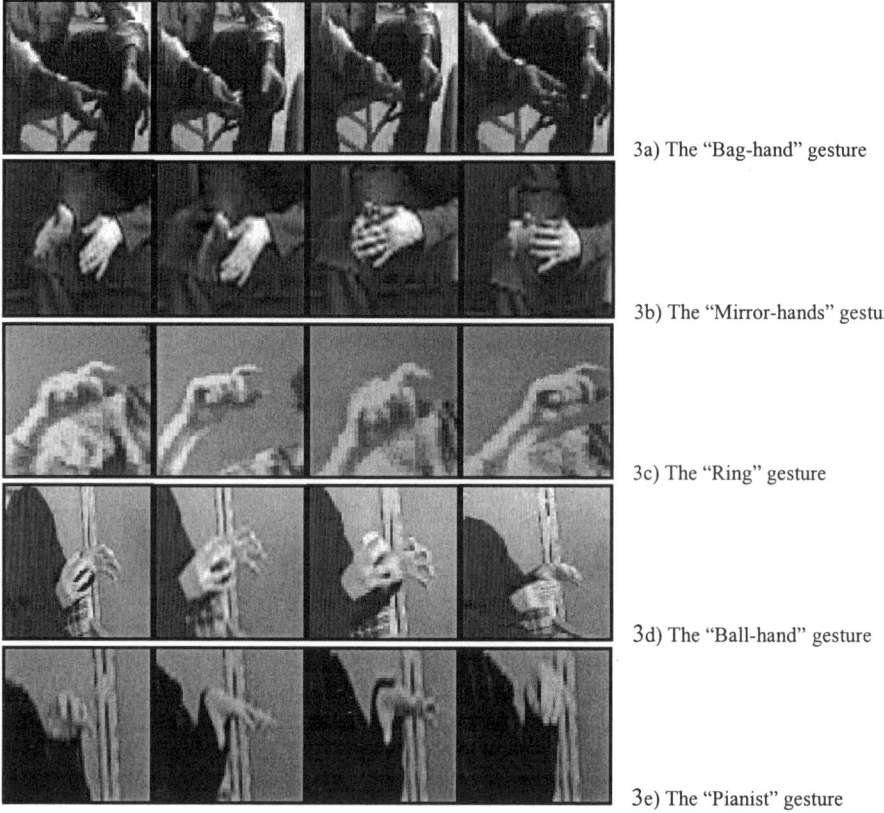

3a) The "Bag-hand" gesture

3b) The "Mirror-hands" gesture

3c) The "Ring" gesture

3d) The "Ball-hand" gesture

3e) The "Pianist" gesture

Figure 15.3 This figure shows the typical Italian (3a-3b-3c) and Icelandic (3d-3e) gestures. In the "Bag-hand" gesture (3a), hands are closed and fingers' tips are joined. In the "Mirror-hands" gesture (3b), hands' palms are facing and joining by fingers' tips. In the "Ring" gesture (3c), thumb and forefinger are joined to form a ring. In the "Ball-hand" gesture (3d), hands are facing and move like a rolling ball. In the "Pianist" gesture, hand's palm is downward and fingers move as playing piano.

In particular, Icelanders turned out to better manage and coordinate their actions in conversation than Italians since the former followed a smoother rhythm, as it was shown by a larger repetition of the same behaviour units in the same critical interval of time.

It is worthwhile to highlight that Icelandic participants showed a specific competence in managing their conversation in a plain and linear way both among known and unknown people. As a rule, they made recourse to few kinds of gestures and body movements during their conversation, and often they repeated them in the course of the same interaction. Furthermore, in conversation Icelandic participants did not move their body as much as Italian ones. Rather, they thoroughly relied on words and gave particular attention to what was said by interlocutors. Such word-based conversation seems to give a peculiar importance to the utterances and linguistic subject, less to the extra-linguistic aspects of conversation.

To put it in a nutshell, Icelandic conversation style may be regarded as more predictable and reliable, although rather monotonic. An Icelandic participant is likely to know which kind of moves he/she may expect from the interlocutor of the same culture, and what kind of answer he/she should communicate. In such a way adjustment and accommodation between participants are made easy, and the conversation turns out to be a smooth and fluent social activity.

Conversely, the data of the current research pointed out that Italian participants produced a wider range of movements in a more chaotic way during their conversation than Icelandic ones. Usually, they moved more not only hands but also arms and trunk, assuming varied body postures in conversation. Moreover, when an Italian participant began to take his/her floor, he/she was prone to exhibit different kind of gestures in a continuous gesticulating manner in order to make what is said clearer and more understandable. In some way, they turned out to not actually trust words, as if words might be ambiguous and not always explicit. Rather, they gave more credit to gestures and movements, considering that these last ones were visible and self-evident. Such gesture-based conversation seems to attribute a specific significance to gestures and, generally, nonverbal actions in conversation, less to linguistic topics.

To sum up, Italian conversation style may be considered as more chaotic and unpredictable, although more affable and friendly. An Italian participant is likely to be interested in sharing a global perspective, in self-disclosing, as well as in displaying more goodwill and warmth.

15.5.2 Icelandic and Italian gestures: two different typologies

The results of the current study gave support to the cultural hypothesis, according to which Icelandic and Italian conversation would be deeply shaped by different typologies of gestures. In particular, usually, Italian participants regularly resorted to wider and more open gestures than Icelandic ones, as, for instance, they opened arms in large movements, put palms up of their hands, inclined their forward or backward, and so on. Conversely, Icelandic participants normally made recourse to close and spatially limited gestures, like folded arms, trunk backward, and so on.

Furthermore, Italian participants produced self-contact gestures more frequently than Icelandic ones. Such gestures may be explained on the ground of a restless and excited style of Italian people in conversation.

Finally, some kinds of gestures, like bag-hand, mirror and ring, were displayed only by Italian participants, while the pianist gesture and the ball-hand were shown only by Icelandic ones.

Summing up, these data seem to give support to the cultural perspective in social pragmatics, as the tangled network between language and body movements is formed in conformity to the cultural standards. In turn, such network comes to frame conversation as social practice, closely depending on the cultural context, as Hayashi [25] recently has pointed out. According to the social pragmatics perspective, participants draw from repertories of behavioural practices those actions suitable to manage conversation and to jointly achieve coordination in their social interaction.

15.5.3 Gaze and overlapping in Icelandic and Italian conversation

With regard to the gaze and turn-taking, the data of the current research point out that in conversation Icelandic participants followed different patterns referring to Italian ones. In particular, as a rule, they took and left their conversational turn more frequently than Italian ones in the same critical interval of time. That means that their turns were shorter with a faster turnover, showing a high level of accommodation and attuning. Their conversations displayed a smooth flow as well.

Conversely, in the Italian conversation a more frequent occurrence of overlapping phenomenon happened. Italian participants often talked together, taking floor before the interlocutor has stopped. It seems that they were able to anticipate the closure of utterance in course and the conclusion of his/her communicative intention. Such condition may suggest that Italian people showed an intense and great participation in conversation, as if the thought of participants would proceed in unison. What for other cultures (like German and Scandinavian) may be regarded as an unpleasant experience and a lack of politeness, in Italian as in French people means involvement and participation. As a matter of fact, for Italian culture overlapping may be interpreted as an advantageous way to make conversation more spontaneous and lively, sometimes rather chaotic and confused.

As regards to gaze, it was observed that in Icelandic interaction, in a similar way to the North and Japanese cultures, participants were used not to gaze the interlocutor in conversation, as it might be regarded as an impolite signal and a cue of challenge. Averting gaze is a way to take respect and show consideration towards interlocutors. In contrast, Italian participants displayed a consistent period of gaze during conversation. Habitually, Italian people, like Arabian and South American cultures, are used to ascribe great importance to gaze as a signal of confidence, sincerity, attention, and trust towards interlocutors.

15.6   Conclusion and future directions

Conversation, as basic social activity, is an intriguing topic due to the intrinsic mixture among universal and local features. Conversation follows a universal format on the whole, considering that essential elements such as temporal partition, turnover, turn-taking, topic sequence and the like occur in every culture. However, although being universal in general format, conversation seems to be shaped by cultural standards which make up a particular style in managing interaction. In the current research it was paid special attention to time management and body movements in conversation. As a main result, conversation turns out to be a domain-specific activity, as Icelandic and Italian participants, all things considered, displayed a deeply different style in conversation management at least as far as it concerns time allocation and gestures. Being a social and cultural practice, conversation should be regarded as a dynamic, multiparty process of production and interpretation of meaning through a sequence of interactions which extend in time [14, 26, and 27].

Needless to say that the current study is not without some limitations. For one, speech was not taken in consideration and, then, it was not possible to connect specific gestures to specific linguistic topics. Further, a limited range of conversation setting was analyzed, as formal contexts were not considered. Additionally, asymmetrical condition, such as teacher-pupil, doctor-patient relationship was not examined. Further limitations concern individual differences which are not taken into consideration in the present study. In particular, some scholars [28] have observed that the range of individual variability, including age, status, educational level, life histories and social factors play an essential role in conversation management. With these limitations in mind, there are, nonetheless, further research implications. A combined analysis of both linguistic and extra-linguistic components of conversation stream should be taken into account, as conversation is a whole activity and, thus, such totality should be recognized in analysis. Specifically, it may be important to consider contextual and individual assortment in conversation management, insofar as only focusing the domain-specific features promotes significant progress in understanding how conversation is organized and managed by participants to reach their personal and social goals.

15.7 References

[1]   C. Goodwin, *Conversational organization: Interaction between speakers and hearers*. New York: Academic Press, 1981.
[2]   R. D. Cherry, Politeness in written persuasion, *Journal of Pragmatics* **12** (1988) 63-81.
[3]   L. Anolli, *Psicologia della comunicazione*. Bologna: Il Mulino, 2002.
[4]   R. E. Nofsinger, *Everyday Conversation*. Newbury Park: Sage Publications, 1991.
[5]   S. C. Levinson, *Pragmatics*. Cambridge: Cambridge University Press, 1983.
[6]   W. Turnbull, An appraisal of pragmatic elicitation techniques for social psychological study of talk: The case of request refusals, *Pragmatics* **11** (2001) 31-61.
[7]   H. Giles, Accent mobility: a model and some data, *Anthropological Linguistics* **15** (1973) 87-105.
[8]   P. Brown and S. Levinson, *Politeness: Some universals in language usage*. Cambridge: Cambridge University Press, 1987.
[9]   H. P. Grice, Logic and conversation, in *Syntax and semantics: Speech acts,* P. Cole and J.L. Morgan, Eds. New York: Academic Press, 1975, pp. 41-58.
[10]   D. Boden and D.H. Zimmerman, *Talk and social structure*. Cambridge: Polity Press, 1991.
[11]   E. Ochs, *Culture and language development: language acquisition and language socialization in a Samoan village*. Cambridge: Cambridge University Press, 1988.
[12]   E. Ochs, Indexing gender, in *Rethinking context: Language as an interactive phenomenon*, A. Duranti, C. Goodwin, Eds. Cambridge: Cambridge University Press, 1992, pp. 336-358.
[13]   M. Grader, Expressive timing and interaction synchrony between mothers and infants: Cultural similarities, cultural differences, and the immigration experience, *Cognitive development* **18** (2003) 533-554.
[14]   C. Goodwin, Action and embodiment within situated human interaction, *Journal of Pragmatics* **32** (2000) 1489-1522.
[15]   E. T. Hall, *The Hidden Dimension*. Garden City: Doubleday, 1966.
[16]   E. T. Hall and M. R. Hall, Monochronic and Polychronic Time, in *The Nonverbal Communication Reader: Classic and Contemporary Readings,* L. K. Guerrero, J. A. De Vito, M. L. Hect, Eds. Waveland press, Prospect Heights, 1990, pp. 237-240.
[17]   F. Moraro, Communication by gestures in Italians and Danes, *Journal of Human Movement Studies* **25** (2000) 85-110.
[18]   J. A. Graham and M. Argyle, A Cross-Cultural Study of the Communication of Extra-verbal Meaning by Gestures, *International Journal of Psychology* **10** (1975) 56-67.
[19]   K. Bartholomew, L. M. Horowitz, Attachment styles among young adults: A test of a four category model, *Journal of Personality and Social Psychology Bulletin* **21** (1991) 394-405
[20]   K. Grammer, K. B. Kruck, M. S. Magnusson, The Courtship Dance: Patterns of Nonverbal Synchronization in Opposite-Sex Encounters, *Journal of Nonverbal Behavior* **22** (1998) 3-29.
[21]   H. G. Wallbott, R. C. Givens, The measurement of human expression in *Aspects of nonverbal communication,* W. von Raffler-Engel, Ed. Lisse: Swets & Zeitlinger, 1980.
[22]   W. C. McGrew, *An ethological study of children's behavior*. New York: Academic Press, 1972.
[23]   M. S. Magnusson, Discovering hidden time patterns in behavior: T-patterns and their detection, *Behavior Research Methods, Instruments and Computer* **32** (2000) 93-110.
[24]   M. S. Magnusson, Hidden real-time patterns in intra- and inter-individual behavior: Description and detection, *European Journal of Psychological Assessment* **12** (1996) 112-123.
[25]   M. Hayashi, Language and the Body as Resources for Collaborative Action: A Study of Word Searches in Japanese Conversation, *Research on Language and Social Interaction* **36** (2003) 109-141.
[26]   C. LeBaron and J. Streeck, Gesture, knowledge and the world, in *Language and Gesture,* D. McNeill, Ed. Cambridge: Cambridge University Press, 2000, pp. 118-138.
[27]   C. Goodwin, Time in Action, *Applied Linguistic* **43** (2002) 1-53.
[28]   P. Clancy, S. Thompson, R. Suzuki, and H. Tao, The conversational use of reactive tokens in English, Japanese and Mandarin, *Journal of Pragmatics* **26** (1996) 355-387.

The Hidden Structure of Interaction
L. Anolli et al. (Eds.)
IOS Press, 2005

16. Temporal Pattern Analysis and its Applicability in Soccer

Jonathan BLOOMFIELD, Gudberg K. JONSSON, Remco
POLMAN, Kenneth HOULAHAN, Peter O'DONOGHUE

Abstract. In order to optimize sports performance it is considered necessary to employ sound scientific principles of physical conditioning and coaching. One of the most critical of these scientific principles is the rule of specificity. To elicit a high degree of transfer from training into competitive scenarios in key performance attributes such as physical capabilities, skill acquisition and cognitive learning a high degree of specificity of competition is desired in practice situations. To this end the specific requirements of the performance must be investigated and reported. A popular method of investigating the physical demands is that of time-motion analysis where various modes of motion are subjectively or objectively chosen and each are recorded throughout the performance. To date, researchers in soccer have often chosen fewer than 8 modes of motion in their investigations, however it is arguable that this does not provide enough detail to report the high degree of specificity required to configure the precise physical demands of the sport. However, the Bloomfield Movement Classification is recognized as the most comprehensive time-motion analysis method in dynamic field-based sports such as soccer, which includes a combination of 17 modes of motion, 14 directional categories, 4 intensity types and other specific instantaneous movement and sport-specific events including turns, swerves and on the ball activity. Historically, time-motion analyses have reported frequencies, totals and means of individual motions and failed to recognize the interaction of movements which cause several different physiological demands. Temporal pattern (T-pattern) analysis can be performed to identify hidden sequences of events and has been used successfully to identify complex playing patterns in soccer matchplay. It is therefore desirable to perform the T-pattern analysis with the movement of the players. In this chapter we offer the work done by our research team at the Department of Sport Science, University of Hull and the use of T-Pattern detection through application of THEME 5.0. The aim of the following sections is, firstly, to review and critique the current research into the physical demands of soccer and secondly to offer an alternative method of detailing the movements performed by the players with an objective of re-producing specific patterns of movement through T-patterns which can be used to enhance physical conditioning and coaching practices.

Keywords: Soccer application; principals of physical conditioning; coaching practices; time motion analysis; Bloomfield Movement Classification.

Contents

16.1   Introduction

Skilled behaviour is fundamental to all sporting activities. This often requires a dynamic co-coordinated process of perception, cognition and action with evidence identifying that skill acquisition and skilled performance share underlying mechanisms across the perceptual, cognitive, and motor domains [1, 2]. In order to produce skilled behavior it is important to identify the discrete requirements of sporting activities, however, coaches are unable to observe and recall all of the discrete incidents and activities that are required for a complete understanding of performance so it is therefore useful to perform video analysis in sport [3]. Skilled sporting behaviour is enhanced through processes of learning, acquisition and physical conditioning. There are several recognized principles for these processes with one of the most important being specificity. Evidence from exercise physiology studies indicates that specific neurophysiological adaptations to physical conditioning are in direct relation to specific exercises performed [4, 5]. Specificity of patterns of movement producing motor skills has been expressed as the fundamental constituent of any movement related to speed and power [6-8]. Many sporting skills require a very precise moment and direction of force application and the neural pattern for the precise force application is acquired only by repetition of the desired skill [9]. Thus, precise movement patterns of specific motor skills are needed to effectively entrain appropriate motor programs for efficient co-ordination of muscular contraction.

Physical conditioning effects are limited to the physiological systems used and overloaded [10, 11]. It is recognized that each sport favours specific biological strategies for success based on the rules of the game and its physiological and biomechanical demands [12]. However, specific movement patterns must be first identified in order to apply the specificity principle in physical conditioning. This can be easier to accomplish in simple actions than in more complex actions. Although the physiological responses to performance and biomechanical analysis of several critical skills have been extensively investigated, it can be argued that there is insufficient knowledge regarding specific detail concerning the physical demands.

In this chapter we offer the work done by our research team at the Department of Sport Science, University of Hull into the investigation of physical demands of dynamic field-based sports and the use of T-Pattern detection through application of THEME 5.0. The aim of the following sections is, firstly, to review and critique the current research into the physical demands of soccer, secondly, to offer an alternative method of detailing the movements performed by the players, and finally the identification of hidden patterns within the movements through use of T-pattern detection with an objective of re-producing specific patterns of movement which can be used to enhance physical conditioning and coaching practices. To this end we will provide exemplar data of specific movement patterns performed in a competitive match by a Football Association Premier League player. We finish this chapter discussing our results and highlighting future directions.

16.2   The physical demands of soccer

Soccer, formally known as Association Football, is one of the six *football* match-play codes which also includes Rugby Union, Rugby League, American Football, Australian Rules, and Gaelic Football [13]. Having begun in England in 1848, it is now played worldwide, with more than 150 countries being registered with FIFA (Federation International de Football Association), the international governing body, which was itself established in 1904 [14, 15]. It is considered to be the most popular sport in the world, both in terms of participation, and as a spectator sport [16]. It was estimated that in 1984, there were 60 million licensed, and an equal number of unlicensed players [14]. Since that time, the number of female players has proliferated, and the game's popularity has increased in the continents of Africa and Asia. As a consequence, soccer has been under scientific investigation for several years in an attempt to understand and improve the sport. A plethora of studies have been performed in areas such as physiology, biomechanics, psychology, notational analysis and kinanthropometry with one key aim to establish the demands of competitive soccer. The following section reviews the studies performed to quantify the physical exertion of players through a method known as time-motion analysis.

16.2.1 Time-Motion analysis

Notational analysis of match-play through use of a timing device is a methodology which has been used to assess the physical and physiological demands of sport. Some of the earliest investigations made using this method were performed in English soccer using various techniques to calculate the total distances players traveled during matches [17-20]. Other studies have investigated the time spent in various modes of motion (time-motion analysis) with the first studies again completed in English Soccer [21, 22]. The main advantages of the paradigm are that it offers a non-intrusive method of analyzing performance during match-play, and that distances covered provide a crude measure of energy expended [22]. Distances can be broken down into discrete motion modalities, which can then be classified according to type, intensity (or quality), duration (or distance), and frequency [23]. This data can then be applied to the construction of research models and in physical conditioning. However, it is critical to continue this form of research in order to re-assess the demands of the modern game due to the rapid evolution of the sport [24-27].

16.2.1.1 Methodological differences
As the game of soccer has evolved, the methods of analyzing performance have also developed (although perhaps not at the same rate). On review of the current studies performed there appear to be large discrepancies between studies in the distances covered by players largely due to methodological differences [22] (Table 16.1). Methods have evolved from the simple use of hand notation tracking of players' movements on scale plans of pitches [17], to the current utilization of video recordings and computerized analyses [48].

Although the production of an overall distance covered may be of some use in establishing the performance demands, it is far removed from identifying the specific demands. It is therefore essential to investigate the movements made which accumulate to cover the total distance in order to reproduce them in practice scenarios and attempt to optimize performance. Unfortunately, however, it is also the area, which is most adversely affected by methodological differences (Table 16.2). There is a need for a much more rigorous analysis of the data, and in particular with reference to identifying the sources of variability resulting from methodological issues, for example those caused by the use of varying methods of data collection used in the studies, the lack of standardized approaches (level of competition, environmental conditions etc), and in particular the considerable differences in the approaches used to classify motion modes.

16.2.1.2 Key findings (including positional differences)
The most frequently cited values in the literature are those from Reilly and Thomas (1976) (walking 24.8%, jogging 36.8%, cruising 20.5%, sprinting 11.2% and backing 6.7%) which were applicable for a total distance covered of 8.68 ± 1.011km.

More recent studies provided a more stringent definition of the utility motion modes relating to walking backwards and jogging backwards/sideways.

Source	Subjects & Level	N	Distance Covered (km)	Method	Ref
Winterbottom, 1959	English	8	3·361	Hand notation using scale plan of pitch.	[17]
Wade, 1962	English	N/A	1·6 – 5·486	N/A	[18]
Zelenka *et al.*, 1967	Italian	1	11.5	N/A	[19]
Agnevik, 1970	Swedish Div I	11	10·2	N/A	[28]
Vinnai, 1973	N/A	N/A	17	N/A	[20]
Saltin, 1977	N/A	9	10·9	Cine-film	[11]
Brookes & Knowles, 1974	English	40	4·886 (4·070 - 7·030)	Hand notation - subjective estimates.	[21]
Reilly & Thomas, 1976	English Div I	40	8·680 (7·069 - 10·921)	Tape Recorder - individual stride lengths	[22]
Smaros, 1980	N/A	7	7.1	TV cameras (2)	[29]
Withers, *et al.*, 1982	Australian National	20	11·527±1·796 (9.731 – 13.323)	Videotape- mean stride lengths	[30]
Ekblom, 1986	Swedish Div I - IV & German Div II	10	9·8	Hand notation.	[14]
Ohashi *et al.*, 1988	Japanese International & League	4	9·845 (9·303 – 10·387)	Trigonometry (2 cameras).	[31]
Ohashi & Togari, 1988	Japanese International & League	N/A	9·971	Trigonometry.	[32]
Van Gool *et al.*, 1988	Belgian University	7	10·245	Cine-film	[33]
Bangsbo *et al.*, 1991	Danish League	14	10·8 (9.49 – 12.93)	Video cameras (24)	[34]
Ohashi *et al.*, 1991	Japanese International & League	50	11·529	Trigonometry	[35]
Miyagi *et al.*, 1999	Yugoslavian International	1	10·460±0.591 (9.869 – 11.051)	Trigonometry	[25]
Rienzi *et al.*, 2000	South American International & English Premier League	17 6	8·638±1·158 (7.480 – 9.796) 10·104±·0.703 (9.401 – 10.807)	Video camera - subjective stride frequency estimation.	[26]
Strudwick & Reilly, 2001	English Premier League	24	11·264	Video camera - subjective stride frequency estimation	[27]

N/A = no data available.
(Adapted and extended from [23]).

Table 16.1 Mean and range of distances covered in match-play and methodologies employed

Investigations have also been made into the physical requirements for the different positions played in soccer. Several time-motion analyses have indicated different work-rate profiles between positions, therefore indicating some degree of positional specificity in the demands of the game [22, 26, 34, 37, 38]. The greatest overall distances are covered by midfield players who act as links between defence and attack [14, 22, 26, 34]. This is mainly due to the midfielders engaging in low speed running more frequently, and for longer duration [37] and standing still for significantly less time than the other outfield players [38]. Bangsbo (1994) [39], in this respect, reported that elite Danish defenders and forwards covered approximately the same distance (10-10.5km), but this was significantly less than that covered by the midfield players (11.5km). In addition, Reilly and Thomas (1976) [22] reported that defenders and forwards covered more distance in walking and sprinting and less in jogging and cruising and the midfield players covered more distance in jogging and cruising and less in walking and sprinting. The increased distance covered by midfielders is also accompanied by higher VO_2max values for these players in comparison to other outfield players [40, 29]. Forwards, on the other hand, have been found to perform the most all out sprints, followed by midfielders and defenders [39]. In addition, it is well documented that playing in different positions constitute different performance demands within the game. For example, forwards and centre backs are significantly more engaged in situations were they have to jump or are required to head the ball whereas defenders tend to make more tackles [37, 41]. Overall, the data seem to indicate that different positions within the game of soccer require different physical and physiological demands.

Classification Method	Examples of Studies	Motions			Ref
Subjective *Description*	Reilly & Thomas (1976) Mayhew & Wenger (1985) Rienzi *et al.,* (2000)	Standing: Walking (forwards/ sideways/backwards): Jogging Running Utility			[22] [36] [26]
Arbitrary *Speed* *Classification*	Bangsbo *et al.,* (1991)	Standing – 0 km·h^{-1} Walking – 6 km·h^{-1} Low-speed jogging – 8 km·h^{-1} Low-speed running – 12 km·h^{-1} Backward running – 12 km·h^{-1} High to moderate-speed running – 15 km·h^{-1} High-speed running – 18 km·h^{-1} Sprint running – 30 km·h^{-1}			[34]
Basic Speed *Classification*	Ohashi, *et al.,* (1988) Van Gool *et al., (*1988)	Speed ranges, from $0 – 1$ m s^{-1}, to $9 – 10$ m s^{-1}, in increments of 1m s^{-1}.			[31] [33]
Individual *Mean Stride* *Lengths*	Reilly & Thomas (1976) Withers *et al.,* (1982) (Figures in parentheses represent reliability & objectivity coefficient values)	[22] Walking: Jogging: Cruising: Sprinting: Sideways: Backing:	[22] 0.64 (0.966) 0.90 (0.962) 1.13 (0.915) 1.24 (0.971) N/A 0.60 (0.915)	[30] 0.82 (0.981) 1.36 (0.979) 1.75 (0.745) 1.76 (0.815) 1.25 (0.904) 0.78 (0.982)	[22] [30]

Table 16.2 Details of motion classification criteria

Due to the crude measures used to index activity patterns and the reporting of totals, frequencies and means in time-motion studies, the information produced is of limited value and provides simply a macroscopic view on the physical demands in soccer (Table 16.3). It has been discovered that there are 1000-1200 discrete movement changes (incorporating rapid and frequent changes in pace and direction) in a game, with the mean duration being 4.5-6s per movement [43]. With the use of computer-based time-motion analysis, it is now possible to control video images and to "enhance sport specific analytical procedures" [44]. Information regarding a complete set of movement categories, directions, intensities, turns and playing activity is needed to thoroughly understand and evaluate the performance requirements. In addition, it is necessary to gain an understanding into the interaction of these motions as this knowledge would make it possible to objectively design training that is highly specific to performance.

Source, Subjects & Level	Ref	Position	Total Distance (km)	Walk (%)	Jog (%)	Cruise (%)	Sprint (%)	Utility (%)
Whitehead	[42]	*Div I :*						
(1975)		Defenders	11.472(1)	22.6	30.9	24.0	22.6	
English		Midfield .	13.827(1)	36.5	33.3	16.5	13.7	
n=n/a		*Div II:*						
		Defenders	10.826(1)	38.7	27.4	19.2	14.7	
		Midfield .	11.184(1)	43.9	37.4	9.8	9.0	
		Top Amateur:						
		Defenders	9.679(1)	42.4	26.6	18.8	12.2	
		Midfield .	9.084(1)	47.4	37.4	10.4	10.0	
		College:						
		Defenders	6.609(1)	47.4	28.3	16.2	8.0	
		Midfield .	8.754 (1)	40.7	33.9	15.4	10.0	
Reilly &	[22]	Central Defs	7.759(7)	27.8	35.2	19.2	9.5	8.1
Thomas (1976)		Full backs	8.245(8)	22.9	37.5	20.6	10.7	8.4
English Div I		Midfield	9.805(110	20.7	41.2	22.0	10.8	5.2
N = 40		Strikers	8.397(14)	27.5	33.0	20.9	12.7	5.9
Withers *et al.*	[30]	Central Defs	10.169(5)	23.7	45.0	14.5	7.9	8.9
(1982)		Full backs	11.980(5)	30.3	37.9	12.5	3.9	15.3
Australian		Midfield	12.194(5)	21.9	49.9	15.1	5.3	7.8
National		Strikers	11.766(5)	29.8	44.4	10.0	5.8	10.1
N = 20								
Rienzi *et al.*	[26]	Defenders(7)						
(2000)		Midfield(6)	8.638±1.158	31	43	11	4	11
S American		Strikers(4)						
Internationals								
n =17		Defenders(2)	10.104±0.703	24	50	9	3	14
English Premier		Midfield(4)						
n= 6								

Unorthodox movements including sideways and backwards movements have been classified as UTILITY movements.
Figures in parentheses equate to numbers of players
N.B. Making comparisons between studies should be avoided due to methodological differences.

Table 16.3 Assessment of positional differences: Total distance and distance covered in each mode of motion as a percentage of total match distance.

16.2.2 The Bloomfield Movement Classification

This method of time-motion, computerized video analysis involves a detailed account of motions, directions, intensities and events (turns, swerves, contact and on the ball activity). The "Bloomfield Movement Classification" (BMC) was designed after several preliminary observations of performances of individual players in team games (soccer, field hockey, rugby union, rugby league, basketball and netball). Movements and game activities were noted, recorded and discussed with participants. The BMC supplied codes for 14 modes of timed-motion, 3 "other" non-timed movements, 14 directions, 4 intensities, 5 turning categories and 7 "On the Ball" activity classifications (see Table 16.4).

The Observer Version 5.0 (Noldus Information Technology, The Netherlands) was chosen as the software to perform the collection, management and presentation of the BMC as observational data could be collected, reviewed and edited with synchronized display of the corresponding video images [45]. Furthermore, the system requires a configuration to be independently composed consisting of states (continuous) and events (discrete) to define how observed behavioural data is to be notated. The Observer 5.0 configuration is comprised of behaviours (state or event) and allows for two further modifiers to be added used to describe the behaviour. Once the initiation of a behaviour was observed, a representative key pressed on a QWERTY (AT Enhanced) keyboard followed by the keys for the appropriate modifiers signify the entry and recording in a Event Log (see figure 16.1).

BEHAVIOURS (Modifiers in parenthesis)	MODIFIERS
1. TIMED *Motion* Sprint (A+B), Run (A+B), Shuffle (A+B), Skip (A+B), Jog (A+B), Walk (A), Stand Still, Slow Down (A+B), Jump (C), Land, Dive (D), Slide (D), Fall, Get Up (B)	*Direction (A)*: Forwards, Forwards Diagonally Right/Left, Sideways Right/Left, Backwards, Backwards Diagonally Right/Left, Arc Forwards Left to Right/Right to Left, Arc Backwards Left to Right/Right to Left, Arc Sideways Right/Left *Intensity (B)*: Low, Medium, High, Very High
2. INSTANTANEOUS (NON-TIMED) *Other Movement* Stop (B), Swerve (E), Impact(F+B)	*Jump (C)*: Vertical, Forwards, Backwards, Sideways (E) *Dive (D)*: Feet first, Head first *Turn (E)*: Right/Left
Turns 0^0-90^0 (E) 90^0-180^0 (E) 180^0-270^0 (E) 270^0-360^0 (E) >360^0 (E)	*Type (F)*: Push, Pull, Pushed, Pulled, Other *Control (G)*: Right/Left foot, Head, Chest, Thigh, Other *Pass/Shoot (H)*: Long Air, Short Air, Long Ground, Short Ground, Other
On the Ball Activity Receive (G), Pass (H+I), Shoot (H+I), Dribble (J+K), Tackle, Trick, Other	*How (I)*: Right/Left Foot, Header, Backheel, Overhead, Other *Dribble (J)*: Start, End *Touches (K)*: Start,1-3, 4-6, 7-10, >10

Table 16.4 The "Bloomfield Movement Classification" Behaviours and Modifiers.

16.2.2.1 The Bloomfield Movement Classification – Reliability
Footage from FA Premier League soccer was collected from Sky Sports Interactive Service (British Sky Broadcasting Group, UK) using the "PlayerCam" facility. This source provided a clear picture, with a separate camera focused solely upon a single player at any time (see Figure 16.2). Footage was recorded on VHS and converted to MPEG format using Dazzle Moviestar Version 4.22 (Fremont, USA). Each MPEG file was edited in M1-Edit Pro Version 4.00.0012 (Mediaware Solutions Pty Ltd, USA) so the opening frame was taken from the start of the player being tracked and the final frame taken when focus changed to a new player or at half or full-time.

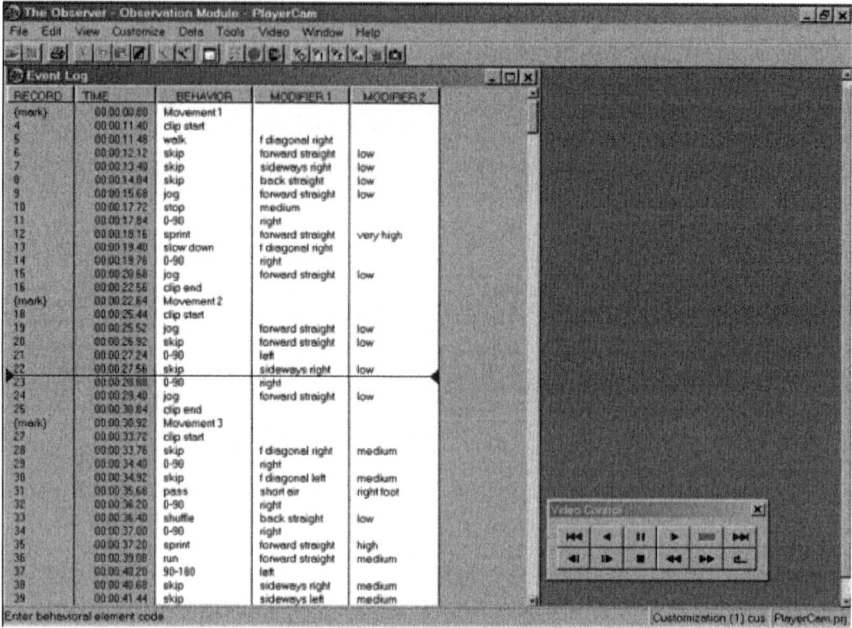

Figure 16.1 The Observer 5.0 Event Log

The BMC was piloted several times in The Observer 5.0 using various "PlayerCam" video clips of players of different positions to ensure that any possible scenario could be coded. Due to the expansive nature of the configuration some impossible scenarios could be coded in the observation (e.g. sprint, backward, low intensity). These impossible scenarios were noted and made aware to the observer.

Figure 16.2 Sky Sports Interactive "PlayerCam" Facility (British Sky Broadcasting Group, UK). Individual Player Camera on right side of screen.

A total of 8 observers (5 semi-professional team games players (soccer, field hockey, basketball), 1 Level Three semi-professional soccer referee and 2 FA Premier League season ticket holders) repeated three 5 minute observations each of 4 FA Premier League players (1 defender, 2 midfielders, 1 forward). This provided an inter- and intra-observer agreement revealing *kappa* values of between 0.64 and 0.78 and 0.79 and 0.92 respectively. This is interpreted as a good to very high level of agreement [46]. Further checks of quality were made using The Observer 5.0 video play list which provides visual highlights of entered data by recalling specified entries from the Event Log. These were constantly performed at random throughout the data collection phase.

16.3   Temporal Pattern Analysis

A Temporal pattern (T-Pattern) is essentially a combination of events where the events occur in the same order with the consecutive time distances between consecutive pattern components remaining relatively invariant with respect to an expectation assuming, as a null hypothesis, that each component is independently and randomly distributed over time. As stated by Magnusson "that is, if A is an earlier and B a later component of the same recurring T-pattern then after an occurrence of A at t, there is an interval [t+d1, t+d2](d2≥d1≥d0) that tends to contain at least one occurrence of B more often than would be expected by chance" [47]. The temporal relationship between A and B is defined as a critical interval and this concept lies at the centre of the pattern detection algorithms.

Through use of the THEME 5.0 software package, pattern detection algorithms can analyze both ordinal and temporal data however, for the algorithms to generate the most meaningful analyses the raw data must be time coded i.e. an event must be coded according to time of occurrence as well as event type. The method of time-motion computerized video analysis therefore lends itself to the use of T-Pattern detection and through use of the Bloomfield Movement Classification detailed and highly complex patterns that are specific to the performance of competition can be identified.

16.3.1 Soccer Match Analysis

T-patterning has been already been used to establish playing patterns in soccer [48]. Thirteen elite level soccer matches were first analyzed through a computerized video method which coded for ball and player pitch location and selected match events and subsequently for T-patterns. The data show that a high number of temporal interactive play-patterns exist in soccer with the number, frequency and complexity of the detected patterns indicating that sport behaviour is more synchronized than the human eye can detect. This synchrony was found to exist on different levels, with highly complex time structures that extended over considerable time spans within performances with patterns occurring in both cyclical and acyclical fashion.

A typical within-team event pattern from the soccer analysis is shown in Figure 16.3a and 16.3b. This figure displays a T-pattern that occurred three times during the first half of a European Championship qualifying match (1998). The pattern describes how player A (Zinedine Zidane) moves the ball towards the opponents goal by receiving the ball in, and then passing it out of, pitch zones 8, 11 and then 14 consecutively. Player A then completes the sequence by passing it on to player B who receives it in zone 15. The pattern describes an attacking movement through the middle of the pitch. Traditional frequency analysis of passing would have identified the ball reception and subsequent pass from each zone as discrete events but would not have linked the consecutive actions in the four zones. The movement from zone 11 to 14 also occurred on another five occasions during the first half

(Fig 16.3a, upper right box) further suggesting that player A was working effectively through the central channel of the pitch.

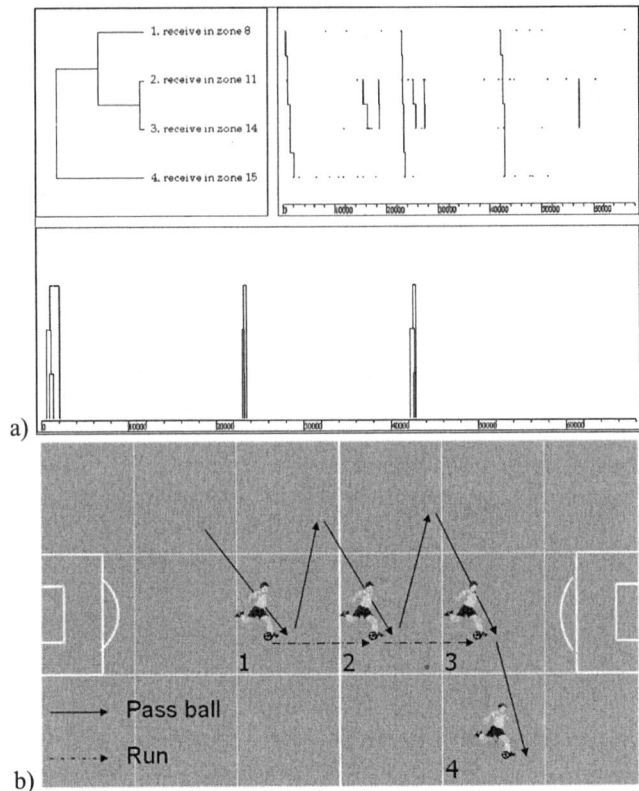

Figures 16.3 A temporal pattern relating to attacking movement of the ball through the centre of the pitch.

Figure 16.4a and 16.4b also show a T-pattern from a club match (Liverpool – Sunderland, English Premiership) in which the pattern involves players from both teams and relates to the critical incident of shots on goal. The pattern occurred on three occasions during the second half of the match and includes two shots on goal within each pattern. The total time period covered the three patterns therefore includes six shots by Team A which represents 75% of their total shot on target during the second half. Even more significantly two of the three pattern occurrences resulted in goals.

It is difficult to conceive of coaching situations in which the type of information identified in Figures 16.3 and 16.4, and the further analyses that they may stimulate, would not be of value in enhancing coach knowledge. At the very least the analyses shown provide a perspective on team performance that is unattainable using traditional frequency counts of discrete events within a match. Another issue addressed in the study was to investigate the potential interrelationship between performance rating by coaches and the degree of structure in team performance. Several soccer coaches were asked to rate the performance of every player (on both teams) on a simple ten point Likert type scale. The data show that the coaches' ratings of team performance were significantly correlated to the number of patterns identified for each team ($r = .81, p < .05$).

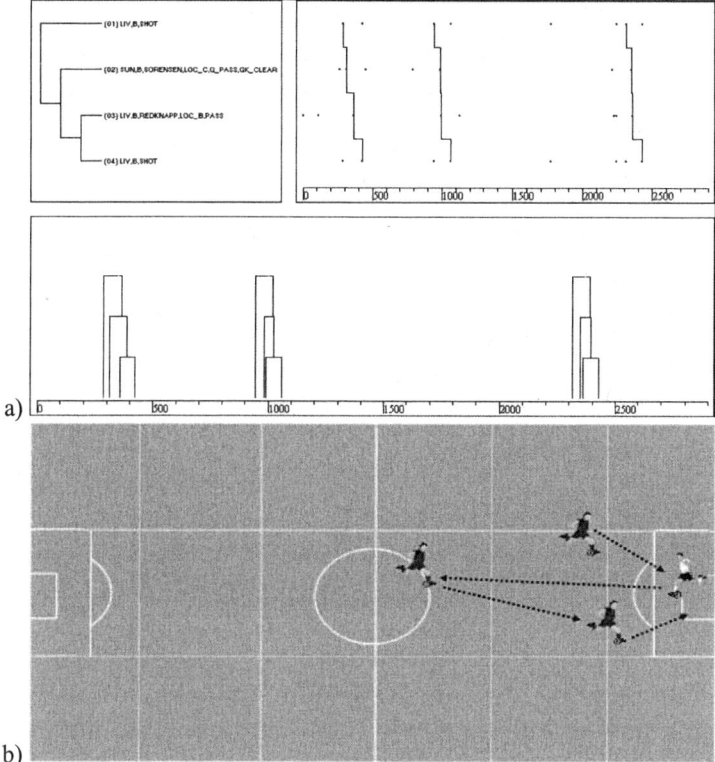

Figures 16.4 A T-pattern incorporating regularity in shots on goal in a F.A. Premiership match. The pattern includes 6 of Team A's 8 shots. Pattern occurrences 2 and 3 resulted in a goal.

16.4   Exemplar Data

Time-Motion analyses have revealed that soccer is a sport that demands a wide range of intermittent bursts of activities and recoveries which involve a range of intensity of movements. Typically, a "burst" in soccer is associated with irregular high intensity movements and subsequent recovery with low intensity activity. However, it may be argued that the "bursts" may also include some low intensity action within and that the more holistic "purposeful" movements should be adopted as opposed to simply the high intensity activity. Purposeful movements may be described as movements performed with deliberate intention to influence the performance (i.e. changing location on the pitch with manifest intent and purpose).

16.4.1 Case Study Using the Bloomfield Movement Classification

Fifteen minutes of footage from an FA Premier League soccer player was collected during an FA Premier League match televised by Sky Sports Interactive Service (British Sky Broadcasting Group, UK) using the "PlayerCam" facility. The player was an international and formed part of a two man strike partnership playing just behind the other forward and in the centre. Firstly, the video footage was separated into purposeful movements (approximately 5 minutes) and recoveries (*kappa* values ranged from 0.91 and 0.98 for intra-reliability and 0.85 and 0.98 for inter-reliability which is interpreted as a very high level of agreement [46]). The purposeful movements were then assessed through using the BMC and The Observer Version 5.0 (Noldus Information Technology, The Netherlands). This was then used to identify temporal patterns in the data through using THEME 5.0. Two complex and highly significant t-patterns detected are displayed in Figures 16.5 and 16.6.

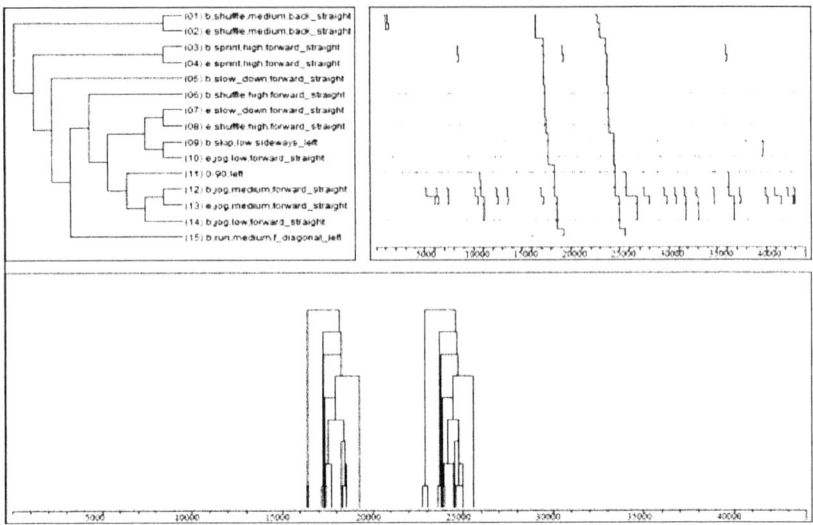

Figure 16.5 A T-pattern incorporating regularity of movements by a centre forward in a F.A. Premiership match.

Figure 16.5 displays a pattern which identifies a varied range of motions but uniformity within the ranges of intensity, beginning with medium, progressing to high, and finally ending in low and medium intensity activity. This correlates strongly with the intermittent nature of the sport. The pattern begins with the player shuffling backwards and then sprinting forwards and slowing down in which he shuffles at high intensity suggesting he slows quite abruptly from his sprint. From this point he skips sideways left at low intensity perhaps preparing for another high intensity burst, turns left and jogs forward at low intensity and gradually increases pace into a run changing direction by moving diagonally left to complete the complex pattern.

Figure 16.6 displays a pattern which begins at high intensity and ends with low intensity movement. The pattern is more simpler than that in Figure 5 and begins with the player sprinting forwards submaximally, slowing down and shuffling at high intensity, again suggesting he slows quite abruptly from his sprint. As illustrated in Figure 5, we can see that this is a common pattern and as both patterns are significant, this deceleration phase should be commonly adopted into physical conditioning. Once the player has completed his deceleration he jogs forward at low intensity and finally skips to his left to complete the pattern.

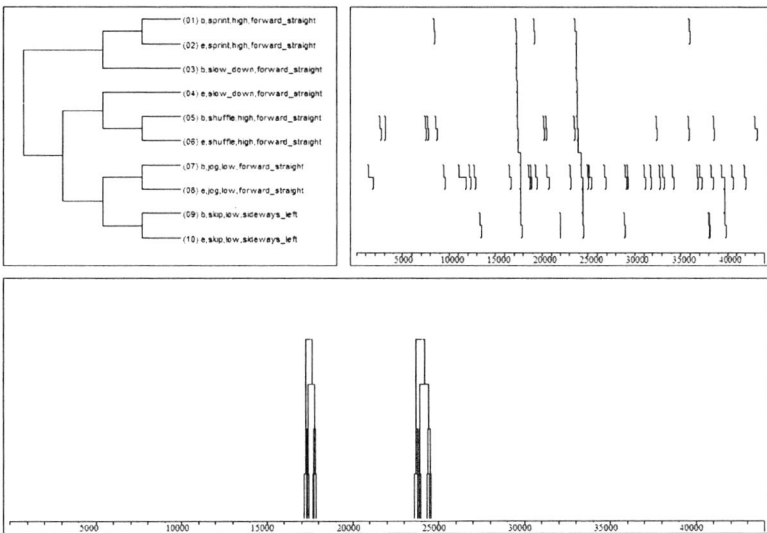

Figure 16.6 A T-pattern incorporating regularity of movements by a centre forward in a F.A. Premiership match.

16.5 Conclusions and future directions

The potential for use of T-pattern detection in soccer is tremendous. The identification of patterns that are not identifiable through simple observation has great benefit not only in match-play but also in establishing the physical demands through time-motion analysis. With regards the latter, highly specific physical conditioning practices can be employed through the use of the Bloomfield Movement Classification and THEME 5.0 which will enhance the condition of the players and optimize time spent in training. A comprehensive study is therefore required investigating the demands between the different positions played in soccer as well as different time phases in a match. This study is ongoing using the BMC and the "PlayerCam" facility provided by Sky Sports Interactive Service (British Sky Broadcasting Group, UK) with televised FA Premier League matches. It is aimed to observe a total of 54 players - 3 from each position (defender, midfielder, forward) and time period (0-15, 15-30, 30-45, 45-60, 6-75, 75-90) and to investigate the differences within hidden pattern analysis. Preliminary investigation of pattern complexity between player positions suggests that a higher number of different patterns and pattern occurrences are detected for Defenders than Forwards and Midfielders. The same also seems to apply for length of patterns. These findings, and their significance, need further examinations.

Once these physical demands have been identified, and the complex hidden patterns that occur it becomes possible to perform further research into establishing the physiological and biomechanical demands which will further assist the enhancement of coaching and physical conditioning practices.

16.6   References

[1]   R. A. Carlson and R.G. Yaure, Practice Schedules and the use of component skills in problem solving, *Journal of Experimental Psychology: Learning, Memory and Cognition* **16** (1990) 484-496.

[2]   D. A. Rosenbaum, Successive approximations to a model of human motor programming, in *The psychology of learning and motivation*, G. H. Bower, Ed. San Diego: Academic Press, 1987, pp. 1-52.

[3]   I. M Franks and G. Miller, Eyewitness testimony in sport, *Journal of Sport Behaviour* **9** (1986) 39-45.

[4]   M. C. Morrissey, E. A. Harman, and M. J. Johnson, Resistance training modes: Specificity and effectiveness, *Medicine and Science in Sports and Exercise* **27** (1995) 648-660.

[5]   D. Sale and D. MacDougall, Specificity in strength training: A review for the coach and athlete, *Canadian Journal of Applied Sport Science* **4** (1981) 56-59.

[6]   T. R. Ackland and J. Bloomfield, Applied Anatomy, in *Science and Medicine in Sport,* J. Bloomfield, P. A. Fricker, and K.D. Fitch, Eds., 2nd ed. Victoria: Blackwell Science, 1996, pp. 2-30.

[7]   D. G. Sale, Neural Adaptations to Strength Training, in *Strength and Power in Sport*, P. V. Komi, Ed. Oxford: Blackwell Scientific Publications, 1992, pp. 249-265.

[8]   D. Schmidtbleicher, Training for Power Events, in *Strength and Power in Sport*, P. V. Komi, Ed. Oxford: Blackwell Scientific Publications, 1992, pp. 381-398.

[9]   C. Poliquin, Theory and Methodology of Strength Training: Part 4, *Sports Coach* **13**(3), (1990) 29-31.

[10]   J. O. Holloszy and E. F. Coyle, Adaptations of skeletal muscle to endurance exercise and their metabolic consequences, *Journal of Applied Physiology* **56** (1984) 831-838.

[11]   B. Saltin, J. Henriksson, E. Nygaard, and P. Andersen, Fiber types and metabolic potentials of skeletal muscles in sedentary man and endurance runners, in *Marathon: Physiological, Medical, Epidemiological, and Psychological Studies*, P. Milvy, Ed. New York: New York Academy of Sciences, 1977, pp. 3-29.

[12]   G. E. McCall, W. C. Byrnes, S. J. Fleck, A. Dickinson, and W. J. Kraemer, Acute and chronic hormonal responses to resistance training designed to promote muscle hypertrophy, *Canadian Journal of Applied Physiology* **24**(1), (1999) 96-107.

[13]   T. Reilly, Football (Soccer), in *Physiology of Sports,* T. Reilly, N. Secher, P. Snell, and C. Williams, Eds. London: E&FN Spon, 1990, pp. 371-401.

[14]   B. Ekblom, Applied physiology of soccer, *Sports Medicine* **3** (1986) 50-60.

[15]   D. Tumilty, Physiological Characteristics of Elite Soccer Players, *Sports Medicine* **16**(2), (1993) 80 – 96.

[16]   R. J. Shephard, Biology and medicine of soccer: An update, *Journal of Sports Sciences* **17** (1999) 757–786.

[17]   W. Winterbottom, *Soccer Coaching.* Kingswood: The Naldrett Press Ltd, 1959.

[18]   A. Wade, The training of young players, *Medicina Dello Sport* **3** (1962) 1245–1251.

[19]   V. Zelenka, V. Seliger, and O. Ondrej, Specific function testing of young football players, *Journal of Sports Medicine and Physical Fitness* **7** (1967) 143-147

[20]   G. Vinnai, *Football Mania.* London: Ocean Books, 1973.

[21]   J. D. Brookes and J. E. Knowles, *A movement analysis of player behaviour in soccer match performance.* Paper presented at the British Society of Sports Psychology Conference, Salford, 1974.

[22]   T. Reilly and V. Thomas, A motion analysis of work-rate in different positional roles in professional football match-play, *Journal of Human Movement Studies* **2** (1976) 87-89.

[23]   T. Reilly, Physiological Aspects Of Soccer, *Biology of Sport* **11**(1), (1994) 3–20.

[24]   B. Drust, T. Reilly, and E. Rienzi, Analysis of work rate in soccer, *Sports Exercise & Injury* **4** (1998) 151–155.

[25]   O. Miyagi, J. Ohashi, and K. Kitagawa, Motion characteristics of an elite soccer player during a game, *Journal of Sports Sciences* **17**(10), (1999) 816.

[26]   E. Rienzi, B. Drust, T. Reilly, J. E. L. Carter, and A. Martin, Investigation of anthropometric and work-rate profiles of elite South American International Soccer Players, *Journal of Sports Medicine & Physical Fitness* **40** (2000) 162–169.

[27]   T. Strudwick and T. Reilly, Work-rate Profiles of Elite Premier League Football Players, *Insight* **2**(2), (2001) 28 – 29.

[28]   G. Agnevic, Fotboll, in *Rapport Idrottsfysiologi*, Stockholm:Trygg-Hansa, 1970.

[29]   G. Smaros, Energy usage during football match, in *Proceedings of the 1st International Congress on Sports Medicine Applied to Football*, L. Vecchiet, Ed. D. Guanello: Rome, 1980, pp. 795-801.

[30]   R. T. Withers, Z. Maricic, S. Wasilewski, and L. O. Kelly, Match Analysis Of Australian Professional Soccer Players, *Journal of Human Movement Studies* **8** (1982) 159 – 176.

[31]   J. Ohashi, H. Togari, M. Isokawa, and S. Suzuki, Measuring movement speeds and distances covered during soccer match play, in *Science and Football*, T. Reilly, A. Lees, K. Davids, and W. J. Murphy, Eds. London: E&F.N. Spon, 1988, pp. 329–333.

[32]   J. Ohashi, H. Togari, and T. Takii, The distance covered during matches of the World Class Soccer Players, *Proceedings of the Department of Sports Science*, College of Arts and Sciences, University of Tokyo, 1991, pp. 1–5.

[33]   D. Van Gool, D. Van Gerven, and J. Boutmans, The Physiological Load Imposed On Soccer Players During Real Match-Play, in *Science and Football*, T. Reilly, A. Lees, K. Davids, and W. J. Murphy, Eds. London: E&F.N. Spon, 1988, pp. 51-59.

[34]   J. Bangsbo, L. Norregaard, and F. Thorso, Activity profile Of Competition Soccer, *Canadian Journal of Sports Science* 16(2), (1991) 110-116.

[35]   J. Ohashi, M. Isokawa, H. Nagahama, and T. Ogushi, The ratio of physiological intensity of movements during soccer match play, in *Science and Football II*, T. Reilly, J. Clarys, and A. Stibbe, Eds. London: E&FN Spon, 1991, pp. 124-127.

[36]   S. R. Mayhew, and H. A. Wenger, Time-motion analysis of professional soccer, *Journal of Human movement Studies* 11 (1985) 49- 52.

[37]   J. Bangsbo, The physiology of soccer with special reference to intense intermittent exercise, *Acta Physiologica Scandinavia* 151 (Suppl. 619), (1994) 1-156.

[38]   P. G. O'Donoghue, Time-motion analysis of work-rate in elite soccer, in *Proceedings of the World Congress of Notational Analysis of Sport IV*, Porto, 1998, pp. 65-71.

[39]   J. Bangsbo, The physiological demands of playing football, in *Football (Soccer)*, B. Ekblom, Ed. London: IOC/Blackwell, 1994, pp. 43-58.

[40]   T. Reilly, Science and Football: An Introduction, in *Science and Football II*, T. Reilly, J. Clarys, and A. Stibbe, Eds. London: E. & F.N. Spon, 1993, pp. 3-11.

[41]   T. Reilly, *Science and Soccer*. London: E & FN Spon, 1996.

[42]   N. Whitehead, *Conditioning for Sport*. London: A. & C. Black Ltd, 1988.

[43]   T. Reilly, N. Secher, P. Snell, and C. Williams, *Physiology of Sports*. London: E&FN Spon, 1990.

[44]   M. D. Hughes, Notational Analysis, in *Science and Soccer*, T. Reilly, and A.M. Williams, Eds., 2nd Ed. London: Routledge, 2003.

[45]   L. P. J. J. Noldus, R. J. H Trienes, A. H. M. Hendriksen, H. Jansen, and R. G. Jansen, The Observer Video-Pro: new software for the collection, management and presentation of time-structured data from videotapes and digital media files, *Behavior Research Methods, Instruments and Computers* 32 (1999) 197-206.

[46]   D. G. Altman, *Practical Statistics for Medical Research*. Chapman & Hall, 1991.

[47]   M. S. Magnusson, Discovering Hidden Time Patterns in Behavior: T-Patterns and their Detection, *Behavior Research Methods, Instruments and Computers* 32(1), (2000) 93-110.

[48]   A. Borrie, G. K. Jonsson, and M. S. Magnusson, Temporal pattern analysis and its applicability in sport: An explanation and exemplar data, *Journal of Sport Sciences* 20 (2002) 845-852.

17. Viewers Viewed: Facial Expression Patterns While Watching TV News

Dagmar C. UNZ, Frank SCHWAB

Abstract. Based on the "Cultivation of emotions" approach in media psychology we explore the emotional processes that occur while people are watching TV-news. Investigation of media reception is done by combining both timeline data of TV-news (describing formats and content of TV-news by using a computer assisted media analysis) and data about facial expressions as indicators of emotional appraisal processes (EmFACS) and searching for hidden patterns with the aid of THEME. Our results show a large number of temporal patterns in facial expressions data. A remarkably high proportion of these patterns can be interpreted as cognitive appraisal-processes according the assumptions of Scherer and colleagues. Furthermore, we find patterns between the formal aspects of TV-news and the facial expressions of the viewers, suggesting that there seems to be a connection between the presentation of TV news events and the emotional processes of the viewer.

Keywords: Facial expressions; TV news; emotional appraisal process; EmFACS; TV viewers.

Contents

17.1   Introduction

Emotions are vitally important in human life. The most impressive stories – in theatre, in literature, in arts, in movies or in our daily life - we tell each other are stories of feelings and emotions [1]. Undoubtly, media attempt to attract the audience by emotions. But little is known, by now, how the audience processes media stimuli emotionally [2-4]. In our studies we examine the elicitation and differentiation of emotional responses induced by media, especially TV-news. Because emotions are complex phenomena, the study of emotions must meet specific requirements: "They involve the need to (a) study ongoing processes over time, (b) study multiple systems and their interaction (cognition, physiology, expression), (c) adopt experimental approaches using well-controlled manipulations, and (d) formalize predictions" [5, p. 95].

The essential focus of this paper is on the temporal course of changes in emotional subsystems. We regard facial expressions as observable indicators of unobservable emotional processes [6]. Investigation of media reception is done combining both timeline data of TV-news (describing formats and content of TV-news by using a computer assisted media analysis; [3, 7, and 8]) and data about facial expressions of the viewers (coded by EMFACS; [9, 10]) and searching for hidden patterns with the aid of THEME. THEME is used as a method to analyse the temporal and sequential structure of facial expressions in order to get deeper insight in the emotional processing of TV viewers. This contribution outlines the theoretical background of the studies, the method and some results. Exemplary patterns of facial expressions are presented to show potential outcomes of THEME-analysis.

17.2   Theoretical background: The component-process-model of emotion

In recent years, the psychology of emotion has been strongly marked by appraisal theories. One prominent representative of appraisal-theory is Klaus R. Scherer [11]. In order to deal with the dynamic nature of emotion, Scherer conceptualizes emotion as a process rather than a steady state. Emotion is defined "as an episode of interrelated, synchronized changes in the states of all or most of the five organismic subsystems in response to the evaluation of an external or internal stimulus event as relevant to major concerns of the organism" [11, p. 93]. "The major aspects of this process are threefold: first, evaluation of the relevance of environmental stimuli or events for the organism's needs, plans or preferences in specific situations; second, the preparation of actions, both physiological and psychological, appropriate for dealing with these stimuli; and finally, the communication of reactions, states, and intentions by the organism to the social surround" [12, p. 557]. The component-process-model of Scherer distinguishes between five sub-systems of an emotion: (1) the cognitive appraisal, (2) the physiological arousal, (3) the motoric system, most notable the facial expression as part of this system, (4) the subjective feeling, and (5) the motivational system. Each of those components has a specific function for the originating emotion:

1.   The function of the cognitive (appraisal-) component is the processing of external and internal stimuli and thereby evaluating objects and events. "Events or internal changes trigger cycles of appraisal running through the evaluation checks … until the monitoring subsystem signals termination of or adjustment to the stimulation that originally elicited the appraisal episode" [11, p. 99]. Individuals constantly evaluate the ongoing situation concerning to relevance (in detail: novelty check, intrinsic pleasantness check, goal relevance check), implications (in detail: causal attribution check, outcome probability check, discrepancy from expectation check, goal/need conduciveness check, urgency check), coping potential (in detail: control check, power check, adjustment check) and

normative significance (in detail: internal and external standard check). The resulting patterns of appraisal are associated with specific emotions, such as joy, fear, sadness or anger.

2.   The (neuro-) physiological arousal component is responsible for the regulation and the management of the functional systems of the body; particularly to generate and provide energy and resources for intended actions.

3.   The motoric component of an emotion serves the aim of expressing and communicating each reaction and each intention of behaviour. Thereby, the reaction to a stimulus can be seen in distinct facial and gesture alterations.

4.   The motivational component serves to prepare and process concrete actions.

5.   The monitoring system, as a component of subjective experience, mirrors the subjective emotional states of an individual. In this subsystem, the alterations/changes of all components are represented.

The model assumes that within an emotional episode there is a component patterning process driven by the cognitive appraisal. The individual appraises an event on a series of sequential stimulus evaluation checks (relating to relevance, implications, coping potential and normative significance). The result of each check modifies the state of each subsystem in the direction of an adjustment to the event. In other words each subsystem gets into a synchronized state of modifications that is typical for the just experienced emotion. The pattern of an emotional reaction is an accumulated result of all these modifications of the status of the subsystems and their synchronisation. The cognitive component that drives the component patterning process is not accessible to direct observation. But each stimulus evaluation check evokes an adequate reaction in the other subsystems. Thus each appraisal has a corresponding reaction in facial expression. For several outcomes of stimulus evaluation checks Scherer and colleagues [6, 13-16] predict related changes in facial expressions. For example, appraising an event as novel is related to raising the eyebrows or frowning, appraising an event as (intrinsic) pleasant is related to pulling the lip corners upwards and raising the cheeks (like in smiling). If a certain appraisal does indeed result in a change of facial expression, as proposed, facial expressions are observable indicators of unobservable emotional processes.

17.3   Objectives

Even though there is a "widespread acceptance of appraisal theory as an appropriate explanation for the elicitation of many, if not all, types of emotional reaction and experience ... the process of appraisal has remained relatively unexplored" – Scherer stated in 1999 [17, p. 764], this is still the case nowadays, and particularly for the case of using media. The aim of our studies is to better.understand the nature of the emotional processing of media stimuli. According to the component-process-model of Scherer, we assume that the emotional processing of stimuli is done in certain sequences – the so called "stimulus evaluation checks", this means "that appraisal occurs in a sequential, serial fashion: and ... that there is a definite, invariant order in which the different stimulus evaluation checks are processed in the repetitive, recursive process that constitutes appraisal" [17, p. 765]. The process of appraisal itself is as a cognitive process not accessible to direct observation and not or only with difficulty accessible to verbalization. But each appraisal evokes an adequate reaction in the other subsystems and so has a corresponding reaction in facial expression. Taking sadness as example, Kaiser and Wehrle [6, p. 292] postulate the following appraisal pattern and related action units: (1) suddenness low, (2) familiarity low related to AU4+AU7 (brow lowering and lids tight), (3) outcome probability very high, (4) conduciveness obstruct related to brow lowering and lids tight (AU4+AU7), (5) urgency low, (6) control very low related to inner brow raise, lip corner depress, lid droop and eyes down (AU1+AU15+AU41+AU64), (7) power very low related to lip stretcher (pulling the lips back laterally) and jaw drop (AU20+AU26). If one accepts these assumptions, then there should be recurring, organized sequences of facial expressions. Furthermore, one can assume that there is a relationship between (formal and content) aspects of the media stimuli and the facial expressions (as indicators of cognitive appraisal). So, we have to ask: What kinds of (hidden) structure exist in facial expressions, and how can we discover effects of independent variables on such structures? The purpose of the study presented here is to analyse the temporal and sequential structure of facial expressions in order to explain the elicitation of emotional responses induced by media.

17.4   Method

Participants were 33 students (19 to 37 years-old). They were videotaped while watching eight news reports from German television (chosen for this study because of their potential to induce emotions; [18]). The news reports were subject to a media content analysis. Content analysis is not confined to text it can also be applied to audio-visual communication. Media content analysis is focussing on quantifying descriptions of what is portrayed or communicated by a movie (audio visual media). Thus it lays important foundations for the examination of effects on the audience. Different from the transcription of speech only there are no binding transcription rules for visual aspects of communication. With the transcription of media communication the problem of transcription is getting even worse: aspects of the portrayed event or news story are interwoven with composition aspects that determine what the audience sees and hears (objects, camera-perspective, camera distance, duration of a single take/shot, etc.). Thus media staging is describable as a complex communicative message that interconnects content and formal presentational techniques. In other words presentational techniques (plot and style) may produce a "narrative form-content-correspondence pattern" within which effects of the film are unfolding [19]. The media content analysis of the news reports focuses on (1) formal visual presentational characteristic (cutting, shot size, camera movement, camera perspective, etc.) and (2) content characteristics that are typical for news reports (issue, location, type of violence, etc.) producing a time series of lasting events with one shot or take as the unit of observation [3, 7, and 8]. By means of this, we can exactly describe the situational context that is presented to the subjects. The facial expression of the viewers was coded using EMFACS (Emotional Facial Action Coding System; the evaluation system EMFACS captures only those action units that have been empirically proven to be connected with emotions) [9, 10, and 20-23] (see also chapter 10, this volume). FACS and EMFACS are objective, reliable tools for the measurement of every single movement in the face. The smallest visible units of muscular activity of the face, the so called "action units" (AU), are derived from a map of all the movable muscles. The focus on an anatomical basis ensures to get a purely descriptive account of the observation, abstracting away from any interpretation, and therefore the objectivity of the observation of the facial activity is assured. The action units referred to by numbers are coded along the timeline as events that report the apex of the observed facial behaviour. Although EMFACS also reports laterality and intensity of each action unit those specifications were unconsidered for THEME-analysis. The EMFACS coding thus produces a second time series of events that is synchronized with the data from the media content analysis. By means of the synchronized time series data we can look at the dynamic process of media reception as a kind of "as if"-interaction between the media and the spectator with the viewers reacting to the ongoing (mass) media communication of the news reports. The analysis of the temporal and sequential structure of facial expressions is based on the process of T-pattern detection [24, 25]. The data of all 33 subjects representing different observation periods were joined in a single data file. Coding included data of selected formal and content features of the news reports. The data were analyzed on a significance level $p = .0005$.

17.5 Results: T-patterns in facial expressions

Our results show a high number of non-random temporal patterns in the event time series of facial expressions. The detected patterns indicate that the facial expression of TV-news viewers is highly temporally structured. The analysis shows different kinds of patterns: patterns connecting certain types of facial expressions (thus indicating a sequence of cognitive emotional processing) and interactive patterns involving features of the media stimuli and facial expressions (thus indicating specific emotional reactions to specific features).

17.5.1 T-Patterns connecting types of facial expressions

We find T-patterns that combine a sequence of certain facial expressions. The example in figure 17.1 shows one of the most frequent patterns. The pattern combines the AU-Combination 14+17+24 (dimpler + chin raiser + lip presser) to a subsequent AU14 (dimpler = tightening the corners of the lips, squeezing inward). Another very frequent pattern connects AU2 (outer brow raise) to AU7 (eye lid tight). Figure 17.2 shows an example of a more complex pattern. Within this pattern AU14+AU17 (dimpler + chin raiser) is connected to a subsequent AU14 (dimpler). At level 2 of the detected T-pattern the AU1+AU2 (inner and outer brow raiser) is integrated with this pattern. This kind of patterns may represent parts of appraisal sequences.

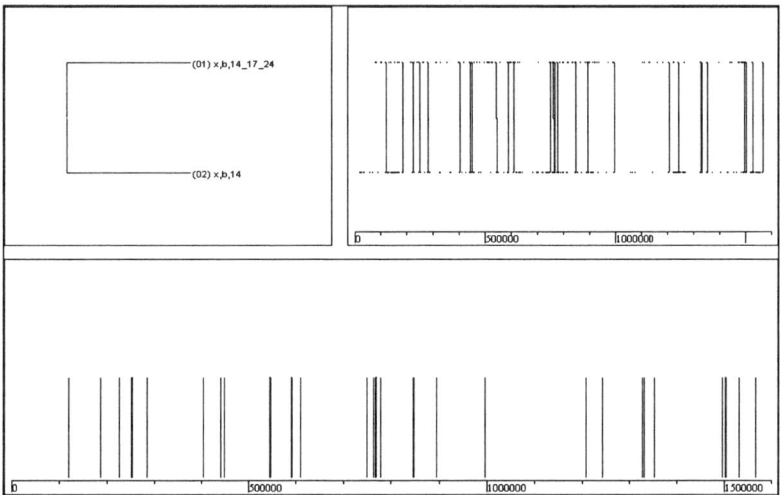

Figure 17.1 Example of a T-pattern connecting types of facial expressions: action unit combination AU14+AU17+AU14 is linked to a subsequent AU14.

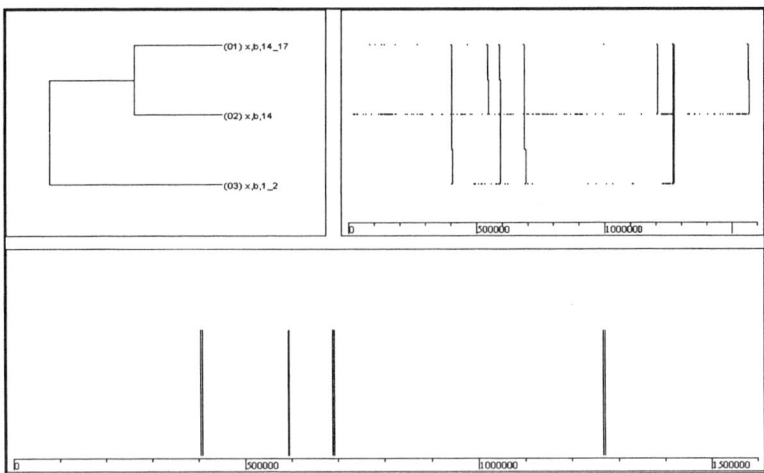

Figure 17.2 Example of a more complex T-pattern connecting types of facial expressions: AU14+AU17 is connected to AU14 and at level 2 to AU1+AU2.

17.5.2 T-Patterns associated with the course of a news report

We find T-patterns that are connecting the end of the news report with the facial behaviour of the viewers. The temporal structure of the news report seems to initate a temporal structuring of the facial expressions of the audience. At the end of each report there is an animated globe as a kind of separator between different messages. The presenting of this globe – and therefore the end of the report – is connected via a T-pattern, for example, with the expression of AU14+AU55 (dimpler and head tilt left) (see figure 17.3). Such patterns could be even more complex, as figure 17.4 shows. T-Patterns that contain the media content event "globe" and a subsequent facial expression may allude to a cognitive-affective appraisal of the before presented news content.

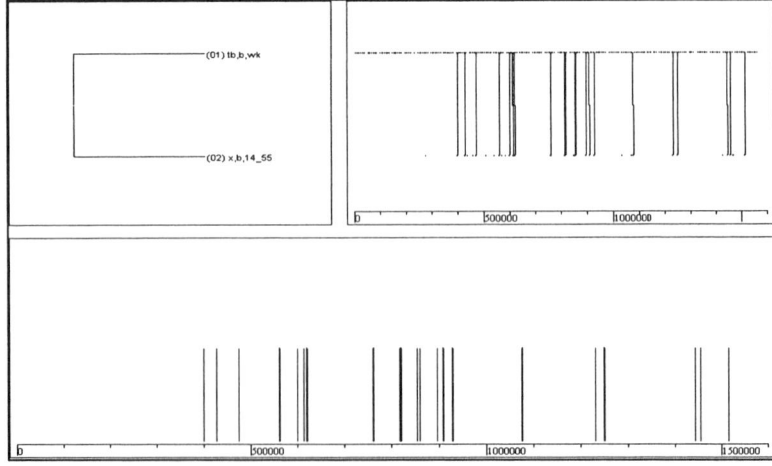

Figure 17.3 Example of T-pattern connecting facial expressions to the course of the news report: AU14+AU55 is connected to the presenting of an animated globe (wk) at the end of the news report.

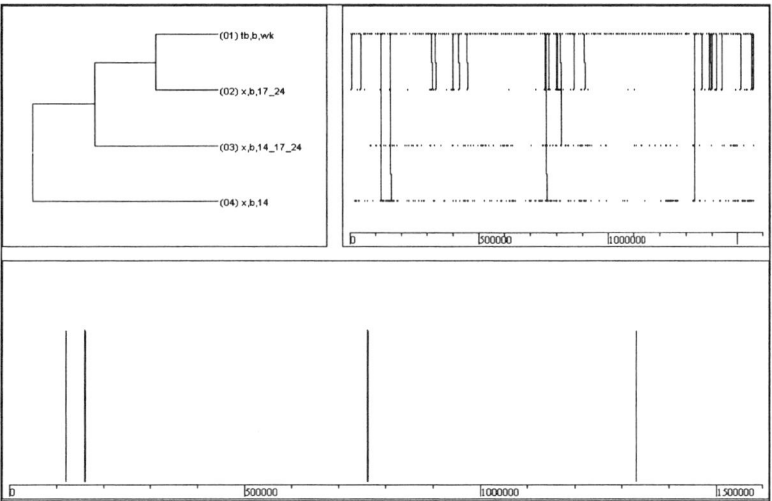

Figure 17.4 Example of a more complex T-pattern connecting facial expressions to the course of the news report: AU17+AU24 is connected to the presenting of an animated globe (wk) at the end of the news report, at higher levels AU14+AU17+AU14 and AU14 are linked.

Another evidence for the existence of a concluding appraisal of the media content may be found within patterns not after the end of the message (when the animated globe is presented), but within the last seconds of a news report just before the animated globe is fading in. An example is shown in figure 17.5, connecting AU20 (lip stretcher = pulling the lips back laterally) to the presenting of the globe. Again, this kind of patterns can be more complex (Figure 17.6).

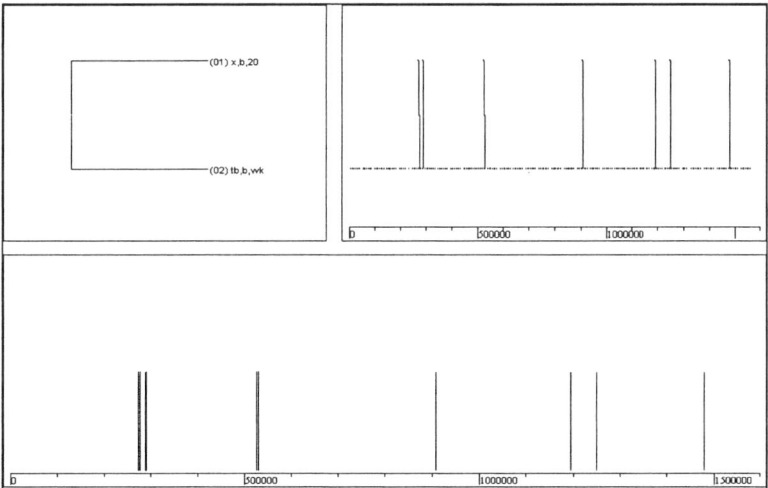

Figure 17.5 Example of T-pattern connecting facial expressions to the course of the news report: AU20 is connected to the subsequent animated globe (wk) at the end of the news report

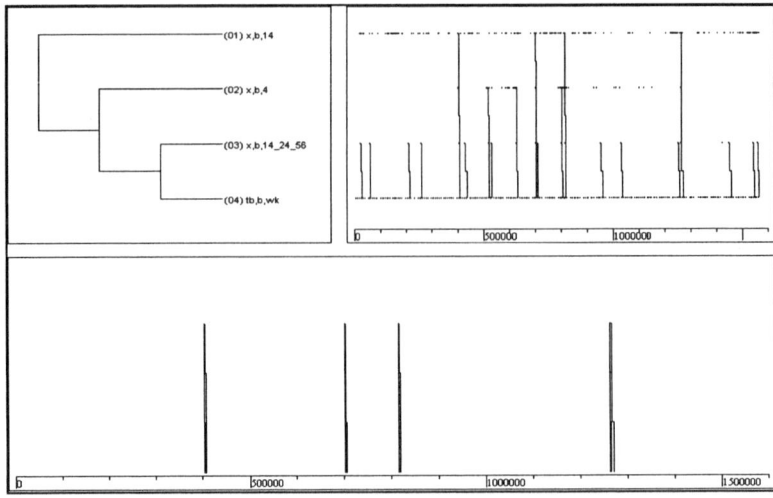

Figure 17.6 Example of a more complex T-pattern connecting facial expressions to the course of the news report: AU14+AU24+AU56 is connected to the subsequent animated globe (wk) at the end of the news report, at higher levels AU4 and AU14 are linked.

17.5.3 Patterns connecting facial expressions to formal features

Further patterns connect facial expression to some formal features of the news. For example, the expression of AU14 (dimpler) is connected to the beginning of the anchorman speaking. It could be supposed, that certain form variables give a kind of cue that provokes appraisal processes.

17.5.4 Patterns connecting facial expressions to certain points in a certain news report

T-patterns, connecting facial expressions to certain points in a certain news report as exemplified in figure 17.7, may demonstrate how verbal information of a news report at a certain point of the told news story generates an appraisal process that is observable through the detected pattern. When we look at what happens at the time in the news report when the pattern occurs, it seems that important information is presented at this time that makes it possible for the viewer to finish the whole or parts of an ongoing emotional appraisal.

Summing up, we find patterns as sequences of facial expressions, patterns linking facial expressions to the course of news reports, patterns connecting facial expressions with form variables, and patterns associating facial expressions with certain points of the story that is presented in a news report.

17.6   Conclusion

Using THEME, we analyzed facial expressions of TV-news viewers in relation to form and content aspects of presented media events. Facial expressions, taken as observable indicators of unobservable appraisal processes, allow the study of emotional processes along the timeline. Considering the multi-functionality of facial behaviour [6, 26-28] we asked: Can facial expressions serve as indicators for processes of cognitive appraisal? Is there a sequence of emotional processing (a sequence of stimulus evaluation checks)?

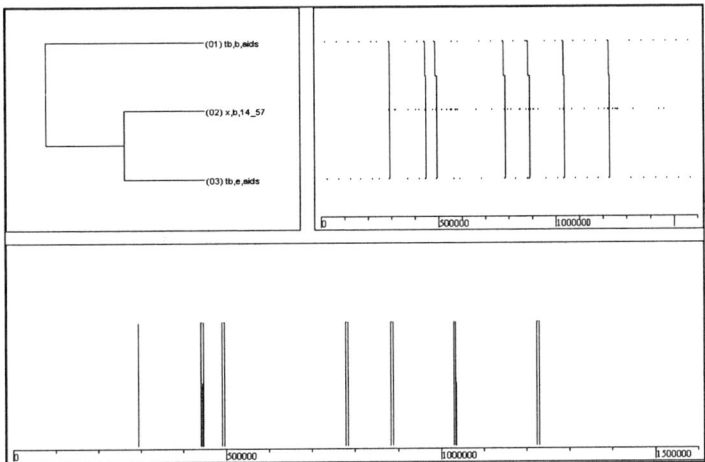

Figure 17.7 Example of a T-pattern connecting facial expressions to certain points in a news report: AU14+AU57 is connected to the beginning and end of a report about aids

Our results show a large number of temporal patterns in the facial behaviour data. We find patterns as sequences of facial expressions. These patterns may be interpreted as parts of appraisal sequences. These results indicate that there seems to be a sequence of emotional processing. Furthermore, we find patterns linking facial expressions to the course of news reports, patterns connecting facial expressions with form variables, and patterns associating facial expressions with certain points of the news story. It seems that the temporal structure as well as formal and content variables of news reports may initiate cognitive-affective appraisal processes.

Due to the fact that Scherer and colleagues propose only some facial behaviour outcomes of certain stimulus evaluation checks [6, 13-16] we are now examining if some of our often found facial expressions (see figure 17.8) may be related to emotional experiences or cognitive appraisals. Looking at the very first preliminary data, we find that AU14 is by most of our subjects associated with a feeling of scepticism (for interpretation of AU14 see also [8]), AU14+AU17+AU24 is linked to a kind of frustration, AU14+AU17 may signal disappointment, while AU1+AU2 is interpreted as some sort of astonishment or amazement (for interpretation of AU1+AU2 see also [29]).

Outlining the results of our studies, we want to illustrate how the study of the temporal structure of facial expressions can help to get a deeper insight into the structure of emotional processing. Using THEME has the potential to make a significant contribution to this examination of emotional processing. It may explain the elicitation and differentiation of emotional responses induced by media. Within the realm of media psychology the analysis of the temporal structure of facial expressive behaviour while using media can contribute to a better understanding of emotional processes of viewers while watching TV, going to the movies or using the Internet.

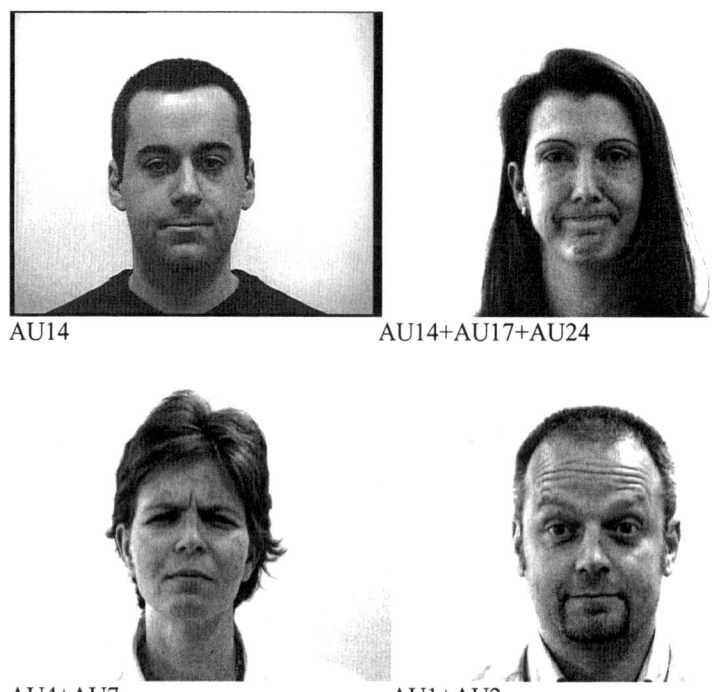

AU14   AU14+AU17+AU24

AU4+AU7   AU1+AU2

Figure 17.8 Examples of frequent action units or action unit combinations expressed by viewers of TV news

17.7   References

[1]   K. Oatley, Why fiction may be twice as true as fact: Fiction as cognitive and emotional simulation. *Review of General Psychology* **3** (1999) 101-117.

[2]   P. Winterhoff-Spurk, Violence in TV news: The cultivation of emotions, in *New Horizons in Media Psychology. Research Cooperations and Projects in Europe*, P. Winterhoff-Spurk and T. van der Voort, Eds. Wiesbaden: Westdeutscher Verlag, 1997, pp. 105-115.

[3]   P. Winterhoff-Spurk, TV news and the cultivation of emotion, *Communications* **23** (1998) 545-556.

[4]   P. Winterhoff-Spurk, *Medienpsychologie. Eine Einführung (2nd edition)*. Stuttgart: Kohlhammer, 2004.

[5]   K. R. Scherer, Emotions as episodes of subsystem synchronization driven by nonlinear appraisal processes, in M. D. Lewis and I. Granic, Eds. *Emotion, development, and self-organization: Dynamic systems approaches to emotional development*, New York and Cambridge: Cambridge University Press, 2000, pp. 70-99.

[6]   S. Kaiser and T. Wehrle, Facial expressions as indicators of appraisal processes, in *Appraisal theories of emotion: Theories, methods, research*, K. R. Scherer, A. Schorr, and T. Johnstone, Eds. New York: Oxford University Press, 2001, pp. 285-300.

[7]   P. Winterhoff-Spurk, D. Unz, and F. Schwab, "In the mood" Zur Kultivierung von Emotionen durch Fernsehen, *Magazin Forschung* **2** (2001) 20-33.

[8]   D. Unz, F. Schwab, and P. Winterhoff-Spurk, Der alltägliche Schrecken? Emotionale Prozesse bei der Rezeption gewaltdarstellender Fernsehnachrichten, in *Empirische Perspektiven der Rezeptionsforschung*, P. Rößler, S. Kubisch, and V. Gehrau, Eds. München: Verlag Reinhard Fischer, 2002, pp. 97-116.

[9]   P. Ekman and W. V. Friesen, *The facial action coding system (FACS). A technique for the measurement of facial action*. Palo Alto: Consulting Psychologists Press, 1978.

[10]   P. Ekman and W. V. Friesen, Measuring facial movement with the Facial Action Coding System, in *Emotion in the human face*, P. Ekman, Ed. Cambridge: Cambridge University Press, 1982, pp. 178-211.

[11]   K. R. Scherer, Appraisal considered as a process of multi-level sequential checking, in *Appraisal processes in emotion: Theory, Methods, Research*, K. R. Scherer, A. Schorr, and T. Johnstone, Eds. New York: Oxford University Press, 2001, pp. 92-120.

[12]   K. R. Scherer, Emotion as a process: Function, origin and regulation, *Social Science Information* **21**(4/5), (1982) 555-570.

[13]   S. Kaiser and T. Wehrle, Ausdruckspsychologische Methoden, in *Emotionspsychologie: Ein Handbuch*, J. H. Otto, H. A. Euler, and H. Mandl, Eds. Weinheim: Beltz, PVU, 2000, pp. 419-428.

[14]   K. R. Scherer, What does facial expression express?, in *International Review of Studies on Emotion Vol. 2*, K. Strongman, Ed. Chichester: Wiley, 1992, pp. 139-165.

[15]   K. R. Scherer, Toward a concept of "modal emotions", in *The nature of emotion. Fundamental questions*, P. Ekman and R. J. Davidson, Eds. New York: Oxford University Press, 1995, pp. 25-31.

[16]   T. Wehrle, S. Kaiser, S. Schmidt, and K. R Scherer, Studying the dynamics of emotional expression using synthesized facial muscle movements, *Journal of Personality and Social Psychology* **78** (1), (2000) 105-119.

[17]   K. R. Scherer, On the sequential nature of appraisal processes: Indirect evidence form a recognition task, *Cognition and Emotion* **13**(6), (1999) 763-793.

[18]   B. Michel, Emotionen bei der Rezeption von TV-Nachrichten, Unveröffentlichte Diplomarbeit der Fachrichtung Psychologie, Saarbrücken: Universität des Saarlandes, 2002.

[19]   P. Ohler and G. Nieding, Kognitive Filmpsychologie zwischen 1990 und 2000, in *Film und Psychologie – nach der kognitiven Phase?*, J. Sellmer and H. J. Wulff, Eds. Marburg: Schüren, 2002, pp. 9-40.

[20]   P. Ekman, *Darwin and facial expression*. New York: Academic Press, 1973.

[21]   P. Ekman, *Unmasking the face*. Englewood Cliffs: Prentice Hall, 1975.

[22]   P. Ekman and W. V. Friesen, The repertoire of nonverbal behavior: Categories, origins, usage and coding, *Semiotica* **1** (1969) 49-98.

[23]   P. Ekman and E. L. Rosenberg, Eds., *What the face reveals*. Oxford: Oxford University Press, 1997.

[24]   M. S. Magnusson, Hidden Real-Time Patterns in Intra- and Inter-individual Behavior: Description and Detection, *European Journal of Psychological Assessment* **12**(2), (1996) 112-123.

[25]   M. S. Magnusson, Discovering Hidden Time Patterns in Behavior: T-Patterns and their Detection, *Behavior Research Methods, Instruments and Computers* **32**(1), (2000) 93-110.

[26]   R. Krause, E. Steimer-Krause, and B. Ulrich, The use of affect research in dynamic psychotherapy, in *Two butterflies on my head: Psychoanalysis in the scientific dialogue*, M. Leutzinger-Bohleber, H. Schneider, and R. Pfeifer, Eds. Heidelberg: Springer, 1992, pp. 277-291.

[27]   J. Merten, Facial-affective behavior, mutual gaze and emotional experience in dyadic interactions. *Journal of Nonverbal Behavior* **21**(3), (1997) 179-201.

[28]   J. Merten, Context-analysis of facial-affective behavior in clinical populations, in *The Human Face: Measurement and Meaning*, M. Katsikitis, Ed. Amsterdam: Kluwer, 2002, pp. 131-147.

[29]   K. Grammer, W. Schiefenhoevel, M. Schleidt, B. Lorenz, and I. Eibl-Eibesfeldt, Patterns on the Face: The Eyebrow Flash in Crosscultural Comparison, *Ethology* **77** (1988) 279-299. http://evolution.anthro.univie.ac.at/institutes/urbanethology/brows.html

The Hidden Structure of Interaction
L. Anolli et al. (Eds.)
IOS Press, 2005

18. Gender at Work: Eavesdropping on Communication Patterns in Two Token Teams

Sabine C. KOCH, Stephanie M. MÜLLER , Antje SCHROEER,
Caja THIMM, Lenelis KRUSE, Joerg ZUMBACH

Abstract. In a national research project we assessed gender-related communicative patterns in 20 teams from diverse organizations. The sub-sample for this study consisted of two teams with one gender token each: a female token in an industrial team of eleven persons and a male token in a kindergarten team of eight persons. We focused on dominance and support-related behaviour in verbal and nonverbal communication. More specifically, we assessed patterns of talking times, back channelling, gaze behaviour, affect display, and movement qualities. Results suggest patterns within and between verbal and nonverbal codes. In the selected sequences, where tasks are negotiated with some underlying conflict potential, we observed that independent of status and token position, women used more nonverbal communication, regarding dominance, support and defensive behaviour. Defensive behaviour is used when the self image of a person is threatened. This seems to apply not only to the female gender-token in the male-dominated team situation, but to a certain degree also to the female leader when interacting with the male gender-token. Self- and other ratings of gender-tokens were biased toward stereotypic perception. Our case studies support and exemplify research findings that gender-token status frequently has negative consequences for women only.

Keywords: Gender; groups; tokenism; language; nonverbal communication; social interaction; video analysis; pattern analysis.

Contents

18.1   Introduction

Team work in organizations has been the focus of a number of recent studies [1, 2]. However, not many of them have placed an emphasis on communication patterns of men and women. Even studies on homogeneity and heterogeneity in teams have mainly focused on social categories other than gender [3, 4]. In interviews men and women quite clearly report gender differences in communication at the workplace [5, 6]. But can these perceived differences be confirmed by behavioural data? Our research project has set out to investigate such differences in behaviour as well as perception, and according constructive effects in gender communication. There are many interesting research questions about gender communication in work teams. Are there differences in communication dependent on speaker's gender? Are there differences dependent on target's gender? Does team leader or team member status of men and women influence communicative patterns? Are there communicative differences in same-sex vs. mixed sex teams? Are there differences in pure male vs. pure female teams? Are there differences in male-dominated vs. female dominated teams? Are there differences in mixed-sex teams vs. token teams where one gender is in the absolute minority? In an attempt to answer some of these questions, we generally work with qualitative and quantitative methods from linguistics and psychology. In this study, we analyzed the communicative patterns in two token teams in order to find out whether the gender tokens have a special position within the teams and whether their gender-role is more salient than that of non-tokens.

18.2   Gender tokens in work teams

In her pioneering work on tokenism, Kanter, 1977 [7], described *tokens* as persons who belong to a social category that constitutes less than 15% of the entire group composition. This criterion applied to a man and to a woman in two out of 20 teams that we observed in our current project. The token-situation is supposed to make gender more salient and thus evoke more pronounced gender-role behaviour than in teams with a balanced gender ratio. It also has implications for self-image and role-expectations. Kanter [7] reported that token women are more likely to have their mistakes amplified, to be socially isolated, and to be found in roles that undermine their status. These results have been documented not only in women managers but also in women police officers, construction workers, fire fighters, military cadets, and law students [8]. While early token research assumed that gender-tokens of both genders would experience negative consequences, recent results indicate that only women are affected by negative outcomes [8]. Researchers found that token women experienced increased visibility, a sense of social distance and isolation from their co-workers, increased stereotypic self-perception and behaviour (assimilation into stereotypes), and heightened pressure to perform well when they are members of a male-dominated work group. Token men generally do not have the same negative outcomes, on the contrary, they may benefit from their token status, for example by being promoted without actively pursuing promotion [9]. This tendency not only affects actual experiences reported on rating-scales, but also *expectations* of men and women for token situations [10]. Cohen and Swim [10] found that token women (particularly those low in self-confidence) had more negative expectations about working in a male-dominated group than did non-token women, whereas gender-token men and non-token men did not differ in their expectations. McDonald et al. [8] experimentally raised the social status of gender-token women and found out that this reduced some of token women's negative expectations. Yoder, Schleicher and McDonald [11] showed that with increasing leadership legitimacy the female token leaders improved group performance and reduced some of the negative consequences associated with tokenism. Thus, status seems to plays an important part for token women. In particular, we were interested in the following research questions: Do the observed interactions in the context of team meetings point to a more pronounced gender-role in gender-tokens? Do the self-ratings and interview data of male and female gender-tokens point in the direction of a more stereotypic gender-role? Do third person ratings point in that direction? Do men and women show different patterns? In order to answer these questions we have conducted this case study with two token teams. We considered verbal and nonverbal indicators of (stereo)typically male attributes such as dominance from the domain of agency, and typically female attributes such as support from the domain of communality [6].

18.3   Behavioural categories

18.3.1 Gaze Behaviour

Gaze is the most important nonverbal dominance signal particularly when related to talking mode [12, 13]. Gaze has an important function in the regulation of social interaction as a correlate of power- and influence-related behaviour [14]. Differences in influence are reflected in communication patterns that lead to the development of hierarchies [15-17]. Dovidio and Ellyson [13] operationalize the influence of person A in a dyad as the ratio of the time A talks and looks at B (looks while talks, lwt) and the time, in which A listens and looks at B (looks while listens, lwl). This value is called the *Visual Dominance Ratio* (VDR). The higher the VDR of person A in relation to person B, the greater is the influence of person A over person B [13]. Persons with relatively little power or status look longer while listening to their partner than while talking, whereas more powerful persons look approximately for the same amount of time both while listening and while talking. Overall, less powerful persons look longer at more powerful persons especially while in the role of the listener than vice versa [12, 18]. In this study we coded *looks while listens* (lwl), *looks while talks* (lwt) along with *actor* and *target* of the observed behaviour.

18.3.2 Talking times

Talking time is a widely used and validated indicator of dominance [16, 17, 19]. In the present study, talking time was selected as the verbal dominance measure. In the THEME behaviour coder we coded *actor* and *target* of speech. We coded *talking onset* when a person started vocalizing and *talking offset* when the person stopped, without taking into account one-word sentences, feedback particles or other brief vocalizations such as laughter (whereas talking times computed from the transcripts included all utterances. In addition, words and turns were counted; see Tables 18.1 and 18.2). Furthermore, for purpose of external validation, we collected group members' reports about how dominant they perceived themselves and each other with the SYMLOG adjective short scale [20]. Results are reported in Tables 18.1 and 18.2. Another frequently used verbal dominance measure are interruptions. They represent a violation of the basic turn-taking rule in conversations [21]. Many research findings show that interruptions are closely linked to the concept of dominance [22, 23]. However, as Schmitt-Mast [17] points out, alternative interpretations of interruptions must be considered as well. Interruptions may, for example, be a consequence of a highly involved conversational style and may thus reflect interest in the discussion topic or the interaction partner, serve as a means to create connections, or indicate feeling at ease with an interaction partner [14]. Because it is still in question whether interruptions are an adequate indicator of dominance, we did not use interruptions as explicit codes here. However, interruptions were coded from transcripts and from action patterns [24] for the statistical analysis. We furthermore classified each sentence and coded them as *control claims* (e.g., the dishes need to be done), *strong control claims* (e.g., you do the dishes, Bob), or *control yields* (e.g., all right, boss). Utterances not related to control were coded with a *neutral* control category

18.3.3 Feedback/Back-channel Behaviour

Feedback can be regarded as a signal of social support of a current speaker [25, 26]. In the research literature it has also been termed back-channel behaviour [27, 28]. We define feedback behaviour as short utterances of the listener that either expresses understanding or non-understanding. Feedback can be either verbal, nonverbal or both. It encourages the speaker to continue or further elaborate on a topic. It is given in speaking pauses or simultaneous without claiming a turn. It can operate at different levels of automaticity and interactivity [27-29]. Feedback or back-channel behaviour is a signal of interest, involvement and of social support. However, missing feedback or back-channelling can also be a signal of social dominance. We coded *positive* and *negative feedback* (without distinguishing verbal and nonverbal channel), *actor* and *target*.

18.3.4 Affect Display

Evaluative affect display (EAD) is a nonverbal expression of agreement or disagreement that signals support or non-support of a current speaker. EAD is conceptualized as the expressive component of an attitude. Research findings support the idea that in many cases attitudes are communicated nonverbally, particularly if they are negative and the target of evaluation has a higher status position than the actor [30-32]. Evaluative affect is an important source of communicating attitudes and thus support in face-to-face interaction [33]. It is mostly communicated non-consciously. Even though facial reaction can be better controlled than any other body reactions [34, 35], the degree of non-deliberateness is much higher than it is for responses on rating scales. We coded *positive, neutral* and *negative affect, affordance* for affect expression (directly preceding stimuli), *actor* and *target*.

18.3.5 Movement Qualities

The four measures just exemplified (two for support and two for dominance, one verbal and one nonverbal each) capture merely quantitative information. In addition, we coded movement qualities with the *Kestenberg Movement Profile* (KMP) [34, 36]. The KMP is a movement analysis tools with a high degree of differentiation in the assessment of nonverbal behaviour. It takes into account more than 72 motion parameters, and is organized in eight profiles, each of which provides a different perspective in a meaning area. For our analysis we used two out of eight profiles: *efforts*, and *pre-efforts* [36, 37].

Efforts are full movement qualities that indicate mastery of the environment in the dimensions of space, weight and time. The effort profile falls into the observational categories of direct use of space vs. indirect use of space, strong use of weight vs. light use of weight, quick use of time vs. sustained use of time [36, 37]. Pre-efforts are a pre-stage of efforts and indicate insecurity, and problems with the environment, the sub-dimensions provide information about learning styles and ego-defences. The pre-effort profile falls into the observational categories of channelling use of space vs. flexible use of space, vehement/straining use of weight vs. gentle use of weight, sudden use of time vs. hesitant use of time [36]. We coded *all 12 sub-categories (six efforts and six pre-efforts), actor* and *target*. Rater reliability for all observational measures was good, except for Cohen's

Kappas [38] of the effort and pre-effort ratings. Reliabilities for talking times, back channelling and gaze observations were very good with Cohen's *Kappa* > .80. For evaluative affect they were good with Cohen's *Kappas* between .64 and .79. For efforts and pre-efforts reliabilities were not satisfactory (with *Kappa* < .45). We attributed this lower *Kappa* to the higher number of categories used and to the heterogeneous KMP training background of the two main raters. Rater 1 corresponded high to a lay rater (*Kappa* > .70) who coded the material in addition. We, therefore, used only the ratings of rater 1 and not of rater 2 for movement qualities.

18.4 Pattern analyses

We analyzed Teams K and O, the only teams who fulfilled the requirements of gender-tokens according to Kanter [7]. Teams were taped during two of their regular team meetings at work. The two teams met about every two weeks. We selected, transcribed, and analyzed 15 minutes out of the entire material from one team. The duration of the selected sessions was four hours for Team K and 1 ½ hours for Team O. Selection criteria for scenes were good general visibility and audibility, the typicality of the interaction for the meeting, and the involvement of as many team members as possible. Additionally, we selected sequences with a definable beginning and end. Within each team persons were labelled alphanumerically, starting with the team leader, who was A, and from there continuing clockwise alphabetically around the table. Analyses were all done with the pattern analysis software THEME 4.0 [40] (see Figure 18.1 for the coding surface).

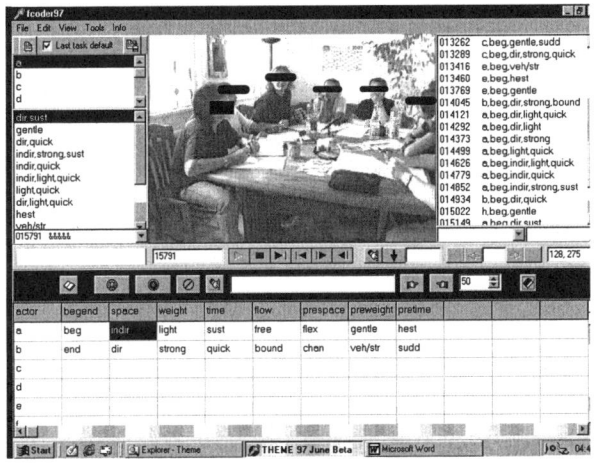

Figure 18.1 Screenshot of Team O with Effort/Pre-effort Codings (Movement Qualities) in the THEME behaviour coder [39][1]

---

[1] The predefined coding scheme appears in the lower half of the screen. Actors were coded with letters A to H/K. The beginning of an action was coded with beg, the end with end (the end was only used for coding of talking times). Efforts were coded by the three variables space, weight and time, pre-efforts were coded by the three variables prespace, preweight and pretime; flow was additionally coded but not analyzed (subcategories were coded as explained under 3). Coding was done by mouse clicks on the according categories on the screen. A time-based coding protocol emerged that can be seen in the upper right window.

18.4.1 Female gender-token (in a male context)

18.4.1.1 Team description

Team K consisted of one woman (K) and 10 men. It was a team in an industrial setting of an international corporation in Southern Germany with a male leader (A). The boss was an assertive and dynamic mid-age family-father. The gender-token was a self-confident mid-age mother. Both were in their 40ies. Both had an academic educational background and were high status team members. The other persons in the team were mostly managers (mostly also high status) from different parts of the corporation. The group planned a joint project with boss A's department. The role of the boss was to coordinate, and to point out potential problems. The role of the gender-token was to represent environmental concerns regarding the industrial affordances and necessities. The atmosphere was quite conflict-loaded as there were many different interests. We selected a scene from the first session where the involvement of the gender-token was particularly high. The involvement in this scene was generally high with many passages of simultaneous talk and many gesture-posture mergers [41] of the main protagonists, indicating involvement on the nonverbal level. While in the selected sequence K dominates the talking time, A dominates the talking time in the longer more representative sequence (here of 53 min, not including the selected 15 min). Within the 15 minutes sequence K interrupts a lot more than anyone else in the team including the boss. K talks twice as fast as the boss (words per seconds) and faster than the other team members. K gives more feedback and displays more control yields than the others. However, she also shows more control claims and strong control claims than the boss in this sequence which applies to no other person of the team. K's and A's visual dominance ratio is almost identical, i.e. she looks a lot at others while talking, while she does not look at the boss very much while listening (lwl to A) (Table 18.1).

Measure	A (male boss)	K (female token)	Others (approx. mean of full team members)
Talking time (min) [a]	3.3 (16.6)	6.1 (3.5)	1.9 (3.5)
Turns (#)	60.6	149,4	37.0
Interruptions (#)	2.7 (7)	16.2 (11)	2.0 (2)
Feedback / Back channel (#) [b]	3.6 / 10.8nv (5)	7.2 / 18.9nv (9)	1.0 / 4.0nv (1)
Control yields; (#)	11	25	4.7
Neutral speech acts; (#)	7	15	6.8
Control claims; (#)	27	29	8.0
Strong control claims; (#)	14	19	3.0
Lwt to group (frames)	-	-	-
Lwl to A (frames)	n.a.	36	2000
Ratio %lwl : %lwt (%)	70:30	70:30	90:10
DomValue (-18 to 18) [c]	13.1	10	6
Dom_Self (-18 to 18)	14.5	5	9
CompValue (-18 to 18)	15	5.0	10.5

[a] values in parenthesis indicate the talking times in a longer, more representative sequence; [b] frequencies: first value from transcript, second value from THEME codings (including nonverbal cues), third value from analysis of action patterns ([24], also *interruption* value in parenthesis); [c] = mean of all other team member's ratings for participant's dominance (on a rating scale from -18 to 18) [20], followed by self-ratings of dominance and mean of all other team member's ratings for participant's competence on the same scale.

Table 18.1: Simple statistics for Team K

18.4.1.2 Pattern analysis (female token)

We conducted a pattern analysis with THEME 4.0. Patterns were taken from data processing without randomization. 46 patterns resulted altogether, 13 patterns included the interaction between A and K.

The following patterns resulted (Figures 18.2, 18.3, 18.4 and 18.5): Those were mostly patterns of talking times and pre-efforts (defensive movement).

Generally, patterns in Team K need to be interpreted with care as in some cases there are only two repetitions of the behaviour in question, whereas some definitions of a pattern include, e.g., a minimum of three repetitions. Taking this into account, across all situations above, K displays defensive gestures of different types (mostly gentleness, an appeasing gesture in the context of conflictive talk; altogether 14 pre-efforts that are part of patterns mostly between A and K: 6x gentle, 3x vehement/straining, 3x sudden, 2x hesitant). When employing defensive behaviour, she frequently uses palm presentation, which is a culturally rather rare gesture in Germany. The KMP-theory assumes that defensive behaviour is displayed when there is a threat for the person, for example, face-saving behaviour in threat of a face-loss. From our observer-perspective the threat for the gender-token here could either result from her role as a control instance for the engineers or it could result from her role as a gender-token. It would therefore be interesting to observe her in a variety of different interaction contexts with boss A.

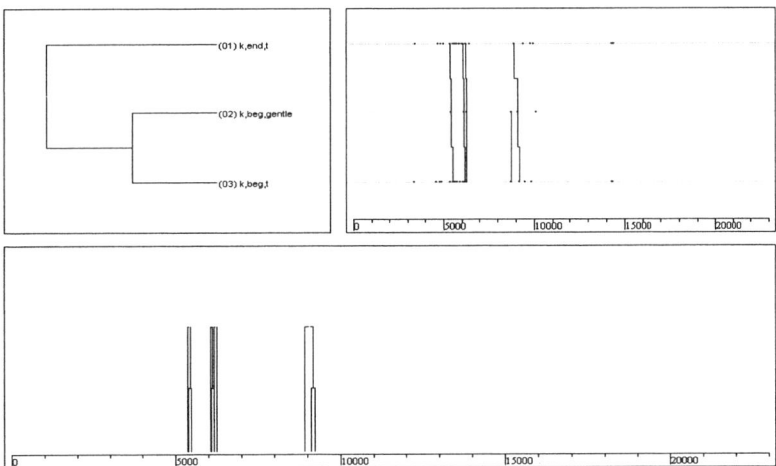

Figure 18.2 Pattern 30: *Appeasing gesture.* At the beginning of the speech acts K tends to gesture. In this case she displays an appeasing, calming gesture five times before she starts to talk, four times this gesture lies in between two turns. The sequence is: K ends to talk (K, end, t), K displays a gentle gesture (K, beg, gentle), and K begins to talk (K, beg, t).

In the entire sequence boss A behaves rather protective toward K. He also used pre-efforts quite frequently, but they do not result in patterns between A and K. K states in the interview (see below) that A behaved as always in the session. A at one point puts his hand softly up to K's upper arm actually touching her; this was the only incident of touch we observed in the entire data of all 20 teams; since it is only one incident it does not result in a pattern, however, because it is so rare it can be seen as a nonverbal cue of special importance, possibly signifying protectiveness or patriarchic behaviour of A towards K [15].

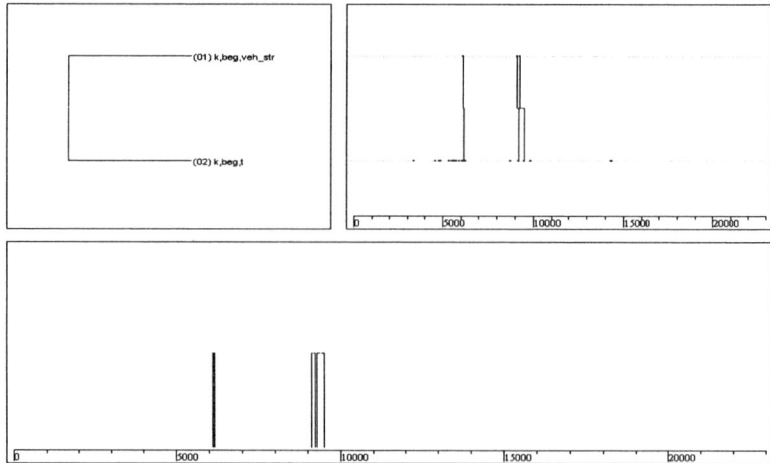

Figure 18.3 Pattern 41: *Nervous gesture "I do not mean to say you are wrong..."* At the beginning of three other speech acts K shows a vehement gesture as a defense (signalling strength drawn back). Similar to the gentle gesture, she uses this gesture in order to appease the other team members. The gesture says what she also verbalizes at one point: "yes, yes, yes, you are right, we have to talk about this, but we do not have to do this now; let's talk about this when we have more time".

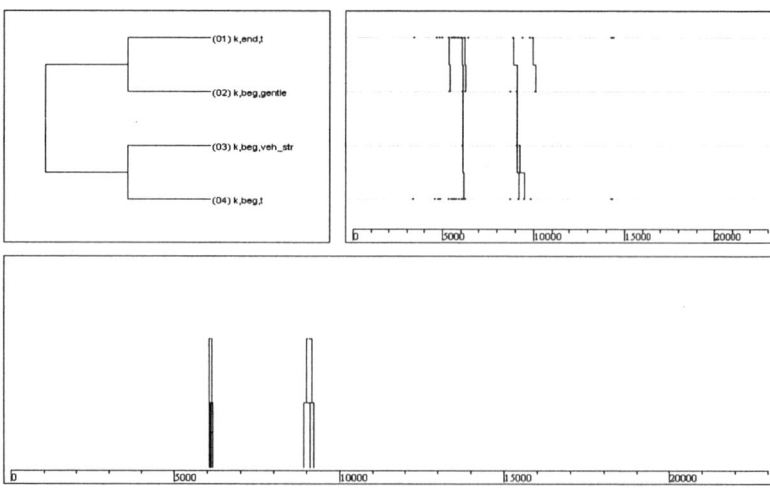

Figure 18.4 Pattern 14: *Nonverbal indicators of subsequent turns.* In two out of the five cases, pattern 30 is directly followed by pattern 41 twice the vehement and the gentle quality are displayed subsequently within one movement phrase. It becomes clear that the movement qualities of K are directly related to the on- and offsets of her talking turns.

However, there is no possibility to validate our interpretation from just one observation. While some team members state that K has the highest emotional warmth and that they have a good relation with her, she is also attributed the lowest influence. Interestingly, she is being called the *scapegoat* of the team by three of the four team members that completed the extra questionnaire about roles in the team. Except for with the gender-tokens, the category *scapegoat* was hardly ever employed by the 130 participants of our project. But what does Mrs. K herself say about her role in the team?

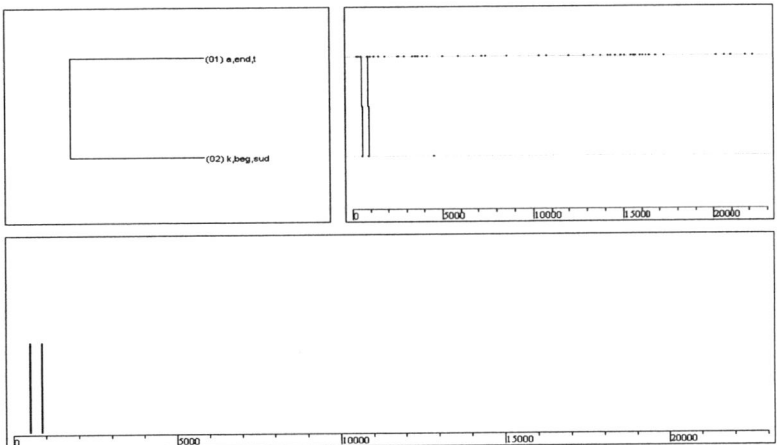

Figure 18.5 Pattern 34: *K reacts defensive towards A.* In the beginning of the scene there is a first hint that the behaviour of K may be related to the behaviour of the boss. When A ends to talk, K reacts with a sudden movement quality, usually either indicating flight or running into danger as a defense mechanism. In this case the latter happens twice: K appears insecure, but she starts out with her professional arguments against what has been talked about.

18.4.1.3 Interview statements Mrs. K, Team K

K reports that she has been working for the organization for 10 years, A has been working there for five years; the team experience of both is high. On rating scales from 1 (very low) to 5 (very high), she rates her *work content* with 3 out of 5 (all other team members with 4 or 5), the *team atmosphere* with 3 (all others with 4), the *identification with the organization* with 3 (all others with 4 or 5). She characterizes herself as feminine in terms of gender-typicality (high expressivity, low instrumentality; as measured with the Gender Typicality Scales (GTS) [42]). A characterizes himself as androgynous. K describes the team as often involved in emotional discussion, the boss is blocking, conflicts are present (none of the men made any comments on this topic), specifically, after having been asked for more information, she talks about derailments, inappropriate behaviour, personal attacks. K states that gender has an influence on the team communication, but also training background of the persons. She differentiates that within the organization gender does not play a role in the hiring policies, but in promotion she experiences career opportunities for women as being lower. K states that gender is not an explicit topic in the team, but has a clear implicit influence: K receives comments about her contributions, "macho, ironic, boorish remarks that have nothing to do with the content". She states that a man would never receive such comments, that they unconsciously slip through. If there were only women in the team, she does not belief that things would change much. If a woman comes into a team of only men, she thinks that *one* woman would probably not make a difference in the team's communication style, but if there were *two women or more* some things might change. For example, topics such as team climate, relationships and personal well-being would maybe enter the team's communication.

18.4.2 Male gender-token (in a female context)

18.4.2.1 Team description

Team O consisted of 7 women and one man (H). It was a typical female-dominated kindergarten team with a female leader (A). The setting was a full time kindergarten by a public administration of a South German town. Boss as well as gender-token, were both in their 40ies with partner but without kids. They both had a non-academic educational background. The other members of the team were all kindergarten teachers or interns. They planned activities and coordinated the daily business. The role of the boss was to take care of topic initiation, structuring and decision making (e.g., task distribution). The role of the gender-token – like of all other persons – was to cooperate and contribute their opinion, articulate their needs and take on some of the task responsibilities. In the first session of Team O, the male gender-token did very much self-related impression management by talking directly into the camera, waving, etc. We decided to select a sequence from the mid-part of the second session we had taped. Before the second session, we had explicitly asked the gender-token not to interact directly with the camera, but to act as if the camera was not present. We selected a typical sequence in terms of A's and H's involvement. H, the gender-token, talks about 1/3 of the time that the boss talks, but has longer talking times than any other team member (Table 18.2). This is representative for the entire team meeting (as measured by the longer, more representative talking times within 60 min). H shows average back channel frequencies, but quite pronounced interruption counts. Compared to A, H shows less control yields and less control claims, but almost as many strong control claims. The visual dominance ratio of A and H are almost identical, others are lower. H talks quite often to the entire group, whereas others in the group do this rarely. H is also particularly attentive to A (lwl to A). Interestingly, Team O is the only team out of 20 where the boss does not have the highest dominance value attributed by the team members. Here, the gender-token has a higher value than the boss. H is also rated higher on competence than the boss by the other team members.

Measure	A (female boss)	H (male token)	Others (approx. mean of full team members)
Talking time (min) [a]	5.1 (19.3)	1.5 (6.1)	0.4 (3.7)
Turns (#)	175	62	40
Interruptions (#)	8.6 (12)	5.7 (11)	0.9 (6.5)
Feedback / Back channel (#) [b]	17.1 / 15.7nv (13)	9.9 / 4.3nv (7)	9 / 10nv (7)
Control yields; (#)	13	5	8
Neutral speech acts; (#)	84	13	10
Control claims; (#)	20	8	4
Strong control claims; (#)	5	4	1
Lwt to group (frames)	4393	1233	170
Lwl to A (frames)	n.a.	3860	2950
Ratio %lwl : %lwt (%)	40:60	43:57	93:07
DomValue (-18 to 18) [c]	11.5	15	6
Dom_Self (-18 to 18)	15	5	8
CompValue (-18 to 18)	7.1	9.0	9

[a] values in parenthesis indicate the talking times in a longer, more representative sequence; [b] frequencies: first value from transcript, second value from THEME codings (including nonverbal cues), third value from analysis of action patterns ([24], also *interruption* value in parenthesis); [c] *mean of all other team member's* ratings for participant's dominance (on a rating scale from -18 to 18) [20], followed by self-ratings of · dominance and mean of all other team member's ratings for participant's competence on the same scale.

Table 18.2: Simple statistics for Team O

18.4.2.2 Pattern Analysis (male token)
Looking at communicative patterns with THEME 4.0, randomized data with 2-3 actors and 1-3 actor switches, 76 patterns resulted. Most of them covered gaze, efforts, pre-efforts and talking time (see figures 18.6, 18.7, 18.8, 18.9 and 18.10).

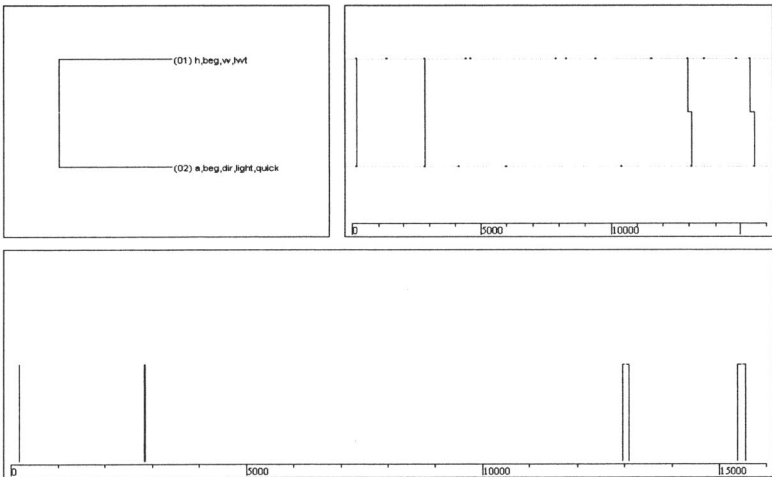

Figure 18.6 Pattern Ob: *A reacts to H.* While H talks A reacts four times with a direct, light and quick gestures. She seems to feel the need to structure the session more. Additionally A reacts directly verbally to H addressing him with lwt, while in half of the cases H looks away, when directly addressed by A (no graphic display for the latter pattern).

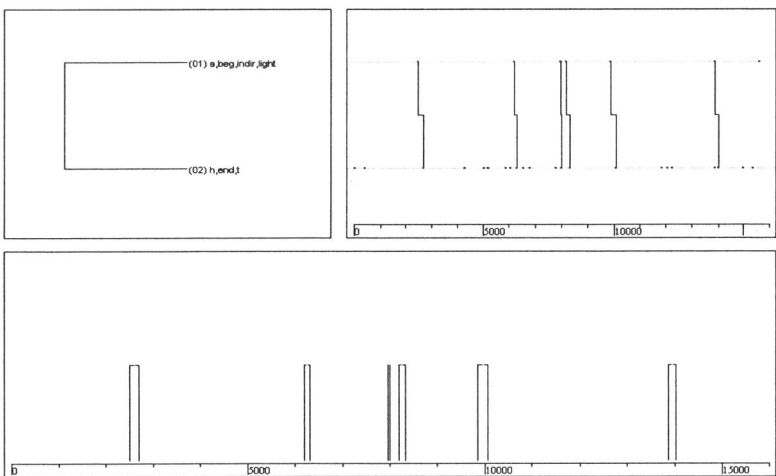

Figure 18.7 Pattern Oc: *H reacts to A: Nonverbal sensitivity of H.* A initiates a gesture and H ends his turn. This happens six times during the entire sequence. She uses indirect and light efforts, two indulgent qualities that include the entire team and are non-threatening. Even though H talks more than other team members, he seems to be attentive to these nonverbal stopping signals of A.

In addition to verbal cues, movement qualities seem to play an important part in the face-to-face interaction in Team O. The boss frequently uses nonverbal cues in order to initiate her contributions, to intervene or to react to the male token. The male token talks, or stops talking. All patterns include verbal and nonverbal cues (in action and reaction), for example, the end of H's talk following the gesture of A in Pattern Oc, or the hesitation of A following H's direct talk to her, four times toward the end of the selected sequence. Defensive gestures are more frequent on the side of the leader (six times vehemence - five of which in interaction with H - and seven times hesitation - the first four in interactions with H). This gives us reason to assume that A needs to defend her self-image vis-à-vis H. Most team members agree that H makes the longest contributions and is the one who can talk much without saying something. While he is estimated as the team member with the highest professional competence and pragmatism, he is also attributed low support and the role of the *scapegoat* of the group by one out of five participants who completed the role questionnaire.

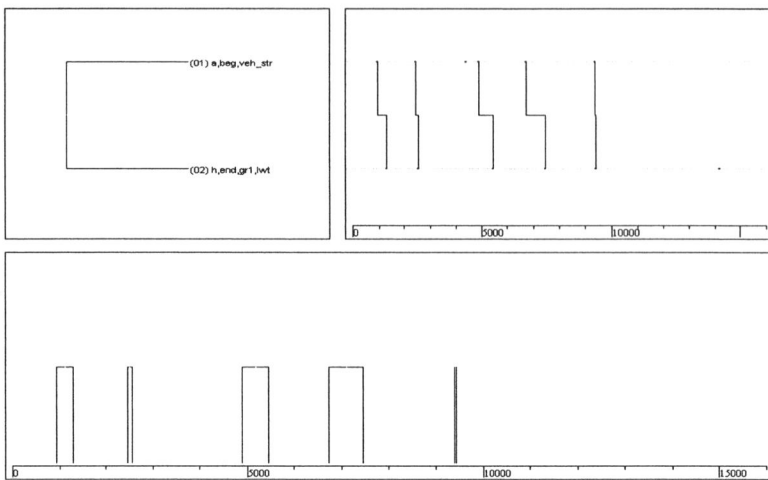

Figure 18.8 Pattern Od: *The boss shows more vehemence in order to structure speaking turns.* This action is possibly a more direct sign of A to H in order to stop his turn. She initiates a defensive movement (vehement) and he ends his talk to the entire group, yet, in three out of five cases with a considerable time lag (which may be just be the time it takes H to actually end his turn).

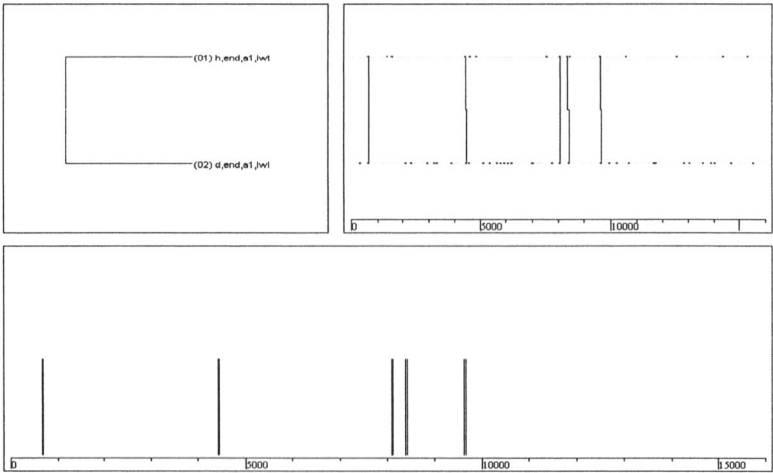

Figure 18.9 Pattern Oe: *Reclaiming the boss's leadership.* Do others in the group reclaim the leadership of the boss by gaze behaviour? D looks at A while H talks to A. She might be looking for A's reactions toward H.

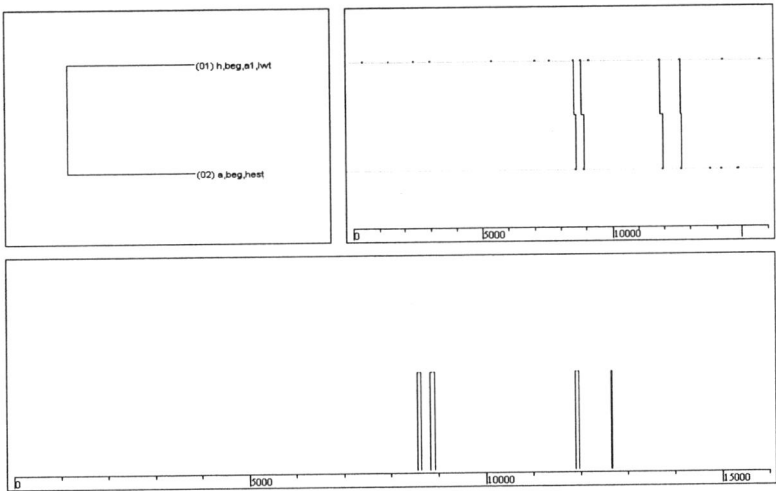

Figure 18.10 Pattern Of: *A reacts to H, when he takes over the lead initiating a topic.* H begins to talk to A, looking at her and A reacts with hesitation. Hesitation indicates the defensive tendency to procrastinate. She seems to be procrastinating stopping him again in order to claim her turn. Whereas in the last incidence of this behaviour, she seems to be procrastinating the initiation of other topics, mentally moving them to the next session due to lack of time.

A is attributed the most frequent turns and the most high quality contributions. Both, A and H, are attributed highest influence by one person only. But what do the protagonists say themselves?

18.4.2.3 Interview Statements (Mr. H, Team O)
H and A have both been working in the team for more than four years, i.e., longer than anybody else. On rating scales from 1 (very low) to 5 (very high), they are both content with their job (4 of 5), rate the team atmosphere as good (4 of 5) and are highly identified with their work (both 5). Other team members mostly have similar or lower values. H rates himself highly androgynous (high expressivity, high instrumentality) and A rates herself as prototypically feminine (high expressivity, low instrumentality), whereas third persons rate her as androgynous. A and H agree on the team atmosphere being good with a good amount of openness, that allows to address all sorts of topics and conflicts. Yet, H adds that some members hold back with their opinion which makes conflict resolution difficult at times. A sees herself as active and demanding, yet, if she does not lead the team session she also catches herself drawing herself back and become uninvolved. Both state that there are conflicts in the team, but that they are openly resolved. H describes his role as partner-like and responsible. People come to him if they need advice. A describes herself as "bitchy", honest and direct. Asked for the influence of gender, H states that in his opinion gender does not play a role in the team and also in the entire job of a kindergarten teacher. A states that gender has an influence in the team, that the only man is very dominant, he is rarely interrupted and that he receives more attention than the other team members. In fact, all eight team members with the exception of the gender-token state that gender is an important factor in their team, that "their" man is dominant, chauvinistic, determining, authoritarian, talks a lot, and that the other team members feel oppressed by him; but also that he is short and precise, rational, direct and that he promotes quick decision-making. As the only team member, H states that gender is not a topic in the team. A states that gender is sometimes a topic in a humorous manner. Another team member adds: "the man does the joking and we get most of the time interrupted if we try to make a joke". However, the male

token also receives a lot of empathy from other team members, "for a man it is hard to work here, because this is a female-dominated profession"; "as a man I would not work here, because it is women's work, a man might have to bring more initiative and work more".

Asked if something would change if there were only men in the team, H states that "yes, women specific personal topics would vanish, but the professional communication would not be affected". Asked for changes, if the team was purely female, others state that "decisions and discussions would take longer", "he brings about quick decisions, he is rational, structured, dominant and reliable." A states that "he gets rarely interrupted... I would perceive it more as one level in a women-only team. He brings diversity to the team...this is enriching, but also challenging. It forces us to face more confrontations".

18.5   Discussion

To be a gender-token seems to play an important role in team communication at the workplace. While our case studies suggest that the behaviour of the gender-token was not consistently biased towards the more stereotypical gender-role behaviour, results from self and other ratings mostly confirmed token research findings. For the male token, stereotypicality was seen in some aspects of behaviour and in other-ratings. For the female token, stereotypicality was rather seen in self- and other-ratings and only somewhat in behaviour.

Results from the *behaviour observations* showed that regarding *dominance behaviour* there was more bias towards the typical gender-role in the male gender-token only. He displayed dominance by talking and interrupting more than the other team members. He also made more power claims than the other team members, but not than the leader. The female token many times signalled the wish to take the talking turn by a nonverbal indicator first, yet, she also interrupted much and displayed many power claims in her speech, partly more than the team leader. She clearly outnumbered the male gender-token with her dominance displays. Regarding *support behaviour* the female token showed more gender-typicality. She displayed many more control yields and back channels than the male token and thus seemed to be more supportive. Regarding *defensive behaviour* the female gender token, but also the female boss showed more patterns including pre-efforts. The female gender-token was attributed the role of the *scapegoat* three times, the male gender-token once.

Results from *self-ratings* confirmed that gender of token seemed to play an important part. K was less satisfied with her job, with the quality of the team atmosphere, and was not as identified with the organization (commitment measure) as any of her colleagues. Furthermore, K rated herself as typically feminine. As this self-observation was neither confirmed in behaviour observation nor in third person ratings of K, it might have been a potential contrast effect to the male peer group. K's interview utterances regarding team improvement also concerned communal qualities. An experienced lack of authenticity can be inferred from K's utterance that in a group with more women the interaction might be more "natural" (3x). O was at least as satisfied with his job and the team atmosphere as the other team members were, and he was highly committed. He rated himself as highly androgynous.

In the ratings by the *other group members* O was described as more dominant but also as more competent than A by all other team members. In his self-description he emphasized his responsibility and his communal traits. K emphasized communal intentions and goals in the interview as well (caring about group wealth and work efficacy). However, she was rated low on dominance and competence by her peers. From the analysis of self- and other-ratings in our study, the female token of Team K was seen as being more gender-stereotypic and experienced more negative consequences than the male token of Team O.

Results from the *pattern analysis* showed the more pronounced use of nonverbal communication patterns in women. There even seemed to be a parallel in behaviour as well as self-perception in the female token of Team K and the female boss of Team O. Both used more nonverbal signals to initiate turns, both used more defensive movement patterns than the male boss and the male gender-token. In brief, defences are used when our self-image is threatened. This seemed to be true for our female gender-token in a male team and for our female-boss in the interaction with a dominant male gender-token. In addition, the frequency data for both women were quite similar.

In sum, much more egalitarian structures have been achieved regarding gender in organization in western societies by the beginning of the 21st century. When it comes to tokenism, however, structures are still characterized by inequality. In our study, gender-tokens partially acted more in line with their gender-role than other team members. The female gender-token perceived herself more in line with her gender-role and was perceived more in line with her gender-role by the other team members. The male token perceived himself as more communal and androgynous and was perceived as more dominant and competent, thus his self-perception was non-stereotypical, whereas perception by others was in line with stereotypes. Generally, behavioural outcomes were not particularly in line with stereotypes. In fact, gender typicality of tokens emerged rather from the pattern analysis than from the frequency counts of behaviour. The use of pattern analysis enabled us to see ongoing patterns at the interface of verbal and nonverbal interactions that we would have been missing otherwise. Pattern analysis can therefore be evaluated as a gain within our multi-methodological approach. The findings have implications for the construction of gender in our two teams: obviously gender-roles are rather anchored in self-image and image of the others than observable from direct behaviour. In line with token research, and independent of the gender-tokens' displayed behaviour, the actual gender of group members seems to influence whether the token status opens or closes perspectives for them, with women reporting and being affected by negative career-related consequences and men reporting and being affected by no or positive consequences.

18.6   Acknowledgments

DFG-Project KR 505/11. We thank the German Science Foundation (Deutsche Forschungsgemeinschaft) for grant support.

18.7   References

[1]   C. Antoni., *Teilautonome Arbeitsgruppen*. Weinheim: Beltz, 1996.
[2]   R. Fisch, D. Beck, and B. Englich, *Projektgruppen in Organisationen*. Göttingen: Verlag für angewandte Psychologie, 2001.
[3]   A. Thomas, Group effectiveness: A balance between heterogeneity and homogeneity, *Psychologische Beiträge* **41** (1999) 226-236.
[4]   S. Hoering, S. Kühl, and A. Schulze-Fielitz, Homogenität und Heterogenität in der Gruppenzusammensetzung – Eine mikropolitische Studie über Entscheidungsprozesse in der Gruppenarbeit, *Arbeit* **10** (2000) 331-351.
[5]   S. C. Koch, S. Schey, C. Thimm, and L. Kruse, *Kommunikationseinstellungen und –erwartungen von Männern und Frauen am Arbeitsplatz*. WorkComm Arbeitsbericht Nr. 1, Universität Heidelberg, Heidelberg: 1999, [Online-Document] http://workcomm.uni-hd.de.
[6]   S. C. Koch, A. Kubat, C. Thimm, and L. Kruse, *Die kommunikative Konstruktion von Geschlecht in beruflichen Settings. Entwicklung der Kodierschemata und erste Ergebnisse*, WorkComm

Arbeitsbericht, Nr. 2, Universität Heidelberg, Heidelberg, 2001, [Online Document] http://workcomm.uni-hd.de.

[7]   R. M. Kanter. *Men and women of the corporation.* New York: Basic Books, 1977.

[8]   T. W. McDonald, L. L. Toussaint, and J. A Schweiger, The influence of social status on token women leaders' expectations about leading male-dominated groups, *Sex Roles* **50** (2004) 401-409.

[9]   J. D. Yoder and J. Sinnett, Is it all iń the numbers? A case study of tokenism, *Psychology of Women Quarterly* **9** (1985) 413-418.

[10]   L. L. Cohen and J. K. Swim, The differential impact of gender ratios on women and men: Tokenism, self-confidence, and expectations, *Personality and Social Psychology Bulletin* **21** (1995) 876-883.

[11]   J. D. Yoder, T. S. Schleicher, and T. W. McDonald, Empowering token women leaders: The importance of organizationally legitimated credibility, *Psychology of Women Quarterly* **22** (1998) 209–222.

[12]   R. V. Exline, S. L. Ellyson, and B. Long Visual behavior exhibited by males differing as to interpersonal control orientation in one and two way communication systems, in *Nonverbal communication of aggression*, P. Pliner, L. Krames, and T. Allowa, Eds. New York: Kluwer Academic Publisher, 1975, pp. 53-759.

[13]   J. F. Dovidio and S. L. Ellyson, *Power, dominance and nonverbal behavior.* New York: Spring Verlag, 1985.

[14]   J. A. Hall, *Nonverbal sex differences. Communication accuracy and expressive style.* London: The John Hopkins University Press, 1984.

[15]   N. M. Henley, *Body politics. Power, sex, and nonverbal communication.* Englewood Cliffs: Prentice Hall, 1977.

[16]   M. Schmid-Mast, *Gender differences in dominance hierarchies.* Lengerich: Pabst Science Publisher, 2000.

[17]   M. Schmid-Mast, Gender differences and similarities in dominance hierarchies in same-sex groups based on speaking time, *Sex Roles* **44** (2001) 537-556.

[18]   J. F. Dovidio, S. L. Ellyson, C. F. Keating, K. Heltman, and C. E. Brown, The relationship of social power to visual displays of dominance between men and women, *Journal of Personality and Social Psychology* **45** (1988) 233-242.

[19]   B. Mullen, E. Salas, and J. E. Driskell, Salience, motivation, and artifact as contributions to the relation between participation rate and leadership, *Journal of Experimental Social Psychology* **25** (1989) 545-559.

[20]   R. F. Bales and S. P. Cohen, *SYMLOG – Ein System für die mehrstufige Beobachtung von Gruppen.* Stuttgart: Klett-Cotta, 1982.

[21]   C. West and D. H. Zimmerman, Doing gender, *Gender & Society* **1** (1987) 125-151.

[22]   E. J. Aries, C. Gold, and R. H. Weigel, Dispositional and situational influences on dominance behavior in small groups, *Journal of Personality and Social Psychology* **44** (1983) 779-786.

[23]   C. L. Ridgeway, J. Berger, and L. Smith, Nonverbal cues and status: an expectation states approach, *American Journal of Sociology* **90** (1985) 955-978.

[24]   C. Thimm, *Dominanz und Sprache. Strategisches Handeln im Alltag.* Wiesbaden: Deutscher Universitätsverlag, 1990.

[25]   R. Schmitt, Unterstützen im Gespräch, *Zeitschrift für Sprachwissenschaft* **16** (1997) 52-82.

[26]   C. R. Rogers, *Client-centered therapy.* Boston: Houghton Mifflin, 1951.

[27]   S. Duncan, On the structure of speaker-auditor interaction during speaking turns, *Language in Society,* **2** (1974) 161-180.

[28]   H. Henne in *Sprache und Pragmatik – Lunder Symposion,* I. Rosengren, Ed. Malmö: Gotab, 1979.

[29]   K. Linser, *Untersuchungen zur Kommunikation von Führungskräften und MitarbeiterInnen in Teambesprechungen,* Unpublished Thesis, Heidelberg, 2004.

[30]   A. Mehrabian, A semantic space for nonverbal behavior, *Journal of Consulting and Clinical Psychology* **35** (1970) 248-257.

[31]   J. K. Burgoon, Nonverbal signals, in *Handbook of Interpersonal Communication,* 2 ed., M. L. Knapp and G. R. Miller, Eds. London: Sage, 1994, pp. 229-285.

[32]   N. C. Krämer, *Bewegende Bewegung. Sozio-emotionale Wirkungen nonverbalen Verhaltens und deren experimentelle Untersuchung mittels Computeranimation.* Lengerich: Pabst, 2001.

[33]   S. C. Koch, *Doing and viewing gender: A lens-model approach to the communicative construction of gender in task-oriented groups.* Heidelberg: University of Heidelberg, 2003.

[34]   J. Kestenberg-Amighi, S. T. Loman, P. Lewis, and M. Sossin, *The meaning of movement. Developmental and clinical perspectives of the Kestenberg Movement Profile.* Amsterdam: Gordon and Breach, 1999.

[35]   R. Rosenthal and B. DePaulo, Sex differences in eavesdropping on nonverbal cues, *Journal of Personality and Social Psychology* **37** (1979) 273-285.

[36]   J. S. Kestenberg, *Parents and Children.* Northvale: Jason Aronson, 1975.

[37]   R. V. Laban and F. C. Lawrence, *Efforts. Economy in body movements*. Boston: Boston Plays, 1974.
[38]   J. Cohen, A coefficient of agreement for nominal scales, *Educational and Psychological Measurement* **20** (1960) 37-46.
[39]   M. S. Magnusson, THEME Software (Version 97), 1997.
[40]   M. S. Magnusson, Discovering hidden time patterns in behavior: T-patterns and their detection, *Behavior Research Method, Instruments and Computers* **32** (2000) 93-110
[41]   W. Lamb, *Posture and Gesture*. London: Gerald Duckworth, 1965.
[42]   C. Altstötter-Gleich, B. Eglau, and J. Kramer, Möglichkeiten der Operationalisierung von Expressivität und Instrumentalität. Entwicklung von Skalen zur Erfassung der Geschlechtstypizität, *Forschungsberichte des Fachbereichs 8: Psychologie* 23, Landau: Universität Koblenz-Landau, 2000.

Author Index